six   n

Action Research

A Guide for the Teacher Researcher

Geoffrey E. Mills

Southern Oregon University

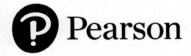 Pearson

330 Hudson Street, NY, NY 10013

Director and Portfolio Manager:
  Kevin M. Davis
Content Producer: Janelle Rogers
Content Project Manager: Pamela D. Bennett
Media Project Manager: Lauren Carlson
Portfolio Management Assistant:
  Anne McAlpine
Executive Field Marketing Manager:
  Krista Clark
Executive Product Marketing Manager:
  Christopher Barry

Procurement Specialist: Carol Melville
Cover Designer: Carie Keller
Cover Photo: Getty Images/Hero Images
Full-Service Project Management:
  Kathy Smith, Cenveo® Publisher Services
Composition: Cenveo® Publisher Services
Printer/Binder: LSC Communications/Crawfordsville
Cover Printer: Phoenix Color/Hagerstown
Text Font: 10.25/12 Sabon LT Std

Library of Congress Cataloging-in-Publication Data
Names: Mills, Geoffrey E., author.
Title: Action research : a guide for the teacher researcher / Geoffrey E.
  Mills.
Description: Sixth Edition. | Boston : PEARSON, [2018] | Includes
  bibliographical references and indexes.
Identifiers: LCCN 2016044280 | ISBN 9780134523033
Subjects: LCSH: Action research in education--United States--Handbooks,
  manuals, etc. | Teaching--United States--Handbooks, manuals, etc.
Classification: LCC LB1028.24 .M55 2018 | DDC 370.72--dc23
LC record available at https://lccn.loc.gov/2016044280

55 2022

ISBN 10:   0-13-452303-2
ISBN 13: 978-0-13-452303-3

*For Ernie Mills, Audrey Mills, Dr. Milton H. Brown, and Catherine S. Brown—
Your love, support, and spirit live with me always.*

A native of Australia, Geoff moved to the United States in 1986 to undertake doctoral studies at the University of Oregon. After completing his PhD in 1988, Geoff accepted his first teaching position at Southern Oregon State College (now Southern Oregon University). After 12 years of teaching, Geoff moved into university administration where he served as dean and professor of education in the School of Education at Southern Oregon University. Most recently, Geoff has returned to the faculty in the School of Education as a professor of education.

Geoffrey Mills

Geoff has traveled extensively and given invited action research presentations in Australia, New Zealand, Greenland, United Kingdom, Canada, Guam, Saipan, Palau, Marshall Islands, American Samoa, U.S. Virgin Islands, and many states in the United States. In addition to *Action Research: A Guide for the Teacher Researcher*, Sixth Edition, Geoff is also the only active author of *Educational Research: Competencies for Analysis and Applications* (2016; with L. R. Gay), now in its eleventh edition.

preface

New to This Edition

The sixth edition of *Action Research* has been revised in response to expert reviewer feedback.

The sixth edition includes the following:

- **"Voices from the Field" sections** For the sixth edition, there are new narrative sections that respond to the video vignettes throughout the text and scaffold the content of each chapter.
- **Expanded Coverage of Mixed-Methods Data Collection and Analysis Techniques** Additional coverage of mixed-methods research has been added throughout the text and reflects six new mixed-methods research designs: explanatory sequential, exploratory sequential, convergent parallel, experimental, social justice, and multistage evaluation.
- **Expanded Coverage of Single-Subject Research Designs** In response to reviewers' comments, single-subject research designs have been expanded for the sixth edition.
- **Expanded Coverage of Digital Research Tools for the Twenty-First Century** Additional coverage of digital research tools that can be used by action researchers through each phase of the action research process.
- **Expanded Coverage of Reviewing the Literature** Additional coverage of using technology to search literature databases that takes advantage of university library consortium agreements as well as the power of technology tools to track references and build bibliographies can be found in this updated stand-alone chapter.

The Role of Action Research in Effecting Educational Change

Action research has the potential to be a powerful agent of educational change. Action research helps to develop teachers and administrators with professional attitudes who embrace action, progress, and reform rather than stability and mediocrity. In addition, the action research process fosters a democratic approach to decision making while, at the same time, empowering individual teachers through participation in a collaborative, socially responsive research activity.

Commitment to action research positions teachers and administrators as learners rather than experts. Those committed to action research will willingly undertake continued professional development because they believe that there is a gap between the real world of their daily teaching practices and their vision of an ideal one.

Incorporating action research into preservice teacher education programs and professional development programs for in-service teachers will help make action research an ongoing component of a professional teacher's practice. Such action will ultimately help teachers incorporate action research alongside other critical components of teaching, such as curriculum development, authentic assessment strategies, classroom management strategies, teaching strategies, and caring for children. Such actions will encourage teachers to embrace change.

It is my hope that this text will, in some small part, help us keep moving forward, even in difficult times. Action research is an invitation to learn, a means to tackle tough questions that face us individually and collectively as teachers, and a method for questioning our daily taken-for-granted assumptions as a way to find hope for the future.

Conceptual Framework and Organization of the Text

This text has evolved over 25 years based on my experience of doing and teaching action research. During this time, I have had the opportunity to work with some outstanding university faculty, classroom teachers, and principals who were committed to looking systematically at the effects of their programs on children's lives. This text's organization has grown out of these experiences and has been field tested by numerous students and colleagues.

Each chapter opens with an action research vignette that illustrates the content that will follow. These vignettes, most of which have been written by teachers and principals with whom I have worked, show readers what action research looks like in practice and who does it. The order of these chapters roughly matches the action research process, an approach that I have found successful when teaching action research.

Contents of This New Edition

Chapter 1, "Understanding Action Research," defines action research and provides historical and theoretical contexts for the rest of the text. The chapter also reviews various models of action research and concludes with the four-step process (identifying an area of focus, collecting data, analyzing and interpreting data, and developing an action plan) and the dialectic model on which this text is based. The remaining chapters mirror these steps.

Chapter 2, "Ethics," provides an expanded discussion of the American Educational Research Association's ethical guidelines and poses an ethical dilemma vignette to spark teacher researchers' thinking about how best to resolve ethical dilemmas if and when they arise. This chapter also provides guidance for seeking and obtaining Institutional Review Board approval.

Chapter 3, "Deciding on an Area of Focus," provides guidelines for selecting an area of focus. The chapter culminates with an action research plan that provides a practical guide for moving teacher researchers through the action research process.

Chapter 4, "Review of Related Literature," offers step-by-step directions for how to do a literature review using many online resources as well as traditional university library resources. The chapter provides an expanded discussion of how to write a literature review.

Chapter 5, "Data Collection Techniques," offers a comprehensive discussion of qualitative data collection that covers the "3 Es" of qualitative data collection: experiencing, enquiring, and examining. It also provides a comprehensive discussion of quantitative data collection techniques that covers collecting data from teacher-made tests, standardized tests, and attitude scales. A section on triangulation covers how to work with multiple sources of data.

Chapter 6, "Data Collection Considerations: Validity, Reliability, and Generalizibility," addresses important data collection considerations to ensure that the data collected will be "trustworthy."

Chapter 7, "Data Analysis and Interpretation," describes selected techniques of data analysis and data interpretation and distinguishes between the goals of the two processes. Included in this chapter is an expanded discussion of data analysis and interpretation with examples of each for qualitative and quantitative data sources.

Chapter 8, "Action Planning for Educational Change," helps teacher researchers take action using a helpful Steps to Action Chart. The chapter also discusses potential obstacles to change and suggests strategies for overcoming these obstacles.

Chapter 9, "Writing Up Action Research," provides practical guidelines for writing up action research and ways that teacher researchers can "get the word out." A reprinted action research article with marginal notations gives researchers an example of the general structure and components of written action research. A self-evaluation rubric helps teacher researchers make sure their write-up is ready for publication. There is also a discussion of using the sixth edition of *Publication Manual of the American Psychological Association* during the writing process.

Finally, Chapter 10, "Evaluating Action Research," is new to this edition and focuses on analyzing and evaluating action research studies. Included in this edition is a new article from an online journal that is analyzed using the new criteria for evaluating action research publications.

Appendix A, "Action Research in Action," contains an extended example of action research through a case study of Curtis Elementary. This case study follows the process described throughout the text and includes an evaluation of the project on the basis of criteria for evaluating action research presented in Chapter 10. Appendix B, "Standard Deviation and Action Research," contains a brief discussion of standard deviation and how it can be applied to the analysis and interpretation of teacher research. Appendix C, "Displaying Data Visually," presents a variety of examples of visual displays of data—bar graphs, tables, and a concept map—from action research projects. Using these display techniques helps teachers "see" data for better analysis and more effective communication of their findings.

Instructor Resources

Online PowerPoint® Slides

To enhance class lectures, Online PowerPoint® slides are available. To access the Online PowerPoint® slides, go to **www.pearsonhighered.com/educator**. Enter the author, title, or ISBN, and click on this text. The PowerPoint® slides are available for download under the "Resources" tab.

Acknowledgments

I would like to thank the reviewers, who invested a great deal of time and provided critical feedback during the development of this text. These reviewers include: Bill Blubaugh, University of Northern Colorado; Susan D. Flynn, Coastal Carolina University; Catherine Kurkjian, Central Connecticut State University; Hector M. Rios, Rowan University; and Yer Jeff Thao, Portland State University. I would also like to acknowledge the staff at Pearson, without whose guidance (and patience!) this text would not have become a reality. In particular, I thank Kevin Davis, Director & Portfolio Manager, for working with me on a sixth edition of the text so as to build on what we achieved with the previous editions. Kevin has been my friend and mentor since he offered my first textbook contract in 1997, and I am indebted to him for his encouragement and support of my writing. Kevin worked diligently to ensure a quality, user-friendly, academically coherent text and patiently kept me on track in order to meet publication deadlines. His feedback on chapter drafts was insightful and important to the development of this sixth edition. As I approach the end of my tenure at Southern Oregon University (Emeritus Professor is in my not-too-distant future) and at the risk of embarrassing Kevin, I can state with confidence that the past 20 years of my professorial career exceeded all of my expectations because of the opportunities Kevin has given me. Thank you.

I would also like to extend my gratitude to the hundreds of students at Southern Oregon University who responded to various drafts of previous editions of this text and also endured my ramblings about the importance of being reflective practitioners and self-renewing professionals. Their insights into what makes a text user friendly have been greatly appreciated and are reflected in the text. Similarly, I have had the pleasure of working with hundreds of teachers throughout Oregon who taught me what needed to be included in a "helpful" text.

This edition has also benefited greatly from interactions and feedback from colleagues who have used the book for many years and who invite me to "google hangout" with their classes. Specifically, I would like to thank Dr. Andrew Hostetler (Vanderbilt University) and Dr. Todd Hawley (Kent State University) for their feedback on previous editions of the book.

Unanticipated consequences of writing textbooks are the invitations to work with groups of educators from around the world. *Action Research* has taken me to many different parts of the world where I have had the honor of working with teachers and principals who are committed to studying the impact of what they do and how it can improve students' lives. For example, during the shelf life of the fifth edition, I have worked in Greenland (with the University of Greenland and Ministry of Education), Guam, Saipan, Palau, American Samoa, and the U.S. Virgin Islands (with McREL). These experiences working with teachers and principals in different (often challenging) contexts continue to push my thinking about how action research can provide a framework to support important school improvement efforts.

Finally, I appreciate the support and encouragement of my wife, colleague, and best friend, Dr. Donna Mills (Emeritus Professor, Southern Oregon University), who endured my weird travel schedules and writing commitments throughout this lengthy process. And I thank my son Jonathan for pushing my thinking about mixed-methods research and how it might be applied to the National Basketball Association! During the writing of this edition, Jonathan engaged in his own research as part of his honors program at the University of Oregon. His thesis focused on decision making in the National Basketball Association and specifically on the interaction of advanced analytics and traditional evaluation methods. It was fun to watch my son struggle with the challenges of being a neophyte researcher and was a good reminder to me of my audience! My sincere thanks to Donna and Jonathan for their love, patience, and support, which are always appreciated and never taken for granted.

—Geoff Mills

brief contents

contents

6 Data Collection Considerations: Validity, Reliability, and Generalizability   147

7 Data Analysis and Interpretation   168

8   Action Planning for Educational Change   212

Writing Up Action Research 238

 Evaluating Action Research 270

Appendix

 Action Research in Action: A Case Study of Curtis Elementary School and an Article Critique 296

Appendix

Standard Deviation and Action Research   310

Appendix

Displaying Data Visually   317

Understanding Action Research

After reading this chapter you should be able to:

1.1 Describe the goal of educational research and the different approaches researchers use.

1.2 Define action research.

1.3 Describe the origins of action research.

1.4 Identify the similarities and differences between critical and practical theories of action research.

1.5 Describe the goals of and rationale for action research.

1.6 Describe the justifications for action research and steps you can take to make it part of your daily teaching practice.

1.7 Describe the four steps of the action research process.

This chapter introduces action research by providing an example of an action research project from a real teacher researcher, an exploration of the historical and theoretical foundations of action research, a discussion of the goals and justification for action research, and an explanation of the action research process.

What Motivates Unmotivated Students?

Deborah South

Deborah South, a teacher in a rural Oregon high school, was a participant in an action research class. She shares the challenges she faced when, owing to a last-minute teaching assignment, she found herself working with a group of "unmotivated" students. Deborah's story illustrates the wide variety of factors that can influence students' learning and a teacher's willingness to critically examine her teaching methods and how they affected the children in her classroom. Although Deborah's interpretation of the results of her study did not validate her practice, it did provide data that Deborah and the school's principal could use to make changes to the existing curriculum for unmotivated students.

Teaching students who are unmotivated and apathetic can be a difficult challenge for any teacher to overcome. These students typically can be disruptive and negative and often require an extraordinary amount of teacher time to manage their behavior. My concern with teaching unmotivated students has existed almost since I began teaching 5 years ago. As an educator, one tries all kinds of possible strategies to encourage students to be successful. However, these strategies do not work with unmotivated students who are apathetic and exhibit unacceptable behavior. Eventually the patience runs out and, as ashamed as I am to admit it, I stop trying to find ways to reach these particular students. It soon becomes enough that they stay in their seats, be quiet, and do not disturb anyone.

However, last term my attitude was forced to change. I was given a study skills group of 20 of the lowest achieving eighth graders in the school. This new class consisted of 16 boys and 4 girls. My task was to somehow take these students and miraculously make them motivated, achieving students. I was trained in a study skills program before the term started and I thought that I was prepared: I had the students, I had the curriculum, and I had the help of an outstanding aide.

Within a week, I sensed we were in trouble. My 20 students often showed up with no supplies. Their behavior was atrocious. They called each other names, threw various items around the room, and walked around the classroom when they felt like it. Their attitudes toward me were negative. I became concerned about teaching these students. In part, I felt bad that they were so disillusioned with school and their future; I also felt bad because the thought of teaching in this environment every day for another 14 weeks made me wish summer vacation were here.

Given this situation, I decided to do some reading about how other teachers motivate unmotivated students and to formulate some ideas about the variables that contribute to a student's success in school. Variables I investigated included adult approval, peer influence, and success in such subjects as math, science, language arts, and social studies, as well as self-esteem and students' views of their academic abilities.

I collected the majority of the data through surveys, interviews, and report card/attendance records in an effort to answer the following questions:

- *How does attendance affect student performance?*
- *How are students influenced by their friends in completing schoolwork?*
- *How do adults (parents, teachers) affect the success of students?*
- *What levels of self-esteem do these students have?*

As a result of this investigation, I learned many things. For example, for this group of students attendance does not appear to be a factor—with the exception of one student, school attendance was regular. Not surprisingly, peer groups did affect student performance. Seventy-three percent of my students reported that their friends never encouraged doing homework or putting any effort into homework.

Another surprising result was the lack of impact of a teacher's approval on student achievement. Ninety-four percent of my students indicated that they never or seldom do their homework to receive teacher approval. Alternatively, 57 percent indicated that they often or always do their homework so that their families will be proud of them.

One of the most interesting findings of this study was the realization that most of my students misbehave out of frustration at their own lack of abilities. They are being obnoxious not to gain attention, but to divert attention from the fact that they do not know how to complete the assigned work.

When I looked at report cards and compared grades over three quarters, I noticed a trend. Between the first and second quarters, student performance had increased. That is, most students were doing better than they had during the first quarter. Between the second and third quarters, however, grades dropped dramatically. I tried to determine why that drop occurred, and the only experience these 20 students shared was that they had been moved into my class at the beginning of the third quarter.

When I presented my project to the action research class during our end-of-term "celebration," I was convinced that the "cause" of the students' unmotivated behavior was my teaching. I had concluded through my data analysis and interpretation that the one experience these 20 children had in common was participation in my study skills class. This conclusion, however, was not readily accepted by my critical friends and colleagues in the action research class, who urged me to consider other interpretations of the data. For example, perhaps the critical mass of negativity present in one classroom provided the children with a catalyst to act out against the teacher. After all, this was the only class shared exclusively by these 20 students. Afterward, I shared the findings of my study with my school principal. As a result,she decided not to group these students together homogeneously for a study skills class the following year.

As you can see, action research is a "wonderfully uncomfortable" (Lytle, 1997) place to be—once we start our journey of investigation, we have no way of knowing in advance where we will end up. Action research, like any other problem-solving process, is an ongoing creative activity that exposes us to surprises along the way. What appears to matter in the planning stages of an action research investigation may provide us with only a hint, a scratching of the surface, of what is really the focus for our investigations. How we deal with the uncertainty of the journey positions us as learners of our own craft, an attitude that is critical to our success. This text attempts to foster an openness in the spirit of inquiry guided by action research.

A Brief Overview of Educational Research

When you hear the phrase *scientific research*, you probably think of a scientist in a white lab coat (usually a balding, middle-age man with a pocket full of pens!) mixing chemicals or doing experiments involving white mice. Traditional scientists, like the one pictured in this rather trite image, proceed with their research under the assumption that "all behaviors and events are orderly" and that all events "have discoverable causes" (Mills & Gay, 2016, p. 5). This traditional belief that natural phenomena can be explained in an orderly way using empirical sciences is sometimes called **positivism.**

Human beings, however, are very complicated organisms, and compared with chemicals—and mice, for that matter—their behavior can be disorderly and fairly unpredictable. This presents a challenge to educational researchers, who are concerned with gaining insight into human behavior in educational environments such as schools and classrooms.

The goal of traditional educational research is "to explain, predict, and/or control educational phenomena" (Mills & Gay, 2016, p. 5). To do this, researchers try to manipulate and control certain **variables** (the factors that might affect the outcomes of a particular study) to test a **hypothesis** (a statement the researcher makes that predicts what will happen or explains what the outcome of the study will be). Educational researchers focus on the manipulation of an **independent variable** and its impact on the **dependent variable.** An independent variable is a behavior or characteristic under the control of the researcher and believed to influence some other behavior or characteristic. A dependent variable is the change or difference in a behavior or characteristic that occurs as a result of the independent variable. The word *control* is not used here in a negative sense; rather, it describes one of the characteristics of traditional, quantitatively oriented research, in which the researcher must control the environment to be able to draw cause-effect relationship conclusions. This cannot occur unless the researcher is able to control the variables in the study that might affect a causal relationship.

For example, researchers might be interested in studying the effects of a certain phonics program (the independent variable) on the rate at which children learn to read (the dependent variable). The researchers may hypothesize that using this phonics program will shorten the time it takes for students to learn to read. To confirm or reject this hypothesis, they might study the reading progress of one group of children who were taught using the phonics program (the **experimental group**) and compare it with the reading progress of another group of children (the **control group**) who were taught reading without the phonics program. Children would be randomly assigned to either the experimental or the control group as a way to reduce the differences that might exist in naturally occurring groups. At the end of the experiment, the researchers would compare the progress of each group and decide whether the hypothesis could be accepted or rejected with a predetermined level of **statistical significance** (e.g., that the difference between the mean for the control group and the mean for the experimental group is large, compared with the standard error). Finally, the researchers would present the findings of the study at a conference and perhaps publish the results.

This process may sound very straightforward. In classroom and school settings, however, controlling all the factors that affect the outcomes of our teaching without disrupting the natural classroom environment can be difficult. For example, how do we know that the phonics program is the only variable affecting the rate at which students learn to read? Perhaps some students are read to at home by their parents; perhaps one teacher is more effective than another; perhaps one group of students gets to read more exciting books than the other; perhaps one group of children has difficulty concentrating on their reading because they all skipped breakfast!

Action researchers acknowledge and embrace these complications as a natural part of classroom life and typically use research approaches that do not require them to randomly assign students in their classes to control and experimental groups. Teacher researchers studying their own practices also differ from traditional educational researchers (studying something other than their own practices) because they are committed to *taking action* and *effecting positive educational change* in their own classrooms and schools based on their findings. Traditional educational researchers may not be able to impact the subjects of their studies because they are outside of their locus of control. That is, traditional educational researchers can share the conclusions of their studies, but it is up to the subjects to determine whether they will take action on the findings. Another difference is that whereas educational research has historically been done by university professors, scholars, and graduate students on children, teachers, and principals, action researchers are often the schoolteachers and principals who were formerly the subjects of educational research. As such, they participate in their own inquiries, acting as both teacher and researcher at the same time. We should note, however, that traditional educational researchers can also collaborate with teacher researchers in **collaborative action research** efforts. As Hendricks (2017) states, "The goal of this type of research is to utilize the expertise of the collaborators and to foster sustained dialogue among educational stakeholders in different settings" (p. 7).

Research is also categorized by the methods the researchers use. Simply put, different research problems require different research designs. These designs to educational research are often classified as either quantitative or qualitative research. **Quantitative research** is the collection and analysis of numerical data to describe, explain, predict, or control phenomena of interest. However, a quantitative research approach entails more than just the use of numerical data. At the outset of a study, quantitative researchers state the hypotheses to be examined and specify the research procedures that will be used to carry out the study. They also maintain control over contextual factors that may interfere with the data collection and identify a sample of participants large enough to provide statistically meaningful data. Many quantitative researchers have little personal interaction with the participants they study because they frequently collect data using paper-and-pencil, noninteractive instruments. Underlying quantitative research methods is the philosophical belief or assumption that we inhabit a relatively stable, uniform, and coherent world that we can measure, understand, and generalize about. This view, adopted from the natural sciences, implies that the world and the laws that govern it are somewhat predictable and can be understood by scientific research and examination. In

table 1–1 ■ Overview of Qualitative and Quantitative Research Characteristics

	Quantitative Research	Qualitative Research
Type of data collected	Numerical data	Nonnumerical narrative and visual data
Research problem	Hypothesis and research procedures stated before beginning the study	Research problems and methods evolve as understanding of topic deepens
Manipulation of context	Yes	No
Sample size	Larger	Smaller
Research procedures	Relies on statistical procedures	Relies on categorizing and organizing data into patterns to produce a descriptive, narrative synthesis
Participant interaction	Little interaction	Extensive interaction
Underlying belief	We live in a stable and predictable world that we can measure, understand, and generalize about.	Meaning is situated in a particular perspective or context that is different for people and groups; therefore, the world has many meanings.

Source: Gay, Lorraine R., Mills, Geoffrey E.; Airasian, Peter W., *Educational Research: Competencies for analysis and applications,* loose-leaf version, 10th Ed., © 2012. Reprinted and electronically reproduced by permission of Pearson Education, Inc., New York, NY.

this quantitative perspective, claims about the world are not considered meaningful unless they can be verified through direct observation. By comparison, **qualitative research** uses narrative, descriptive approaches to data collection to understand the way things are and what the research means from the perspectives of the participants in the study. Qualitative approaches might include, for example, conducting face-to-face interviews, making observations, and video recording interactions.

Table 1–1 provides an overview of quantitative and qualitative research characteristics. Despite the differences between quantitative and qualitative research, you should not consider them to be oppositional. Taken together, they represent the full range of educational research methods.

Although quantitative and qualitative research designs need not be considered mutually exclusive, a study might incorporate both quantitative *and* qualitative techniques. Studies that combine the collection of quantitative and qualitative data in a single study are called **mixed-methods research designs**. Mixed-methods research designs combine quantitative and qualitative approaches by including both quantitative and qualitative data in a single study. The purpose of mixed-methods research is to build on the synergy and strength that exist between quantitative and qualitative research methods to understand a phenomenon more fully than is possible using either method alone. Although this approach to research may appear obvious (i.e., of course we want a complete understanding of any phenomenon worthy of investigation), it requires a thorough understanding of both quantitative and qualitative research. Table 1–2 provides a summary of the key characteristics of mixed-methods research and an example of how it might be applied to an action research study.

table 1–2 ■ Mixed-Methods Research Summary

Definition	*Mixed-methods research* combines quantitative and qualitative approaches by including both quantitative and qualitative data in a single study. The purpose of mixed-methods research is to build on the synergy and strength that exist between quantitative and qualitative research methods to understand a phenomenon more fully than is possible using either quantitative or qualitative methods alone.
Design(s)	There are three common, basic types of mixed-methods research design: <ul><li>Explanatory sequential (also known as the QUAN–>qual) design</li><li>Exploratory sequential (also known as the QUAL–>quan) design</li><li>Convergent parallel (also known as the QUAN+QUAL) design</li></ul> The method in uppercase letters is weighted more heavily than that in lowercase, and when both methods are in uppercase, they are in balance. Three advanced types of mixed-methods research designs are also frequently used: <ul><li>Experimental design</li><li>Social justice design</li><li>Multistage evaluation design</li></ul>
Types of appropriate research questions	Questions that involve quantitative and qualitative approaches in order to better understand the phenomenon under investigation.
Key characteristics	The differences among the basic designs are related to the priority given to the following areas: <ul><li>The weight given to the type of data collected (i.e., qualitative and quantitative data are of equal weight, or one type of data has greater weight than the other)</li><li>The sequence of data collection (i.e., both types of data are collected during the same time period, or one type of data is collected in each sequential phase of the project)</li><li>The analysis techniques (i.e., either an analysis that combines the data or one that keeps the two types of data separate)</li></ul>

(Continued)

table 1–2 ■ (Continued)

Steps in the process	1. Identify the purpose of the research. 2. State research questions that require both quantitative and qualitative data collection strategies. 3. Determine the priority to be given to the type of data collected. 4. Determine the sequence of data collection (and hence the appropriate mixed-methods design). 5. Data collection. 6. Conduct data analysis that combines both kinds of data. 7. Write a report that is balanced in terms of qualitative and quantitative approaches.
Potential challenges	■ Few researchers possess all the knowledge and skills to master the full range of research techniques encompassed in quantitative and qualitative research approaches. ■ Researchers who undertake a mixed-methods study must have the considerable time and resources needed to implement such a comprehensive approach to research. ■ Analyzing quantitative and qualitative data sources concurrently or in sequence and attempting to find points of intersection as well as discrepancies requires a high level of skill.
Example	Nguyen (2007) investigated the factors that support Black male students' achievement in the Madison Metropolitan School District (MMSD). Nguyen's study used MMSD databases for information about the success rates of high school Black males and discovered interesting patterns about minority student achievement. Based on these quantitative patterns, Nguyen followed up with interviews of a sample of young Black men whose standardized test scores indicated potential for academic success. Nguyen's mixed-methods action research resulted in the identification of strategies teachers can use to be more intentional in their efforts to connect with their Black male students.

Source: Mills, Geoffrey E.; Gay, Lorraine R., *Educational Research: Competencies for Analysis and Applications*, Loose-Leaf Version, 11th Ed., © 2016. Reprinted and electronically reproduced by permission of Pearson Education, Inc., New York, NY.

Quantitative research designs also include; survey research, correlational research, causal-comparative research, experimental research, and single-subject experimental research (Mills & Gay, 2016). In the field of special education, it is common for action researchers to utilize a **single-subject experimental research design**. Single-subject experimental research designs (also referred to as single-case experimental designs) are designs that can be applied when the sample size is one or when a number of individuals are considered as one group. These designs are typically used to study the behavior change an individual exhibits as a result of some treatment. In single-subject designs, each participant serves as his or her own control.

In general, the participant is exposed to a nontreatment and a treatment phase, and performance is measured during each phase. The nontreatment phase is symbolized as A, and the treatment phase is symbolized as B. For example, if we (1) observed and recorded a student's out-of-seat behavior on five occasions, (2) applied a behavior modification procedure and observed behavior on five more occasions, and (3) stopped the behavior modification procedure and observed behavior five more times, our design would be symbolized as A-B-A. Although single-subject designs have their roots in clinical psychology and psychiatry, they are useful in many educational settings, particularly those involving studies of students with disabilities. Table 1–3 provides a summary of the key characteristics of single-subject experimental research designs and an example of how it might be applied to an action research study.

table 1–3 ■ Single-Subject Experimental Research Summary

Definition	*Single-subject experimental research designs are designs* that can be applied when the sample size is one or when a number of individuals are considered as one group.
Design(s)	Single-subject designs are classified into three major categories: A-B-A withdrawal, multiple-baseline, and alternating treatment designs.
Types of appropriate research questions	These designs are typically used to study the behavior change an individual exhibits as a result of some treatment. Although single-subject designs have their roots in clinical psychology and psychiatry, they are useful in many educational settings, particularly those involving studies of students with disabilities.
Key characteristics	■ Study includes a sample size of one, or the study considers a number of individuals as one group. ■ In single-subject designs, each participant serves as his or her own control. ■ In general, the participant is exposed to a nontreatment and treatment phase, and performance is measured during each phase. ■ Single-subject designs are applied most frequently in clinical settings where the primary emphasis is on therapeutic impact, not contribution to a research base.
Steps in the process	1. Select and define a problem. 2. Select participants and measuring instruments. 3. Prepare a research plan, including selection of the appropriate single-subject research design (A-B-A withdrawal, multiple-baseline, and alternating treatment). 4. Execute procedures. 5. Analyze the data. 6. Formulate conclusions.

(Continued)

table 1–3 ▪ *(Continued)*

Potential challenges	A major criticism of single-subject research studies is that they suffer from low external validity; in other words, results cannot be generalized to a population of interest.
Example	What is the impact of a functional mobility curriculum on five elementary-age students with severe, multiple disabilities?

Source: Mills, Geoffrey E.; Gay, Lorraine R., *Educational Research: Competencies for Analysis and Applications*, Loose-Leaf Version, 11th Ed., © 2016. Reprinted and electronically reproduced by permission of Pearson Education, Inc., New York, NY.

It is important to note that the area of focus or research question identified by the action researcher will determine the most appropriate research design (quantitative and/or qualitative) to use. While most published action research studies use narrative, descriptive methods, some studies are more quantitatively oriented and use survey and quasi-experimental research designs, mixed-methods research designs, and single-subject experimental research designs. Therefore, while this text emphasizes the use of qualitative research designs, data collection, and data analysis, it also includes quantitative research designs, data collection, and analysis (using descriptive statistics).

Defining Action Research

Over the past decade, the typical "required" research course in many schools, colleges, and departments of teacher education has changed from a traditional survey class on research methods to a more practical research course that either focuses on or includes the topic of action research. But what is action research, and why has it captured the attention of teachers, administrators, and policymakers?

Action research is any systematic inquiry conducted by teacher researchers, principals, school counselors, or other stakeholders in the teaching/learning environment to gather information about how their particular schools operate, how they teach, and how well their students learn. This information is gathered with the goals of gaining insight, developing reflective practice, effecting positive changes in the school environment (and educational practices in general), and improving student outcomes and the lives of those involved.

Action research is research done *by* teachers *for* themselves; it is not imposed on them by someone else. Action research engages teachers in a four-step process:

1. Identify an area of focus.
2. Collect data.

KEY CONCEPTS BOX 1–1

A Summary of Action Research

What?	Action research.
Who?	Conducted by teachers and principals on children in their care.
Where?	In schools and classrooms.
How?	Using a variety of research designs to match the study's area of focus, including qualitative methods to describe what is happening and to understand the effects of some educational intervention, quantitative methods to test hypotheses that rely on numerical analyses, and mixed-methods designs that combine quantitative and qualitative approaches to data collection in a single study.
Why?	To take action and effect positive educational change in the specific school environment that was studied.

3. Analyze and interpret data.
4. Develop an action plan.

Before we elaborate on these four steps, however, we will explore the historical antecedents of action research and the theoretical foundations of current action research practices. As you read these descriptions, consider which philosophy best fits your beliefs about action research, teaching, and learning. Then consider how you might incorporate action research into your professional life. Key Concepts Box 1–1 provides a summary of action research.

Origins of Action Research

The history of action research has been well documented and debated (cf. Adelman, 1993; Gunz, 1996; Kemmis, 1988; Noffke, 1994). Kurt Lewin (1890–1947) is often credited with coining the term *action research* around 1934. After a series of practical experiences in the early 1940s, he came to view action research as a process that "gives credence to the development of powers of reflective thought, discussion, decision and action by ordinary people participating in collective research on 'private troubles' that they have in common" (Adelman, 1993, p. 8).

The many "descendants" of early action researchers follow different schools of action research thought, including the American action research group, with its roots in the progressive education movement, particularly in the work of John Dewey (Noffke, 1994); the efforts in the United Kingdom toward curriculum reform and greater professionalism in teaching (Elliott, 1991); and Australian efforts located within a broad-ranging movement toward collaborative curriculum planning (Kemmis, 1988).

As is evident, the geographical locations and sociopolitical contexts in which action research efforts continue to evolve vary greatly. The primary focus of all these efforts, however, regardless of the context, is on enhancing the lives of students. As Noffke (1994) reminds us, reading the accounts of action research written by people housed in universities does little to illuminate the classroom experiences of teachers and what they hope to gain from participating in action research activities. Therefore, this text focuses on teachers examining issues related to the education of children and on partnering with teachers, administrators, counselors, and parents in the action research process.

Theoretical Foundations of Action Research

The theoretical perspectives and philosophies that inform the practices of today's teacher researchers are as varied as the historical roots for action research. The following sections briefly review the two main theories of action research: critical (or theory based) and practical.

Critical Action Research

Critical action research is also known as *emancipatory action research* because of its goal of liberation through knowledge gathering. Critical action research derives its name from the body of critical theory on which it is based, not because this type of action research is critical, as in "faultfinding" or "important," although it may certainly be both! The rationale for critical action research is provided by critical theory in the social sciences and humanities and by theories of postmodernism.

Critical theory in action research shares several fundamental purposes with critical theory in the social sciences and humanities (Kemmis, 1988). These similar interests or "commonalities of intent" include the following:

1. A shared interest in processes for enlightenment.
2. A shared interest in liberating individuals from the dictates of tradition, habit, and bureaucracy.
3. A commitment to participatory democratic processes for reform.

In addition to its roots in the critical theory of the social sciences and humanities, critical action research also draws heavily from a body of theory called **postmodernism**, which challenges the notions of truth and objectivity on which the traditional scientific method relies. Instead of claiming the incontrovertibility of fact, postmodernists argue that truth is relative, conditional, and situational and that knowledge is always an outgrowth of previous experience. For example, historically there has been little or no connection between research and practice in education—an apparent failure of research to affect teaching. This is not news for teachers! Research has been viewed as something done *on* them, not *for* them. According to Kennedy (1997), the lack of influence of research on practice has been attributed to the following qualities of educational research:

- It is not persuasive and has lacked the qualities of being compelling to teachers.
- It has not been relevant to teachers' daily practices—it has lacked practicality.
- It has not been expressed in ways that are accessible to teachers.

The postmodern perspective addresses many of these concerns by advocating for research that challenges the *taken-for-granted assumptions* of daily classroom life and presenting *truths* that are relative, conditional, situational, and based on previous experience. So, although research may provide insights into promising practices (from research conducted in *other* teachers' classrooms and schools), action research conducted in one's *own* classroom/school is more likely to be persuasive and relevant and to offer findings expressed in ways that are meaningful for teachers themselves.

Postmodern theory dissects and examines the mechanisms of knowledge production and questions many of the basic assumptions on which modern life is based. Thus, it inspires us "to examine the ordinary, everyday, taken-for-granted ways in which we organize and carry out our private, social, and professional activities" (Stringer, 1996, p. 156). Action research gives us a means by which we can undertake this examination and represent the classroom teachers' experiences that are contextually and politically constructed.

The values of critical action research dictate that all educational research should be socially responsive and exhibit other important characteristics:

1. Democratic—Enabling participation of people.
2. Participatory—Building a community of learners.
3. Empowering—Providing freedom from oppressive, debilitating conditions.
4. Life enhancing—Enabling the expression of people's full human potential. (Stringer, 2004, p. 31)

Although this critical theory-based approach has been criticized by some for lack of practical feasibility (Hammersley, 1993), it is nonetheless important to consider because it provides a helpful heuristic, or problem-solving, approach, for teachers committed to investigate through action research the taken-for-granted relationships and practices in their professional lives. Key Concepts Box 1–2 summarizes the most important components of a critical perspective of action research.

KEY CONCEPTS BOX 1–2

Components of a Critical Perspective of Action Research

Key Concept	Example
Action research is participatory and democratic.	You have identified an area in your teaching that you believe can be improved (based on data from your students). You decide to investigate the impact of your intervention and to monitor whether it makes a difference.
Action research is socially responsive and takes place in context.	You are concerned that minority children (e.g., ESL [English as a Second Language] students) in your classroom are not being presented with curriculum and teaching strategies that are culturally sensitive. You decide to learn more about how best to teach ESL children and to implement some of these strategies.
Action research helps teacher researchers examine the everyday, taken-for-granted ways in which they carry out professional practice.	You have adopted a new mathematics problem-solving curriculum and decide to monitor its impact on student performance on open-ended problem-solving questions and students' attitudes toward mathematics in general.
Knowledge gained through action research can liberate students, teachers, and administrators and enhance learning, teaching, and policy making.	Your school has a high incidence of student absenteeism in spite of a newly adopted district-wide policy on absenteeism. You investigate the perceptions of colleagues, children, and parents toward absenteeism to more fully understand why the existing policy is not having the desired outcome. Based on what you learn, you implement a new policy and systematically monitor its impact on absenteeism levels and students' attitudes toward school.

Practical Action Research

Practical action research places more emphasis on the "how-to" approach to the processes of action research and has a less "philosophical" bent. It assumes, to some degree, that individual teachers or teams of teachers are autonomous and can determine the nature of the investigation to be undertaken. It also assumes that teacher researchers are committed to continued professional development and

Voices from the Field
Critical Action Research

In this video, we see a teacher researcher embrace many of the principles that underlie critical action research. For example, the teacher researcher is willing to challenge the taken-for-granted assumptions about the implementation of technology in her classroom and acknowledges that knowledge about the "best effective strategies" will be developed through her own action research focused on student growth. In this way, the teacher researcher is living a commitment to a participatory research process that provides "liberation" through knowledge creation that is relative, conditional, situational, and an outgrowth of previous experience in her classroom.

ENHANCEDetext
video example 1–1
How do the opinions of the researcher in this video reflect the principles that underlie critical action research?

school improvement and that teacher researchers want to systematically reflect on their practices. Finally, the practical action research perspective assumes that as decision makers, teacher researchers will choose their own areas of focus, determine their data collection techniques, analyze and interpret their data, and develop action plans based on their findings. These beliefs are summarized in Key Concepts Box 1–3.

KEY CONCEPTS BOX 1–3

Components of a Practical Perspective of Action Research

Key Concept	Example
Teacher researchers have decision-making authority.	Your school has adopted a school-based decision-making approach that provides teachers with the authority to make decisions that most directly impact teaching and learning. Given this decision-making authority, you decide as part of your continued professional development to investigate the effectiveness of a newly adopted science curriculum on students' process skills and attitudes.

(Continued)

KEY CONCEPTS BOX 1–3 (*Continued*)

Components of a Practical Perspective of Action Research

Key Concept	Example
Teacher researchers are committed to continued professional development and school improvement.	Based on the results of statewide assessment tests and classroom observations, the teachers and principal at your school determine that reading comprehension skills are weak. Collaboratively, the staff determines the focus for a school improvement effort and identifies the necessary professional development that will be offered to change the ways teachers teach reading.
Teacher researchers want to reflect on their practices.	You are a successful classroom teacher who regularly reflects on your daily teaching and what areas could be improved. You believe that part of being a professional teacher is the willingness to continually examine your teaching effectiveness.
Teacher researchers will use a systematic approach for reflecting on their practice.	Given a schoolwide reading comprehension focus, you have decided to monitor the effectiveness of a new reading curriculum and teaching strategies by video recording a reading lesson (once per month), administering reading comprehension "probes" (once per week), interviewing children in your classroom (once per term), and administering statewide assessment tests (at the end of the school year).
Teacher researchers will choose an area of focus, determine data collection techniques, analyze and interpret data, and develop action plans.	To continue the example presented earlier, you have focused on the effectiveness of a new reading curriculum and teaching strategies. You have decided to collect data using video recordings of lessons, regular "probes," interviews, and statewide assessment tests. During the year, you try to interpret the data you are collecting and decide what these data suggest about the effectiveness of the new curriculum and teaching strategies. When all of the data have been collected and analyzed, you decide what action needs to be taken to refine, improve, or maintain the reading comprehension curriculum and teaching strategies.

Goals and Rationale for Action Research

Although the critical and practical theories of action research draw on vastly different worldviews, these two distinctly different philosophies are united by common goals that go a long way toward bridging whatever philosophical, historical, social, and regional variations exist.

Action research carried out according to both philosophies creates opportunities for all involved to improve the lives of children and to learn about the craft of teaching. All action researchers, regardless of their particular school of thought or theoretical position, are committed to a critical examination of classroom teaching principles and the effects that teachers' actions have on the children in their care. The reality of classroom life is that teachers are constantly confronted with practical and critical challenges, and it is up to the individual action researcher to seek out approaches that provide both practical solutions and empowerment to address the critical social and cultural issues of classrooms today.

By now it should be evident that educational change that *enhances the lives of children* is a main goal of action research. But action research can also *enhance the lives of professionals.*

Osterman and Kottkamp (1993) provide a wonderful rationale for action research as a professional growth opportunity in their "credo for reflective practice":

1. Everyone needs professional growth opportunities.
2. All professionals want to improve.
3. All professionals can learn.
4. All professionals are capable of assuming responsibility for their own professional growth and development.
5. People need and want information about their own performance.
6. Collaboration enriches professional development. (p. 46)

Action research is largely about developing the *professional disposition* of teachers, that is, encouraging teachers to be continuous learners—in their classrooms and in their practice. Although action research is not a universal panacea for the intractability of educational reform, it is an important component of the professional disposition of teachers because it provides teachers with the opportunity to model for their students how knowledge is created.

Action research is also about incorporating into the daily teaching routine a *reflective stance*—the willingness to critically examine one's teaching in order to improve or enhance it. It is about a commitment to the principle that as a teacher one is always far from the ideal but is striving toward it anyway—it's the very nature of education! Action research significantly contributes to the professional stance that teachers adopt because it encourages them to examine the dynamics of their classrooms, ponder the actions and interactions of students, validate and challenge existing practices, and take risks in the process. When teachers gain new understandings about both their own and their students' behaviors through action research, they are empowered to improve teaching in several ways:

- Make informed decisions about what to change and what not to change.
- Link prior knowledge to new information.
- Learn from experience (even failures).
- Ask questions and systematically find answers. (Fueyo & Koorland, 1997)

The goal of teachers and principals to be professional problem solvers committed to improving both their own practice and student outcomes provides a powerful reason to practice action research.

Justifying Action Research: The Impact of Action Research on Practice

At the beginning of a course on action research, I often ask teachers to reflect on what they do in their schools and classrooms; that is, what are the assumptions they take for granted in their schools and what are the origins of those practices? Often the responses include the following:

> In elementary grades, it is important to do the "skill" subjects in the morning and the "social" subjects in the afternoon because that is when young children can concentrate better and learn more.

> The best way to do whole-group instruction with young children (grades K–3) is to have them sit on the "mat" in a circle. That way, they are close to the teacher and pay more attention to what is being said.

> In high schools, the optimal time for a learning period is 43 minutes. Anything longer than that, and the students get restless and lose concentration. Therefore, I think that the proposal for "block scheduling" is just an attempt to make us more like elementary school teachers.

> If you simply share scoring guides with children, they will automatically do better on the test. There's no need to change instructional approaches.

> In a science laboratory, if children spend less time collecting data, they will develop a deeper understanding of the science concepts being taught.

Although these are real examples of just a few of the naïve theories about teaching and learning that I have heard, they also indicate the gap that has existed between research and practice in the field of education. To what extent has teaching practice been informed by research? Is teaching informed by folklore? Do teachers acquire the culture of teaching through years of participation and observation, first as students and then as neophyte teachers? How did teachers get to be the way they are? Are some of the derogatory Hollywood portrayals of teachers and teaching (as characterized, e.g., in *Ferris Bueller's Day Off* or *Mr. Holland's Opus*) really warranted? What is it about research that makes teachers, in general, snicker at the thought that it can in some way improve practice? What is the potential for this discussion to put action into action research efforts?

According to Kennedy (1997), studies of the connection between research and practice and the apparent failure of research to affect teaching has provided the following insights:

- Teachers do not find research persuasive or authoritative.
- Research has not been relevant to practice and has not addressed teachers' questions.
- Research findings have not been expressed in ways that are comprehensible to teachers.
- The education system itself is unable to change, or, conversely, it is inherently unstable and susceptible to fads.

Many teacher researchers may consider Kennedy's hypotheses to be statements of the obvious; however, these statements provide yet another rationale for why many teachers have chosen to be reflective practitioners: to address the intractability of the educational system. These hypotheses also speak to the desire to put action into ongoing action research efforts.

Action Research Is Persuasive and Authoritative

Research done by teachers for teachers involves collection of persuasive data. These data are persuasive because teachers are invested in the legitimacy of the data collection; that is, they have identified data sources that provide persuasive insights into the impact of an intervention on student outcomes. Similarly, the findings of action research and the actions recommended by these findings are authoritative for teacher researchers. In doing action research, teacher researchers have developed solutions to their own problems. Teachers—not outside "experts"—are the authorities on what works in their classrooms.

Action Research Is Relevant

The relevance of published research to the real world of teachers is perhaps the most common concern raised by teachers when asked about the practical applications of educational research—either the problems investigated by researchers are not the problems teachers really have or the schools or classrooms in which the research was conducted are vastly different from their own school environment. In reviewing the past two decades of research on schools and teaching, however, Kennedy (1997) cites the seminal works of Jackson's (1968) *Life in Classrooms* and Lortie's (1975) *Schoolteacher* as ways to illustrate the relevance of the findings of these studies. Kennedy's review found that classroom life was characterized by crowds, power, praise, and uncertainty:

Crowds—Students are always grouped with 20 or 30 others, which means that they must wait in line, wait to be called on, and wait for help.

Power—Teachers control most actions and events and decide what the group will do.

Praise—Teachers give and withhold praise, so students know which of their classmates are favored by the teacher.

Uncertainty—The presence of 20 to 30 children in a single classroom means there are many possibilities for an interruption in one's work.

Kennedy (1997) argues that one of the aims of research is to increase certainty by creating predictability within the classroom because "routines increase predictability and decrease anxiety for both teachers and students" (p. 6).

One of the outcomes of action research is that it satisfies the desire of all teachers to increase the predictability of what happens in their classrooms—in particular, to increase the likelihood that a given curriculum, instructional strategy, or use of technology will positively affect student outcomes. And although these desirable outcomes come at the initial expense of predictability—that is, they have emerged from the implementation of a *new* intervention or innovation—the findings of your action research inquiries will, over time, contribute to the predictability of your teaching environments.

Voices from the Field
Action Research Is Relevant

In this video, the teacher researcher talks about the important role action research plays in keeping her focused on making sure that the students in her classroom are learning. Using an action research process, the teacher is able to satisfy her desire for predictability in her classroom knowing that when issues arise in her teaching related to the implementation of curriculum and instructional strategies, she is able to have confidence in her research findings. This knowledge is relevant to her classroom setting and contributes to her understanding of "best practices" in her classroom and their positive impact on student outcomes.

ENHANCEDetext
video example 1–2
The researcher in this video states clearly why she thinks action research is relevant.

Action Research Allows Teachers Access to Research Findings

Kennedy (1997) also hypothesizes that the apparent lack of connection between research and practice is due to teachers' poor access to research findings. This apparent lack of impact of research on teaching is, in part, credited to teachers' prior beliefs and values and the realization that teachers' practices cannot be changed simply by informing them of the results of a study. After all, if we reflect on how we currently teach and what we hold to be sacred teaching practices, we are likely to find that our beliefs and values stem from how we were taught as children ("It worked for me and I'm successful. I'm a teacher.") and how we have had teaching modeled for us through our teaching apprenticeships (student teaching).

Simply informing teachers about research is unlikely to bring about change. Therein lies the beauty, power, and potential of action research to positively affect practice. As a teacher researcher, you challenge your taken-for-granted assumptions about teaching and learning. Your research findings are meaningful to you because *you* have identified the area of focus. *You* have been willing to challenge the conventional craft culture. In short, *your* willingness to reflect on and change your thinking about your teaching practices has led you to become a successful and productive member of the professional community.

Action Research Challenges the Intractability of Reform of the Educational System

Kennedy's final hypothesis is that the lack of connection between research and practice can be attributed to the educational system itself, not the research. Kennedy (1997) characterizes the American educational system as follows:

- It has no consensus on goals and guiding principles.
- It has no central authority to settle disputes.
- It is continually bombarded with new fads and fancies.
- It provides limited evidence to support or refute any particular idea.
- It encourages reforms that run at cross-purposes to each other.
- It gives teachers less time than most other countries do to develop curricula and daily lessons.

Given this characterization, it is little wonder that the more things change, the more they stay the same! Again, action research gives teacher researchers the opportunity to embrace a problem-solving philosophy and practice as an integral part of the culture of their schools and their professional disposition and to challenge the intractability of educational reform by making action research a part of the system rather than just another fad.

Action Research Is Not a Fad

One insight that Kennedy does not address when discussing the apparent failure of research to affect teachers' practices is the belief of many classroom teachers that researchers tend to investigate trendy fads and are interested only in the curricular approach or instructional method *du jour*. Therefore, it is not surprising to hear critics of action research say, "Why bother? This is just another fad that, like other fads in education, will eventually pass if I can wait it out!" But action research is decidedly not a fad for one simple reason: *Good teachers have always systematically looked at the effects of their teaching on student learning.* They may not have called this practice action research, and they may not have thought their reflection was formal enough to be labeled research, but action research it was!

Making Action Research a Part of Daily Teaching Practices

The first step in making action research a part of daily teaching practices is to become familiar with the process and recognize how much action research is already a part of your daily life as a classroom teacher. Consider this analogy that reveals how similar the act of teaching is to the act of doing action research. In any individual lesson, you plan, implement, and evaluate your teaching, just as a teacher researcher does when undertaking action research. You develop a list of objectives (a focus area), implement the lesson, reflect on whether the children achieved the objectives through summative evaluation statements (data collection), spend time at the end of a lesson reflecting on what happened (data analysis and interpretation), and spend time at the end of the day considering how today's lesson will affect tomorrow's lesson (action planning). Like action research, the act of teaching is largely an intuitive process carried out idiosyncratically by both experienced and novice teachers.

I was recently reminded by a teacher enrolled in one of my action research classes that in my fervor and enthusiasm to illustrate data analysis and interpretation in practice (based on some of my own research), I had unwittingly made her feel that research was something that could realistically be done only by a full-time researcher who did not have a "real" job to contend with—namely, teaching 28 very lively first graders! The teacher felt that action research was so difficult and time consuming that it was unreasonable to expect a mere mortal to undertake the activity. She felt as if she needed "Super Teacher" to burst into the classroom and take over business! Not so. If the process of action research cannot be done without adversely affecting the fundamental work of teaching, then it ought not to be done at all.

Throughout this text, we will explore practical, realistic ways in which action research can become a normative part of the teaching-learning process. There will be an initial commitment of time and energy as one learns the process, but that time is an investment in enriching the education of students. To realistically incorporate the process of action research into daily teaching practices, a few things need to happen:

- *Try the process and be convinced that the investment of time and energy is worth the outcomes.* First, undertake an action research project that is meaningful to you and addresses the needs of your students. Once the project is completed, you will see the contribution that your new understanding of the subject will make to your teaching or your students' learning (or, ideally, both!). Only then will you be fully confident that action research is a worthwhile investment of your time and energy. Your beliefs and attitudes about action research will be changed after you have tried it for yourself.
- *Know that action research is a process that can be undertaken without having a negative impact on your personal and professional life.* For example, action research, as it is described in this text, is not intended to be just "one more thing" for you to do. Teachers already have too much to do and not enough time in which to do it! The action research process advocated in this text is intended to provide you with a systematic framework that can be applied to your daily teaching routines. The investment of time as you learn how to do action research will be worth the outcomes. The process may also produce unexpected positive outcomes by providing opportunities for collaborative efforts with colleagues who share a common area of focus. This text provides strategies you can use to develop your *reflective practice* utilizing many of the existing data sources in your classroom and school. It will provide you with a model that can be shared with like-minded colleagues who also are committed to improving the teaching-learning process in their classrooms.
- *Ask your professional colleagues for support with implementation.* Although such strategies as studying theory, observing demonstrations, and practicing with feedback enable most teachers to develop their skills to the point that they can use a model fluidly, skills development by itself does not ensure that skills transfer. Relatively few persons who learn new approaches to teaching will integrate their skills into regular practice unless they receive coaching (Joyce, Hersh, & McKibben, 1983). That is why seeking support and guidance from other teacher researchers is critical to your success as an action researcher. These suggestions are summarized in Research in Action Checklist 1–1.

The Process of Action Research

Now that we have defined action research, described its historical and theoretical foundations, and explained why teachers do it, let's explore the process of action research. Many guidelines and models have been provided over the years for teacher researchers to follow:

- Kurt Lewin (1952) described a "spiraling" cyclical process that included planning, execution, and reconnaissance.
- Stephen Kemmis (1988) created a well-known representation of the action research "spiral" that includes the essential characteristics of Lewin's model. Kemmis's model includes reconnaissance, planning, first action step, monitoring, reflecting, rethinking, and evaluation.
- Emily Calhoun (1994) described an Action Research Cycle that includes selecting an area or problem of collective interest, collecting data, organizing data, analyzing and interpreting data, and taking action.
- Gordon Wells (1994) described what he calls an Idealized Model of the Action Research Cycle, that includes observing, interpreting, planning change, acting, and "the practitioner's personal theory" (p. 27), which informs and is informed by the action research cycle.
- Ernest Stringer (2004) described an Action Research Helix that includes looking, thinking, and acting as "phases of the research [are] repeated over time" (p. 10).
- John Creswell (2015) described action research as a dynamic, flexible process that involves the following steps: determining if action research is the best design to use, identifying a problem to study, locating resources to help address the problem, identifying necessary information, implementing the data collection, analyzing the data, developing a plan for action, and implementing the plan and reflecting on whether it makes a difference.
- Richard Sagor (2005) described a four-step process that includes clarifying vision, articulating theories, implementing action and collecting data, and reflecting and planning informed action.
- Cher Hendricks (2017) described an action research process that follows the principle of "systematic inquiry based on ongoing reflection" (p. 2), that is heavily influenced by the work of Lawrence Stenhouse (1981) from the Center for Applied Research in Education at the University of East Anglia in England.

✓ RESEARCH IN ACTION CHECKLIST 1–1

Making Action Research a Part of Your Daily Teaching Practice

_____Actually *try* the process to convince yourself that the investments of time and energy are worth the outcomes.

_____Recognize that action research is a process that can be undertaken without negatively affecting your personal and professional life.

_____Seek support from your professional colleagues.

Voices from the Field
Making Action Research a Part of Daily Teaching Practices

This teacher researcher states a strong case for embedding action research as a natural part of the teaching and learning process. In particular, she links action research (and teaching) to a clear focus (parallel to a learning objective) and the ongoing data collection that occurs as part of teaching: keeping records, daily charts, student observations, teacher-made checklists, and so on. And in the same way that teachers "monitor and adjust" their teaching, action researchers sometimes experience the need for a new area of focus based on their data collection, analysis, and interpretation. This vignette makes it clear that action research can be embedded in daily teaching practices, especially given a clear focus and with the support of like-minded colleagues.

ENHANCEDetext
video example 1–3
The researcher in this video discusses her views on making action research part of daily teaching practices.

All these models have enjoyed varying degrees of popularity, depending on the context in which they have been applied. For example, these action research models have been applied to agriculture, health care, social work, factory work, and community development in isolated areas.

Clearly, these action research models share some common elements: a sense of purpose based on a "problem" or "area of focus" (identification of an area of focus), observation or monitoring of practice (collection of data), synthesis of information gathered (analysis and interpretation of data), and some form of "action" that invariably "spirals" the researcher back into the process repeatedly (development of an action plan).

These shared elements are what we will focus on in this text. The following chapters will address in detail how to proceed with an action research process that includes the four elements just mentioned: **identifying an area of focus, collecting data, analyzing and interpreting data,** and **developing an action plan.**

Key Concepts Box 1–4 illustrates the action research process used by Deborah South, described at the beginning of this chapter .

figure 1–1 ■ **The Dialectic Action Research Spiral**

```
                    ┌─────────────────┐
                    │  Identify an    │
                    │  Area of Focus  │
                    └─────────────────┘

  ┌─────────────┐                        ┌──────────────┐
  │ Develop an  │───────────────────────▶│ Collect Data │
  │ Action Plan │                        └──────────────┘
  └─────────────┘
                    ┌─────────────────┐
                    │  Analyze and    │
                    │  Interpret Data │
                    └─────────────────┘
```

      This four-step process, which I have termed the **Dialectic Action Research Spiral,** is illustrated in Figure 1–1. It provides teacher researchers with a practical guide and illustrates how to proceed with inquiries. It is a model for research done *by* teachers and *for* teachers and students, not research done *on* them, and as such is a dynamic and responsive model that can be adapted to different contexts and purposes. It was designed to provide teacher researchers with "provocative and constructive ways" of thinking about their work (Wolcott, 1989, p. 137).

Voices from the Field
The Process of Action Research

This teacher researcher provides a clear illustration of the action research process: developing an area of focus, collecting data, analyzing and interpreting data, and action planning through his discussion of studying student interests and engagement. The teacher researcher asserts that most teachers are already doing action research as a part of their normal teaching practice given their commitment to implementing and monitoring best practices. "Meticulous data collection" speaks to the teacher's need to understand what works and what doesn't work with different groups of students and, based on implementing the cyclical action research process, to better understand the best practices for his own classroom setting.

ENHANCEDetext
video example 1–4
In this video, a new researcher provides a nice summary of the process of action research.

KEY CONCEPTS BOX 1–4

Steps in the Action Research Process Based on Deborah South's Example of "Unmotivated" Students

Key Concept	Example
Identifying an area of focus	The purpose of this study was to describe the effects of a "study skills" curriculum on student outcomes. In particular, the study focused on the variables of student attendance, peer influence, adult influence, and students' self-esteem.
Collecting data	Data were collected through surveys, interviews, and report card/attendance records.
Analyzing and interpreting the data	Attendance did not appear to be an issue—children attended school regularly. Peer groups did affect performance. Students encouraged each other not to complete homework assignments. Teacher approval of student work appeared to have little effect on students' work habits, whereas about half the children indicated that they were motivated to complete their homework to receive parental approval. On average, student grades had dropped dramatically during the term in which they were enrolled in the study skills class. Interpretation: The study skills class was having a negative impact on student outcomes, behavior, and attitudes.
Developing an action plan	It was determined that students would not be homogeneously grouped for a study skills class the following year because of a "critical mass of negativity" that appeared to emerge from the students as they fed off each other's lack of motivation. The study skills curriculum would continue to be used and monitored with a heterogeneous grouping of students.

SUMMARY

A Brief Overview of Educational Research

1. The goal of traditional educational research is "to explain, predict, and/or control educational phenomena" (Mills & Gay, 2016, p. 5). To do this, researchers try to manipulate and control certain variables (the factors that might affect the outcomes of a particular study) to test a hypothesis (a statement the researcher makes that predicts what will happen or explains what the outcome of the study will be).

2. Positivism is the belief that natural phenomena can be explained in an orderly way using empirical sciences.

3. At the end of an experiment, researchers would compare the progress of each group in the study and decide whether the hypothesis could be accepted or rejected with a predetermined level of statistical significance (e.g., that the difference between the mean for the control group and the mean for the experimental group is large, compared with the standard error).

4. Collaborative action research utilizes the expertise of the collaborators and fosters sustained dialogue among educational stakeholders in different settings (Hendricks, 2017, p. 7).

5. Quantitative research focuses on controlling a small number of variables to determine cause-effect relationships and/or the strength of those relationships. This type of research uses numbers to quantify the cause-effect relationship.

6. Qualitative research uses narrative, descriptive approaches to data collection to understand the way things are and what the research means from the perspectives of the participants in the study. Qualitative approaches might include, for example, conducting face-to-face interviews, making observations, and video recording interactions.

7. Studies that combine the collection of quantitative and qualitative data in a single study are called mixed-methods research designs. The purpose of mixed-methods research is to build on the synergy and strength that exists between quantitative and qualitative research methods to understand a phenomenon more fully than is possible using either method alone.

8. Single-subject experimental research designs (also referred to as single-case experimental designs) are designs that can be applied when the sample size is one or when a number of individuals are considered as one group. These designs are typically used to study the behavior change an individual exhibits as a result of some treatment. In single-subject designs, each participant serves as his or her own control. In general, the participant is exposed to a nontreatment and a treatment phase, and performance is measured during each phase.

9. The area of focus or research question identified by the action researcher will determine the most appropriate approach (quantitative and/or qualitative) to use.

Defining Action Research

10. Action research is any systematic inquiry conducted by teacher researchers, principals, school counselors, or other stakeholders in the teaching/learning environment to gather information about how their particular schools operate, how they teach, and how well their students learn.
11. Action research engages teacher researchers in a four-step process (referred to in this text as the *Dialectic Action Research Spiral*):
    a. Identify an area of focus.
    b. Collect data.
    c. Analyze and interpret data.
    d. Develop an action plan.

Origins of Action Research

12. Kurt Lewin (1890–1947) is often credited with coining the term *action research* around 1934.
13. The many "descendants" of early action researchers follow different schools of action research thought, including the American action research group with its roots in the progressive education movement, particularly the work of John Dewey (Noffke, 1994); the efforts in the United Kingdom toward curriculum reform and greater professionalism in teaching (Elliott, 1991); and Australian efforts located within a broad-ranging movement toward collaborative curriculum planning (Kemmis, 1988).

Theoretical Foundations of Action Research

14. Critical action research is also known as *emancipatory action research* because of its goal of liberation through knowledge gathering. Critical action research derives its name from the body of critical theory on which it is based, not because this type of action research is critical, as in "faultfinding" or "important," although it may certainly be both!
15. Postmodernism challenges the notions of truth and objectivity on which the traditional scientific method relies. Instead of claiming the incontrovertibility of fact, postmodernists argue that truth is relative, conditional, and situational and that knowledge is always an outgrowth of previous experience.
16. The values of critical action research dictate that all educational research should be socially responsive and have the following characteristics:
    a. Democratic
    b. Participatory
    c. Empowering
    d. Life enhancing
17. Practical action research places more emphasis on the "how-to" approach to the processes of action research and has a less "philosophical" bent.
18. It assumes, to some degree, that individual teachers or teams of teachers are autonomous and can determine the nature of the investigation to be undertaken.

Goals and Rationale for Action Research

19. Action research carried out according to both philosophies creates opportunities for all involved to improve the lives of children and to learn about the craft of teaching. All action researchers, regardless of their particular school of thought or theoretical position, are committed to a critical examination of classroom teaching principles and the effects teachers' actions have on the children in their care.
20. The goal of teachers to be professional problem solvers committed to improving both their own practice and student outcomes provides a powerful reason to practice action research.

Justifying Action Research: The Impact of Action Research on Practice

21. Action research is persuasive and authoritative.
22. Action research is relevant.
23. Action research allows teachers access to research findings.
24. Action research challenges the intractability of reform of the educational system.
25. Action research is not a fad.

Making Action Research a Part of Daily Teaching Practices

26. The first step in making action research a part of daily teaching practices is to become familiar with the process and recognize how much action research is already a part of your daily life as a classroom teacher.
27. Try the process and be convinced that the investment of time and energy is worth the outcomes.
28. Know that action research is a process that can be undertaken without having a negative impact on your personal and professional life.
29. Ask your professional colleagues for support with implementation.

The Process of Action Research

30. The Dialectic Action Research Spiral includes the following four elements:
    a. Identifying an area of focus
    b. Collecting data
    c. Analyzing and interpreting data
    d. Developing an action plan

TASKS

1. How would you describe the purpose(s) of action research?
2. How do the tenets of the critical perspective support the need for action research?

3. Suppose that the students in your class are not progressing in essay writing as you had hoped. Using the four steps in the action research process described in this chapter, sketch out briefly what you might do to systematically examine this issue.
4. Your school has received a large professional development grant focused on improving children's scores on a national reading test. You believe that your existing reading program is strong. What kind of action research study might you conduct to address the differences between your current reading program's outcomes and the concepts tested on the national test?

2

Ethics

After reading this chapter you should be able to:

2.1 Clarify ethical issues involved in conducting action research.

2.2 Recognize the challenges and procedures for obtaining Institutional Review Board (IRB) approval.

2.3 Recognize the ethical obligations that educational researchers have and describe the codes and procedures they follow to ensure they adhere to them.

This chapter describes the ethical issues that confront teacher researchers and suggests a series of ethical guidelines to help ensure that your research is conducted in an ethical manner.

The Use of Technology to Enhance Mathematics Achievement

Geoff Mills

Children learn at an early age the concept of light refraction. Peering into fishbowls, children see that the fish, rocks, plants, and toys appear larger than life—their movement, shape, and size distorted by the refraction of light. We have all been puzzled at some time in our lives by this illusion and the contradiction between what we see and what we get as we attempt to reach in and touch the inhabitants of the fishbowl. Can the same be said for the use of technology in mathematics reform? Is what we see in classrooms really what we get? Are students and teachers developing a functional and appropriate use of the technology, or are they just playing at the computer? Are teachers and students making connections between the use of technology for presenting models and the concepts that the models represent? How is the use of technology to enhance curriculum and instruction in mathematics affecting student outcomes in mathematics? It is this final question that drove the schoolwide action research project at Billabong Elementary School.

*B*illabong elementary school is a large K–7 school that has embraced the use of technology as a key component of its mathematics curriculum reform efforts. Visitors to the school—and there are many—are given tours. The teachers at Billabong Elementary consider that they "teach in a fishbowl," constantly on display to the outside world. In many ways, the school looks different from traditional schools, and visitors to the school are invited to look into classrooms through the large windows that provide them with snapshots into the inner sanctum of our classrooms.

The principal of Billabong Elementary is described by his teachers as a "visionary leader," and the school has a large collection of computer hardware and software because of the principal's grant-writing efforts. One key component of the principal's vision has been the introduction of technology to the school. In large part, this technology has been made possible through school-business partnerships that he has forged. The principal is committed to the use of technology at Billabong because of what he sees as the gap between the "real world" and the "school world"; he thinks that one way to bridge this gap is to embrace technology in an effort to prepare children for the twenty-first century.

As a site council responsible for guiding staff development efforts in the school, we decided to focus on the impact of our extensive investment in technology on student achievement in mathematics. In particular, we wanted to know the following:

1. Whether our use of technology was successfully meeting the National Council of Teachers of Mathematics (NCTM) Standards
2. How those Standards were being interpreted into classroom practice and student outcomes

Our action research team decided that we would collect data by observing in each other's classrooms, interviewing teachers and children, analyzing mathematics test data, and comparing the mathematics curriculum taught in the school with the NCTM Standards. When we presented our project to the faculty, all of the teachers and the principal appeared to want to cooperate with the research team's requests for access to classrooms, curriculum materials, and so on. Our hope was to learn more about our technology intervention and how we might continue to evolve as a faculty in this area.

As you move through the halls at Billabong, there is a great deal to be seen—classrooms are open for the inquiring eye. Kindergarten through third-grade classrooms characteristically have six computers, as well as scanners, color printers, and networking with the school's library (thus having access to the extensive CD-ROM collection). The fourth- through seventh-grade classrooms have all of these resources and another six computers per classroom. In one class, all of the children are given an individual laptop computer to use for the year. Children can be seen using computers as part of their class assignments, busying themselves with creating HyperCard stacks for creative writing, "playing" math games, and so on. Math learning centers are evident, and each child is given varied opportunities to interact with a number of different math manipulatives: base 10 blocks, place value charts, construction materials, colored chips, tangrams, and geo-boards, to name a few.

What we saw from the inside of each other's classrooms, however, was distinctly different from what we had seen from the outside "looking in." For example, in many of the classrooms children could be seen busily engaged with the computers playing math mazes. For the most part, however, children were engaged in low-level activities, and the purpose of the tasks was lost. Many of the children were engaged in "drill-and-kill" activities that had little relevance to their math learning. The computers had taken on the role of an electronic work sheet to keep children busy once they had completed other assigned math tasks.

Interviews with children were revealing. When we interviewed the children, we did so with a guarantee that their responses would be confidential and asked that they be honest with us—after all, our goal was to provide the best possible mathematics learning environment for them that we possibly could. Some children were brutally honest, telling in great detail the kinds of math activities some teachers used on the computers. Some activities were singled out by children as being a "waste of time," and others described some teachers as "not having a clue" about how the computers were really being used. Indeed, some of this information was confirmed by our own observations of classrooms where children had become proficient at "scribbling" on the computer screen using the mouse and a graphics program and quickly returning to the "drill-and-kill" screen when the teacher approached.

While the computers were being heavily used, the appropriateness of their use was questionable. This was nowhere more evident than in classrooms where the calculator function had been removed from the computers. As one teacher explained, "The children are unable to mentally compute, and their basic skills have deteriorated . . . so we can't have them using calculators until they master the basic skills!" There appeared to be consensus among the teachers that there was a direct relationship between providing children with access to computers and children's lack of ability to recall basic math facts.

The interviews with teachers revealed other problems. Many of the teachers knew very little about the NCTM Standards and continued to use their old "tried and proven" curriculum in spite of a new textbook adoption promoted by the principal. In fact, some teachers were very unhappy about the textbook adoption because no teachers had been consulted in the process—the textbook had been selected by the principal, who was a good friend of the author. In return for piloting the curriculum materials in the school, the principal secured free copies of the textbook.

Compared to other schools in the district, our children appeared to be doing below average on statewide assessments. This came as quite a surprise to some teachers who felt that their children were doing well in most math strands with the exception of open-ended problem-solving and algebraic relationships. In these teachers' views, the problem was with the appropriateness of the tests, not the use of technology to enhance teaching and learning.

The findings of our schoolwide action research effort raised some difficult ethical dilemmas for the action research team:

1. What do we do with the data that provided a negative picture of individual teachers in the school? Do we share data on an individual basis with teachers who were singled out by students? What risks do we run in sharing this information? How can we promote professional development without hurting anyone?

2. *What do we do with the data that indicated a great deal of dissatisfaction with how the principal had mandated the choice of curriculum? Do we risk alienating the teachers from the administration? Could some teachers be hurt professionally by action the principal might take?*

3. *How can we improve student achievement through the use of technology without hurting teachers (and the principal) in the process?*

The action research team decided to adopt a "hold harmless" approach to dealing with the findings of the study. We shared the general findings of the study with teachers at a faculty meeting and invited teachers, on a voluntary basis, to meet with us to discuss the data for their classrooms. Similarly, we invited the principal to meet with us to discuss implications of the findings for future professional development opportunities.

This vignette provides an excellent illustration of the unpredictable events that can occur during the conduct of educational research. It is intended not to frighten action researchers but rather to provide an example of the kinds of challenges teacher researchers can face in conducting research in their own classroom and school. This chapter will help action researchers develop their own list of ethical guidelines so that they will act appropriately if and when confronted with a difficult ethical question. The chapter will also provide guidelines to help action researchers obtain Institutional Review Board (IRB) approval.

The Ethics of Research

All research studies involve ethical considerations. Therefore, all researchers must be aware of and attend to the ethical considerations related to their studies. In research, the ends do not justify the means, and researchers must not put their need to carry out their study above their responsibility to maintain the well-being of the study participants. Research studies are built on trust between the researcher and the participants, and researchers have a responsibility to maintain that trust, just as they expect participants to maintain it in the data they provide. Two overriding rules of ethics are that participants should not be harmed in any way—physically, mentally, or socially—and that researchers obtain participants' informed consent, as described in the following sections.

To remind researchers of their responsibilities, professional organizations have developed codes of ethical conduct for their members. The general principles from the Ethical Principles of Psychologists and Code of Conduct adopted by the American Psychological Association (June 1, 2010) provide guidelines and contain specific ethical standards in 10 categories, which are not limited to research: (1) Resolving Ethical Issues, (2) Competence, (3) Human Relations, (4) Privacy and Confidentiality, (5) Advertising and Other Public Statements, (6) Record Keeping and Fees, (7) Education and Training, (8) Research and Publication, (9) Assessment, and (10) Therapy. You may read the full text online at the website for the American Psychological Association (http://www.apa.org).

The American Educational Research Association (AERA) approved a code of ethics in February 2011 (for a comprehensive discussion, see *Educational Researcher*, 40(3), 145–156). The code of ethics of AERA outlines a set of values on which educational researchers should build their research practices. Included in the code of ethics are five principles and 22 ethical standards. The principles are intended to serve as a guide for education researchers in determining ethical behavior in various contexts and include (a) Professional Competence, (b) Integrity, (c) Professional, Scientific, and Scholarly Responsibility, (d) Respect for People's Rights, Dignity, and Diversity, and (e) Social Responsibility. The 22 ethical standards set forth the rules for ethical conduct by education researchers and, while not intended to be an exhaustive list, aim to cover most situations encountered by education researchers. The list is as follows:

1. Scientific, Scholarly, and Professional Standards
2. Competence
3. Use and Misuse of Expertise
4. Fabrication, Falsification, and Plagiarism
5. Avoiding Harm
6. Nondiscrimination
7. Nonexploitation
8. Harassment
9. Employment Decisions
10. Conflicts of Interest
11. Public Communications
12. Confidentiality
13. Informed Consent
14. Research Planning, Implementation, and Dissemination
15. Authorship Credit
16. Publication Process
17. Responsibilities of Reviewers
18. Teaching, Training, and Administering Education Programs
19. Mentoring
20. Supervision
21. Contractual and Consulting Services
22. Adherence to the Ethical Standards of the American Educational Research Association

Of particular importance to action researchers is the ethical standard of informed consent, and AERA provides considerable guidance for how and when informed consent with children should be sought (cf. pp. 151–152). This will be discussed further in the section on ethical guidelines later in the chapter. Action researchers should consider membership of AERA and, in particular, membership of the Action Research Special Interest Group (SIG), that provides a forum for experienced and novice action researchers alike. Membership information and benefits can be found at aera.net.

In 1974, the U.S. Congress put the force of law behind codes of ethical research and passed the **National Research Act of 1974**, which authorized the creation of the National Commission for the Protection of Human Subjects of Biomedical and Behavioral Research. This commission was charged with developing an ethical code and guidelines for researchers. The need for legal restrictions was graphically illustrated by a number of studies in which researchers lied to or put research participants in harm's way in order to carry out their studies. For example, in a study on the effects of group pressure (conducted some years ago), researchers lied to participants while they participated in and watched what they thought was actual electric shocking of other participants (Milgram, 1964). In another study, men known to be infected with syphilis were not treated for their illness because they were part of a control group in a comparative study (Jones, 1998). Incidents such as these prompted governmental regulations regarding research studies, and today, most universities, research centers, and medical centers adhere to ethical guidelines that prohibit such methods. Most universities have a review group, usually called the *Human Subjects Review Committee (HSRC)* or *IRB*.

Institutional Review Boards and Action Researchers

Teacher researchers conducting action research as part of a university program of study face unique challenges associated with obtaining IRB approval and must meet standards that go beyond what most schools and school districts require as part of their own research protocols. IRBs are charged by universities to ensure the ethical conduct of research involving human subjects. The key issue for teacher researchers studying their own practices and, hence, collecting data based primarily on student outcomes relates to the fact that they are acting not only as researchers but also as the change agents who have the power and authority to bring about change in their classrooms. According to Nolen and Vander Putten (2007), "These potentially conflicting roles can confound the individual's primary objective in the classroom or school: student learning" (p. 402). Given this potential conflict, Nolen and Vander Putten raise a number of questions, the answers to which provide guidance for action researchers seeking to obtain IRB approval:

- At what point does teaching become research?
- Where does the accountability for this research lie?

- Are teachers properly trained to see the possible ethical pitfalls in such research?
- How are the rights and freedoms of the research participants (the students) protected?

Given the emancipatory nature of action research (and the definition of action research used in this text), it is clear that the answer to the first question is that teaching and research are intertwined. For action researchers studying their own practices and their impact on student outcomes, the inquiry lens of action research pervades the teaching process: Teacher researchers are the data collection instruments constantly monitoring what is going on in their classrooms.

The accountability for this research lies not only with the teacher researcher but also, in a university context, with the researcher's mentor/teacher, who must ensure that proposed action research studies are ethical in their conduct. As such, it is the responsibility of the university instructor to teach neophyte teacher researchers about the potential ethical pitfalls associated with classroom/school-based action research. It is the responsibility of the IRB to ensure that action researchers address potential ethical challenges in their written proposals and (when called for) in supplementary oral presentations.

In many ways, the most complex issue action researchers face is how to safeguard the rights and freedoms of the students in the classrooms. How do teachers negotiate informed consent with students (and their parents)? Are students really in a position to opt out of any research their classroom teachers are conducting? Similarly, this question raises concerns about the role of power and authority in a classroom environment and whether students can reasonably be expected to opt out of a study without being concerned about possible censure by the classroom teacher. It should be noted that these kinds of concerns are not new to action researchers or any other qualitatively oriented community-based researchers. IRBs (which are often populated by quantitatively oriented researchers) often struggle with social science research proposals that invariably focus on "insider" research, where the research process is inherently open ended and intimate. Teachers are active participant observers of their classrooms, continually monitoring and adjusting their teaching based on formal and informal observations of their students. Nevertheless, IRBs have been condoning this kind of research for many years, and action researchers should not be intimidated by the prospect of answering important ethical questions, even if the accompanying frustration of "these quantitative researchers really don't understand what we do" threatens to sideline the research.

Given this context, I offer the following recommendations for action researchers wishing to obtain IRB approval (adapted from Nolen and Vander Putten, 2007):

- Action researchers should provide IRBs with all the necessary university-based IRB requirements (which vary slightly from university to university).

- Action researchers should provide IRBs, school district administrators, and parents with data collection plans that clearly minimize data sources that could be construed as providing evidence that could be used in a coercive manner.
- Action researchers should provide IRBs, school district administrators, and parents with cover letters that explain their studies and include statements about the dual role of teacher and researcher and the sensitivity it takes to conduct research into one's own practice.
- Action researchers should provide IRBs, school district administrators, and parents with parental consent forms that clearly state how they will guarantee that students will be protected from harm, that is, that students will not be penalized for not participating in a study.
- Action researchers should include in all data collection instruments a final "yes or no" option, such as "Please include my answers in the study," which unobtrusively allows the student to opt out of the study while appearing to participate.

It is the burden of the action researcher to provide the IRB with evidence that the proposed study clearly addresses issues of informed consent, protection from harm, student autonomy, and the potentially coercive nature of action research.

The National Research Act of 1974 was also designed to protect the privacy of students' educational records. Among its provisions is the specification that data that actually identify students may not be made available unless written permission is acquired from the students (if of age) or a parent or legal guardian. The consent must indicate what data may be disclosed, for what purposes, and to whom. If part of your study requires obtaining information from individual elementary students' record files, you would need to obtain written permission from each student's parent or guardian, not a blanket approval from the school principal or classroom teacher. Note that if you are interested in using only class averages (in which no individual student is identified), individual consent from the principal would likely suffice. If you calculate the class average from individual student records, however, individual permission would be necessary because you have access to individual records.

There are some exceptions that may not require written consent. For example, school personnel with a "legitimate educational interest" in a student would not need written consent to examine student records. In other cases, the researcher could request that a teacher or guidance counselor either remove names from students' records completely or replace them with a coded number or letter. The researcher can then use the records without knowing the names of the individual students. Again, this adherence to providing anonymity offers other instructional challenges for the teacher researcher who wishes to use formative and summative evaluation data to develop specific instructional interventions designed to meet students' needs.

It is also worth noting that some IRBs do not require IRB approval for action research conducted as part of a university course. Be sure to check with your

Voices from the Field
Institutional Review Boards and Action Researchers

The teacher researcher in this video vignette was a student teacher who was conducting action research as a coursework requirement. At this student's university coursework assignments were not required to have IRB approval. However, the student was proactive in notifying the parents of children in his class about the research that was being done and providing assurances of confidentiality and anonymity through the use of a cover letter. The student also sought informed consent from the students in his class. Given that this research was being done as a coursework assignment, the student should have also checked with the local school district to determine if there was a policy covering classroom based research and whether any IRB and/or informed consent requirements existed.

ENHANCEDetext
video example 2–1
The researcher in this video discusses submitting his research materials for review, but he does not mention an Institutional Review Board. How might a classroom teacher who is not affiliated with a university seek a formal, unbiased, and timely review of his or her study design?

instructor and/or IRB to determine if IRB approval is required at your university. Sometimes the determining factor in this decision relates to whether the outcomes of the proposed study will be published or presented at a professional conference.

The sources and advice offered in this chapter will help you to conceive and conduct your research ethically. The suggestions provided do not cover all the ethical issues you are likely to encounter in your research. Perhaps the fundamental ethical rule is that participants should not be harmed in any way, real or possible, in the name of science. Respect and concern for your own integrity and for your participants' dignity and welfare are the bottom lines of ethical research.

Doing the Right Thing: The Role of Ethics in Action Research

Simply stated, the role of ethics in action research can be considered in terms of how each of us treats the individuals with whom we interact at our school setting: students, parents, volunteers, administrators, and teaching colleagues. As Nolen and Vander Putten (2007) contend, "Like the physician and the counselor, the teacher cannot abandon the role of practitioner but must always exercise professional judgment and skill in the best interest of the student" (p. 403). Similarly, Smith (1990) stated, "At a commonsense level, caring, fairness, openness, and truth seem to be the important values undergirding the relationships and the activity of inquiring" (p. 260). However, values such as these invariably take on a different meaning for different people with whom we interact. Nevertheless, the success of your action research project depends on a clear understanding of the intimate nature of the research process and on not harming participants in the name of research.

The vignette of Billabong Elementary School that opened this chapter is a good reminder of why it is important to think about ethical dilemmas before they occur. And although I have seen few instances of where ethical dilemmas have threatened to stall a collaborative action research effort, the very nature of the enterprise provides the potential for conflict and harm. Considering the ethics of action research before commencing the work (and as part of your IRB approval) is one way to ensure that you are prepared to respond in an ethical, caring manner to difficult situations that may arise.

The issue of ethics in qualitative research and action-oriented research has received considerable attention in recent years (cf. Christians, 2000; Creswell, 2015; Eisner, 1991; Flinders, 1992; Mills & Gay, 2016; Nolen & Vander Putten, 2007; Smith, 1990; Soltis, 1990; Wolcott, 1990). Most of this literature describes mistakes made in the research process and how the ethics of the situation were addressed. What makes the subject of ethics particularly challenging for teacher researchers is the intimate and open-ended nature of action research.

Action research is intimate because there is little distance between teacher researchers and their subjects, the students in their classrooms and schools. Qualitatively oriented action research is open ended because the direction of the research often unfolds during the course of the study. This significantly complicates the ability of teacher researchers to obtain students' "fully informed consent" to participate in the research process. Informed consent is central to research ethics. It is the principle that seeks to ensure that all human subjects retain autonomy and the ability to judge for themselves what risks are worth taking for the purpose of furthering scientific knowledge.

In action research, the key participants in a study are often the students in our classrooms. How does the concept of informed consent apply to them? Do we need to obtain written permission from parents/guardians before collecting naturally occurring data, such as test scores, observations, work samples, and so on? As stated previously, it will depend on whether you need to obtain IRB approval in addition to meeting the local school district protocols. But as you will see in the following discussion, regardless of the kinds of mandatory research approvals, it is important that you develop your own criteria for what you consider to be ethical behavior.

Ethical Guidelines

The following commonsense ethical guidelines may help teacher researchers respond appropriately when faced with ethical decisions before, during, and after an action research inquiry.

Informed Consent and Protection from Harm

Informed consent should take the form of a dialogue that mutually shapes the research and the results. Informed consent ensures that research participants enter the research of their free will and with an understanding of the study and any possible dangers that may arise. It is intended to reduce the likelihood that participants will be exploited by a researcher persuading them to participate without fully knowing the study's requirements. Be clear about whether you need to seek permission from participants in the study. For example, if you are using photographs or video recordings as data collection techniques and intend to use these artifacts in a public forum, such as a presentation at a conference, make sure that you have checked whether written permission is necessary. The answer may vary from district to district and university to university depending on how the materials are to be used.

Similarly, consider how to inform students that they are subjects in a study. For example, you may decide to interview a small group to determine how a problem-solving curriculum is being implemented in different classrooms as a follow-up to a survey or an observation. How will you ensure the anonymity of the respondents to protect their privacy? How will you protect the confidentiality of participants? In the case of Billabong Elementary School (from the opening vignette), the action research team wrestled with the issue of informed consent. When they initially presented their project to the faculty at the school, all of the teachers and the principal appeared to want to cooperate with the research team's requests for access to classrooms, curriculum materials and so on. The research team had not collected data without their knowledge. Still, the team wondered if they had done enough. Would the presentation of their data harm the teachers, especially if the teachers had expressed disapproval of the principal? Were the teachers adequately prepared for the risks? After debate, the researchers resolved to share the general findings of the study rather than singling out any individual teacher's comments. That way, the researchers could protect the confidentiality of participants while at the same time sharing the themes that emerged from the study.

Freedom from harm is focused on not exposing students to risks. It involves issues of confidentiality (to protect students from embarrassment or ridicule) and issues related to personal privacy. Collecting information on participants or observing them without their knowledge or without appropriate permission is not ethical. Furthermore, any information or data that are collected, either from or about a person, should be strictly confidential, especially if it is at all personal. Access to data should be limited to persons directly involved in conducting the research. An individual participant's performance should not be reported or made public using the participant's name, even for an innocuous measure such as an arithmetic test. For example, individuals identified as members of a group that performed poorly on a research instrument might be subjected to ridicule, censure by parents, or lowered teacher expectations.

The use of anonymity or confidentiality to avoid privacy invasion and potential harm is common. **Anonymity** means that the researcher does not know the identities of the participants in the study. On the other hand, confidentiality is when the researcher knows the identities of participants but promises not to release them to anyone else. If the researcher knows participants' identities, there can be confidentiality but no anonymity. Removing names or coding records is one commonly used way to maintain anonymity. When planning your study, you must indicate to participants (students and parents) whether you will provide confidentiality (you will know but will not tell) or anonymity (you will not know the participants' names) and be sure they know the difference. Clearly, this is a challenge in action research when the focus of the research is on the outcomes of students in the teacher researcher's classroom.

Confidentiality usually involves the use of pseudonyms to conceal identities. However, protecting confidentiality in a qualitatively oriented action research effort is sometimes more problematic than just assigning pseudonyms. For example, a team of teacher researchers who are responsible for driving a schoolwide action research effort will likely be made privy to the intimate details of their colleagues' classrooms. It will be their challenge to make sure that they protect their colleagues from stress, embarrassment, or unwanted publicity that may come from sharing the action research findings. Of course, all of this must be balanced against their commitment to improve the learning experiences of the students in their school.

Figure 2–1 presents a cover letter written by a principal in support of a doctoral student's proposed study. Note that the student secured not only the principal's permission but also his strong support and cooperation by sharing the potential benefits of the study with the principal's students. Figure 2–2 presents the parental consent form that accompanied the cover letter. It addresses many of the ethical and legal concerns discussed in this chapter.

Clearly, human relations are an important factor in conducting research in applied settings. That you should be your usual charming self goes without saying. But you should keep in mind that you are dealing with sincere, concerned educators who may not have your level of research expertise. Therefore, you must make a special effort to discuss your study in plain English (it is possible!) and to never give the impression that you are talking down to them. Also, your task is not over once the study begins. To maintain your participants' initial level of cooperation, monitor their feelings and respond as necessary.

figure 2–1 ▪ Sample Cover Letter

SCHOOL OF EDUCATION

BOSTON COLLEGE

January 17, 2005

Mr. Dennis Yacubian
Vice-Principal
Westside High School
Westside, MA 00001

Dear Mr. Yacubian,

The Department of Measurement and Evaluation at Boston College is interested in determining the types of testing, evaluation, research, and statistical needs high school administrators in Massachusetts have. Our intent is to develop a master's level program that provides graduates who can meet the methodological needs of high school administrators. The enclosed questionnaire is designed to obtain information about your needs in the areas of testing, evaluation, research, and statistics. Your responses will be anonymous and seriously considered in developing the planned program. We will also provide you a summary of the results of the survey so that you can examine the responses of other high school administrators. This study has been approved by the university's Human Subjects Review Committee.

We would appreciate your completion of the questionnaire by January 31. We have provided a stamped, addressed envelope for you to use in returning the questionnaire. You do not need to put your name on the questionnaire, but we request that you sign your name on the enclosed postcard and mail it separately from the questionnaire. That way we will know you have replied and will not have to bother you with follow-up letters.

We realize that your schedule is busy and your time is valuable. However, we hope that the 15 minutes it will take you to complete the questionnaire will help lead to a program that will provide a useful service to school administrators.

Thank you in advance for your participation. If you have questions about the study, you can contact me at 555-555-4444.

Yours truly,

James Jones
Department Chair

Deception

There is no room for deception in action research (or any other research for that matter). For example, if during an interview a colleague, parent, or student

figure 2–2 ■ **Parental Consent Form for a Proposed Research Study**

PARENTAL CONSENT FORM

The information provided on this form and the accompanying cover letter is presented to you in order to fulfill legal and ethical requirements for Northwest Eaton College (the institution sponsoring this doctoral dissertation study) and the Department of Health and Human Services (HHS) regulations for the Protection of Human Research Subjects as amended on March 26, 1989. The wording used in this form is utilized for all types of studies and should not be misinterpreted for this particular study.

The dissertation committee at Northern University and the Research Review Committee of Knox County Public Schools have both given approval to conduct this study, "The Relationships Between the Modality Preferences of Elementary Students and Selected Instructional Styles of CAI as They Affect Verbal Learning of Facts." The purpose of this study is to determine the effect on achievement scores when the identified learning styles (visual, audio, tactile/kinesthetic) of elementary students in grades 3 and 5 are matched or mismatched to the instructional methods of specifically selected computer assisted instruction (CAI).

Your child will be involved in this study by way of the following:

1. Pretest on animal facts.
2. Posttest on animal facts.
3. Test on learning styles.
4. Interaction with computer-assisted instruction (CAI-software on the computer)— visual, audio, tactile CAI matching the student's own learning style.

All of these activities should not take more than two hours per student. There are no foreseeable risks to the students involved. In addition, the parent or researcher may remove the student from the study at any time with just cause. Specific information about individual students will be kept *strictly confidential* and will be obtainable from the school principal if desired. The results that are published publicly will not reference any individual students since the study will only analyze relationships among groups of data.

The purpose of this form is to allow your child to participate in the study, and to allow the researcher to use the information already available at the school or information obtained from the actual study to analyze the outcomes of the study. Parental consent for this research study is strictly voluntary without undue influence or penalty. The parent signature below also assumes that the child understands and agrees to participate cooperatively.

If you have additional questions regarding the study, the rights of subjects, or potential problems, please call the principal, Ms. Gwen Gregory, or the researcher, Ms. Joleen Levine (Director of Computer Education, Northern University, 555-5554).

_____

Student's Name

_____   _____

Signature of Parent/Guardian   Date

Voices from the Field
Informed Consent and Protection from Harm

The teacher researcher in this vignette asserts that because she was using "regular test data," it was not necessary to seek informed consent from the parents and the students. Furthermore, she claims that the students were not fearful that their test results would be published in the local newspaper. Informed consent can be a moving target throughout the action research process, and given the context in which this teacher researcher was working (student teacher), an argument could be made to the student that seeking informed consent from students in the form of a signed letter should be considered standard operating procedure and a necessary step in protecting students from any harm. Further, teacher researchers should always check local school district policies covering the conduct of research in classrooms.

ENHANCEDetext
video example 2–2
In your view, did the researcher in this video do the right thing by not directly seeking student consent?

confides in you "off the record," then the substance of the conversation should remain off the record. Regardless of how meaningful the comments, you have a responsibility to act with integrity and to honor your interviewees' requests for confidentiality. Similarly, there is no place for hidden microphones in order to capture interviewees "on tape." If you wish to record a conversation, seek verbal and/or written permission. It is recommended that you not do your action research studies using a topic that requires deception. Your advisor and the Human Subjects Review or IRB Committee at your institution will provide suggestions about ethical ways to carry out your research plan. Note that as the teacher researcher in an action research study, it is your responsibility to maintain ethical standards in the research.

Personal Ethical Perspective

Researchers should have an ethical perspective that is very close to their personal ethical position. This may seem like a statement of the obvious except for this caveat: As teacher researchers, we may find ourselves in situations that are foreign to us. For example, in a collaborative action research project focused on the effects of a new math problem-solving curriculum on student achievement and attitude, teachers are asked to administer a student attitude survey. The

Voices from the Field
Deception

This teacher researcher was clearly trying to deceive the school principal by not wanting to share the purpose of her action research. It appears as though the teacher researcher was fearful that she would not be allowed to conduct the research if she shared the purpose of her study focused on the use of basal readers and the inherent gender bias in these materials. The context of the teacher researcher as a student teacher completing a coursework requirement is not an excuse for failure to seek informed consent, especially if the researcher intended to disclose the findings of her study. The conduct of any research with the intent to disclose the findings to a wider audience requires that the teacher researcher seek informed consent and work within the local school district's policy for school-based research.

ENHANCEDetext

video example 2-3
Was the researcher in this video engaging in deception? What is the relationship between deception and disclosure of the findings?

surveys are then analyzed by a team of teacher researchers representing different grades or benchmark levels in the school. During the analysis, it becomes clear that one group of students is very unhappy with their math instruction and have supported their assertions with negative comments about the teacher. What will you do with the data? Should they be shared in an unedited form with the teacher? Who might be hurt in the process? What potential good can come from sharing the data? Or perhaps the principal hears that there is a problem with one teacher and asks for access to the data so that the teacher can be placed on a "plan of assistance." How should the research team respond? What assurances of confidentiality were given to the participants before collecting the data? How will you respond to the principal when you are stopped in the hallway and asked for your opinion?

This scenario is not meant to scare you away from doing action research. However, these are the kinds of unexpected outcomes that occasionally face teacher researchers who have been made privy to information about their own teaching and that of their colleagues. Smith's (1990) lesson is an important one: You will potentially avoid such awkward situations if you have clarified your own ethical perspectives at the outset. This might take the form of a values clarification activity that can be undertaken individually or collectively (see Task 1 at the end of

Voices from the Field
Personal Ethical Perspective

This teacher researcher did not seek informed consent and argued that the practice of making sure all data collection was anonymous was analogous with informed consent. The teacher researcher embraces a core ethical value of avoidance of harm as an integral part of her classroom life. While this core value/personal ethical perspective is critical to the successful conduct of classroom-based research, it does not protect the teacher if faced with an unanticipated ethical dilemma. There are no circumstances under which informed consent is a bad idea.

ENHANCEDetext

video example 2–4
Notice how the researcher in this video made efforts to conduct her research in a way that fit with her own personal ethical perspective.

this chapter). The point is this—be prepared to respond in a manner that is comfortable and natural for you. When you are placed in the "hot seat," there may not be time to give a well-thought-out, rational response. This situation will be easier if you can respond in a personal manner.

Social Principles

You should be able to identify broader social principles that are an integral part of who you are as a teacher and a contributing member of the community in which you live. These broader social principles should dictate your ethical stance. For example, democratic processes, social justice, equality, and emancipation may be the principles that guide your ethical behavior in a given situation.

Accuracy

Ensuring the accuracy of your data is a central concern of action research. It is unethical and unscientific to fabricate data in order to substantiate a personal belief or value. For example, your study may have focused on the effectiveness of a newly adopted reading program. Although you personally like the program, the data suggest that it is not effective in improving test scores. You must be able to accept the findings of the study despite your bias toward the reading program. Any attempt to manipulate the data to support a personal position is unethical.

The purpose of this discussion on ethics in action research has been to prepare you to think about a whole range of issues that face any researcher. Carefully consider how you will respond when confronted with difficult questions from colleagues,

RESEARCH IN ACTION CHECKLIST 2-1

Ethical Guidelines for Action Researchers

_____ Determine whether you require IRB approval and/or school district approval.

_____ If necessary, obtain IRB approval.

_____ Seek your action research participants' informed consent.

_____ Consider confidentiality, anonymity, and avoidance of harm.

_____ Deception is unacceptable.

_____ Develop an ethical research perspective that is close to your personal, ethical position.

_____ Determine the broader social principles that affect your ethical stance.

_____ Ensure that you accurately record data.

parents, students, and administrators. Taking time to clarify your values and ethical perspectives will help you to respond in a professional, personal, and caring fashion.

As you embark on your action research journey and data collection efforts, remember that you are ultimately condemned to freedom in matters of ethics (Eisner, 1991). There are few absolutes. Working with colleagues through issues related to confidentiality, anonymity, informed consent, and rational judgment in matters of ethics will ensure that you avoid potentially difficult situations that may arise in implementing your action research effort. Mills and Gay (2016) summarize ethical issues as follows:

> Perhaps the fundamental rule of ethics is that participants should not be harmed in any way, real or possible, in the name of science. Respect and concern for your own integrity and for your participants' dignity and welfare are the bottom lines of ethical research. (p. 23)

Remember, you will be undertaking your action research in your own classroom and school—this is the place where you will continue to conduct your professional and personal life long after you have changed your current area of focus. Attention to the fundamental ethical guidelines presented in this chapter will help ensure that, regardless of your area of focus, life in school will not be adversely affected by your quest for excellence. (See Research in Action Checklist 2–1 for ethical guidelines for teacher researchers.)

SUMMARY

The Ethics of Research

1. In research, the ends do not justify the means, and researchers must not put their need to carry out their study above their responsibility to maintain the well being of the study participants.

2. Many professional organizations have developed codes of ethical conduct for their members, such as the American Psychological Association (APA, updated June, 2010) and the American Educational Research Association (AERA updated February 2011).

3. The National Research Act of 1974 requires that, to ensure protection of participants, proposed research activities involving human participants be reviewed and approved by an authorized group before the execution of the research.

4. Institutional Review Boards (IRBs) are charged by universities to ensure the ethical conduct of research involving human subjects.

5. The key issue for teacher researchers studying their own practices and, hence, collecting data primarily based on student outcomes relates to the fact that they are acting not only as the researchers but also as the change agents who have the power and authority to bring about change in their classrooms.

6. Teachers are active participant observers of their classrooms, continually monitoring and adjusting their teaching based on formal and informal observations of their students.

7. Action researchers should provide IRBs with all the necessary university-based IRB requirements (which vary slightly from university to university).

8. Action researchers should provide IRBs, school district administrators, and parents with data collection plans that clearly minimize data sources that could be construed as providing evidence that could be used in a coercive manner.

9. Action researchers should provide IRBs, school district administrators, and parents with cover letters that explain their studies and include statements about the dual role of teacher and researcher and the sensitivity it takes to conduct research into one's own practice.

10. Action researchers should provide IRBs, school district administrators, and parents with parental consent forms that clearly state how they will guarantee that students will be protected from harm, that is, that students will not be penalized for not participating in a study.

11. Action researchers should include in all data collection instruments a final "yes or no" option, such as "Please include my answers in the study," which unobtrusively allows the student to opt out of the study while appearing to participate.

Doing the Right Thing: The Role of Ethics in Action Research

12. The role of ethics in action research can be considered in terms of how each of us treats the individuals with whom we interact at our school setting: students, parents, volunteers, administrators, and teaching colleagues.

13. Action research is intimate because there is little distance between teacher researchers and their subjects: the students in their classrooms and schools. This significantly complicates the ability of teacher researchers to obtain students' informed consent to participate in the research process.

Ethical Guidelines

14. Perhaps the most basic and important ethical issues in research are concerned with participants' informed consent and freedom from harm.
15. Informed consent should take the form of a dialogue that mutually shapes the research and the results.
16. Informed consent ensures that research participants enter the research of their free will and with an understanding of the study and any possible dangers that may arise.
17. The use of confidentiality or anonymity to avoid privacy invasion and potential harm is common.
18. Anonymity means that the researcher does not know the identities of the participants in the study.
19. Confidentiality is when the researcher knows the identities of participants but promises not to release them to anyone else.
20. There is no room for deception in action research.
21. Researchers should have an ethical perspective that is very close to their personal ethical position.
22. You should be able to identify broader social principles that are an integral part of who you are as a teacher and a contributing member of the community in which you live.
23. Ensuring the accuracy of your data is a central concern of action research.
24. Teacher researchers should, to the best of their ability, recognize their own personal biases and develop an ethical perspective that ensures they will do the right thing when confronted with a difficult ethical dilemma.

TASK

1. Using the ethical guidelines provided in Research in Action Checklist 2–1, determine what remains to be done to address all possible ethical dilemmas in your study.

3

Deciding on an Area of Focus

After reading this chapter you should be able to:

3.1 Select an appropriate area of focus.
3.2 Do reconnaissance.
3.3 Write an action plan to guide your work.

This chapter provides guidelines for clarifying a general idea and an area of focus for action research efforts. This chapter also describes how to create an action research plan.

Interactive Teen Theater

Cathy Mitchell

Cathy Mitchell is a substitute teacher who also works with teen theater companies. Her story helps us to see how serendipity can play a role in developing an area of focus. At the beginning of the action research process, Cathy was unsure of her area of focus. As the result of an unexpected "intervention" to her teen theater production, however, when an actor did not turn up for a performance, Cathy decided to systematically investigate the effects of improvisation on audience participation.

For the past 10 years, I have directed peer education teen theaters. These companies create and perform original plays based on company members' experiences and ideas. The plays are collections of dramatic scenes, comic sketches, and songs; the topics are current issues of concern to young people, including self-esteem, substance abuse, teen pregnancy, love versus lust, violence, family relationships, and sexually transmitted diseases. We tour extensively, performing for high schools and middle schools as well as at juvenile detention facilities.

Although the company is generally very well received, I have felt that there is something stale in the actor/audience relationship. The audience sits attentively, laughs in recognition, and enjoys the variety in their class day but remains essentially passive. Question sessions after the show, initially planned to generate discussion about important topics, frequently degenerated into boring adulation questions, such as "How long have you been rehearsing this?" or "Do you want to be an actor when you grow up?"

Two years ago, a few actors had to miss a performance. When we arrived at the high school at which we were scheduled to perform, we realized the opening scene had two small roles that we could not eliminate but didn't have enough actors to fill. I asked two children from the audience to volunteer and taught them their lines backstage while the rest of the scene was going on, and they walked on stage and finished the scene. The audience was instantly galvanized. Even with this very small change, we had broken the division between actor and audience.

Thus began my experience with interactive theater. For me, this has meant bringing some of the improvisation techniques that we use to develop material during rehearsals onto the stage and inviting the audience to participate in limited ways. I found that involving the audience changed the dynamics from those of a passive spectator sport to those of a more participatory dialogue.

Through my research, I have arrived at a working description for interactive theater: A short scene is played by workshop actors. The audience is asked to look for opportunities to improve the resolution. The scene is played again, and any time anyone wants to intervene and take any character's place to show a better way of handling the situation, they just shout "Stop!" and take over the role. One scene may be played many times. Often no closure is evident, and the scene ends in unresolved issues and heightened emotions. The actors and audience then discuss the issues generated by the scene.

The purpose of my study was to determine how audience interaction with the actors in teen theater productions affected their ability to identify issues and transfer learnings into similar problems in their lives. For example, in the current production of Duct Tape Theater, a company I direct, there is a well-written scene called "Sticks and Stones," which is a collage containing poetry, a song, short monologues, and scenes. It lasts about 20 minutes and confronts issues of prejudice, discrimination, and violence. I decided, as my intervention, to replace this scene with an interactive theater piece developed with the audience. For three performances, we included "Sticks and Stones" (my control groups), and for three other performances, we included what became known as the "Violence Improv" audience interaction scene. This gave us six audiences: three control groups and three interactive groups.

Some of my methods of data collection for this project—my personal journal and the actors' journals, which are required for actors receiving credit for the class—were already in place. I also asked each teacher to write me a letter commenting on what they observed during the performance. None of these gave me the data I really wanted but which was most difficult to collect—data from the audience. I decided to have my acting company develop this data collection source with me. The actors and I developed a questionnaire to be filled out directly after the performance and a group interview technique that involved three company members meeting with a small group of audience members for about 15 minutes. The goal was to generate as many responses as possible to the scenes about teen violence and harassment. One actor served as the interviewer, one served as the scribe, and one kept a running tally of comments and responses.

The data showed four clear themes:

1. The audience clearly judged the performance containing the "Violence Improv" as more relevant to their lives than the control performance of "Sticks and Stones."
2. More individuals participated in discussing the issues of violence and harassment, with more overall comments and more comments that were considered "right on." This data showed that more audience members were able to both identify issues in the performance and relate these issues to their own lives.
3. The clearest negative response was that the interactive piece made the performance feel "rushed." These data told me that the interactive material threw off the timing of the show. I often wrote in my own journal that I felt exhausted at the end of performances, and teachers wrote to me that we were running into break time and past the end of the period "trying to squeeze everything in."
4. The biggest letdown to me was that there wasn't any significant increase in the number of different issues identified or solutions suggested between the two audiences. Even though the interactive improvisation generated more answers and much more participation, the issues and solutions were pretty much the same.

My action research project confirmed to me that my methods for making teen theater work more meaningful are on the right track. It also became clear, however, that the format I am using is not the best one. I plan to continue working with the teen theater groups, to modify the format I have used in the past, and to monitor the effects of the changes on participants' transfer of learning to their real lives. For me, this is critical work, and the most important result of this project is that I feel renewed energy for my work. Last year at this time, I was busily seeking a replacement for myself and announcing to everyone that I wasn't going to direct teens anymore. I didn't even consider that I could examine the problem, address it, and remedy it. It feels really good to expect something to happen in my working life as a result of my own research and reflection.

Not everyone comes to an action research setting with an area of focus in mind. In fact, many teachers initially resist participating in the process. It is not uncommon for teachers and administrators to skeptically claim, "I'm only here because I have to be: No action research—no teaching/administrator license!" In this teen theater example, the "intervention" and "area of focus" emerged quite unexpectedly and led to some important understandings about how to increase audience understanding and participation.

We'll assume, then, that you haven't identified an area of focus. However, you probably do have several interests and concerns: perhaps your content area, a self-contained special education classroom, an at-risk program, an alternative education program, a multigrade classroom, a single fourth-grade classroom, a reading specialist program, a block-scheduled team teaching program, or even a one-room schoolhouse, to name a few!

Every teacher and administrator who undertakes an action research project starts at the same place: making explicit a question or problem to investigate or defining an area of focus. Finding an area of focus can be hard work if your action research inquiry is going to be engaging and meaningful for you. Taking time in the beginning to ensure that your topic is important—for you—is a critical step in the action research process. No one should tell you what your area of focus is or ought to be. The following guidelines can help you focus your research question.

Clarifying a General Idea and an Area of Focus

In the beginning of the action research process, you need to clarify the general idea that will be the area of focus. The general idea is a statement that links an idea to an action and refers to a situation one wishes to change or improve on (Elliott, 1991). Here are some examples, phrased in the form of a statement based on an observation and followed by a question about how the situation could be improved:

- *Statement/Observation*: Students do not seem to be engaged during teen theater productions.
- *Question*: How can I improve their engagement?
- *Statement/Observation*: Students take a lot of time to learn problem solving in mathematics, but this process doesn't appear to transfer to their acquisition of other mathematics skills and knowledge.
- *Question*: How can I improve the integration and transfer of problem-solving skills in mathematics?
- *Statement/Observation*: Parents are unhappy with regular parent-teacher conferences.
- *Question*: How can I improve the conferencing process using student-led conferences?

Taking time in the beginning of the action research process to identify what you feel passionate about is critical. For some, this will be a relatively short activity—you may have come to an action research setting with a clear sense of a student-centered, teacher-centered, or parent-driven area of focus. For others, gaining a sense of the general idea will be more problematic. Don't rush it. Take time to talk to colleagues, reflect on your daily classroom life, and carefully consider what nags at you when you prepare for work every day.

Voices from the Field
Clarifying a General Idea and an Area of Focus: Video 1

This teacher researcher based his area of focus on observations of his classroom. Specifically, the teacher noticed a general lack of student engagement and motivation. These observations led the teacher researcher to a working hypothesis about the relationship between students' perceived lack of control over their education and corresponding levels of engagement and motivation. The next step for the teacher researcher would be to develop a research question related to this general idea about student engagement and motivation. For example, how can I improve student engagement and motivation? This area of focus in clearly within the teacher's locus of control and is something he is passionate about.

ENHANCEDetext
video example 3–1
In this video, Doug presents the questions that guided his review of the literature in his area of interest. Note that the first of these questions is a different sort of question than the others—he can answer it based on his review of the literature. For the others, he will need to collect data to help provide an answer. These last three research questions form the basis of his action research project.

Voices from the Field
Clarifying a General Idea and an Area of Focus: Video 2

Based on this teacher researcher's observations of her classroom, a general idea for an area of focus emerged related to the general classroom "atmosphere." Further, this teacher researcher focused on the role of formative assessments in classroom morale, summative assessment scores, and the general classroom climate. A next step for this teacher researcher would be to develop research questions, such as "How do formative assessments affect classroom climate?" This area of focus is in the teacher's locus of control and is something she is willing to improve on.

ENHANCEDetext
video example 3–2
In this video, Rachelle, a teacher researcher, describes how an observation led to a question and then led to an action research project.

Criteria for Selecting a General Idea/Area of Focus

There are some important criteria you should keep in mind while identifying your general idea and subsequent area of focus (Creswell, 2014; Elliott, 1991; Sagor, 2000):

- The area of focus should involve teaching and learning and should focus on your own practice.
- The area of focus is something within your locus of control.
- The area of focus is something you feel passionate about.
- The area of focus is something you would like to change or improve.

Applying these criteria early in the process will keep you on track during the early stages of the action research process. They will also remind you of the vital and dynamic dimensions of action research—that it is important work done by teacher researchers for themselves and their students, the results of which will ultimately improve student outcomes. (See Research in Action Checklist 3–1.)

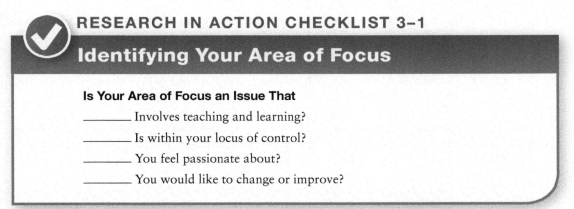

RESEARCH IN ACTION CHECKLIST 3–1

Identifying Your Area of Focus

Is Your Area of Focus an Issue That

_____ Involves teaching and learning?

_____ Is within your locus of control?

_____ You feel passionate about?

_____ You would like to change or improve?

Voices from the Field
Criteria for Selecting a General Idea and an Area of Focus

This teacher researcher is interested in the integration of technology into teaching and learning but based on classroom observations is surprised to find that the 10 computers in the classroom are not being used by the teacher or the students. As a result, this teacher researcher is searching for research-based computer practices that she can implement with her students and to better understand the effect of computer use on student achievement.

ENHANCEDetext
video example 3–3
In this video, Jureen describes working with peers to establish reliable definitions for the variables in her action research study.

Reconnaissance

The next important step in the action research process is reconnaissance, or preliminary information gathering. More specifically, reconnaissance is taking time to reflect on your own beliefs and to understand the nature and context of your general idea. Doing reconnaissance takes three forms: self-reflection, description, and explanation.

Gaining Insight into Your Area of Focus Through Self-Reflection

First, try to explore your own understanding of the following:

- The *theories* that impact your practice
- The *educational values* you hold
- How your work in schools fits into the *larger context* of schooling and society
- The *historical* contexts of your *school* and *schooling* and how things got to be the way they are
- The *historical* contexts of how you arrived at your *beliefs* about *teaching* and *learning* (Kemmis, 1988)

If your general idea for your action research inquiry is the question "How can I improve the integration and transfer of problem-solving skills in mathematics?," you might think about the following:

- Based on my experience teaching mathematics and my reading of the subject, I have been influenced by Van de Walle's (2003) *theory* about teaching and learning mathematics developmentally. In particular, the goal of mathematics is *relational understanding*, which is the connection between *conceptual* and *procedural knowledge* in mathematics. This theory of mathematics directly affects the ways in which I think about teaching mathematics to my students.
- I hold the *educational value* that children ought to be able to transfer problem-solving skills to other areas of mathematics as well as to life outside of school. That is, I am committed to relevancy of curriculum.
- I believe that mathematical problem solving—and problem solving in general—fits the *larger context* of schooling and society by providing children with critical lifelong learning skills that can be transferred to all aspects of their life.
- The *historical context* of mathematics teaching suggests a rote method of memorizing facts and algorithms. Although this approach to teaching mathematics worked for me (as a child and young teacher), it no longer suffices as a teaching method today.

- The historical context of how I came to *believe* in the importance of changing how I teach mathematics to children has grown out of my own frustration with knowing what to do to solve a problem but not knowing *why* I need to use a particular approach or algorithm.
- Given this self-reflection on an area of focus related to the integration and transfer of problem-solving skills in mathematics, I can now better understand the problem before I implement an intervention that addresses my concern for how to best teach a *relevant* problem-solving curriculum.

This is part of the "mind work" or "mental gymnastics" of action research. It is not an activity that will immediately produce new and exciting curricula and/or teaching materials—things that may follow later in the process when you become clearer about an intervention.

Gaining Insight into Your Area of Focus Through Descriptive Activities

Next, try to describe as fully as possible the situation you want to change or improve by focusing on *who, what, when, where,* and *how.* Grappling with these questions not only will clarify the focus area for your action research efforts but also will prevent you from moving ahead with an investigation that was too murky to begin with. For example, at this stage, you might answer these questions:

- What evidence do you have that this issue (the problem-solving skills of math students) is a problem?
- Which students are not able to transfer problem-solving skills to other mathematics tasks?
- How is problem solving presently taught?
- How often is problem solving taught?
- What is the ratio of time spent teaching problem solving to time spent teaching other mathematics skills?

Gaining Insight into Your Area of Focus Through Explanatory Activities

Once you've adequately described the situation you intend to investigate, try to explain it. Focus on the *why.* Can you account for the critical factors that have an impact on the general idea? In essence, this is the step in which you develop a hypothesis stating the expected relationships between variables in your study (Elliott, 1991).

In this case, you might hypothesize that students are struggling with the transfer of problem-solving skills to other mathematics tasks because they are not getting enough practice, they lack fundamental basic math skills, or they have not had sufficient opportunity to use math manipulatives. Given these possible explanations for why children have not been successfully transferring problem-solving skills to other areas of mathematics, you might develop the following hypotheses:

- A relationship exists between a mathematics curriculum that emphasizes the children's ability to know *what* to do and *why* to do it and children's abilities to transfer problem-solving skills.
- A relationship exists between a mathematics curriculum that emphasizes the use of manipulatives (to help children create meaning) and children's abilities to transfer problem-solving skills.

These reconnaissance activities (self-reflection, description, and explanation) help teacher researchers clarify what they already know about the proposed focus of the study; what they believe to be true about the relationships of the factors, variables, and contexts that make up their work environment; and what they believe can improve the situation. Research in Action Checklist 3–2 summarizes the critical activities for reconnaissance that you should perform at this point in the action research process.

RESEARCH IN ACTION CHECKLIST 3–2

Critical Activities for Doing Reconnaissance

Self-Reflection:

_____ Reflect on your area of focus in light of your values and beliefs; your understandings about the relationships among theory, practice, school, and society; how things got to be the way they are; and what you believe about teaching and learning.

Description:

_____ Describe the situation you wish to change or improve.

_____ Describe the evidence you have that the area of focus is a problem.

_____ Identify the critical factors that affect your area of focus.

Explanation:

_____ Explain the situation you intend to investigate by hypothesizing how and why the critical factors you've identified affect that situation.

The Action Research Plan

Ideally, your investment of time and energy in the reconnaissance and literature review stages will allow you to synthesize the related literature so that you can see your project more clearly. In addition, it may have helped you identify promising practices that can become an integral part of your ongoing action research efforts.

At this stage of the action research process, you should create an action plan. An action plan summarizes your action research thoughts in a plan that will guide you through your action research work and includes the following nine steps (Elliott, 1991; Kemmis, 1988):

1. Write an area-of-focus statement.
2. Define the variables.
3. Develop research questions.
4. Describe the intervention or innovations.
5. Describe the membership of the action research group.
6. Describe negotiations that need to be undertaken.
7. Develop a time line.
8. Develop a statement of resources.
9. Develop data collection ideas.

Write an Area-of-Focus Statement

An area of focus identifies the purpose of your study. To start, write a statement that completes the following sentence: "The purpose of this study is to . . ." For example:

- The purpose of this study is to describe the effects of an integrated problem-solving mathematics curriculum on student transfer of problem-solving skills and the retention of basic math facts and functions.
- The purpose of this study is to describe the impact of bringing audience members into an interactive relationship with teen theater productions on participants' abilities to identify issues and incorporate solutions to similar problems in their own lives.
- The purpose of this study is to describe the effects of student-led conferences on parent and student satisfaction with the conferencing process.

Define the Variables

As part of the area-of-focus statement construction process, write definitions of what you will focus on in the study. These definitions should accurately represent what the factors, contexts, and variables *mean to you*. A variable is a

Voices from the Field
Defining the Variables

In a collaborative action research project, this teacher researcher worked with colleagues to assist in the data collection process. In so doing, Jureen needed to operationally define the variables in her study: terms such as "off-task behavior" and "engagement" needed to be defined in order to ensure validity and reliability in the data collection process. All participants needed to agree on the definitions in order for consistent and trustworthy observations to be conducted by multiple participants in the study.

ENHANCEdetext
video example 3–4
In this video, Jureen describes working with peers to establish reliable definitions for the variable in her action research study.

characteristic of your study that is subject to change. That is, it might be the way you are going to change how you teach, the curriculum you use, and student outcomes. Definitions may also emerge from the literature, but it is important that you own whatever you are defining and communicate that ownership with others. In the preceding examples, the researchers would define what they mean by transfer of solutions to life's situations, an integrated problem-solving curriculum, transfer of problem-solving skills, the retention of math facts and functions, interactive participation in teen theater, student-led conferences, and parent and student satisfaction with the conferencing processes. If you are clear about what you are examining, it will be easy to determine how you will know it when you see it! That is, your data collection ideas will flow more freely, and there will be no confusion when you communicate with your action research collaborators about your purpose.

Develop Research Questions

Develop questions that breathe life into the area-of-focus statement and help provide a focus for your data collection plan. These questions will also help you validate that you have a workable way to proceed with your investigation. For example:

- What is the effect of teen theater audience participation strategies on audience comprehension of issues?

- How does the "Violence Improv" affect the audience's understanding of the issues of violence and harassment?
- What is the effect of incorporating math manipulatives into problem-solving activities on student performance on open-ended problem-solving tests?
- In what ways do students transfer problem-solving skills to other areas of mathematics?
- How do students incorporate problem-solving skills into other curriculum areas?
- How do students transfer problem-solving skills to their life outside of school?

Describe the Intervention or Innovation

Describe what you are going to do to improve the situation you have described; for example, "I will implement a standards-based, integrated problem-solving mathematics curriculum," "I will include audience improvisation as part of the

Voices from the Field
Develop Research Questions (Video 1)

In this vignette, the teacher researcher describes her desire to evaluate the basal readers being used in the district and to determine if they constitute a "gender-biased" reading program. This raises the question of whether this study meets the tenets of action research: involves teaching and learning, in the teacher's locus of control, displays passion for, and is willing to change or improve. It could be argued that a district-mandated curriculum in not in the teacher's locus of control; however, if the teacher is aware of gender-biased messages in the required curriculum, a targeted effort could be made to eliminate or counter the messages. Jeannette is clearly passionate about this area of focus, and, depending on what her analysis of the basal readers reveals, she would be able to pose specific action research questions related to the perceived gender-biased basal readers.

ENHANCEDetext
video example 3–5
Jeannette conducted a study to evaluate the content of the basal reader system used in her district. She did not study children in the classroom at all. Reflect on the research questions she presents in this video. Why is her project considered action research?

Voices from the Field
Develop Research Questions (Video 2)

In this vignette, the teacher researcher outlines a number of possible research questions that evolved from his classroom observations. However, not all of these questions "breathe life" in the area of focus. For example, "What does an unmotivated student look like?" could be answered by defining the term "unmotivated" through a review of related literature. Similarly, Doug could easily identify "current options for freshmen" by looking at the school's master schedule. The other questions described by Doug form the basis for his action research project and suggest data collection strategies that can be developed.

ENHANCEDetext
video example 3–6
In this video, Doug, a teacher researcher, briefly describes the process by which he developed a general idea into an area of focus for an action research project.

teen theater performances I direct," and "I will incorporate student participation in student-parent-teacher conferences." Remember, this is simply a statement about what you will do in your classroom or school to address the teaching/learning issue you have identified.

Describe the Membership of the Action Research Group

Describe the membership of your action research group and discuss why its members are important. Will you be working with a site council team? A parent group? If so, what will be the roles and responsibilities of the group's participants? For example:

> I will be working with seven other high school math teachers who are all members of the math department. Although we all have different teaching responsibilities within the department, as a group we have decided on problem solving as an area of focus for the department. Each of us will be responsible for implementing curriculum and teaching strategies that reflect the new emphasis on problem solving and for collecting the kinds of data that we decide will help us monitor the effects of our teaching. The department chair will be responsible for keeping the principal informed about our work

Voices from the Field
Describe the Membership of the Action Research Group

This teacher researcher describes her action research group as a group that was "already chosen for me." In a sense, this is true for all action researchers: members of our action research group are the children we teach. However, the group can be expanded to include colleagues with whom we work and to involve them in the action research process. In Jureen's example, she included her cooperating teacher, educational assistant, and computer lab assistant in the action research group.

ENHANCEDetext
video example 3–7
Jureen, in this video, identifies her action research group, which includes both the colleagues working with her and the students in her classroom. In action research, it is important to think of the students as active participants in the research, not just subjects to be observed.

and securing any necessary resources we need to complete the research. The chair will also write a description of our work to be included in the school newsletter (sent home to all parents), thus informing children and parents of our focus for the year.

Describe Negotiations That Need to Be Undertaken

Describe any negotiations that you will have to undertake with others before implementing your plan. Do you need permission from an administrator? Parents? Students? Colleagues? All this assumes that you control the focus of the study and that you undertake the process of negotiation to head off any potential obstacles to implementation of the action plan. It is very frustrating to get immersed in the action research process only to have the project quashed by uncooperative colleagues or administrators.

Develop a Time Line

In developing a time line, you will need to decide who will be doing *what* and *when*. Although not part of a time line in the strictest sense, you can also use this stage to anticipate *where* and *how* your inquiry will take place. For example:

- Phase 1 (August–October). Identify area of focus, review related literature, develop research questions, reconnaissance.
- Phase 2 (November–December). Collect initial data. Analyze video recordings of lessons, do first interviews with children, administer first problem-solving probe.
- Phase 3 (January–May). Modify curriculum and instruction as necessary. Continue ongoing data collection. Schedule two team meetings to discuss early analysis of data.
- Phase 4 (May–June). Review statewide assessment test data and complete analysis of all data. Develop presentation for faculty. Schedule team meeting to discuss and plan action based on the findings of the study. Assign tasks to be completed prior to year 2 of the study.

Voices from the Field
Describe Negotiations That Need to Be Undertaken

In this vignette, Rachelle (a student teacher at the school) was teaching multiple sections of Spanish 1 and Spanish 2 and was working with multiple cooperating teachers. Given this context, it would be critical that Rachelle negotiate informed consent with all of the participants in the study (teachers, students, and parents) prior to starting her research. This is easily done using cover letters to each group to clearly explain the purpose of the study and how the data will be used to positively impact student outcomes.

ENHANCEDetext
video example 3–8
As she describes in this video, Rachelle collected data in classes other than her own. What negotiations would you expect that Rachelle needed to undertake prior to beginning?

Develop a Statement of Resources

Briefly describe what resources you will need to enact your plan. This is akin to listing materials in a lesson plan. There is nothing worse than starting to teach and finding that you don't have all the manipulatives you need to achieve your objectives. For example, to participate in the study of math problem-solving skills, the team determines that it will need teacher release time for planning the project, reviewing related literature, and completing other tasks; funds to purchase classroom sets of manipulatives; and a small budget for copying and printing curriculum materials. After all, there is no sense in developing a study that investigates the impact of a new math problem-solving curriculum if you don't have the financial resources to purchase the curriculum.

Develop Data Collection Ideas

Give a preliminary statement of the kinds of data that you think will provide evidence for your reflections on the general idea you are investigating. For example, brainstorm about the kind of intuitive, naturally occurring data that you find in your classroom or school, such as test scores, attendance records, portfolios, and anecdotal records. As you learn more about other types of data that can be collected, this list will grow. In the early stages, however, you should think about what you already have easy access to and then be prepared to supplement it with interviews, surveys, questionnaires, video and audio recordings, maps, photos, and observations as the area of focus dictates.

These activities can be undertaken whether you are working individually, in a small group, or as part of a schoolwide action research effort. The resolution of these issues early in the action research process will ensure that you do not waste valuable time backtracking (or even apologizing) once you are well down the action research path. The process of developing an action plan is summarized in the Research in Action Checklist 3–3.

RESEARCH IN ACTION CHECKLIST 3–3

Developing an Action Plan

_____ Write an area-of-focus statement.

_____ Define the variables.

_____ Develop research questions.

_____ Describe the intervention or innovation.

_____ Describe the membership of the action research group.

_____ Describe negotiations that need to be undertaken.

_____ Develop a time line.

_____ Develop a statement of resources.

_____ Develop data collection ideas.

Put the Action Plan into Action

Kemmis (1988) provides the following conclusion to the process of developing a plan:

> Your plan orients you for action, of course; but it is also a reference point for reflection later on, and it is something which you can modify and develop in later plans. Since you have done so much hard thinking to put your plan together, don't skimp when it comes to drafting and redrafting it before you go into action. It represents the fruits of one round of reconnaissance and thinking ahead—it provides you with a benchmark for later reflection and replanning. (p. 77)

With the plan complete, it's time to determine what information (data) you can collect that will increase your understanding about your own practice and its impact on your students. You are now ready to decide how you will monitor the effects of the innovation or intervention you are going to implement and to develop your data collection techniques.

SUMMARY

Clarifying a General Idea and an Area of Focus

1. In the beginning of the action research process, you need to clarify the general idea that will be the area of focus of your study.
2. The general idea is a statement that links an idea to an action and refers to a situation one wishes to change or improve on.
3. Taking time in the beginning of the action research process to identify what you feel passionate about is critical.
4. The area of focus should involve teaching and learning and should focus on your own practice.
5. The area of focus is something within your locus of control.
6. The area of focus is something you feel passionate about.
7. The area of focus is something you would like to change or improve.

Reconnaissance

8. Reconnaissance is taking time to reflect on your own beliefs and to understand the nature and context of your general idea. Doing reconnaissance takes three forms: self-reflection, description, and explanation.
9. Try to explore your own understanding of:
   a. The theories that impact your practice.
   b. The educational values you hold.

    c. How your work in schools fits into the larger context of schooling and society.

    d. The historical contexts of your school and schooling and how things got to be the way they are.

    e. The historical contexts of how you arrived at your beliefs about teaching and learning.

10. Try to describe as fully as possible the situation you want to change or improve by focusing on the who, what, when, where, and how questions.

11. Try to explain the situation you intend to investigate by hypothesizing how and why the critical factors that you have identified affect the situation.

The Action Research Plan

12. Ideally, your investment of time and energy in the reconnaissance and literature review stages allows you to synthesize the related literature so that you can see your project more clearly. In addition, it may help you identify promising practices that can become an integral part of your ongoing action research efforts.

13. At this stage of the action research process, you should create an action research plan that summarizes your action research thoughts in a plan that will guide you through your action research work. It should include the following nine steps:

    1. Write an area-of-focus statement.

    2. Define the variables.

    3. Develop research questions.

    4. Describe the intervention or innovations.

    5. Describe the membership of the action research group.

    6. Describe negotiations that need to be undertaken.

    7. Develop a time line.

    8. Develop a statement of resources.

    9. Develop data collection ideas.

TASKS

1. Complete an action plan that includes an area-of-focus statement, definitions, research questions, a description of the intervention, membership of the action research group, negotiations to be undertaken, a time line, the necessary resources for the project, and data collection ideas.

4

Review of Related Literature

After reading this chapter you should be able to:

4.1 Define the purpose and scope of a review of related literature.

4.2 Describe the role of the literature review in qualitative research.

4.3 Differentiate between a keyword and subject/descriptor search.

4.4 Identify, evaluate, and annotate sources.

4.5 Describe the steps involved in analyzing, organizing, and reporting a review of the literature.

4.6 Write a review of related literature.

This chapter provides guidelines for reviewing related literature using online resources, such as the Education Resources Information Center (ERIC), the Internet, university library resources, or articles found in journals published by professional organizations for educators.

Review of Related Literature

At this point, you should make an initial foray into the professional literature, the formal record of other people's experiences, to try to better understand the problem on which you are focusing. The literature may suggest other ways of looking at your problem and help you to identify potential promising practices that you might use in your classroom to correct the problem. To borrow the words of Kemmis (1988), "Can existing research throw any light on your situation and help you see it more clearly?" (p. 55).

*R*eviewing the literature is a valuable contribution to the action research process that could actually save you time. Often, teacher researchers think that they know what their problem is but become stymied in the process because they weren't really sure what they were asking. Taking time to immerse yourself in the literature allows you to reflect on your own problems through someone else's lens. You can locate *yourself within the research literature and find support for what you are doing or be challenged by what other researchers have done and how they have tackled a particular problem.*

At the end of the process, you ought to be informed enough about the literature that you could talk to colleagues about the major themes that emerged. Similarly, you should be able to talk about "promising practices" that were discussed.

Sometimes, teacher researchers will claim that they cannot find any published research related to their area of focus. This invariably leads to questions of relevance and importance. After all, if nobody else has researched the problem, perhaps it is not worthy of investigation! However, as the following personal and serious illustration demonstrates, lack of published research on a topic does not mean that the topic is not important. About 20 years ago my son, who was five years old at the time, inexplicably began to pass blood in his urine—a pretty scary sight for any parent. After many invasive medical tests over a six-month period, we finally opted for a procedure that required general anesthesia in order to determine the cause of the blood. The surgeon emerged from the operating room and pronounced, "I have some good news, and I have some bad news!" The good news was that the surgeon was able to diagnose the cause of the internal bleeding—a rare, benign, and non–life-threatening condition called trigonitis. *The bad news was that the surgeon was unable to tell us why our son had developed the condition or how to treat it! I was shocked at this revelation from the surgeon, a pediatric urology specialist. How could my son be bleeding internally and there not be a medical explanation? The surgeon responded that, because the condition was rare, benign, and non–life-threatening, it simply did not warrant research! My point here is not to be melodramatic but rather to make a case for the importance of your own research, regardless of whether it has been researched (and published) by other professionals. Just because your area of focus is unique to you does not make it any less important. It is your problem, and you own it. Do not be disheartened if your review of the literature fails to provide you with helpful insights.*

Too often, the review of related literature is seen as a necessary evil to be completed as fast as possible so that one can get on with the "real research." This perspective reflects a lack of understanding of the purposes and importance of the review and a feeling of uneasiness on the part of students who are not sure how to report the literature. Nonetheless, the review of related literature is as important as any other component of the research process and can be conducted quite painlessly if approached in an orderly manner. Some researchers even find the process quite enjoyable! A good place to start is to focus on what the literature says about your topic as a way of discovering the focus and content of other scholars.

The review of related literature involves the systematic identification, location, and analysis of documents containing information related to the research problem. The term is also used to describe the written component of a research plan or report that discusses the reviewed documents. These documents can include articles, abstracts, reviews, monographs, dissertations, books, other research reports, and electronic media efforts. The major purpose of reviewing the literature is to determine what has already been done that relates to your topic. This knowledge not only prevents you from unintentionally duplicating another person's research but also gives you the understanding and insight you need to place your topic within a logical framework. Previous studies can provide the rationale for your research hypothesis, and indications of what needs to be done can help you justify the significance of your study. Put simply, the review tells you what has been done and what needs to be done.

Another important purpose of reviewing the literature is to discover research strategies and specific data collection approaches that have or have not been productive in investigations of topics similar to yours. This information will help you avoid other researchers' mistakes and profit from their experiences. It may suggest approaches and procedures that you previously had not considered. For example, suppose your topic involved the comparative effects of a brand-new experimental method versus the traditional method on the achievement of eighth-grade science students. The review of literature may reveal 10 related studies that found no differences in achievement. Several of the studies, however, may suggest that the brand-new method is more effective for certain kinds of students than for others. Thus, you may reformulate your topic to involve the comparative effectiveness of the brand-new method versus the traditional method on the achievement of a subgroup of eighth-grade science students—those with low aptitude.

Being familiar with previous research also facilitates interpretation of your study results. The results can be discussed in terms of whether and how they agree with previous findings. If the results contradict previous findings, you can describe differences between your study and the others, providing a rationale for the discrepancy. If your results are consistent with other findings, your report should include suggestions for the next step; if they are not consistent, your report should include suggestions for studies that may resolve the conflict.

Beginning researchers often have difficulty determining how broad and comprehensive their literature reviews should be. At times, all the literature will seem directly related to the topic, so it may be difficult to decide when to stop. Determining whether an article is truly relevant to the topic is complicated and requires time. Unfortunately, there is no simple formula to solve the problem. You must decide using your own judgment and the advice of your teachers or advisors.

The following general guidelines can assist you:

- Avoid the temptation to include everything you find in your literature review. Bigger does not mean better. A smaller, well-organized review is definitely preferred to a review containing many studies that are only tangentially related to the problem. Initially, a literature search may be very inclusive so as not to miss potential research related to your subject, but as you evaluate the information, you will refine your list of sources.
- When investigating a heavily researched area, review only those works that are directly related to your specific problem. You will find plenty of references and should not have to rely on less relevant studies. For example, the role of feedback for verbal and nonverbal learning has been extensively studied in both

nonhuman animals and human beings for a variety of different learning tasks. Focus on those using similar subjects or similar variables—for example, if you were concerned with the relation between frequency of feedback and chemistry achievement, you would probably not have to review feedback studies related to nonhuman animal learning.

■ *When investigating a new or little-researched problem area, review any study related in some meaningful way to your problem. Gather enough information to develop a logical framework for the study and a sound rationale for the research hypothesis. For example, suppose you wanted to study the effects of an exam for non–English-speaking students on grade-point average. The students must pass the exam to graduate. Your literature review would probably include any studies that involved English as a Second Language (ESL) classes and the effects of culture-specific grading practices as well as studies that identified strategies to improve the learning of ESL students. In a few years, there will probably be enough research on the academic consequences of such an exam on non–English-speaking students to permit a much more narrowly focused literature review.*

A common misconception among beginning researchers is that the worth of a topic is directly related to the amount of literature available about it. This is not the case. For many new and important areas of research, few studies have been published. The effects of technology and social media on student writing is one such area. The very lack of such research often increases the worth of its study. On the other hand, the fact that a thousand studies have already been done in a given problem area does not mean there is no further need for research in that area. Such an area will generally be very well developed, and subtopics that need additional research will be readily identifiable.

Action Research and the Review of Related Literature

Action researchers disagree about the role of the literature review in the research process. Some researchers have argued that reviewing the literature curtails inductive analysis—using induction to determine the direction of the research—and should be avoided at the early stages of the research process (Bogdan & Biklen, 1998). Others suggest that the review of related literature is important early in the action research process because it serves the following functions:

■ The literature review demonstrates the underlying assumptions (i.e., propositions) behind the research questions that are central to the research proposal.

■ The literature review provides a way for the novice researcher to convince the proposal reviewers that he or she is knowledgeable about the related

table 4–1 ■ **Conducting a Literature Review**

1. Identify and make a list of keywords to guide your literature search.
2. Search appropriate databases using your keywords and identify authoritative subject headings to locate primary and secondary sources pertaining to your research problem.
3. Review list of subject headings to identify related subheadings.
4. Check the links to authors of relevant sources for additional related sources.
5. Check any links to the cited references or any listings of other articles that have cited a specific source.
6. Evaluate your sources for quality. The sources you choose to reference establishes your credibility and authority as a researcher.
7. Create citations from the database and abstract your sources. All databases, such the Education Resources Information Center (ERIC), Education Full Text, and others, have citation generators within the database that are mostly accurate. Remember to double-check that accuracy of your citations.
8. Analyze and organize your sources using a literature matrix.
9. Write the literature review.

Source: Mills, Geoffrey E.; Gay, Lorraine R., *Educational Research: Competencies for Analysis and Applications*, Loose-Leaf Version, 11th Ed., © 2016. Reprinted and electronically reproduced by permission of Pearson Education, Inc., New York, NY.

research and the intellectual traditions that support the proposed study (Marshall & Rossman, 1995).

■ The literature review provides the researcher with an opportunity to identify any gaps that may exist in the body of literature and to provide a rationale for how the proposed study may contribute to the existing body of knowledge.

■ The literature review helps the researcher to refine the research questions and embed them in guiding hypotheses that provide possible directions the researcher may follow.

Conducting a literature review follows a basic set of steps. Table 4–1 outlines the basic process you take when reviewing the literature.

Identifying Keywords and Identifying, Evaluating, and Annotating Sources

Identifying Keywords

The words you select for your searches will dictate the success of your research. Before you begin your research, make a list of possible keywords to guide your literature search. As you progress through your searching, add keywords and subject headings related to your search. Most of the initial source works you consult will have an alphabetical subject index or thesaurus to help you generate words to describe your research problem. You can look in these indexes for the keywords you have selected. Another option is to search databases such as ERIC and Education Full Text to generate subject headings or descriptors from the search results.

For example, if your research topic concerns the effect of interactive multimedia on the achievement of tenth-grade biology students, the logical keywords would be "interactive multimedia" and "biology." When beginning with a keyword search for interactive multimedia in a database such as ERIC, however, you will see a list of possible subject headings, such as multimedia instruction, computer-assisted instruction, multimedia materials, games, or hypermedia. These subject headings may also be called *descriptors*. It is important that you understand the difference between the keyword search and a subject heading—and, perhaps more important, why you want to connect to the subject headings.

Every article indexed in a database such as ERIC or Education Full Text is read by a human being who determines what topics are addressed in the article. The topics are listed as subject headings or descriptors in the article citation. Therefore, a subject search is more precise than a keyword search that searches for the words anywhere in the complete record of an article. If the words appear one time in the full text of an article, you will retrieve that article even though it may not be very relevant to your search. Subject headings or descriptors connect you with concepts that you are searching for, not just the words. You may have to mix and match your search terms to retrieve more accurate and relevant results. At times, the keywords and subject headings will be obvious for some searches, such as biology.

For others, you may have to play detective. Giving a bit of thought to possible keywords and subject headings should facilitate an efficient beginning to an effective search. As you progress through your search, try to identify additional keywords and subject headings that you can use to reformulate a search to produce different and more relevant results or results that address specific aspects or subheadings about the topic.

Identifying Your Sources

For your review, you will examine a range of sources that are pertinent to your topic. To start, it is best to consult educational encyclopedias, handbooks, and annual reviews found in libraries. You may also search the Internet for government publications or organizational sites that address your research topic. These resources, some of which were mentioned earlier in the discussion on narrowing your topic, provide summaries of important topics in education and reviews of research on various topics. They allow you to get a picture of your topic in the broader context and help you understand where it fits in the field. You may also find these sources useful for identifying search terms and aspects related to your topic that you may not have considered.

The following are some examples of handbooks, encyclopedias, and reviews relevant to educational research:

- The International Encyclopedia of Education
- Encyclopedia of Curriculum Studies
- Handbook of Research on Teacher Education: Enduring Questions in Changing Contexts

Voices from the Field
Identifying Keywords

This teacher researcher is interested in understanding the impact of technology on student engagement and motivation in the classroom. In order to identify a research-based "technology intervention," the teacher researcher reviewed the related literature using keywords such as "educational technology," "access to computers" and "academic achievement," or "achievement" (all terms taken from the ERIC Thesaurus of Descriptors). A useful way for Jureen to narrow or broaden her search would be to use Boolean operators (words that tell the computer the keywords you want to include or exclude). Common Boolean operators are the words AND, OR, and NOT.

ENHANCEDetext
video example 4–1
Watch as Jureen states her research question. She notes in the video that she used library resources to conduct a review of previous research. What sorts of keywords might she have used in a computerized search?

- Handbook of Research on the Education of Young Children
- Handbook of Latinos and Education: Theory, Research, and Practice
- Handbook of Research on Practices and Outcomes in E-Learning: Issues and Trends
- Handbook of Research on the Education of School Leaders
- Handbook of Research on New Media Literacy at the K–12 Level: Issues and Challenges
- Handbook of Education Policy Research
- Handbook of Research on School Choice
- Handbook of Research on Literacy and Diversity
- Handbook of Education Finance and Policy
- Research in the Social Foundations of Education
- Handbook of Research on Schools, Schooling, and Human Development
- Handbook of Reading Disability Research
- Handbook of Research on Children's and Young Adult Literature
- Handbook on the Research of Teaching the English Language Arts

It is important to distinguish between two types of sources used by educational researchers: primary and secondary sources. A primary source contains firsthand information, such as an original document or a description of a study written by the person who conducted the study. The data are factual rather than interpretive, so the study is more valued than secondary research. Research reports, dissertations, experiments, surveys, conference proceedings, letters, and interviews are some examples of primary sources. There is a difference between the opinion of an author and the results of an empirical study. The latter is more valued in a review.

A secondary source is a source that interprets or analyzes the work of others—either a primary source or another secondary source, such as a brief description of a study written by someone other than the person who conducted it. Secondary sources are often used to review what has already been written or studied. Education encyclopedias, handbooks, and other reference works typically contain secondhand information summarizing research studies conducted on a given topic. Secondary sources usually give complete bibliographic information for the references cited, so they can direct you to relevant primary sources, which are preferred over secondary sources. In fact, a primary source may have a literature review section that contains secondary source information. A good researcher can use the literature review to track down the original primary research.

Searching for Books on Your Research Topic in the Library

Having identified your keywords and some potential resources, you are ready to make an initial foray into your university library. Because the library will be a second home to you, at least for a while, you should become familiar with it. The time you spend here initially will save more in the long run. You should learn about the references available and where they are located. You should be able to completely navigate your library's website and know how to access resources from any location with a connection to the Internet. Most libraries, especially university libraries, provide help and education in the use of their resources. You should be familiar with services offered by the library as well as the rules and regulations regarding the use of library materials. Libraries also provide access to materials through interlibrary loan for articles and to collective library catalogs to find books that are available from other institutions.

Most university libraries have a librarian on duty to help with requests. More importantly there also is a librarian who is the liaison to the education department. This librarian has experience in both K–12 and graduate education and is very skilled in helping track down resources. Most libraries offer 24/7 online chat to assist you with your research if you are not in the building. Librarians usually are very willing to help you, but you should also learn to navigate the library on your own. The librarian is available to work with you, not to do your research. With or without a librarian's help, you should take advantage of the resources available from the library, such as the online catalog, databases like ERIC and Education Full Text, and government publications. Most libraries have subject-specific online research guides that help organize the resources for a specific discipline. Also, learn to browse the stacks to search for books on your problem. Most of all, make a point to know the education librarian. Generally, if you are taking more than 15 to 20 minutes trying to finding something, then you should ask for assistance. You may even want to set up an appointment with the education librarian.

Using Library Catalogs

Although significant technological advances have changed the way research is conducted in the library, individual libraries vary greatly in their ability to capitalize on increasingly available options. In today's academic libraries, card catalogs of previous generations have been replaced with online catalogs. These online catalogs provide access to the resources in the library as well as to collective catalogs accessing materials from other libraries within a particular region as part of a library's consortium agreement with other institutions. For students, getting books through the collective catalog and having them delivered to a particular library is generally free. These electronic catalogs are extremely user friendly and provide a good place to start your search for literature related to your area of focus. In addition, electronic books are becoming increasingly popular both for their immediate availability and for their ease of use.

To locate books, video, and other materials, such as government documents, you need to conduct a search of the library catalog. To search by topic, begin with a keyword search. In library catalogs, a keyword search will search the entire record of an item that includes the content notes—the chapter headings or titles of essays within a book. If you see a book relevant to your search, check the subject headings that are listed. You may be able to refine your search or find additional materials. For example, to find summaries of research previously conducted in an area of psychology, you may enter the keywords "handbook" and "psychology" or "encyclopedia" and "psychology." If you search for a particular topic, such as transformative learning, enter that term as a keyword search. The keyword search is important when you are looking for books because the search retrieves items with your keywords in the title, subject heading, and content notes. Since the content notes provide a listing of essays and chapter headings within a book, a keyword search could retrieve an essay about transformative learning in a book about adult learning. Always check the subject headings of any relevant item that you locate. You will find the subject headings important for finding similar items and further information. If you know a title of a book, then you can also search for the specific title.

If you are at the beginning of your search for primary sources, add search terms slowly and thoughtfully. Refrain from searching phrases, such as "developing active learning activities in the classroom." Choose the main concepts from your research question—"active learning" and "classroom activities." Add additional search terms concept by concept depending on the amount of materials you retrieve and how narrow you want your search to be. If you need a relatively small number of references and a significant amount of research has been published about your topic, a narrow search will likely be appropriate. If you need a relatively large number of references and very little has been published about your topic, a broad search will be better. If you do not have a sense of what is available, your best strategy is to start narrow and broaden as necessary. For example, if you find very few references related to the effect of interactive multimedia on the achievement of tenth-grade biology students, you can broaden your search by including all sciences or all secondary students.

A useful way to narrow or broaden a keyword search is to use Boolean operators, words that tell the computer the keywords you want your search results to include or exclude. Common Boolean operators are the words AND, OR, and NOT. Put simply, using the connector AND or NOT between keywords narrows a search, whereas using the connector OR broadens one. Searching "multiple intelligences AND music" will provide a list of references that refer to both multiple intelligences and music. Searching "multiple intelligences NOT music" will retrieve references pertaining to multiple intelligences but will exclude references pertaining to music. A search for "multiple intelligences OR music" retrieves references that relate to either or both concepts. By using various combinations of the AND and OR connectors, you can vary your search strategy as needed. Note that it is difficult to develop a search model that can be followed in every library and every catalog or database. You must get acquainted with the unique search strategies and methods that are successful within your library environment. It is a good idea to check with the education librarian to determine if additional Boolean operator strategies are best suited to your search.

Browsing the Stacks

With access to online catalogs, many new researchers may not consider an older strategy for locating books: browsing the stacks. This strategy is similar to the kind of activity you undertake at a public library when looking for a new fiction book to read. When the area of the library with books related to your area of focus is located, it can be productive to browse and pull interesting books off the shelves. You may also find leads to related materials if you initiate your search on the computer. Remember, libraries try to organize like objects with like objects. Accordingly, when you spot a relevant item on the shelves, or in the results of an online search, always look at the other items nearby.

Steps for Searching Computer Databases

The online catalog found in a library is an example of a database—a sortable, analyzable collection of records maintained on a computer representing books, documents, DVDs, and videos. Other types of subject specific databases also are used in research to search indexes for scholarly and peer-reviewed journal articles—some of which are available in full text, abstracts, or other documents. These databases—such as ERIC, Education Full Text, PsycINFO, and others—provide an excellent way to identify primary sources and secondary sources.

The steps involved in searching a research database are similar to those involved in a book search, except that it is more critical to identify appropriate subject headings or descriptors to retrieve highly relevant material:

1. Identify keywords related to your topic.
2. Select the appropriate databases—some databases using the same interface may allow you to search multiple databases simultaneously.

figure 4–1 ▪ **Sample of EBSCO Keyword Search**

Source: Mills, Geoffrey E.; Gay, Lorraine R., *Educational Research: Competencies for Analysis and Applications,* Loose-Leaf Version, 11th Ed., © 2016. Reprinted and electronically reproduced by permission of Pearson Education, Inc., New York, NY.

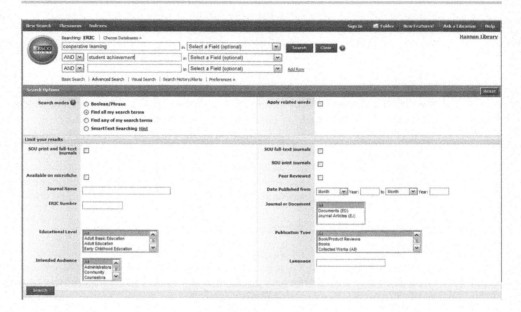

3. Initiate a search using your keywords selectively. Some databases will map to subject headings or descriptors, requiring you to build your search term by term. Other databases will provide a list of subject headings or descriptors based on the results of your search. For example, in Figure 4–1, you can see the results of a keyword search using "cooperative learning" and "student achievement" with a possible 1,761 articles. These initial "hits" will require additional sorting to determine their relevancy for your review of related literature.

4. Reformulate your search using appropriate subject headings or descriptors, combining terms as appropriate. Remember that combining too many terms may result in few or no retrieved items. If this occurs, mix and match search terms or broaden the search to produce better results. For example, in Figure 4–2, "student achievement" is called "academic achievement" and results in a more targeted list of references.

5. Once you have found a relevant article, check the item record for links to additional subject headings or descriptors, author(s), cited references, times cited in the database, or other references for finding additional related items using the features within the database. For example, the record in Figure 4–3 gives other descriptors used to classify the article and other articles in the database that are written by the same author.

figure 4–2 ■ **Sample of ERIC/EBSCO Search: Reformulating with Subject Descriptors**

Source: Mills, Geoffrey E.; Gay, Lorraine R., *Educational Research: Competencies for Analysis and Applications*, Loose-Leaf Version, 11th Ed., © 2016. Reprinted and electronically reproduced by permission of Pearson Education, Inc., New York, NY.

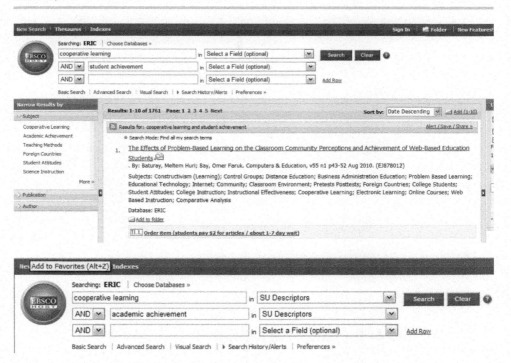

6. Most databases provide a link that will create a citation in various formats, including APA. Although the citations still need to be checked for correctness, they will provide an excellent start to creating your list of references. It is highly recommended that you begin your list of references and populate the list with citations from any relevant articles. This will save you time in either going back later to retrieve the citation or in creating a citation. For example, in Figure 4–4, ERIC/EBSCO allows you to create an account and to save your references in APA, AMA, Chicago, or MLA formats.

7. Many databases allow you to create an account, so you can log in to save and manage your searches and your relevant research articles. This feature is an important part of using a particular database to not only retrieve relevant research but also manage your sources.

For example, in Figure 4–5, you can return to your MyEBSCO*host* account at any time to copy your references, which can finally be pasted into your review

figure 4–3 ▪ Sample ERIC/EBSCO: Sample Record

Source: Mills, Geoffrey E.; Gay, Lorraine R., *Educational Research: Competencies for Analysis and Applications*, Loose-Leaf Version, 11th Ed., © 2016. Reprinted and electronically reproduced by permission of Pearson Education, Inc., New York, NY.

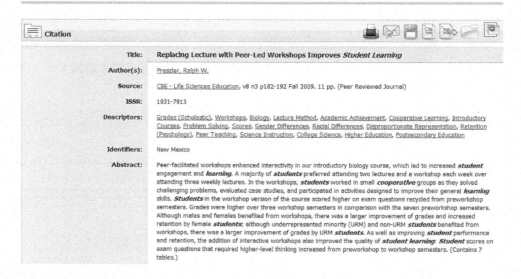

figure 4–4 ▪ Sample APA Citation

Source: Mills, Geoffrey E.; Gay, Lorraine R., *Educational Research: Competencies for Analysis and Applications*, Loose-Leaf Version, 11th Ed., © 2016. Reprinted and electronically reproduced by permission of Pearson Education, Inc., New York, NY.

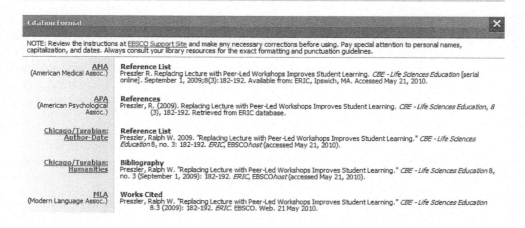

figure 4–5 ■ Managing References in a Database

Source: Mills, Geoffrey E.; Gay, Lorraine R., *Educational Research: Competencies for Analysis and Applications*, Loose-Leaf Version, 11th Ed., © 2016. Reprinted and electronically reproduced by permission of Pearson Education, Inc., New York, NY.

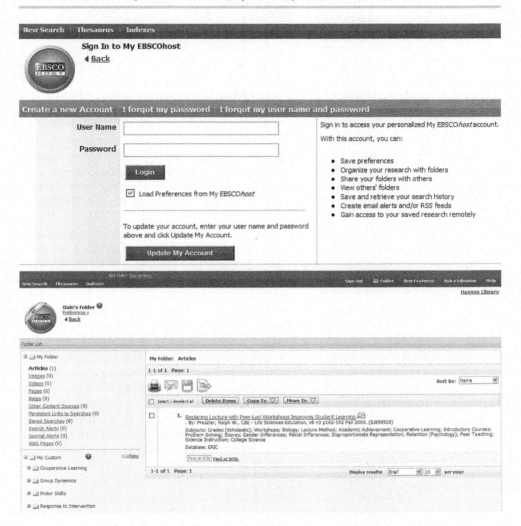

of related literature document. When you write your review of related literature, you will be very thankful that you have created this account!

The following sections describe some of the commonly used databases for searches of education literature.

Education Resources Information Center (ERIC)

ERIC, the largest digital library of education literature in the world, was established in 1966 by the National Library of Education as part of the U.S. Department of Education's Office of Educational Research and Improvement and is now sponsored by Institute of Education Sciences of the U.S. Department of Education. The online database provides information on subjects ranging from early childhood and elementary education to education for gifted children and rural and urban education. ERIC is used by more than 500,000 people each year, providing access to more than 1.5 million bibliographic records of journal articles, research reports, curriculum and teaching guides, dissertations, theses, conference papers, books, and technical reports. ERIC indexes content published by more than 1,000 selected centers, agencies, programs, associations, non-profit organizations, and initiatives.

In 2004, the ERIC system was restructured by the Department of Education. The ERIC database is available at almost every academic library or via the ERIC website at http://www.eric.ed.gov. The website uses the most up-to-date retrieval methods for the ERIC databases, but it is no match for the database interfaces provided by your academic library. Given a choice, search ERIC via the interface available through your library—such as EBSCO or ProQuest. Doing so will allow you to automatically link automatically to full-text articles when they are available through your library and to save your articles and cite the articles in the appropriate style guide, such as APA. Regardless of whether you use your library's database interfaces or the government-sponsored ERIC website, ERIC is a formidable database for searching educational materials that is relatively quick and easy to search.

When you search ERIC, you may notice that documents are categorized with an ED or EJ designation. An ED designation is generally used for unpublished documents, such as reports, studies, and lesson plans. Usually, ED references are available in academic libraries as full-text online documents or, if they are very old, via microfiche. An EJ designation is used for articles published in scholarly or professional journals as well as discipline-related magazines. EJ articles are often available in full text from the ERIC database at an academic library. If you are using the ERIC collection on the Web at http://www.eric.ed.gov, the full text may not be available and must be tracked down in the periodicals collection of a library or purchased from article reprint companies.

ERIC is the largest computer database for searches of education literature, but it is not the only source available. Other commonly used databases in education are described next.

Education Full Text

The Education Full Text database contains articles historically available within the Wilson Education Index and references articles published in educational periodicals since 1983. The database provides references to many full-text articles that are not available in the ERIC database, so it is important to search both databases for more comprehensive research. In addition to article abstracts, the database includes citations for yearbooks and monograph series, videotapes, motion picture and computer program reviews, and legal cases.

Education Source

Education Source is a more comprehensive database that duplicates the Education Full Text database with additional full-text journals previously not available in other databases. Coverage dates back to 1929 with full-text for more than 2,000 journals, 550 books, and 1,200 education-related conference papers encompassing all levels of education from early childhood to higher education including adult education, continuing education, distance learning, multicultural education, social issues, counseling, and vocational education.

PsycINFO

The PsycINFO database is the online version of *Psychological Abstracts,* a former print source that presented summaries of completed psychological research studies (see http://apa.org/psycinfo) *Psychological Abstracts* ceased its print publication in December 2006. PsycINFO contains full text and abstracting of journal articles, technical reports, book chapters, and books in the field of psychology. Approximately 90% of the articles are from peer-reviewed sources. The database centers on psychology but also explores the interdisciplinary aspects of behavioral and social science literature, including clinical case reports, empirical studies, and some dissertations. It is organized by subject area according to the Thesaurus of Psychological Index Terms codes describing the content of the database rather than the field of psychology. The classification codes can be accessed at http://apa.org/pubs/databases/training/thesaurus.aspx. These classification codes allow you to retrieve abstracts for studies in a specific category—for example, Learning and Memory (2343), Developmental Disorders and Autism (3250), or Speech and Language Disorders (3270).

Dissertation Abstracts

Dissertation Abstracts contains bibliographic citations and abstracts from all subject areas for doctoral dissertations and master's theses completed at more than 1,000 accredited colleges and universities worldwide. The database dates back to 1861, with abstracts included from 1980 forward. If after reading an abstract you want to obtain a copy of the complete dissertation, check to see if it is available in your library. If not, speak to a librarian about how to obtain a copy. You can request a dissertation from your library through interlibrary loan. Be aware that there may be charges to get the dissertation from the lending library. Dissertations may be able to be obtained by searching the Internet for an online copy or by contacting the author.

Searching the Internet and the World Wide Web

An abundance of educational materials is available on the Web—from primary research articles and educational theory to lesson plans and research guides. Currently, a proficient researcher can access information in a variety of formats, such as video, images, multimedia, PowerPoint presentations, screen captures, tutorials, and more. Blogs, RSS feeds, podcasts, wikis, e-mail, and other Web 2.0 tools offer researchers a variety of alternative means for finding information. Also, as search engines develop to include more sophisticated methods for finding research, both "digital natives" and traditional researchers can find primary sources using tools such as Google Scholar, Google Books, and more. Even Wikipedia can provide background information to help a researcher understand fundamental concepts and theory that lead to better keywords and strategies for searching. For further discussion of using Google, see the section titled "Digital Research Tools for the 21st Century: Google Searches" later in the chapter.

Internet search engines are structured and function differently than databases. The essential difference is that a search engine is compiled and organized through programming. Search results are retrieved using complex algorithms that establish an essential relevancy for each site or page. No person reads or reviews the list of sites compiled within a search engine. This somewhat explains why an Internet search breaks down after the second or third page and begins to contain more and more irrelevant information. A research database like ERIC or Education Full Text is also compiled through programming, but it is organized by humans who have read the contents, such as the articles. It is essential to connect with the human organization of a database by using the appropriate subject headings and descriptors that are not present in an Internet search engine. On the Internet, using multiple keywords and experimenting with search terms is essential for successfully retrieving useful information. It is also important to specify a date range when searching a source like Google Scholar because the algorithms of Internet search tools do not use date of publication as a criteria for relevancy.

The resources you can find on the Web are almost limitless. More and more print material is being digitized, and new sites are constantly being developed and tested to provide more and more access to information. Academic social network sites like Research Gate and other sites are providing an online space for scientists and researchers to connect and share publications and other works for free. With just a few clicks, you can access electronic educational journals that provide full-text articles, bibliographic information, and abstracts. You can obtain up-to-the-minute research reports and information about educational research activities undertaken at various research centers, and you can access education sites with links to resources that other researchers have found especially valuable. But be warned—there is little quality control on the Internet, and at times, the sheer volume of information can be overwhelming. Some Internet sites post research articles selected specifically to promote or encourage a particular point of view or even an educational product. Blogs and wikis provide excellent modes of creating and manipulating content to share and communicate ideas and concepts, but they are not always as robust as peer-reviewed academic research. Make sure you understand the strengths and limits of the sources you use.

The following websites are especially useful to educational researchers:

CSTEEP: The Center for the Study of Testing, Evaluation, and Educational Policy (http://www.bc.edu/research/csteep/html). The website for this educational research organization contains information on testing, evaluation, and public policy studies on school assessment practices and international comparative research.

National Center for Education Statistics (http://www.nces.ed.gov). This site contains statistical reports and other information on the condition of U.S. education. It also reports on education activities internationally.

TeachersFirst: State Education Standards (http://teachersfirst.com/statestds .cfm). This site contains a wealth of up-to-date information regarding state-by-state educational standards and curriculum frameworks.

Developing Educational Standards (http://www.edstandards.org/Standards .html). This site contains a wealth of up-to-date information regarding educational standards and curriculum frameworks from all sources (e.g., national, state, local, and other). Information on standards and frameworks can be linked to by subject area, state, governmental agency, or organization. Entire standards and frameworks are available.

U.S. Department of Education (http://www.ed.gov). This site contains links to the education databases supported by the U.S. government (including ERIC). It also makes available full-text reports on current findings on education and provides links to research offices and organizations as well as research publications and products.

Becoming a Member of Professional Organizations

Another way to find current literature related to your research topic is through membership in professional organizations. The following list gives the names of a few U.S.-based professional organizations that can be valuable resources for research reports and curriculum materials. In countries other than the United States, similar organizations likely can also be accessed through an Internet search. This list of professional organizations is not intended to be comprehensive, for there are as many professional organizations as there are content areas (e.g., reading, writing, mathematics, science, social studies, music, health, and physical education) and special interest groups (e.g., Montessori education). Search the Education Resource Organizations Directory or browse the About ED—Educational Associations and Organizations site (http://www2.ed.gov/about/contacts/gen/othersites/ associations.html) to discover and learn about some of the associations that support teachers and specific disciplines in education. Also try searching the Education Oasis site (http://www.educationoasis.com.) to discover and learn about some of the associations that support teachers and specific disciplines in education.

ASCD: Association for Supervision and Curriculum Development

(http://www.ascd.org). Boasting 160,000 members in more than 135 countries, ASCD is one of the largest educational organizations in the world. ASCD publishes books, newsletters, audiotapes, videotapes, and some excellent journals that are valuable resources for teacher researchers, including *Educational Leadership* and the *Journal of Curriculum and Supervision*.

DIGITAL RESEARCH TOOLS FOR THE 21ST CENTURY

Google Searches

Google Books (http://books.google.com)

Google Books searches for books and within the content of books in Google's digital book collection. The searchable collection of digitized books contains full text as well as limited selections, previews, or snippet views of the content—including front cover, table of contents, indexes, and other relevant information, such as related books, posted reviews, and key terms. As such, Google Books offers an alternative search mechanism to a library catalog for finding and previewing books and information inside books. Google Books searches full-text content, so a search can often retrieve more specific information that a library catalog will not retrieve.

In most cases, however, Google Books does *not* replace the full text of all the books that it finds, so it is best used in conjunction with a library catalog or the collective catalog from a consortium of libraries. For example, you may search Google Books and find a relevant book. After reviewing information such as the table of contents and the limited preview of the book, you may want to search your library catalog to obtain the book. On the other hand, you may find an item record of a book using your library catalog that does not contain much information about the book; that is, you may not be able to see the table of contents or any information other than the title and the subject headings. As an alternative, you could search the title of the book in Google Books to find additional information, such as a table of contents or even a preview of the contents of the book.

Google Books began in 2004, and as more and more content is digitized into the Google Books database, its usefulness to researchers will continue to expand. You may want to consider limiting the publication date of a search using the advanced feature to retrieve more current materials. The default search is set to relevancy, but the most relevant material may be too old for the research you are doing.

Google Scholar (http://scholar.google.com)

Google Scholar offers simple and free access to scholarly information. Originally released in a beta version in November 2004, Google Scholar searches for full-text articles, citations, and abstracts. It also searches the Google Books database for books. To take full advantage of Google Scholar, you should click on Scholar Preferences and set the Library Links feature to access your library. This will allow you to obtain the full text of the articles you find through your library and your library databases. You may also want to set your preferences to retrieve only articles. Google Scholar also includes links to other articles that have cited a specific article and related articles.

Again, for finding scholarly and peer-reviewed journal articles, ultimately you will want to use your library's access to the ERIC or Education Full Text databases. Google Scholar, however, often can help you tease out the correct descriptors or subject headings for finding articles in your library databases. This is especially true if you find the full text of an article in a database from your library. Just like Google, searching Google Scholar allows you to find relevant information using the simple and familiar search strategies you use to search the Web. Starting with Google Scholar can lead you to more sophisticated searching in library databases.

USA.gov (https://www.usa.gov)

USA.gov is a powerful online search tool for finding U.S. federal government and state government information. For education research, USA.gov refines a typical search by limiting the results to information from federal and state domains. For example, you may search for "standards aligned curriculum" to determine what activities are happening in various states. You can also limit a search to a particular state, such as Oregon, to retrieve information specifically from sites such as the Oregon Department of Education. Because so much educational information and decision making can be found on government sites, a USA.gov search is a good option for finding relevant primary information not found in books and journal articles.

NCTM: National Council of Teachers of Mathematics

(http://nctm.org). With more than 80,000 members and 230 affiliates in the United States and Canada, NCTM is dedicated to the teaching and learning of mathematics and offers vision and leadership for mathematics educators at all age levels. NCTM provides regional and national professional development opportunities and publishes the following journals: *Teaching Children Mathematics*, *Mathematics Teaching in the Middle School*, *Mathematics Teacher*, *Mathematics Teacher Education*, and the *Journal for Research in Mathematics Education*.

NCSS: National Council for the Social Studies

(http://www.socialstudies.org). The NCSS supports and advocates social studies education. Its resources for educators include the journals *Social Education* and *Social Studies and the Young Learner*.

NEA: National Education Association

(http://www.nea.org). The mission of the NEA is to advocate for education professionals and fulfill the promise of public education to prepare students to succeed in a diverse and interdependent world.

NSTA: National Science Teachers Association

(http://nsta.org). The NSTA, with more than 55,000 members, provides many valuable resources for science teachers. It develops the National Science Education Standards and publishes the journals *Science and Children*, *Science Scope*, *The Science Teacher*, and the *Journal of College Science Teaching*.

ILA: International Literacy Association

(http://www.literacyworldwide.org). The ILA provides resources to an international audience of reading teachers through its publication of the journals *The Reading Teacher*, the *Journal of Adolescent and Adult Literacy*, and *Reading Research Quarterly*.

About ED—Educational State Contacts

(http://www2.ed.gov/about/contacts/gen/othersites/associations.html). This U.S. Department of Education site lists a variety of state-by-state educational departments and contacts.

Education Resource Organizations Directory

(http://wdcrobcolp01.ed.gov/Programs/EROD). The Education Resource Organizations Directory can help you identify and contact a wide range of educational organizations in the discipline.

Evaluating Your Sources

When you have retrieved a list of sources, you will need to evaluate them to determine not only whether these sources are relevant but also whether they are reliable and legitimate. Good researchers must be able to discern the quality and limitations of a source, so good research requires excellent judgment. The statements in Table 4–2 can serve as a rubric for evaluating your sources regardless of whether those sources are from scholarly journals, magazines, or websites. A note of caution: Anyone can post a "professional" looking website on the Internet. Do not be fooled by looks. Apply the same criteria for evaluating Web-based materials that you would use for print materials. Critically evaluating your sources will save you time and energy reading and annotating sources that may contribute little to your understanding of a research topic. This section includes an evaluation rubric using the categories of relevancy, author, source, methodology, date, validity, and references.

Relevancy

- What was the purpose or problem statement of the study? Obviously, the first thing to do is to determine whether the source really applies to your research topic and qualifies to be included in a review of related literature. Does the title of the source reflect research related to your work? Is there a well-refined question or statement of purpose? The problem statement is often found in the abstract and will allow you to determine the relevance of the research to your own research.

Author

- Who was the author? What are the qualifications, reputation, and status of the author? In most databases, the name of the author links to any other published

table 4–2 ▪ Rubric for Evaluating Print and Internet Resources

Dimension	Evaluation Criteria				
	1 Poor	2 Below Average	3 Average	4 Above Average	5 Excellent
Relevancy	The source does not address the research interests of your study.	The source addresses one of the research interests of your study.	The source addresses most of the research interests of your study.	The source meets all of the research interests of your study.	The source meets all of the research interests of your study and provides a conceptual framework for a study that is replicable.
Author	Unclear who authored the study.	Author name and contact information is provided.	Author name, contact information, and some credentials are included in the article.	Author name, contact information, and full credentials are included in the article.	Author is a well-known researcher in the research area under investigation and provides links to other research related to the current study.
Source	Source is a nonrefereed website and is a summary of the author's opinion.	Source is a nonrefereed website and must be closely examined for bias, subjectivity, intent, accuracy, and reliability before inclusion in the review of related literature.	Source is a scholarly or peer-reviewed journal, an education-related magazine, or a popular magazine.	Source is a scholarly or peer-reviewed journal.	Source is a scholarly or peer-reviewed journal with links to related literature by the same author(s) and the ability to download fully online versions of articles.

(Continued)

table 4–2 ■ **(Continued)**

Dimension	Evaluation Criteria				
	1 Poor	2 Below Average	3 Average	4 Above Average	5 Excellent
Methodology	It is not possible to determine from the description of the study whether an appropriate methodology was used to investigate the research problem.	The description of the methodology does not include sufficient information to determine whether the sample size was acceptable given the research problem.	The source includes a full description of the research problem and the appropriateness of the methodology to investigate the problem.	The source includes a full description of the research problem and the appropriateness of the methodology to investigate the problem. The results are presented objectively and can be connected to the data presented in the study.	The source includes a full description of the research problem and the appropriateness of the methodology to investigate the problem. Issues of validity and reliability are discussed along with limitations of the study. There is sufficient information in the source to enable a replication of the study.
Date	No date of publication is included in the source.	Date of publication is included but is too old to be helpful for the current research problem.	Current date of publication.	Current date of publication with a list of references consulted by the author.	Current date of publication with a list of references consulted by the author, including links to fully online articles.

Source: Mills, Geoffrey E.; Gay, Lorraine R., *Educational Research: Competencies for Analysis and Applications,* Loose-Leaf Version, 11th Ed., © 2016. Reprinted and electronically reproduced by permission of Pearson Education, Inc., New York, NY.

works in the database. Check to determine what other works, if any, have been published by the author and whether any other others cite the works of the author. Is the subject matter a primary interest in the published works of the author? Is the author affiliated with any institution or organization? Most important, can you contact the author? Does the author have a personal website with vitae?

Source

- Where was the source published? Does the information come from a scholarly or peer-reviewed journal, an education-related magazine, or a popular magazine? Is the information personal opinion or the result of a research study? Clearly, sources of different types merit different weight in your review. For example, did you find your source in a refereed or a nonrefereed journal? In a refereed journal, articles are reviewed by a panel of experts in the field and are more scholarly and trustworthy than articles from nonrefereed or popular journals. Research articles in refereed journals are required to comply with strict guidelines regarding format and research procedures. Review the submission guidelines at the journal website to determine the criteria for publication. Special care and caution must also be taken when evaluating websites because anyone can post information on the Internet. Websites must be closely examined for bias, subjectivity, intent, accuracy, and reliability. These important quality-control questions will help you determine whether a source is worthy of inclusion in your review of related literature.

Methodology

- How was the study conducted? It is important to verify that the information presented in a particular source is objective and impartial. What methodology was used to investigate the problem or test the hypothesis? Was an appropriate method used? Can the research be replicated by others? Was the sample size suitable for the research? Does the source add to the information you have already gathered about your topic? Is the information presented in the source accurate? It is important to verify that the information presented in a particular source is objective and impartial. Does the author present evidence that supports the interpretations? Does the content of the article consist mainly of opinion, or does it contain appropriately collected and analyzed data? How accurate are the discussion and conclusions of the findings? Do the findings present any contrary data or assumptions?

Date

- When was the research conducted? The date of publication is of primary importance in evaluating a source. Look at the copyright date of books and the dates when articles were published. Websites should always include a reference to the last updated or revised date, but in general, Web search tools do not incorporate date as a relevancy factor. Research in areas of current interest and continuing development generally requires recent, up-to-date references. Searching for recent references does not mean disregarding older research. Often, older research as opposed to out-of-date research is pertinent to your worldview as an educator and is still relevant. The importance of seminal theoretical works is evident throughout this text, such as the theoretical work conducted in educational psychology by Jean Piaget.

■ What other sources were referenced? Check the bibliography of a source to help determine the quality of the research. Do the references reflect current, scholarly, or peer-reviewed research? Are they robust enough for the subject matter? Do they reflect original sources and alternative perspectives? Who are the authors? The list of references can yield an abundance of information when evaluating the quality of a source. Remember, the quality of your research will also be judged by the references you choose, so you should be careful to select the best research to support your work.

Conducting effective library and Internet searches will yield an abundance of useful information about your topic. By using multiple search methods and strategies, you can collect information that is current, accurate, and comprehensive. As you become more experienced, you will learn to conduct more efficient and effective searches, identifying better sources that focus on your topic and accurately represent the information needed for your research. For the most part, research conducted in databases that access primary, scholarly and peer-reviewed sources will produce high-quality information and therefore should be the emphasis of your research.

Annotating Your Sources

After you have identified the primary references related to your topic, you are ready to move on to the next phase of a review of related literature—annotating the references. Many databases include an abstract or summary of a study that describes the hypotheses, procedures, and conclusions. An abstract is descriptive in nature and does not assess the value or intent of the source. An annotation assesses the quality, relevance, and accuracy of a source. Additionally, the annotation describes how the source relates to the topic and its relative importance. Basically, annotating involves reviewing, summarizing, and classifying your references. Students sometimes ask why it is necessary to read and annotate original, complete articles or reports if they already have perfectly good abstracts. By assessing the quality and usefulness of a source, annotations articulate your response to a source and why the source is important to your research. After completing annotations, many students discover that these same annotations contributed heavily to the writing of their review of related literature.

To begin the annotation process, arrange your articles and other sources in reverse chronological order. Beginning with the latest references is a good research strategy because the most recent research is likely to have profited from previous research. Also, recent references may cite preceding studies that you may not have identified. For each reference, complete the following steps:

1. If the article has an abstract or a summary, as most do, read it to determine the relevance of the article to your problem.
2. Skim the entire article, making mental notes of the main points of the study.
3. If you were searching research databases, then you should have a Word document already that contains a complete bibliographic reference for the work. Include the library call number if the source work is from a book. This step can be tedious but is important. You would spend much more time trying to find the complete bibliographic information for an article or book that you failed to annotate completely than annotating it in the first place. If you know that your final report must follow a particular editorial style, such as that described in the *Publication Manual of the American Psychological Association* (APA), put your bibliographic reference in that form. Remember, most databases put the citation of a source in a citation style. For example, an APA-style reference for a journal article looks like this:

Snurd, B. J. (2007). The use of white versus yellow chalk in the teaching of advanced calculus. *Journal of Useless Findings, 11,* 1–99.

In this example, "2007" is the date of publication, "11" is the volume number of the journal, and "1–99" are the page numbers. A style manual provides reference formats for all types of sources. Whatever format you select, use it consistently and be sure your bibliographic references are accurate. You never know when you may have to go back and get additional information from an article.

4. Classify and code the article according to some system and then add the code to the annotation in a conspicuous place, such as an upper corner. The code should be one that can be easily accessed when you want to sort your notes into the categories you devise. Any coding system that makes sense to you will facilitate your task later when you have to sort, organize, analyze, synthesize, and write your review of the literature. You may use abbreviations to code variables relevant to your study (e.g., "SA" in the upper corner of your abstract may signify that the article is about student achievement). Coding and keeping track of articles is a key to organization. Programs such as RefWorks, EndNote, and others can help you manage, organize, annotate, and create bibliographic citations. They also allow you to add keywords or descriptors to your citations. Database vendors, such as ProQuest and EBSCO, allow you to create an account to store references from the ERIC and Education Full Text databases. To manage citation with ProQuest's My Research or MyEBSCO, you must create a profile account that allows you to save individual citation records, create folders to organize citations, and save searches. In addition, you can request RSS feeds and search alerts that automatically retrieve newer articles that meet your search criteria.
5. Annotate the source by summarizing the central theme and scope of the reference, why the source is useful, strengths and limitations, the author's conclusions, and your overall reaction to the work. If the work is an opinion article, write the main points of the author's position—for example, "Jones believes

parent volunteers should be used because [list the reasons]." If it is a study, state the problem, the procedures (including a description of participants and instruments), and the major conclusions. Make special note of any particularly interesting or unique aspect of the study, such as use of a new measuring instrument. Double-check the reference to make sure you have not omitted any pertinent information. If an abstract provided at the beginning of an article contains all the essential information (and that is a big if), by all means use it.

6. Indicate any thoughts that come to your mind, such as points on which you disagree (e.g., mark them with an X) or components that you do not understand (e.g., mark them with a question mark). For example, if an author states that he or she used a double-blind procedure and you are unfamiliar with that technique, you can put a question mark next to that statement in your database entry, on your index card, or on a photocopy of the page. Later, you can find out what it is.

7. Indicate any statements that are direct quotations or personal reactions. Plagiarism, intentional or not, is an absolute no-no with the direst of consequences. Put quotation marks around direct quotations and add the in-text citation information, or you may not remember later which statements are direct quotations. You must also record the exact page number of the quotation in case you use it later in your paper. You will need the page number when citing the source in your paper. Direct quotations should be kept to a minimum in your research plan and report. Use your own words, not those of other researchers. Occasionally, a direct quotation may be quite appropriate and useful.

Whatever approach you use, guard your notes and digital records carefully. Save more than one copy so that you will not lose your work. Also, when your annotations are complete, save the information for future reference and future studies (nobody can do just one!).

Literature Matrix

A helpful way to keep track of your annotations is to record them, by author and date, on a matrix (see Figures 4–6 and 4–7). The matrix is a powerful organizer when you are committing your thoughts to text. Along the Y-axis, list the authors' names and year of publication. Along the X-axis, list the kinds of variables/themes/ issues addressed by the studies. The matrix will provide you with a mental map of what you are reading and what the studies share in common.

Analyzing, Organizing, and Reporting the Literature

For beginning researchers, the hardest part of writing the literature review for a plan or report is thinking about how hard it is going to be to write the literature review. More time is spent worrying about doing it than actually doing it.

figure 4–6 ■ Literature Matrix

Author/s	Year	Variables Considered in the Study						

figure 4–7 ■ Sample Literature Matrix

Author/s	Year	Academic Achievement	Military Personnel	Social Adjustment	Attitude to Change	Discontinuous Education	Caravan Parks	S.E.S.	I.Q.	School Counselors	Solutions Provided
Carmer, W., & Dorsey, S.	1970	•	•								
Bourke, S. F., & Naylor, D.R.	1971	•	•								
Collins, R. J., & Coulter, F.	1974	•	•	•							
Mackay L. D., & Spicer, B. J.	1975	•	•	•							
Lacey, C., & Blare, D.	1979	•				•					
Parker, L.	1979	•				•	•				
Parker, L.	1981	•		•			•	•			
Bell, D. P.	1962	•					•				
Smith, T. S., Husbands, L. T., & Street, D.	1969	•							•		
Whalen, T. C., & Fried, M. A.	1973	•						•	•		
Black, F. S., & Bargar, R. R.	1975	•									
Goodman, T. L.	1975	•									
Splete, H., & Rasmussen, J.	1977									•	•
de Noose, D. A., & Wells, R. M.	1981	•		•						•	•
Allan, J., & Bardsley, P.	1983									•	•
King, M.	1984	•							•		•
Thomas, B. D.	1978	•				•					•
Rahmani, Z.	1987		•								•
Mills, G. E.	1989	•		•		•					•

This hesitancy stems mostly from a lack of experience with the type of writing needed in a literature review—a technical form of writing unlike most of the writing we do. In technical writing, facts must be documented and opinions substantiated. For example, if you say that the high school dropout percentage in Ohio has increased in the last 10 years, you must provide a source for this information. Technical writing is precise, requiring clarity of definitions and consistency in the use of terms. If the term *achievement* is important in your review, for example, you must indicate what you mean by it and be consistent in using that meaning throughout the written review. Figure 4–8 summarizes these and other important technical writing guidelines useful in a literature review.

If you have annotated the literature related to your problem efficiently and if you approach the task in an equally systematic manner, then analyzing, organizing, and reporting the literature will be relatively painless. To get warmed up, you should read quickly through your annotations and notes to refresh your memory and identify references that no longer seem sufficiently related to your topic. Do not force references into your review that do not really fit; the review forms the background and rationale for your hypothesis and should contain only references that serve this purpose. The following guidelines—based on experience acquired the hard way—should be helpful to you.

Make an Outline

Don't groan; your eighth-grade teacher was right about the virtues of an outline. However you construct it, an outline will save you time and effort in the long run and will increase the probability of having an organized review. The outline does not have to be excessively detailed. Begin by identifying the main topics and the order in which they should be presented. For example, the outline of the review for the problem concerned with salaried paraprofessionals versus parent volunteers may begin with these headings: "Literature on Salaried Paraprofessionals," "Literature on Parent Volunteers," and "Literature Comparing the Two." You can always add or remove topics in the outline as your work progresses. The next step is to differentiate each major heading into logical subheadings. The need for further differentiation will be determined by your topic; the more complex it is, the more subheadings you will require. When you have completed your outline, you will invariably need to rearrange, add, and delete topics. It is much easier, however, to reorganize an outline than it is to reorganize a document written in paragraph form.

Analyze Each Reference in Terms of Your Outline

In other words, determine the subheading under which each reference fits. Then sort your references into appropriate piles. If you end up with references without a home, there are three logical possibilities: (1) something is wrong with your outline, (2) the references do not belong in your review and should be discarded, or (3) the references do not belong in your review but do belong somewhere else in your research plan and report introduction. Opinion articles or reports of descriptive research often are useful in the introduction, whereas formal research studies are most useful in the review of related literature.

figure 4–8 ■ Guidelines for Technical Writing

Source: From "Educational Research: Competencies for Analysis and Applications." By Geoffrey E. Mills, Lorraine R. Gay. Published by Pearson Education © 2016.

1. *Document facts and substantiate opinions.* Cite references to support your facts and opinions. Note that facts are usually based on empirical data, whereas opinions are not. In the hierarchy of persuasiveness, facts are more persuasive than opinions. Differentiate between facts and opinions in the review.

2. *Define terms clearly, and be consistent in your use of terms.*

3. *Organize content logically.*

4. *Direct your writing to a particular audience.* Usually the literature review is aimed at a relatively naïve reader, one who has some basic understanding of the topic but requires additional education to understand the topic or issue. Do not assume your audience knows as much as you do about the topic and literature! They don't, so you have to write to educate them.

5. *Follow an accepted manual of style.* The manual indicates the style in which chapter headings are set up, how tables must be constructed, how footnotes and bibliographies must be prepared, and the like. Commonly used manuals and their current editions are *Publication Manual of the American Psychological Association*, Sixth Edition, and *The Chicago Manual of Style*, Sixteenth Edition.

6. *Evade affected verbiage and eschew obscuration of the obvious.* In other words, limit big words and avoid jargon.

7. *Start each major section with a brief overview of the section.* The overview may begin like this: "In this section, three main issues are examined. The first is. . . ."

8. *End each major section with a summary of the main ideas.*

Analyze the References Under Each Subheading for Similarities and Differences

If three references say essentially the same thing, you will not need to describe each one; it is much better to make one summary statement and cite the three sources, as in this example:

> Several studies have found white chalk to be more effective than yellow chalk in the teaching of advanced mathematics (Snurd, 1995; Trivia, 1994; Ziggy, 1984).

Give a Meaningful Overview of Past Research

Don't present a series of abstracts or a mere list of findings (Jones found A, Smith found B, and Brown found C). Your task is to organize and summarize the references in a meaningful way. Do not ignore studies that are contradictory to most other studies or to your personal bias. Analyze and evaluate contradictory studies and try to determine a possible explanation, as in this example:

> Contrary to these studies is the work of Rottenstudee (1998), who found yellow chalk to be more effective than white chalk in the teaching of trigonometry. However, the size of the treatment groups (two students per group) and the duration of the study (one class period) may have seriously affected the results.

Discuss the References Least Related to Your Problem First and Those Most Related to Your Problem Just Before the Statement of the Hypothesis

Think of a big V. At the bottom of the V is your guiding hypothesis; directly above your hypothesis are the studies most directly related to it, and so forth. The idea is to organize and present your literature in such a way that it leads logically to a tentative, testable conclusion, namely, your hypothesis. Highlight or summarize important aspects of the review to help readers identify them. If your problem has more than one major aspect, you may have two Vs or one V that logically leads to two tentative, testable conclusions.

Conclude the Review with a Brief Summary of the Literature and Its Implications

The length of this summary depends on the length of the review. It should be detailed enough to clearly show the chain of logic you have followed in arriving at your implications and tentative conclusions.

SUMMARY

Review of Related Literature

1. The review of related literature involves systematically identifying, locating, and analyzing documents pertaining to the research topic.
2. The major purpose of reviewing the literature is to identify information that already exists about your topic.
3. The literature review can point out research strategies, procedures, and instruments that have and have not been found to be productive in investigating your topic.
4. A smaller, well-organized review is preferred to a review containing many studies that are less related to the problem.

5. Heavily researched areas usually provide enough references directly related to a topic to eliminate the need for reporting less related or secondary studies. Little-researched topics usually require review of any study related in some meaningful way so that the researcher may develop a logical framework and rationale for the study.

Action Research and the Review of Related Literature

6. Action researchers disagree about the role of the literature review in the research process. Some researchers have argued that reviewing the literature curtails inductive analysis—using induction to determine the direction of the research—and should be avoided at the early stages of the research process.
7. Others suggest that the review of related literature is important early in the action research process because it helps action researchers identify underlying assumptions behind their research questions and helps the researcher refine research questions and embed them in guiding hypotheses that provide possible directions to follow.

Identifying Keywords

8. Most sources have alphabetical subject indexes to help you locate information on your topic. A list of keywords should guide your literature search.

Identifying Your Sources

9. A good way to start a review of related literature is with a narrow search of pertinent educational encyclopedias, handbooks, and annual reviews found in libraries. These resources provide broad overviews of issues in various subject areas.
10. An article or report written by the person who conducted the study is a primary source; a brief description of a study written by someone other than the original researcher is a secondary source. Primary sources are preferred in reviews.

Searching for Books on Your Research Topic in the Library

11. Most libraries use an online catalog system as well as collective catalogs to access materials from other libraries. You should familiarize yourself with your library, the library website, and the resources available within and beyond your library.
12. A keyword search uses terms or phrases pertinent to your topic to search for and identify potentially useful sources.
13. Keyword searches can be focused by using the Boolean operators AND, OR, and NOT. Using AND or NOT narrows a search and reduces the number of sources identified; using OR broadens the search and increases the number of sources. It is often best to start with a narrow search.

Steps for Searching Computer Databases

14. Identify keywords related to your research topic.
15. Select the appropriate databases—some databases using the same interface may allow you to search multiple databases simultaneously.
16. Initiate a search using your keywords selectively.
17. Reformulate your search using appropriate subject headings or descriptors combining terms as is appropriate.
18. Once you have found a relevant article, check the item record for links to additional subject heading or descriptors, author(s), cited references, times cited in database, or other references for finding additional related items using the features within the database.

Searching the Internet and the World Wide Web

19. The Internet links organizations and individuals all over the world. The World Wide Web is on the Internet.
20. To access the Internet, you need a computer with a modem or Ethernet/cable line and a browser that connects to the Web.
21. The available resources on the World Wide Web are almost limitless, so the best way to become familiar with its use is to "surf" in your spare time.
22. The Web contains a variety of sites relevant to an educational researcher. Each site is reached through its Internet address. Addresses containing "ed" or ending in ".edu" are related to educational institutions, those ending in ".com" are related to commercial enterprises, those ending in ".org" refer to organizations (including professional organizations), and those ending in ".gov" link to government sites.
23. Search engines have established subcategories and also allow keyword searches to review large portions of the World Wide Web quickly.

Becoming a Member of Professional Organizations

24. The websites for professional organizations maintain links to current research in a particular discipline.
25. Popular professional organizations include the Association for Supervision and Curriculum Development, the National Council of Teachers of Mathematics, the National Council for the Social Studies, the National Science Teachers Association, and the International Literacy Association.

Evaluating Your Sources

26. It is important to evaluate all literature sources by asking the following questions: What was the problem statement of the study? Is the study relevant given your research interests? Who was studied? Where was the source published? When was the study conducted? How was the study conducted?

Annotating Your Sources

27. Annotating your sources involves creating summaries by locating, reviewing, summarizing, and classifying your references. Annotations assess the quality, relevance, and accuracy of a source; articulate your response to a source; and indicate why the source is important to your research.

28. The main advantage of beginning with the latest references on your topic is that the most recent studies are likely to have profited from previous research. References in recent studies often contain references to previous studies that you have not yet identified.

29. For each source work, list the complete bibliographic record, including author's name, date of publication, title, journal name or book title, volume number, issue number, page numbers, and library call number. Briefly list main ideas. Put quotation marks around quotes taken from the source and include page numbers. Keep all references in the citation format required for research reports or dissertations.

30. Make a copy of your references and put it in a safe place.

31. A helpful way to keep track of the literature is to use a matrix.

Analyzing, Organizing, and Reporting the Literature

32. Describing and reporting research call for a specialized style of writing. Technical writing requires documenting facts and substantiating opinions, clarifying definitions and using them consistently, using an accepted style manual, and starting sections with an introduction and ending them with a brief summary.

33. When organizing a review, make an outline; sort references by topic; analyze the similarities and differences between references in a given subheading; give a meaningful overview in which you discuss references least related to the problem first; and conclude with a brief summary of the literature and its implications.

TASKS

1. Identify 10 to 15 good references (sources) that directly relate to your area of focus. The references should include a variety of source types (e.g., books, articles, Internet reports, etc.).

2. Evaluate and abstract those references.

3. Write a review of related literature.

Data Collection Techniques

After reading this chapter you should be able to:

5.1   Identify and appropriately utilize qualitative data collection techniques.
5.2   Identify and appropriately utilize quantitative data collection techniques.

This chapter introduces qualitative and quantitative data collection techniques that can be used to systematically investigate an area of focus. These techniques include using direct observation, interviews, questionnaires, attitude scales, new and existing records, artifacts, teacher-made tests, standardized tests, and school-generated report cards.

Reflection on Action Research
James Rockford

James Rockford is an elementary teacher in a rural school district in Oregon. James is responsible primarily for teaching music and computer keyboarding skills to young children and initially became involved with action research as part of a statewide action research initiative. As a result of his first attempt at doing action research and his effort to make it a standard part of his teaching, James has also worked as a mentor for other teachers in his region. James's story highlights the importance of collecting data from a variety of sources to fully understand the effects of an intervention on student outcomes.

It seemed to be a perfect match. I had charge of a new computer lab and a mandate to develop a program of instruction to match the curriculum guide, and I needed a "problem" for a collaborative action research class.

The only software that came with the computers was a popular program to teach keyboarding and ClarisWorks. It didn't make any sense to spend several thousand dollars to teach keyboarding, so the problem became, "How does keyboarding instruction enhance students' ability to use word processing, database, spreadsheet, and draw functions?"

Looking at the literature proved to be a formidable problem because there wasn't a good academic library in the area. The local community college had one online computer to access ERIC (Educational Resources Information Center) through the World Wide Web if I gave search terms to the librarian. A little help came, but I preferred to do the search myself. Our school was not yet online, so I resorted to using my son's computer. A quick survey of the literature showed plenty of research on keyboarding but not much focused on young children. Opinions ranged from "Start them as early as possible" to "Avoid bad habits" to "Don't bother because they can hunt and peck as fast as they can type."

The problem proved to be a little overwhelming in that I had just started an instructional program to teach all the keyboarding skills, and it became obvious that results would be harder to get for database, spreadsheet, and draw functions. As a result, I decided to look initially only at the effect of teaching keyboarding on word processing for students in grades 4 through 6.

This was supposed to be a collaborative venture, so my first task was to enlist the help of the teachers in grades 4 through 6. We met after school one afternoon so I could explain the purpose of the project. They agreed to help gather data, but only one class actually got into the lab every day. This was disappointing, but it helped make the project more manageable since I would be handling data from only one class instead of three.

What variables might have an effect on students' success in learning to keyboard? I conducted a survey of teacher attitudes and a survey to assess whether students had any prior knowledge, how much time they spent on a computer at home and at school, and whether they had a computer at home. Records were kept for time on computers at school in instructional and free-choice situations.

A well-designed action research project should, as its name declares, lead to some kind of action. The purpose of my action research project was to determine if teaching keyboarding skills to sixth-grade students had enough of an impact on their word processing skills to warrant spending the time and money. It seemed rather obvious that it would, but several students had developed their own unique "hunt-and-peck" system and could already approach the district-mandated target of 20 words per minute. There are many variables that might affect word processing rates, and that led to the following questions:

1. *Do students have a computer at home? How much time do they spend at it per week?*
2. *What preexisting knowledge do students have about computers?*
3. *How much time do students spend at the computer when they're at school? How does it affect word processing rates?*
4. *What is the effect of the keyboarding software used in the lab at school?*

Student Self-Evaluation Survey

1. Do you have a computer that you use outside of school?

    (a) Yes   (b) No

2. How many hours a day do you spend at the computer outside of school?

    (a) 0   (b) 1 or less   (c) 1–2   (d) 2–3

3. How much time do you spend at the computer while you're at school?

    (a) 0   (b) 15 minutes   (c) 30 minutes   (d) more than 30 minutes

4. When you type on a keyboard, do you look at the

    (a) monitor (b) keyboard   (c) rough draft   (d) your neighbor

5. I use the computer to (circle all that apply)

    (a) play games   (b) write stories and reports
    (c) draw pictures   (d) collect information and store it
    (e) find information in the library

6. Learning to keyboard in the lab made my life with computers

    (a) easier   (b) more frustrating   (c) no different

7. If I had the chance to do more with computers, I would

    _____

8. The best thing about learning to keyboard is

    _____

9. The hardest thing about learning to keyboard is

    _____

The questions were then placed in a data matrix and triangulated as follows (Note: D.S. = data source):

Questions	D.S. 1	D.S. 2	D.S. 3
Preexisting knowledge?	Students' survey	Computer knowledge pretest	
Keyboarding speed?	Pretest	Posttest	Teacher help
Appropriate use (WP)?	Pretest software	Posttest software	Timed typing teacher constructed
Time on computers?	School lab records	Student survey	Parent survey

I collected data using surveys that I developed to measure the following areas:

- *Student self-evaluation questionnaire*
- *Teacher-constructed vocabulary/facts pretest of general computer knowledge*
- *Teacher-constructed timed typing test rates*
- *A classroom teacher survey of knowledge/attitudes about technology*
- *A teacher observation record for the computer lab*
- *Existing records of students' word processing rates with software*
- *Parent survey of student computer use outside of school*

Data were compiled as follows:

- *The three variables of time, prior knowledge, and use of keyboarding software were analyzed using a scatter plot graph to determine any correlation to word processing speed.*
- *Surveys were compiled to show tendencies.*
- *Keyboarding rates between October and May were compiled in graph form to show progress over time.*

In general, the data indicated the following:

- *Student time spent on computers out of school had no effect on word processing rate. (They love those computer games!)*
- *Time spent on computers at school was critical.*
- *In only 1 month, the class word processing rate mean had increased 300 percent.*

As a result, it was apparent that the keyboarding software was effective, and on that basis I continued its use. Because time on task is critical, teachers were urged to take students to the lab every day and monitor keyboarding habits as well as install keyboarding software on classroom computers so that each student received a minimum of 10 minutes' practice per day. Timed typing tests require greater and different skills than are called for on keyboarding software. In the future, timed typing tests will be given weekly to provide an authentic assessment of student progress, and a tracking system will be used to monitor the acquisition of skill development.

Any research worth its salt appears to generate more questions than it answers. At the completion of this project, I was left wondering if a student's learning style had any impact on the ability to learn word processing skills. Would keyboarding instruction improve students' use of database, spreadsheet, and draw/paint functions? Could other types of authentic assessment be used to determine skill/concept development? These are questions I will continue to investigate.

The project became a springboard to address issues in setting up a computer lab. Instead of being behind the eight ball, I was able to anticipate problems and find solutions. Collaboration was an important part of the process. But perhaps the most powerful part of the action research process was the extent to which I became more reflective about what I was doing in the computer lab. The lab at my school has received a lot of praise from administrators, board members, and teachers, and I believe that going through the action research process has had much to do with the continued success of the lab.

I don't look at classroom problems quite the same way now. For example, I also teach middle school choir and began to notice that the weeks on which I saw eighth graders on Mondays (we're on block scheduling), it was usually a difficult, if not unproductive rehearsal. Keeping some informal data about those days and reflecting about why they were so difficult led me to try some interventions that might help alleviate the problem. It may be a bit corny, but action research has changed my life—in the classroom anyway. Student learning is enhanced, I approach problems more systematically, I gather data more carefully and accurately, and my practice is more reflective.

The year following my word processing action research project, I had the good fortune to be a mentor for other teachers learning the action research process. Based on this experience, two observations come to mind. Problem formulation is a difficult process. Extra time spent in this phase of the action research cycle will prevent backtracking, headaches, and frustration down the road. When teachers do identify something that needs addressing, there appears to be a measurable difference between problems that are student centered and those that arise from a teacher complaint about a teaching situation. It appeared that the problems that are student centered are more likely to result in the improvement of instruction.

Making action research a natural part of the teaching process, in the classroom and the school, is critical to success. Traditionally, teachers are not researchers. The school routine isn't geared to provide teachers with the time and resources that research demands. Teachers are considered to be working only when they're in front of a class. On the other hand, teachers need to develop the attitude that improvement of the teaching/learning process can and should be addressed with data-based decision making formalized through action research.

Teacher Survey

1. I take my class to the lab

    (a) once a week   (b) twice a week   (c) 3 times a week
    (d) 4 times a week   (e) every day   (f) only when Mr. Rockford
                                                            is there

2. I expect my students to (circle all that apply)

    (a) compose reports/stories   (b) revise reports from written copies
    (c) practice keyboarding   (d) other:_____

3. If I rated my comfort level with computers it would be

    Use it every   Don't want to be in the
    chance I get   same room as one

    5   4   3   2   1

4. I monitor my students' keyboarding technique

    (a) only during lab sessions   (b) any time they're at the computer
    (c) never

5. My students' abilities to use the computer have been enhanced by learning
    to keyboard

    They're experts!   They're still looking
                                                 for the on switch!

    5   4   3   2   1

6. I would like my students to be able to

    _____

The decision about what data are collected for an action research area of focus is determined largely by the nature of the problem. There is no one recipe for how to proceed with data collection efforts. Rather, the individual or group must determine what data will contribute to their understanding and resolution of a given problem. Hence, data collection associated with action research is largely an idiosyncratic approach fueled by the desire to understand one's practice and to collect data that are appropriate and accessible.

This chapter will discuss qualitative (experience-based) data collection techniques and quantitative (number-based) techniques. The former includes data sources such as field notes, journals, questionnaires (surveys), maps, and digital recordings, whereas the latter focuses on the collection of teacher-made tests (criterion-referenced tests), standardized tests (norm-referenced tests), school-generated report cards, attitude scales, and the results of student achievement reported on statewide assessment tests.

One approach is not *better* than the other. Your area of focus and research questions will determine the best data collection techniques for your research. As discussed earlier, this may involve *qualitative* data sources and *quantitative* sources using a **mixed-methods** design. However, the literature on action research supports the assertion that qualitative designs are more appropriately applied to action research efforts compared with the application of an experimental pretest-posttest control group design in which the teacher researcher randomly assigns children to either a control group or an experimental group in order to receive a "treatment." Qualitative research is not the "easy" way out for teacher researchers who fear statistics (a.k.a. sadistics!). As you will see, the rigor of good qualitatively oriented action research equals the rigor of doing good quantitatively oriented action research. If your area of focus necessitates a more quantitative, experimental approach, then you should consult more quantitatively oriented references, such as Mills and Gay (2016, chapters 7 to 11) or Creswell (2015).

Qualitative Data Collection Techniques

The receptivity among educators in general and among action researchers in particular to a qualitative (descriptive) way of examining problems is reflected in the action research literature that emphasizes the following data collection techniques and sources:

- Existing archival sources within a school
- Tools for capturing everyday life
- Tools for questioning
- Conventional sources (surveys, questionnaires, etc.)
- Inventive sources (exhibits, portfolios, etc.)
- Interviews
- Oral history and narrative stories
- Rating scales
- Inventories
- Observation
- Mapping
- Visual recordings

- Photography
- Journals and diaries

(Anderson, Herr, & Nihlen, 1994; Calhoun, 1994; Hendricks, 2017; Sagor, 2000; Stringer, 2004; Wells, 1994)

As you can see from these examples, the kinds of data you collect would include descriptive, narrative, and even nonwritten forms. In many cases, these data occur naturally and are regularly collected by teachers and administrators. In simple terms, we are engaging in an activity that seeks to answer the question, "What is going on here?" It is not a mysterious quest but is quite simply an effort to collect data that increase our understanding of the phenomenon under investigation. The three primary fieldwork strategies we will discuss in this chapter are *experiencing*, *enquiring*, and *examining* (Wolcott, 1992, p. 19). Each of these strategies will be discussed in the context of actual teacher researchers' experiences.

Voices from the Field
Qualitative Data Collection Techniques

The teacher researcher in this video vignette describes a variety of qualitative data collection techniques and strategies that she believed would contribute to her understanding of the impact of classroom computers on students' attitudes toward learning and how they actually use computers in their own learning. Jureen uses multiple qualitative data collection techniques, including; classroom observations (recorded as field notes), student surveys (prior to and after implementing computers in her classroom instruction), attitude surveys (semantic differentials), and surveys of her cooperating teacher and educational assistant focused on their observations of implementing technology in the classroom. The teacher researcher's specific research questions help guide the decision about which multiple qualitative data collection techniques will provide a comprehensive picture about "what is going on" in the classroom during the implementation of a technology innovation. While survey results can be analyzed using descriptive statistics, their use in this study is clearly as a qualitative indicator about changes in students' attitudes toward the use of technology in teaching and learning.

ENHANCEdetext
video example 5–1
Watch as Jureen, a teacher researcher, describes her data collection techniques in this video. As you listen, reflect on the difference between qualitative and quantitative techniques. Why does she consider her survey to be a qualitative measure?

Experiencing Through Direct Observation

Teachers who undertake action research have countless opportunities to observe in their own classrooms. They observe as a normal component of their teaching, monitoring and adjusting instruction based on the verbal and nonverbal interactions in their classrooms. Therefore, using direct observation as a data collection strategy is familiar and not overly time consuming. As teachers, we are constantly observing our environment and adjusting our teaching based on what we see. Action research gives us a systematic and rigorous way to view this process of observation as a qualitative data collection technique.

Participant Observation

The action research vignettes shared in Chapters 1 to 3 illustrate how teachers "experience" their teaching through observation. James Rockford observed the "hunt-and-peck" keyboarding strategies of his students as a natural part of his teaching. Cathy Mitchell observed audience reactions to the "Violence Improv" and recorded field notes in her daily journal. Deborah South observed the interpersonal interactions of her "study skills" students and recorded her observations in a journal—observations that quickly confirmed the presence of major problems in the classroom. These experiences are all examples of participant observation.

If the researcher is "a genuine participant in the activity being studied," then the researcher is called a **participant observer** (McMillan, 1996, p. 245). According to Spradley (1980), participant observation is undertaken with at least two purposes in mind:

- To observe the activities, people, and physical aspects of a situation
- To engage in activities that are appropriate to a given situation that provide useful information

Participant observation can be done to varying degrees depending on the situation being observed and the opportunities presented: A participant observer can be an *active participant observer*, a *privileged, active observer*, or a *passive observer* (Pelto & Pelto, 1978; Spradley, 1980; Wolcott, 1982, 1997). Depending on the problem, teachers have many opportunities to be active participants in the observation process as they go about their work. However, the tendency with observing is to try to see it all! A good rule of thumb here is to try to do less but to do it better. That is, as you embark on some degree of participant observation, do not be overwhelmed with the task. It is not humanly possible to take in everything that you experience. Be content with furthering your understanding of your area of focus through *manageable* observations. Avoid trying to do too much, and you will be happier with the outcomes.

Active Participant Observer

Teachers, by virtue of teaching, are active participant observers of their teaching practice. When they are actively engaged in teaching, teachers observe the

Voices from the Field
Participant Observation

In this video vignette, our teacher researcher Jureen talks candidly about the challenges facing action researchers studying their own practices. As Jureen states, "It's hard to collect data and teach at the same time." Teachers are always engaged in naturalistic, ongoing data collection efforts as they "monitor and adjust" their instruction. Teachers are always in the role of participant observer to varying degrees, and Jureen shares some helpful participant observation strategies: working collaboratively with colleagues to record classroom observations, "teaching" and then "observing" students engaged in guided practice or other student-centered work, and using digital recordings that can be viewed at a later time. Experienced action researchers become competent observers of their own practice and use participant observation techniques as the cornerstone of their data collection efforts to better understand what is happening in their classrooms.

ENHANCEDetext
video example 5–2
In this video, Jureen offers suggestions to make observation easier for teachers, who are always participants in their own classrooms.

outcomes of their teaching. Each time we teach, we monitor the effects of our teaching and adjust our instruction accordingly. As an active participant observer of our own teaching practices, however, we may be so fully immersed in what we are doing that we don't have time to record our observations in a systematic way during the school day. Such recording is a necessary part of being an active participant observer.

In the action research vignettes from Chapters 1 to 3, we saw teachers who were active participant observers of their own teaching. Deborah South observed the "off-task" behavior of her "unmotivated" students during the study skills lessons. Cathy Mitchell observed the nature of the audience participation while she directed the teen theater. James Rockford observed the "hunt-and-peck" strategies used by keyboarding students while he was teaching keyboarding skills. As researchers of our own teaching practices, active participant observation is likely to be the most common "experiencing" data collection technique that we use.

Privileged, Active Observer

Teachers may also have opportunities to observe in a more privileged, active role. That is, they may wish to observe their children during a time when they are not directly responsible for the teaching of a lesson, for example, during a "specialist's" time in music, library, or physical education. These times provide opportunities for teachers to work as a "teacher's aide" while at the same time allowing them to withdraw, stand back, and watch what is happening during a particular teaching episode, moving in and out of the role of teacher, aide, and observer.

Many teachers comment on how valuable these experiences have been in allowing them time to observe the social interactions of students and the impact of a particular instructional strategy on those interactions. By necessity, these privileged, active observer opportunities require teachers to give up valuable time that is often dedicated to duties other than teaching, such as planning, attending team meetings, reading, visiting other classrooms, and relaxing (the all-important "downtime" during a day, if they are fortunate enough to have such a schedule). Taking time to observe one's class is a valuable use of nonteaching time that honors a teacher's effort to improve practice based, in part, on observational data.

Passive Observer

Teachers also have opportunities to be passive observers in classrooms and schools. When teachers take on the role of passive observer, they no longer assume the responsibilities of the teacher—they should focus only on their data collection. A privileged, active observer could be transformed into a passive observer by making explicit to the students and a teaching colleague that the classroom teacher is present only to "see what's going on around here." Students will quickly learn that there are times when their teacher is not going to interact with them as the teacher normally does. The teacher might simply announce, "Today I am going to watch and learn from what you are doing!" Taking a step back from the daily rigor of being "onstage" and performing can be refreshing and provide an insightful opportunity for teachers who are unaccustomed to watching their students in a different setting, through a different lens.

Field Notes

The written records of participant observers are often referred to as **field notes**. For teachers undertaking participant observation efforts in their classrooms, these field notes may take the form of anecdotal records compiled as part of a more systematic authentic assessment or portfolio effort. So, what do you write down in these field notes? Well, it depends on what you are looking for! I can offer only limited guidance to help quell your concerns about the "how-to" of writing field notes. But first let me start with an example of how *not* to do field notes!

During my graduate studies at the University of Oregon, I took a class on ethnographic research in education, and as part of learning how to do ethnography (qualitative research), I was required to conduct a "beginning ethnography" of something that was "culturally different" for me. As an Australian studying in the United States, I had a number of opportunities to study a culturally different phenomenon while at the same time having fun with the project. I chose to study a sorority. As part of this study, I participated in one of the regular ceremonies that was part of the sorority members' lives—a formal dinner held each Monday night at which members were required to wear formals and male guests were expected to wear a jacket and tie.

During the course of the dinner, I frequently excused myself to visit the restroom, stopping along the way to take out my notebook so I could try to record quotes and reconstruct events as they were happening, as I tried to capture in great detail all that I was observing. Of course, the irony in this strategy was that I was missing a great deal of the dinner by removing myself from the setting in a futile effort to record everything. The ridiculousness of the situation became evident when one of my dinner hosts asked me if I was feeling well or if the meal was to my satisfaction. After all, why did I keep leaving the dinner table?!

The message here for teacher researchers who wish to use field notes as part of their data collection efforts is clear: You can't physically record everything that is happening during an observational episode, nor should you try to. The following options for observing and recording field notes are useful ways to proceed (adapted from Wolcott, 1994).

Observe and Record Everything You Possibly Can

If you knew exactly what you wanted to observe when you went into an observation, you would find this data collection process inefficient. Engaging in an effort to "record everything" will quickly attune you to what is of most interest to you. During these observational periods, you can start with a broad sweep of the classroom and gradually narrow your focus as you gain a clearer sense of what is most pressing. You can also decide on your strategies for recording observations. You might choose verbatim conversations, maps and illustrations, photographs, video or audio recordings, or even writing furiously in the fashion of a principal or university professor undertaking an evaluation. It is a very idiosyncratic activity but follow one rule: Don't run off to the restroom every five minutes—you *will* miss something! Do try to maintain a running record of what is happening in a format that will be most helpful for you.

For example, in my study of a school district attempting multiple change efforts (see Mills, 1988), I attended the 37th Annual McKenzie School District Teacher In-Service Day. Part of my field notes from this observation were as follows:

8:30 A.M.   An announcement is made over the public address system requesting that teachers move into the auditorium and take a seat in preparation for the in-service. As the teachers file into the auditorium, the pop song "The Greatest Love of All" is played.

8:41 A.M.   The assistant superintendent welcomes the teachers to the in-service with the conviction that it is also the "best district with the best teachers." The brief welcome is then followed by the Pledge of Allegiance and the introduction of the new assistant superintendent.

8:45 A.M.   The assistant superintendent introduces the superintendent as "the superintendent who cares about kids, cares about teachers, and cares about this district."

The next hour of the in-service is focused on introducing new teachers to the district (there were 60 new appointments) and the presentation of information about how a new focus for the district would be at-risk children.

10:00 A.M.   The superintendent returns to the lyrics of "The Greatest Love of All" and suggests that the message from the song may be suitable as the district's charge: "Everyone is searching for a hero. People need someone to look up to. I never found anyone who fulfilled my needs . . ." The superintendent compels the teachers to be the heroes for their students and wishes them a successful school year before closing the in-service.

As you can see from this abbreviated example, there is nothing mystical about field notes. They serve as a record of what an observer attended to during the course of an observation and help guide subsequent observations and interviews. This was the beginning of my yearlong fieldwork in the McKenzie School District, and this initial observation helped me to frame questions that guided my efforts to understand how central office personnel, principals, and teachers manage and cope with multiple innovations.

Observe and Look for Nothing in Particular

Try to see the routine in new ways. If you can, try to look with "new eyes" and approach the scene as if you were an outsider. Wolcott (1994) offers helpful advice for teachers conducting observations in classrooms that are so familiar that everything seems ordinary and routine:

Aware of being familiar with classroom routines, an experienced observer might initiate a new set of observations with the strategy that in yet another classroom one simply assumes "business as usual. . . ." The observer sets a sort of radar, scanning constantly for whatever it is that those in the setting are doing to keep the system operating smoothly. (p. 162)

Look for "Bumps" or Paradoxes

In this strategy, you consider the environment you are observing as if it were "flat"; nothing in particular stands out to you. It is an opportunity for observers to look for the "bumps" in the setting. In action research projects, these "bumps" might be unexpected student responses to a new curriculum or teaching strategy or an unexpected response to a new classroom management plan, seating arrangement, monitoring strategy, or innovation.

For example, the "bumps" observed by a teacher concerned with gender inequity may become painfully evident when the "locus of control" in a classroom is on one or two boys. That is, by keeping a tally of who commanded most of the teacher's attention by answering and asking questions, it became clear that one or two dominant boys were the focus of the activity during a lesson.

This strategy also suggests that teacher researchers look for contradictions or paradoxes in their classrooms. In a sense, this is not dissimilar to the "looking for bumps" strategy because a paradox will often stand out in an obvious way to the teacher who has taken the time to stand back and look at what is happening in the classroom. (See Key Concepts Box 5–1 for a description of the components of effective observation.)

For example, teacher researchers often comment on the unintended consequences of a particular teaching strategy or a curriculum change that have become evident only when they have had an opportunity to stand back and observe the results of their actions. These consequences often present themselves in the form of a paradox—a contradiction in terms. For example, as one teacher researcher commented after attempting to incorporate manipulatives into her math instruction in a primary classroom, "I thought that the use of manipulatives in teaching mathematics would also lead to increased cooperation in group work. Instead, what I saw were my kids fighting over who got to use what and not wanting to share."

KEY CONCEPTS BOX 5–1

Components of Effective Observation

DEGREES OF PARTICIPATION

Participant observer	Engage in activities and observe activities, people, and physical aspects
Privileged observer	A teacher's aide during specialists' time
Passive observer	Present only to observe what's going on

FIELD NOTES

Observe and record everything	Attune to what you actually record through verbatim conversations, maps and illustrations, photos, and video and audio recordings
Observe and look for nothing	Try to see beyond the routine and look with a fresh perspective
Look for paradoxes	What are the unintended consequences of action?

Voices from the Field
Field Notes

The teacher researcher in this video vignette claims that she used observations and field notes as part of her mixed-methods research design with an area of focus on the impact of formative and summative assessments on student achievement and attitude. It appears as though Rachelle "looked for bumps" in student behavior in order to capture verbatim comments in response to announcements about upcoming formative and summative assessments. In order to see how "students were reacting" in the classroom, Rachelle could have conducted more sustained observations and considered the use of digital recordings in order to gather a comprehensive picture of what was going on in the classroom. This would have also been aided by the use of maps to capture who was interacting with whom in response to the announcement that formative and summative assessments would be administered and the specific nature of those interactions.

ENHANCEDetext
video example 5–3
Rachelle, the teacher researcher shown in this video, used both qualitative and quantitative data collection methods. As she describes her procedures for taking field notes, think about whether she followed the guidelines given in the text.

Enquiring: When the Researcher Asks

A second major category of data collection techniques can be grouped as data that are collected by the teacher through the asking of questions. Teacher researchers may ask questions of students, parents, and other teachers using **interviewing** and **questionnaire** techniques.

As Agar (1980) suggests, information from interviews can serve as the "methodological core" against which observational data can be used to "feed" ongoing informal interviews. That is, observational data (collected through the "experiencing" techniques described earlier) can suggest questions that can be asked in subsequent interviews with children, parents, teachers—whoever the participants in the study might be. Participants in an interview may omit things. Pairing observation and interviewing provides a valuable way to gather complementary data. For example, Cathy Mitchell's Teen Theater Group (see Chapter 3) developed a group interview technique based on observations of audience reactions to performances. This technique involved three company members meeting with a small group of audience members for about 15 minutes following a performance so that they could gauge the audience response to the scenes about teen violence and harassment. One actor served as the interviewer, one served as the scribe, and one kept a running tally of comments and responses.

Informal Ethnographic Interview

The **informal ethnographic interview** is little more than a casual conversation that allows the teacher, in a conversational style, to inquire into something that has presented itself as an opportunity to learn about their practice. Agar (1980) suggests strategies that allow teacher researchers to have a ready set of questions to ask participants in a study, for example, the "5 Ws and H": *who, what, where, when, why,* and *how.* Using these prompts, teachers will never be at a loss for a question to add to their understanding of what is happening in their classrooms. For example, in considering the example of the teacher researching the impact of manipulatives on math performance and through observation recognizing the unanticipated consequence of poor sharing of manipulatives, the teacher might ask questions such as these:

- *Who* should be responsible for rotating the materials through the group?
- *What* was the cause of the problem?
- *Where* did the problem originate?
- *When* did the problem of sharing begin?
- *Why* don't you want to share the manipulatives with each other?
- *How* do you think we can solve this problem?

Following the episode, the teacher might briefly jot down in a plan book a summary of what the students had to say and refer back to it later as a valuable data source. Alternatively, the teacher researcher may keep anecdotal records on each student and simply make an entry on the student's file. An example of a student anecdotal record form is presented in Figure 5–1.

Structured Formal Interviews

Teacher researchers may also want to consider formally interviewing children, parents, or colleagues as part of their data collection efforts. Using a structured interview format allows the teacher to ask all the participants the same series of questions. However, a major challenge in constructing any interview is to phrase questions in such a way that they elicit the information you really want. Although this may seem obvious, teacher researchers often feel compelled by tradition and history to ask a lengthy set of questions of which only a part is really their focus. When planning interviews, consider the following options for ensuring the quality of your structured formal interviews:

figure 5–1 ▪ **Student Anecdotal Record Form**

Student Anecdotal Record Form

Name: ___Mary Smith_____

Grade: ___K_____

Date: _10/23_   Comments: ___Writing table_____

observation: Mary appears unhappy during the time

she spends at the writing table. Her explanation:

"I don't have time to think about my story."

Date: _____   Comments: _____

_____

_____

_____

- **Pilot questions on a similar group of respondents.** That is, if you have developed an interview schedule to use with the students in your classroom, try it out on some similarly aged students (not in your class) to see if it makes sense. Their feedback will quickly confirm—or challenge—the assumptions you have made about appropriate language. Using the feedback from the students, revise the questionnaire before administering it to your class.
- **Use questions that vary from convergent to divergent.** That is, use both "open-ended" and "closed" questions in a structured interview or questionnaire.

For example, a closed (convergent) question allows for a brief response, such as "Yes/No." Alternatively, an open-ended (divergent) question can conclude with an "Other Comments" section or a request for the interviewees to "add anything else" they would like to. In so doing, you will provide students with opportunities to elaborate on questions in ways that you had never anticipated. However, the information gathered through open-ended questions is often more difficult to make sense of. But it does allow the teacher researcher to obtain information that might otherwise be considered "outlying" or "discrepant."

- **Persevere with silence and "wait time" to elicit a response.** Otherwise, it becomes too easy to answer your own question!
- **Consider using a digital recorder to capture the interview responses.** One way to ensure that you capture verbatim responses during an interview is to use a digital recorder. After all, you can't write down everything that is said and still maintain rapport with your interviewee. But be warned—this will add to the amount of time that it takes to "write up" your interview. You will need to listen to the recording and transcribe the responses. Furthermore, I seem to suffer from Murphy's Law when it comes to the use of digital recorders! (That is, if something is going to break or malfunction, it will develop a terminal illness on my shift!) I have also interviewed teachers, principals, and superintendents who are very uncomfortable with being recorded. After all, who else will listen to the recording?! Check the body language of whomever you are interviewing to determine if they are okay with the use of the recorder. You may find that your interviewees eventually loosen up!
- **Locate a private place to interview.** Whether you are conducting one-on-one or focus group interviews, be sure to conduct the interview in a private place where you are not likely to be interrupted and where you have the tools for the interview (audio recorder and notepad). You may choose to use your classroom, another teacher's classroom, a study room in the library—anywhere will work as long as you have privacy and your interviewee feels comfortable in the environment. Alternatively, in an informal interview, you may choose to talk to students outside during a recess and play a game of some sort. Some of your colleagues may be very comfortable being interviewed in a faculty lounge or lunchroom. Take your cues from your interviewees as to where they are most comfortable being interviewed.
- **Carefully choose whom you will interview.** Teacher researchers have considerable flexibility about how they will choose whom they interview. The decision to interview will depend largely on the questions you are trying to answer and whether the interviewee is "information rich" (Patton, 1990, p. 169). This is perhaps a statement of the obvious—it doesn't make a lot of sense to interview folks who don't know anything about your area of focus! But at some point you will make a conscious decision about whom you will interview. Will you interview all the children in your class/school? All the teachers? The answer is probably "No." Therefore, you will choose whom to talk

to based on a number of factors: knowledge and experience of the area of focus, verbal skills, and willingness to be interviewed. For most teacher researchers, the choice will be fairly limited—the students in their classes will be the primary targets for interviews. Depending on the number of students in your classes, you may choose to conduct a combination of focus group and individual interviews in order to develop a comprehensive understanding of your area of focus.

- **Take notes during the interview.** Regardless of whether you use a digital recorder during an interview, be sure to take notes to capture the essence of the conversation. This is also an antidote for Murphy's Law! No matter how quickly you can write, you will not be able to capture everything that transpires during the interview. The notes taken during the interview will serve as a road map for you so that you can fill in the blanks as soon as possible after the actual interview. Your interviewees will also appreciate the rapport that you establish with them and not be distracted by your fervent scratching on a notepad! Note taking is largely an idiosyncratic activity. What works for one person may not work for another. I tend to use a combination of verbatim quotes (taken in longhand), abbreviations, and sketches (uses of arrows to link comments that are repeated, smiley faces to capture the interviewee's body language, etc.) to enable me to reconstruct an interview. Given my increasing number of "senior moments," it also speaks to the importance of taking time *as soon as possible after the interview* to write up the field notes for the interview! (The components of interviewing are listed in Key Concepts Box 5–2.)

KEY CONCEPTS BOX 5–2

Components of Interviewing

Informal Interviews	5 WS And H: *Who, What, Where, When, Why*, and *How*?
Structured formal interviews	Pilot the interview.
	Use a variety of question formats.
	Use divergent and convergent questions.
	Allow ample "wait time" to elicit a response.
	Consider using an audio recorder to capture the interview responses.
	Locate a private place to conduct the interview.
	Carefully choose whom you will interview.
	Take notes during the interview.

Focus Groups

Another valuable interview technique is the use of focus groups with several individuals who can contribute to your understanding of your area of focus. One way to think of focus groups is as a group interview where you are trying to "collect shared understanding from several individuals as well as to get views from specific people" (Creswell, 2012, p. 218). Focus groups are a particularly useful technique when the interaction among individuals will lead to a shared understanding of the questions being posed by the teacher researcher. For example, James Rockford may have conducted a focus group with the parents of students in his word processing classes to determine a collective view of computer use in the home.

When conducting focus groups, it is important to ensure that all participants have their say and to nurture a group agreement to take turns; that is, participants should understand that the focus group is a sharing activity and that one or two participants should not dominate it. Using a structured or semistructured interview schedule, the teacher researcher can pose questions to the group and encourage all participants to respond. To use sporting metaphors, use a basketball versus a ping-pong questioning style. That is, ask the question, elicit a response, and pass it off to another participant (basketball) versus ask the question, accept the response, and ask another question. Get as much information out of each question as you possibly can and, in the process, ensure that all group participants have an opportunity to respond.

Ideally, the teacher researcher will use an interview to capture the responses from the focus group and then later transcribe the discussion. This is a time-consuming process—perhaps even more so than individual interviews—so be prepared to allocate time to ferreting out the nuances of the focus group interview and the shared understandings that emerge.

E-Mail Interviews

Another approach to interviewing that can be used effectively by teacher researchers is the use of e-mail interviews. With schools becoming increasingly networked, it is easy to use e-mail to interview colleagues and students. For busy teachers, it may be a far more effective use of time to engage in an ongoing conversation using e-mail. Busy professionals can respond to an e-mail either synchronously (during a "live" conversation) or asynchronously (at some other time when you are not sitting at your computer).

There are some pros and cons associated with the use of e-mail interviews. For example, one advantage of the e-mail interview is that the transcription of the interview has already been done for you by the respondent! That is, you don't have to transcribe a recorded interview with a colleague or student. However, there are ethical issues associated with assuring your respondent that his or her text response will be confidential and anonymous. I am not an expert when it comes to technology, but I do not trust that, once I have sent an e-mail to someone, it is not sitting on a server somewhere that is accessible to other, curious folks! This paranoia is further enhanced by the amount of spam (junk e-mail) I receive that has been forwarded from someone else's computer.

In spite of these technical and ethical challenges associated with the use of e-mail interviews, such interviews may be a useful tool to use at your school. If your colleagues are like mine, it is difficult to find time during a day when we can sit down face-to-face to talk. Using e-mail will allow your colleagues and students to respond on their own time line—perhaps from the comfort of their home or the quiet of their classroom or library after school.

Questionnaires

Perhaps the major difference between a structured interview schedule and a questionnaire is that the student or parent will write out the responses on the form provided. Clearly, there are positives and negatives with each approach: Questionnaires allow the teacher researcher to collect large amounts of data in a relatively short amount of time (compared with interviewing the same number of students or parents), whereas interviews allow an opportunity for the teacher to intimately know how each student (and parent) feels about a particular issue but in a time-consuming fashion that few teacher researchers feel is justified. A compromise is to use a questionnaire (when appropriate) and to conduct follow-up interviews with students who have provided written feedback that warrants further investigation. For example, in a conversational way, teachers, as part of their regular teaching, may ask, "Mary, in the questionnaire you returned you commented that. . . . Can you tell me a little more about that?" Similarly, as part of a parent-teacher conference, the teacher may follow up with parents who have returned questionnaires.

Clearly, one major assumption associated with the use of a questionnaire is that the student can read and write. Many teacher researchers exclude the use of a questionnaire on this basis alone but also compromise the time it takes to interview all their students by interviewing only a "representative sample" in their class.

A solid data collection instrument will help to ensure useful responses. Consider the following guidelines for developing and presenting questionnaires:

1. **Carefully proofread questionnaires** (or, better still, have a "critical" friend read your questionnaire) before sending them out. Nothing will turn parents off more quickly than receiving a message from their child's teacher that is filled with errors. Alternatively, students may be thrilled by the chance to point out that there is an error in their teacher's written work.
2. **Avoid a sloppy presentation.** Make the survey attractive and consider using BIG print if necessary.
3. **Avoid a lengthy questionnaire.** Piloting the instrument will give you a realistic sense of how long it will take for your students (or parents) to complete the task. Remember, no matter how much they want to help you, if the questionnaire is too long, it will find its way into the "circular file" instead of back into your hands.

4. **Do not ask unnecessary questions.** This is akin to teachers developing tests that don't match what was taught—a common complaint directed toward the administration of standardized tests. Often, we feel compelled to ask a great deal of trivial information on a questionnaire that is tangential to our stated purpose.

5. **Use structured items with a variety of possible responses.** (See the discussion of Likert scales in this chapter.) Indicate what you mean by "often" and "frequently" and how they differ from each other. Otherwise, your respondents will interpret the meaning of the terms in quite different ways.

6. **Whenever possible, allow for an "Other Comments" section.** This provides respondents with an opportunity to respond openly to your questions. These comments also provide you with an excellent source of "discrepant" data ("I hadn't expected someone to say that!") and an opportunity to follow up with an informal interview to elicit more information from the respondent as your time, energy, and inquisitiveness allow. For example, "In your response to question 3 you stated that. . . . Can you tell me a little more about what you meant?"

7. **Decide whether you want respondents to put their names on the questionnaires or whether you will use a number to keep track of who has responded.** You should assure respondents (students, parents, colleagues) that their confidentiality will be protected throughout the process. However, you can protect respondents while also keeping track of who has responded and deciding whether they have made comments that you feel warrant a follow-up conversation. The key issue here is to assure the students, parents, and colleagues that they will not suffer any negative consequences for anything they might share with you. If we want respondents to be honest and forthright in their answers, we must assure them that they will not be persecuted if they tell us something we don't want to read or hear. (For further discussion of this matter, see the discussion of ethics in Chapter 2.) See Research in Action Checklist 5–1 for guidelines for devising a questionnaire.

Examining: Using and Making Records

This third category for data collection techniques suggests a catchall term to describe everything else that a teacher researcher may collect. Again, many of these data sources are naturally occurring and require only that teachers locate them within their school setting.

Archival Documents

Like classrooms, schools are repositories for all sorts of records—student records, minutes of meetings (faculty, PTA, school board), newspaper clippings about

RESEARCH IN ACTION CHECKLIST 5–1

Guidelines for Devising Questionnaires

_____ Proofread the questionnaire carefully.

_____ Avoid a sloppy presentation.

_____ Avoid a lengthy questionnaire.

_____ Do not ask unnecessary questions.

_____ Use structured items with a variety of possible responses.

_____ Include an "Other Comments" section.

_____ Decide whether to use respondents' names.

_____ Pilot the questionnaire.

_____ Use a variety of question formats.

significant events in the community, and so on. With permission, the teacher researcher can use these sources of data to gain valuable historical insights, identify potential trends, and explain how things got to be the way they are. Clearly, there are many archival data sources that can be accessed by teacher researchers if indicated by their focus areas. Often, clerical assistants, school aides, and student teachers are happy to help with uncovering archival data and organizing them in a way that is most useful to the classroom teacher if they believe that it is contributing to the collective understanding of a pressing educational issue. Don't be bashful about asking for assistance with this task.

Calhoun (1994) lists several archival data sources that exist in schools:

- Attendance rates
- Retention rates
- Discipline referrals
- Dropout rates
- Suspension rates
- Attendance rates at parent-teacher conferences
- Disaggregated data by grade level for student performance on statewide assessments in math, reading, writing, and so on
- Standardized test scores
- Student participation rates in extracurricular activities

Journals

Daily journals kept by both students and teachers are also a valuable data source. As Anderson et al. (1994) point out,

> The journal acts as a narrative technique and records events, thoughts, and feelings that have importance for the writer. As a record kept by a student, it can inform the teacher researcher about changing thoughts and new ideas and the progression of learning. (p. 153)

Students' journals can provide teachers with a valuable window into the students' world (in much the same way that homework assignments provide parents with insights into their children's daily experiences). Teachers can also use daily journals to keep a narrative account of their perspectives of what is happening in their classrooms.

Cochran-Smith and Lytle (1993) have incorporated teachers' journals as a central part of their work with teacher researchers and offer a somewhat expanded definition of what journals might incorporate:

- Journals are records of classroom life in which teachers write observations and reflect on their teaching over time.
- Journals are a collection of descriptions, analyses, and interpretations.
- Journals capture the essence of what is happening with students in classrooms and what this means for future teaching episodes.
- Journals provide teachers with a way to revisit, analyze, and evaluate their experiences over time.
- Journals provide windows on what goes on in school through teachers' eyes (pp. 26–27).

Journals, conceptualized in this way, are more than a single data source—they are an ongoing attempt by teachers to systematically reflect on their practice by constructing a narrative that honors the unique and powerful voice of the teachers' language. Regardless of your specific area of focus, journaling is recommended as a way to keep track of not only observations but also feelings associated with the action research process.

Making Maps, Digital Recordings, and Artifacts

These nonwritten sources of data can also be extremely helpful for teacher researchers trying to monitor movements in a classroom—data that are not always easily recorded in a narrative form.

Construction of Maps

Teacher researchers find class maps and school maps useful for a number of reasons. They provide contextual insights for people who have not visited the school, and they provide the teacher researcher with a reflective tool—a way of rethinking

figure 5–2 ■ Classroom Map Example

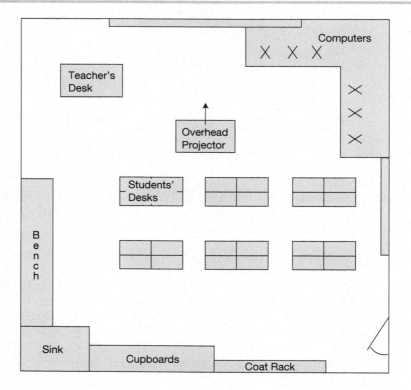

the way things are in their classrooms. For example, why are the computers in the classroom placed in a "bank" along one wall, and what are the effects of individual student computer time on other seat-work activities? A map can also record traffic flow in a classroom as well as teacher movement during instruction.

The school map may also prove useful for teams of teachers who are concerned about the movement and interactions of different grade levels of students and any problems that emerge from the traffic flow. Quite simply, maps are easy, useful tools that help teacher researchers and the people with whom they are sharing their research locate particular teaching episodes in the space of the teacher's classroom or school. For qualitatively oriented classroom researchers, context is everything! Figure 5–2 shows an example of a classroom map.

Digital Recordings

Digital recordings provide teacher researchers with another data source when the teacher is fully engaged in teaching but still wants to capture classroom events and interactions. Of course, there are drawbacks to these techniques. For example, their presence may elicit the usual "funny faces" and bizarre comments that we normally associate with the presence of such technology in a classroom for the first time. One way of moving ahead with these efforts is to introduce them into a classroom early in an action research project and provide the illusion that the "camera is running" when, in fact, there is no film in the camera. Alternatively, be prepared to make a lot of recordings! However, with the move to outcome-based performance assessment and "capstone" experiences, children are often required to demonstrate knowledge and skills through presentations to peers or panels of teachers and parents. A digital recording is an excellent way to capture these events and to provide an opportunity for teachers and students alike to reflect on content, skills, and attitudes demonstrated by the students. Similarly, I have seen teacher researchers effectively use digital photographs (I mean, who doesn't have a camera on their phone?!) to capture events in their classrooms that are central to their given area of focus. For example, James Rockford might have considered the use of photographs to capture the kinds of activities engaged in by students learning word processing.

Assuming there are no technical problems (and that is a pretty big assumption!), using digital recordings also raises the serious issue of time—the time it takes to watch, listen, and record observations from these sources. Although finding enough time is probably the number one challenge for teachers doing action research, it is important for us to weigh the potential benefits and drawbacks of these data sources. These techniques have the potential to be more time consuming and, thus, potentially threatening to the goodwill of any action research endeavor. However, many teacher researchers use these methods to great advantage—which only confirms the idiosyncratic nature of data collection efforts!

DIGITAL RESEARCH TOOLS FOR THE 21ST CENTURY

Speech Recognition Tools

Dragon Mobile Assistant, Dragon Dictation, and Dragon Dictate for Mac 3

Speech recognition programs have been available for many years but were often cumbersome to use and expensive to purchase. However, there are now many smartphone and computer applications available that will save the narrative researcher some of the time spent writing field notes and transcribing interviews. Three such applications are Dragon Mobile Assistant, Dragon Dictation, and Dragon Dictate for Mac 3.

Dragon Mobile Assistant

A new app for your mobile phone, Dragon Mobile Assistant combines the easy-to-use voice recognition software application with a host of other tools for the on-the-go researcher. Need help scheduling an interview? Check your calendar and send an e-mail to your research participants while driving to another research site. This free app can help record your field notes, send e-mails and texts, and make your dinner reservations while automatically detecting the need for hands-free operation.

(Continued)

DIGITAL RESEARCH TOOLS FOR THE 21ST CENTURY

Speech Recognition Tools (*Continued*)

Dragon Dictation

Dragon Dictation is an easy-to-use voice recognition software application that allows you to speak and instantly see your content in a text form that can be edited, e-mailed, or even posted to blogs. With a little practice, Dragon Dictation gives the researcher the potential to record observations, field notes, and interviews at five times the speed of typing on a keyboard. This is also a great tool to use to record your thoughts in the car while you are driving to your home or office, and, best of all, it's a free application for smartphone users. As Dragon Dictation claims, "Turn talk into type while you are on the go."

Dragon Dictate for Mac 3

If you're not comfortable with talking and driving and you are looking for a more advanced software package, Dragon Dictate for Mac 3 allows you to convert talk to type at a computer (and to interact with your Mac applications by using only your voice). This program could be used to record interviews with research participants and would therefore save the researcher time spent transcribing. Unlike Dragon Dictation, it is not free, but it may become your favorite computer application and narrative research time-saving tool.

(Mills & Gay, 2016, p. 355)

Artifacts

Classrooms are rich sources of what we might call **artifacts**—written or visual sources of data that contribute to our understanding of what is happening in our classrooms and schools. The category of artifact can include almost everything else that we haven't already discussed. For example, there has been a trend in schools to move toward "authentic assessment" techniques, including the use of student portfolios—a presentation of work that captures individual students' work samples over time and the relative growth of that work. Portfolios, although difficult to quantify, provide the teacher with valuable outcome data that get at the heart of the qualitatively different samples of work. Such artifacts are a valuable data source that teachers may use as a starting point for conversation with their students. For example, a teacher may ask students to explain the differences they see between the work they included in their portfolios earlier and later in the school year. Key Concepts Box 5–3 shows the components of using and making records.

Hence, we have gone full circle in looking at how teacher researchers could use the contents of student portfolios as the basis for an informal interview with their students as they search for greater understanding of the students' perspectives of their learning. For example, a teacher may ask a student to elaborate on the thinking behind a piece of creative writing, artwork, or explanation of an open-ended

KEY CONCEPTS BOX 5-3

Components of Using and Making Records

Archival sources

Minutes of meetings
Attendance rates, retention rates, dropout rates, suspension rates
Discipline referrals
Statewide assessment scores
Newspaper clippings

Journals

Daily observations and analysis
Reflections
Record keeping

Artifacts

Maps and seating charts
Photographs, audio recordings, and video recordings
Portfolios or less formal examples of student work

KEY CONCEPTS BOX 5-4

Qualitative Data Collection Techniques

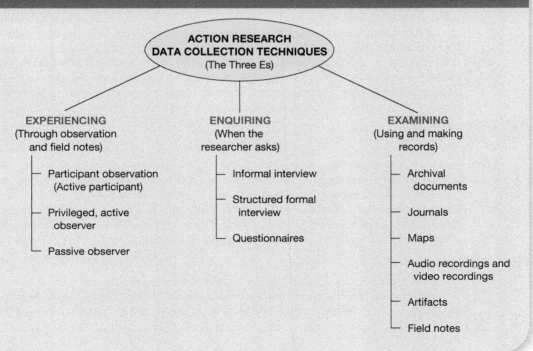

mathematics problem-solving solution. Utilize Agar's "5 Ws and H" to informally engage students in conversation about their work—you'll be pleased with the outcome and the return for your investment of time. Key Concepts Box 5–4 shows the taxonomy of action research qualitative data collection techniques.

The following section illustrates how digital research tools such as wikis, blogs, and Skype can contribute to your qualitative data collection strategies in an ever-changing digital environment. Tools such as these allow action researchers to interact with research participants (colleagues, students, and parents who may be geographically remote) in ways that were not previously thought possible.

DIGITAL RESEARCH TOOLS FOR THE 21ST CENTURY

Wiki, Blog, and Skype

In addition to survey tools (e.g., SurveyMonkey), e-mail, and digital voice and video recordings, there are new Web-based tools that can provide the qualitative researcher with additional data collection strategies.

Wiki

A wiki is a website that allows the easy creation of a Web page that can provide a forum for collaborative research. For example, you could create a wiki focused on an aspect of your research and invite participants (your sample) into a secure setting where they could participate in an open forum. Similarly, you can provide links to other websites, as well as use the wiki as a communication tool through which you can communicate with the study's participants. One popular, free wiki provider is Wikispaces (www.wikispaces.com). Creation of a wiki is simple and secure and provides a new data collection possibility for qualitative researchers who wish to invite Generation X and Generation Y research participants into a collaborative forum.

Blog

A blog (a blend of the term "Web log") is a type of personal website where you can share information about your research and solicit responses from participants while capturing the discourse in chronological order. It is possible to embed photos and videos within your blog as part of the creation of a collaborative research space. A popular, free blog provider is Blogger (www.blogger.com), and getting started is as simple as creating an account and following the template designer. Blogs provide an excellent opportunity for engaging research participants in a collaborative, secure conversation.

Skype

Skype is a proprietary software application that allows users to make voice calls and hold videoconferences over the Internet. Founded in 2003 by Danish and Swedish developers, by 2010 Skype boasted 663 million registered users. By that same year, 13%

of all international call minutes (54 billion minutes) were used by Skype calls. In short, with the proliferation of computers with cameras and cell phones with forward-facing cameras (like the iPhone 6S), Skype provides a new, relatively inexpensive (if not free) qualitative data collection tool for action researchers who are unable to personally visit with research participants

(Mills & Gay, 2016, p. 555).

Quantitative Data Collection Techniques

Many data collection techniques can be used by action researchers that represent common "evaluation" practices in schools and provide the teachers with data that can be reduced to numbers. Action researchers must not confuse the quantitative collection of data with the application of a quantitative research design. Experimental quantitative research requires students to be randomly assigned to a control group or an experimental group and involves manipulation of the independent variables in order to control group assignments. In classrooms, it is usually not feasible for classroom teachers to structure their classroom instruction in this way. However, even if action researchers can't control all of the variables in their classrooms, they can still make use of quantitative data collection techniques to gather useful information about their students that can be analyzed and interpreted using the descriptive statistical techniques.

Teacher-Made Tests

Perhaps one of the most common quantitative data collection techniques used by teachers to aid them in their ability to monitor and adjust instruction is the use of teacher-made tests. That is, teachers will not rely solely on the unit tests provided by textbook companies to determine whether their students have achieved mastery of specific goals and objectives. Often, teachers *adapt* rather than *adopt* commercial curriculum materials and therefore cannot rely on the unit test accompanying the curriculum to be a valid measure of student performance. Similarly, teachers are expert at developing innovative curricula to address a particular area of focus and must make their own tests from scratch. Gathering data from teacher-made tests provides classroom teachers with accessible information about how well their students are responding to a particular teaching or curriculum innovation.

Standardized Tests

Teachers are all too familiar with the kind of standardized tests that swept the nation as a result of the reauthorization of the Elementary and Secondary Education

Voices from the Field
Teacher-Made Tests

The teacher researcher in this video vignette explains the challenges facing an action researcher who is tasked with teaching a required Spanish curriculum and using the associated formative assessments. This scenario is also complicated by the fact that a student teacher/ action researcher does not necessarily have the authority to modify the classroom teacher's assessment strategies. However, Rachelle was able to develop a series of formative assessments based on her own lesson planning in the hope that she would be able to collect meaningful data focused on student achievement and attitude throughout the teaching of her Spanish I and Spanish II curriculum. The challenges of using another teacher's teacher-made tests rest with the validity of those tests to accurately measure what Rachelle is teaching in her classes. In this scenario, Rachelle had limited input on the structure and content of these formative assessments, and it is not clear what impact the lack of control had on her findings.

ENHANCEDetext
video example 5–4
In this video, Rachelle describes two different types of teacher-made tests—those she made herself and those that other classroom teachers were already using in their classes. What challenges arise in action research when using tests made by the other teachers to collect data?

Act (ESEA) in 2001, touted as the "No Child Left Behind" (NCLB) legislation. These standardized tests were intended to provide teachers, principals, parents, and state and federal education officials with individual student achievement data. These data are often reported as percentile ranks or stanines (see Appendix B) and provide teachers with data about the relative performance of their students. That is, these data provided teachers with a snapshot of how their students were performing on a given subject test relative to all other students taking the test. These data were also aggregated to provide policymakers (e.g., principals and superintendents) with information about whether groups of students and schools were meeting adequate yearly progress (AYP). In the United States, AYP was a critical component of the federal NCLB act. In July 2015, the federal government reauthorized the ESEA after 15 years with the new Every Student Succeeds Act

(ESSA). The ESSA returns responsibility to the states to grapple with issues of teacher quality and student achievement and specifically allows states to use non-academic measures as part of school scores. Regardless of this move, it appears unlikely that schools will be free of standardized test scores as a key measure of student achievement and that teachers will find these quantitative data sources to be a critical component of any action research data collection plan.

Teacher researchers are often pressured or required to use standardized tests. It is not possible to list here all of the standardized tests that exist. We should acknowledge, however, that standardized test scores are another data source that contributes to our understanding of how teaching practices affect our students. A good source for teachers who are investigating standardized tests is the *Mental Measurements Yearbook* (MMY). The MMYs are published by the Buros Institute of Mental Measurements and are a major source of test information for educational researchers. The yearbooks, which can be found in most large libraries, provide information and reviews of published tests in various school subject areas (such as English, mathematics, and reading) as well as personality, intelligence, aptitude, speech and hearing, and vocational tests. The Web addresses for the Buros Institute and its catalogs are at www.unl.edu/buros and www.unl.edu/buros/bimm/html/catalog.html.

School-Generated Report Cards

I was at one time the parent of a high school-aged child (Time and tide stand still for no one! He is now a college graduate.), and I had intimate knowledge of the kind of report cards provided to children and parents to map student progress. My son, Jonathan, was proud to display his report cards on the front of our refrigerator along with all the other important family artifacts commonly found on the family refrigerator (e.g., pictures of family and friends and special vacation places). Along with the teachers' comments (e.g., "Jonathan is an awesome writer," a chip off the old block I would say!), there were the all-important credits earned and the even more important *grade*! At Jonathan's school, grades were reported as letters (A–F) that were ultimately translated into numbers (0–4) in order to calculate a grade-point average (GPA). Students who earned a 3.5 GPA or higher, with a minimum of four credits, qualified for the Honor Roll, and their names appeared in the local newspaper. Hence, school-generated report cards are a valuable data source for teachers (who can quantify student achievement) and for students and parents (who can interpret the data and set goals accordingly).

Attitude Scales

Many teacher researchers are curious about the impact of their work on students' attitudes. Scales that are often used to measure attitudes, such as Likert scales and semantic differentials, are useful tools for the action researcher. The use of attitude scales allows teacher researchers to determine "what an individual believes, perceives, or feels" (Mills & Gay, 2016, p. 164). Nearly all of the action research vignettes in this text include examples of how teacher researchers wanted to know how children "felt" about something (a keyboarding software program, the violence and harassment scenes presented by the Teen Theater group, the absenteeism policy at the school, and the deemphasis of grades). In some cases, these teacher researchers used an attitude scale, whereas others used open-ended questions, such as "How do you feel about the school's absenteeism policy?"

Likert Scales

A **Likert scale** asks students to respond to a series of statements indicating whether they strongly agree (SA), agree (A), are undecided (U), disagree (D), or strongly disagree (SD) with each statement. Each response corresponds with a point value, and a score is determined by adding the point values for each statement. For example, the following point values might be assigned for positive responses: SA = 5, A = 4, U = 3, D = 2, SD = 1. As Mills and Gay (2016) point out, "A high point value on a positively stated item would indicate a positive attitude and a high total score on the test would be indicative of a positive attitude" (p. 164).

Although these instruments provide teacher researchers with quantitative (numerical) data, these data can still be considered descriptive. The responses to such a survey can be reduced to numbers (e.g., the average response was 4.2), but the data are still largely descriptive and analyzed using descriptive statistics, such as mean and standard deviation (see Appendix B) and an accompanying narrative (e.g., "The average response was 4.2 and was supported by the following comments . . .").

To illustrate, students experiencing a new math curriculum that emphasizes problem-solving strategies may be asked to respond to the following item on a questionnaire:

Please respond to the following items by drawing a circle around the response that most closely reflects your opinion: strongly agree (SA), agree (A), undecided (U), disagree (D), or strongly disagree (SD).

1. I believe that the problem-solving skills I learn in class help me make good problem-solving decisions outside of school.

    SA   A   U   D   SD

By assigning the following point values, SA = 5, A = 4, U = 3, D = 2, SD = 1, the teacher researcher would be able to infer whether the students felt positively or negatively about the effect of math problem-solving skills outside the classroom.

Semantic Differential

A **semantic differential** asks a student (or parent) to give a quantitative rating to the subject of the rating scale on a number of bipolar adjectives. For example, following the implementation of a new math curriculum, students might be asked to rate the curriculum in terms of whether it was exciting or boring, relevant or irrelevant, or enjoyable or unenjoyable.

Each location on the continuum between the bipolar words has an associated score:

Boring	___	___	___	___	___	___	___	Exciting
	-3	-2	-1	0	1	2	3	
Irrelevant	___	___	___	___	___	___	___	Relevant
	-3	-2	-1	0	1	2	3	
Unenjoyable	___	___	___	___	___	___	___	Enjoyable
	-3	-2	-1	0	1	2	3	

By totaling scores for all items on the semantic differential, the teacher researcher can determine whether a child's attitude is positive or negative. Semantic differential scales usually have five to seven intervals, with a neutral attitude being assigned a value of zero.

A child who checked the first interval on each of these items would be expressing a positive attitude toward mathematics (for further discussion of semantic differentials, see Mills & Gay, 2016; Pelto & Pelto, 1978). Key Concepts Box 5–5 lists quantitative data collection techniques.

If you are comfortable using the Internet, you can find a veritable smorgasboard of online, Web-based survey tools to the design and analysis of your Likert scale and semantic differential quantitative data collection strategies. See "Digital Research Tools for the 21st Century: Web-Based Survey Tools" to learn more.

KEY CONCEPTS BOX 5–5

Quantitative Data Collection Techniques

- Teacher-made tests
- Standardized tests
- School-generated report cards
- Attitude scales
- Likert scales
- Semantic differential

DIGITAL RESEARCH TOOLS FOR THE 21ST CENTURY

Web-Based Survey Tools

Web-Based Survey Tools

Many Web-based survey tools support the design and analysis of survey research instruments, and many commercial survey research providers have popular online products that cater to educational researchers' needs for the development and analysis of survey instruments. Universities often provide students with free access to survey tool software hosted on the university server. However, do not be lured into a false sense of security by these user-friendly online providers. Remember the guiding principle of "garbage in, garbage out"! The survey researcher must still follow the steps in the research process to ensure that a survey tool based on an existing (commercially available) instrument collects the information necessary to answer the research questions.

What follows is a brief description of four selected online survey sites. However, a simple Google search of "online survey tools" will provide a comprehensive list of free and subscriber services.

SurveyMonkey.com

SurveyMonkey.com provides templates for the development of questionnaires using a variety of response strategies (e.g., multiple choice, rating scales, drop-down menus, etc.) as well as the ability to administer the survey using e-mail invitations, with a record of respondents and nonrespondents, and the ability to analyze results as soon as data arrive. Data are easily downloaded into statistical and spreadsheet programs such as SPSS and Excel but can also be viewed through SurveyMonkey.com in graphic or table form. For detailed information, including pricing and guided tutorials for the development of a survey instrument, visit the home page at www.surveymonkey.com. SurveyMonkey.com also provides links to other online providers so that potential users can conduct a comparison of the services provided.

Zoomerang

Zoomerang provides survey researchers with a free trial to create an online survey, including the ability to pilot test the tool on a small sample and to analyze the results of the trial. Like other commercial online survey providers, Zoomerang provides users with survey templates and the ability to conduct sophisticated statistical analyses of the results. Zoomerang charges users for its regular services but provides a discount for educational institutions. For detailed information, including pricing and a free trial, visit the home page at www.zoomerang.com.

LimeSurvey

LimeSurvey is an open-source, free survey tool that the developers claim "contains everything you need for doing nearly every survey with grace." LimeSurvey has an impressive list of features, including multilingual versions of surveys currently available in 50 languages and access to 20 different question types. The words easy and free are important descriptors for this source, which is available at www.limesurvey.org.

eSurveyspro

eSurveyspro is another open-source, free survey tool that provides 18 different question types and the ability to export your survey data to Excel or SPSS. Like other "free" services, eSurveyspro offers subscriptions for users with advanced survey needs. Visit www.esurveyspro.com for a complete list of survey features.

Qualtrics

Qualtrics is an open-source, free (up to a point), sophisticated survey tool that provides users with over 100 different question types and uses interactive question types and rich media sources in the hope of increasing survey response rates. Qualtrics also provides access to a large library of existing surveys to save time in the development process. Visit www.qualtrics.com for a complete list of survey features and a free account.

(Mills & Gay, 2016, p. 202)

Triangulation

In research terms, the desire to use multiple sources of data is referred to as **triangulation**. It is generally accepted in action research circles that researchers should not rely on any single source of data, interview, observation, or instrument. Sagor (2000) has suggested that action researchers complete a "triangulation matrix—a simple grid that shows the various data sources that will be used to answer each research question" (pp. 19–20). In the vignette that opened this chapter, you can see how Rockford has laid out his triangulation matrix to address issues related to bias in the data collection. (See Figure 5–3 for an example of a triangulation matrix.) We will adopt a less prescriptive approach here, but we support the triangulation principle. That is, the strength of educational research lies in its triangulation, collecting information in many ways rather than relying solely on one (Wolcott, 1988). Pelto and Pelto (1978) have described this as a "multi-instrument" approach (p. 122). For our purposes in doing action research, this suggests that the teacher is the research instrument who, in collecting data, utilizes a variety of techniques over an extended period of time, "ferreting out varying perspectives on complex issues and events" (Wolcott, 1988, p. 192).

It should be noted that this "ferreting out" may involve the combination of qualitative and quantitative approaches by including both qualitative and quantitative data in a single study. For example, a teacher may be shocked to see the steady decline of student performance on statewide reading assessments. In order to better understand the reasons behind the decline, the teacher develops and

figure 5–3 ■ Triangulation Matrix Example

Research Questions	Data Source		
	1	**2**	**3**
1. Preexisting Knowledge?	Student Survey	Computer Knowledge Pretest	
2. Keyboarding Speed?	Pretest	Posttest	Teacher Help
3. Appropriate Use (WP)?	Pretest Software	Posttest Software	Timed Typing Teacher Constructed
4. Time on Computers?	School Lab Records	Student Survey	Parent Survey

administers a survey to students that is focused on out-of-school reading behaviors. Analysis of the survey may reveal that students do not like the choice of reading materials provided by the school and as a result have stopped reading after school. The teacher uses these data as the basis for interviews with some of the students (and, perhaps, parents) in order to better understand the kinds of reading materials that students would find interesting to read out of school. Therefore, our triangulation of data may involve collecting qualitative and quantitative data, allowing us to build on the synergy and strength that exist between qualitative and quantitative research methods. This approach will enable us to understand a phenomenon more fully than is possible using either qualitative or quantitative methods alone. As we begin to focus our data collection efforts, we must keep in mind the principle of triangulation and apply it to our regular data collection efforts.

Realign Your Area of Focus and Action Research Plan When Necessary

By this point in the action research process, teacher researchers have already articulated their area of focus in a problem statement and reviewed the literature based on that idea. However, once they start their data collection, many teacher researchers find themselves drawn into other directions that appear more interesting, relevant, or problematic. That is the very nature of action research; it is intimate, open ended, and often serendipitous. Being clear about a problem is critical in the beginning, but once teacher researchers begin to systematically collect their data, the area of focus will become even clearer.

Be prepared to modify and adjust your action research plan if necessary. For example, a group of teachers started their action research project with an area of focus on the impact of early literacy development on problem-solving skills in mathematics. As their study evolved, it became clear to the participants that their real focus was not on the transfer of literacy to problem solving but rather on the effects of a phonemic skills curriculum on early literacy development. When this focus became clear after some initial data collection, the group decided to change their research questions to more accurately reflect the real nature of their work.

There is nothing wrong with realigning your inquiry midway through it. Remember, action research is done to benefit you and the students in your classroom. The process is a spiral. If you discover a question or a method that seems more fruitful than the one you are currently using, adjust your action research plan and continue on!

Voices from the Field
Realign Your Area of Focus and Action Research Plan When Necessary

In this video vignette, our teacher researcher explains some of the challenges of being able to realign her area of focus and to make changes given the context of being a student teacher working in a cooperating teacher's classroom while also completing an academic program requirement: an action research project. However, the vignette provides a good example of the need for teacher researchers to reflect on their area of focus and data collection strategies and to be prepared to make changes "on the fly." In this scenario, our teacher researcher reflects on her desire to add to her data collection strategies by incorporating student interviews into her plan and in so doing, to better understand students' perceptions and attitudes toward assessment strategies in the classroom.

ENHANCEDetext
video example 5–5
Rachelle was required to follow through with her original action research plan to meet a requirement for graduate school. In this video, she notes changes she would make in future studies. One advantage for most teacher researchers is that they can make many of these types of changes right away, realigning the area of focus or the action research plan instead of completing a first study and then planning a new, separate study.

SUMMARY

1. The decision about what data are collected for an action research area of focus is determined largely by the nature of the problem.
2. Qualitative data collection techniques include data sources such as field notes, journals, interviews, maps, and audio and video recordings.
3. Quantitative data collection techniques include data sources such as questionnaires (surveys), attitude scales, teacher-made tests (criterion-referenced tests), standardized tests (norm-referenced tests), school-generated report cards, and the results of student achievement reported on statewide assessment tests.
4. One approach is not better than the other. Your area of focus and research questions will determine the best data collection techniques for your research.
5. A research project might use both qualitative and quantitative sources of data using a mixed-methods design. Mixed-methods research designs combine qualitative and quantitative approaches by including both qualitative and quantitative data in a single study.

Qualitative Data Collection Techniques

6. Qualitative data collection techniques may include the following: existing archival tools within a school, tools for capturing everyday life, tools for questioning, conventional sources (e.g., surveys and questionnaires), inventive sources (e.g., exhibits and portfolios), interviews, oral history and narrative stories, rating scales, inventories, observation, mapping, visual recordings, photography, journals, and diaries.
7. Three qualitative fieldwork strategies include experiencing, enquiring, and examining.
8. In action research, the teacher researcher is the primary data collection instrument.

Experiencing Through Direct Observation

9. When qualitative researchers obtain data by watching the participants, they are observing.
10. A researcher who becomes a part of and a participant in the situation under observation is called a *participant observer*.
11. A researcher can be an active participant observer; a privileged, active observer; or a passive observer.
12. A passive observer watches but does not participate in the situation while observing it.
13. Field notes are the records of what the observer has seen or heard. Field notes contain literal descriptions as well as personal reactions and comments on what the observer has experienced and thought about during an observation session. Field notes may be guided by a protocol developed before the observation session.

Enquiring: When the Researcher Asks

14. The unstructured interview is like a casual conversation and allows the qualitative researcher to inquire into and learn about something that is going on at the research setting.
15. In a structured interview, the researcher has a specified set of questions designed to elicit the same kind of information from all respondents.
16. For interviews, researchers should include convergent and divergent questions and pilot test them with a group of respondents similar to the target sample.
17. Interviewers should take notes during the interview, write notes after the interview, or (preferably) audio or video record the interview and later transcribe it.
18. A focus group is a group interview. Researchers conducting focus groups should ensure that all participants have a chance to state their points of view.
19. An e-mail interview can be used to elicit responses from busy professionals, who can respond to an e-mail either synchronously or asynchronously.
20. A questionnaire is a written collection of self-report questions to be answered by a selected group of research participants.
21. Developing and presenting questionnaires take care; questions should be relevant, and the presentation should be attractive. Be sure to protect participants' confidential information.
22. The Internet offers a veritable smorgasbord of Web-based survey tools to support the design and analysis of survey (questionnaire) research instruments, and many commercial survey research providers have popular online products that cater to action researchers' needs for survey instruments.
23. SurveyMonkey.com provides templates for the development of questionnaires using a variety of response strategies (e.g., multiple choice, rating scales, and drop-down menus) as well as the ability to administer the survey using e-mail invitations, with a record of respondents and nonrespondents and the ability to analyze results as soon as data arrive.
24. Zoomerang provides survey researchers with a free trial to create an online survey, including the ability to pilot test the tool on a small sample and to analyze the results of the trial. Like other commercial online survey providers, Zoomerang provides users with survey templates and the ability to conduct sophisticated statistical analyses of the results.
25. LimeSurvey is an open-source, free survey tool that the developers claim "contains everything you need for doing nearly every survey with grace." The words *easy* and *free* are important descriptors for this source, which is available at www.limesurvey.org.
26. eSurveyspro is another open-source, free survey tool that provides 18 different question types and the ability to export your survey data to Excel or SPSS. Like other "free" services, eSurveyspro offers subscriptions for users with advanced survey needs. Visit www.esurveyspro.com for a complete list of survey features.

27. Qualtrics is an open-source, free (up to a point) sophisticated survey tool that provides users with over 100 different question types and uses interactive question types and rich media sources in the hope of increasing survey response rates. Qualtrics also provides access to a large library of existing surveys to save time in the development process. Visit www.qualtrics.com for a complete list of survey features and a free account.

Examining: Using and Making Records

28. Useful educational records include archival documents, journals, maps, digital recordings, and artifacts.

29. There are many archival data sources that teacher researchers can access: student records, minutes of meetings (faculty, PTA, school board), newspaper clippings about significant events in the community, and so on.

30. Students' journals can provide teachers with a valuable window into the students' world (in much the same way that homework assignments provide parents with insights into their children's daily experiences). Teachers can also use a daily journal to keep a narrative account of their perspectives of what is happening in their classrooms.

31. Maps can also be extremely helpful for teacher researchers trying to monitor movements in a classroom—data that are not always easily recorded in a narrative form.

32. Video and audio recordings provide teacher researchers with another data source when the teacher is fully engaged in teaching but still wants to capture classroom events and interactions.

33. Classrooms are rich sources of what we might call *artifacts*—written or visual sources of data that contribute to our understanding of what is happening in our classrooms and schools.

Quantitative Data Collection Techniques

34. Many data collection techniques can be used by action researchers that represent common "evaluation" practices in schools and provide the teachers with data that can be reduced to numbers. Action researchers must not confuse the quantitative collection of data with the application of a quantitative research design.

35. Quantitative data collection techniques include teacher-made tests, standardized tests, school-generated report cards, attitude scales, Likert scales, and semantic differentials.

36. Teacher-made tests are perhaps one of the most common quantitative data collection techniques used by teachers to aid them in their ability to monitor and adjust instruction. That is, teachers will not rely solely on the unit tests provided by textbook companies to determine whether their students have achieved mastery of specific goals and objectives.

37. Standardized tests are intended to provide teachers, principals, parents, and state and federal education officials with individual student achievement data. These data are often reported as percentile ranks or stanines (see Appendix B) and provide teachers with data about the relative performance of their students.

38. A good source for teachers who are investigating standardized tests is the *Mental Measurements Yearbook* (MMY). The MMYs are published by the Buros Institute of Mental Measurements and are a major source of test information for educational researchers.

39. School-generated report cards are a readily available data source for teachers. Different schools will use different approaches to how student success data are reported but will usually include a letter grade and narrative teacher comment.

40. Attitude scales allow teacher researchers to determine what an individual believes, perceives, or feels; they often use a Likert scale or semantic differential.

41. A Likert scale asks students to respond to a series of statements indicating whether they strongly agree (SA), agree (A), are undecided (U), disagree (D), or strongly disagree (SD) with each statement. Each response corresponds with a point value, and a score is determined by adding the point values for each statement.

42. A semantic differential asks a student (or parent) to give a quantitative rating to the subject of the rating scale on a number of bipolar adjectives.

Triangulation

43. In research terms, the desire to use multiple sources of data is referred to as *triangulation*. It is generally accepted in action research circles that researchers should not rely on any single source of data, interview, observation, or instrument.

Realign Your Area of Focus and Action Research Plan When Necessary

44. Be prepared to modify and adjust your action research plan if necessary.

45. There is nothing wrong with realigning your inquiry midway through it. Remember, action research is done to benefit you and the students in your classroom. The process is a spiral. If you discover a question or a method that seems more fruitful than the one you are currently using, adjust your action research plan and continue on.

TASKS

1. Identify data collection techniques you can use to answer each of your research questions.
2. Identify data collection instruments you need to locate or develop.

figure 5–4 ▪ Triangulation Matrix Exercise

Research Questions	Data Source		
	1	2	3
1.			
2.			
3.			
4.			
5.			

3. Complete a triangulation matrix (Figure 5–4) for your proposed study. (Reminder: Don't force the issue of three data sources for each question. In some cases, you may have more than three data sources that you wish to use, and in other cases, such as standardized test scores, it may not be possible to include more than one data source.)

Data Collection Considerations: Validity, Reliability, and Generalizability

After reading this chapter you should be able to:

6.1 Understand the concept of validity as it applies to quantitative research.

6.2 Understand the concept of validity as it applies to qualitative research.

6.3 Understand the concepts of reliability and generalizability as they apply to action research.

This chapter addresses the importance of validity, reliability, and generalizability as ways to ensure the quality of qualitatively oriented action research.

Improving Student Understanding and Motivation of Multiplication Facts

Alyson Marland

Alyson Marland, a student teacher in a fourth-grade classroom, was a participant in an action research class. Like many elementary teachers, Alyson was challenged about how best to teach elementary students basic number facts while at the same time keeping the children motivated to learn. Alyson's story illustrates the importance of using multiple data sources (qualitative and quantitative) to address issues of validity and reliability that ensured the quality—and robustness—of her action research findings.

*T*his action research project focuses on promoting student understanding and motivation while teaching the basic multiplication facts (0–9). The study examined the effectiveness of teaching methods with an emphasis on rote memorization, compared to those focusing on problem solving. Research advocates the use of problem solving when introducing and teaching basic facts and holding off on drill and practice methods until after students have developed an understanding. The participants in the study consist of 35 fourth-grade students. The students participated in lessons on arrays and multiplication games, and they discussed efficient versus inefficient counting strategies. Data were collected from their old timed tests, state math scores, interviews, and work sheets. The results of the study suggest a positive relationship between balancing conceptual understanding and procedural skills and student success with basic facts. The results also show a positive relationship between playing games and student motivation for studying the basic facts.

Introduction

Research suggests that for every time you do something wrong, you have to do it right 17 times before your brain gets used to doing it correctly. These findings are startling when you consider the vast amount of drill and practice methods used in the classroom to teach students their basic math facts. The purpose of my action research project was to seek out and examine effective and efficient methods for teaching the basic facts. My second objective for this project was to develop effective strategies for increasing student motivation in terms of studying their multiplication facts. Students are often frustrated and bored when studying things they don't understand or when using tedious study methods.

Background

According to the 2004–2005 Oregon State Standards, by the end of fourth grade, students are expected to have developed efficient strategies for solving multiplication problems. They should be fluent with these strategies and able to solve all basic fact problems mentally within three seconds. Unfortunately, researchers have found that an alarming number of eighth-grade students still resort to finger counting and other inefficient strategies when solving simple problems (Isaacs, Carroll, & Bell, 2001). These strategies are inefficient because they take too much time and are not done mentally.

One promising practice is to reduce the use of drill and practice methods (Jones, 1995). These methods include timed tests, flash cards, and work sheets with rows of basic facts. One reason researchers advise educators to stay away from drill and practice methods is because they don't aid in students' conceptual understanding of multiplication. These methods provide students with procedural skills that they are taught to mimic. Teaching in this way makes it hard for students to apply multiplication concepts to word problems or real-life situations.

Effective strategies for teaching basic facts include balancing procedural skills and conceptual knowledge. Teaching with balance includes the use of word problems, arrays, and open-ended problem-solving assignments. Isaacs et al. (2001) recommend practicing multiplication in a variety of contexts and situations to increase the students' ability to transfer the skill/concept.

Other promising practices suggest three components to use when teaching basic facts. The first component is developing a strong understanding of the operations of number relationships. The second focuses on trading inefficient strategies for efficient ones, and the third component is providing students with drill and practice assignments. Van de Walle (2003) stresses the importance of not moving to the third step until after the students have developed efficient strategies. If you introduce drill before the students have mastered one or more efficient strategies, the practice will only reinforce the inefficient strategies (counting on fingers, adding the numbers instead of multiplying them, using manipulatives, drawing pictures, etc.). Inefficient methods are inefficient because they take a long time and cannot be done mentally. Efficient methods include skip counting, simplifying the problem, and, ultimately, memorization.

Intervention

My planned intervention to address students' understanding of and motivation to learn basic number facts included the following:

- *Lessons focused on building students' conceptual understanding of the multiplication process*
- *Teaching students efficient strategies for solving basic facts*
- *Introducing students to fun games they could play while studying their basic number facts*

Data Collection

The data collection tools I used were the following:

1. *Students' scores on state math tests*
2. *Results of timed tests*
3. *Informal interviews*
4. *Students' written work*

Data Analysis

The data I collected from the students' state math test was surprising. I was shocked to find that 11 students (about 35 percent of the class) did not meet the state standards in math. The students who did not meet state standards were consistent with the students who were not passing their timed tests. I decided I would need to spend some extra time working with these 11 students.

The data I collected from students' timed tests were by far the most helpful in planning my intervention and understanding where students were having the most trouble. The data I collected from the timed tests focused on the types of errors students were making. Edelman, Abdit, and Valentin (1995) describe four types of errors humans make when multiplying—operand, table, operation, and nontable errors. Operand errors occur when the incorrect answer given is correct for another problem that shares an operand (e.g., $4 \times 2 = 16$, when 16 is the correct answer for 4×4). Table errors occur when the incorrect answer given does not share an operand with the correct answer but the answer given does reside in the multiplication table (e.g., $6 \times 9 = 56$). Humans make operation errors when they perform a different operation, such as adding or subtracting when solving a multiplication problem (e.g., $9 \times 0 = 9$). The final error is a nontable error, and it occurs when the incorrect answer is not an answer to any problem in the multiplication table (e.g., $5 \times 6 = 31$). Operand errors were by far the most common error made by the students. They accounted for 55 percent of the error total. These data told me that students were associating the incorrect answer with one of the operands, and the early emphasis on drill and practice has reinforced these wrong answers. Nontable errors accounted for 23 percent of the errors. I believe students are making a high amount of nontable errors because they are miscounting on their fingers. Solving 6×7 on your fingers is both hard and confusing, so I assumed students who rely on their fingers make the majority of the table errors. Operation errors occur mostly in problems containing an operand of zero or one. The students often switch to addition and solve the problem by adding zero or one to the other number. This error occurs mostly when the zero or one is on the bottom. I didn't feel the error occurred consistently enough to be considered a problem, so I decided not to focus on it during my intervention.

I also used the students' timed tests to identify which multiplication facts they were having the most trouble with. The problems I found that gave students the most trouble were 6×7, 7×6, 7×4, 7×7, 8×8, 8×7, 6×6, 8×6, and 6×8. In general, though, any problem including an operand of 6, 7, 8, and/or 9 was answered incorrectly by the majority of students. These data were especially helpful in adjusting my interventions because they allowed me to focus on the problems with which students were having the most trouble.

The informal interviews provided me with insight into what the students thought about timed tests, what strategies they used to solve basic fact problems, and how well they could transfer their skills to real-world situations. I was surprised to find that every student answered "yes" to the question about whether they felt timed tests were helpful. The majority of students supported their answer, stating that timed tests gave them a chance to practice their multiplication facts. The interviews also allowed me to discover which strategy each student relied on when solving multiplication facts.

Discussion

The purpose of my action research project was to seek out and examine effective and efficient methods for teaching basic math facts. On completion of my action research project, I feel confident that I will be able to effectively and efficiently teach basic facts to any grade, first through sixth. I am now aware of the common misconceptions regarding rote memorization and the premature use of timed tests.

My results tell me that timed tests can be beneficial when used as a form of practice. Students should be able to correct their own tests, allowing for immediate feedback on which problems they got wrong and what the correct answer should have been. Teachers should also consider not grading the tests so that students can focus on improving their skills and not on a grade.

From my research, experience, and results, I was also able to infer that effective teaching strategies center around balancing conceptual understanding and procedural skills. To provide this balance, educators should emphasize problem-solving strategies at an early age. Problem-solving methods provide students with flexibility in their learning, making it easier for them to transfer their knowledge to various math problems and real-life situations. Also, teachers should teach one concept at a time and teach it to mastery before moving on.

To motivate their students, educators must first develop their understanding of the multiplication procedure and concept. This understanding will boost the students' self-esteem, giving them confidence and motivating them intrinsically. The second step in motivating students is introducing fun ways for them to learn, study, and memorize the basic facts. In my experience, students preferred competitive games, especially when playing against the teacher. The participants in my study were really excited about having a "multiplication bowl," where the two fourth-grade classes would face off in a multiplication competition. I am excited to continue to test these teaching strategies in the next cycle of my action research journey.

References

- *Edelman, B., Abdit, H., & Valentin, D. (1995). Multiplication number facts: Modeling human performance with connectionist networks.* Psychologica Belgica, 36, 31–63.
- *Isaacs, A., Carroll, W., & Bell, M. (2001). UCSMP Everyday Mathematics Curriculum.* Journal of Mathematical Behavior, 19, 49–62.
- *Jones, S. C. (1995). Review of cognitive research.* Educational Memory Aids, 2, 57–60.
- *Van de Walle, J. A. (2003).* Elementary and middle school mathematics: Teaching developmentally. *Upper Saddle River, NJ: Pearson, 156–176.*

Attention to the three important concepts of validity, reliability, and generalizability will help teacher researchers ensure the quality of their work. These concepts are also important for teacher researchers who are reviewing published and unpublished research. That is, to both do action research and measure the quality of the action research you'tre reading about, you need a basic understanding of the concepts of validity, reliability, and generalizability.

Validity

The word *validity* is common in our everyday professional language. For example, teachers will ask, "Are the results of the California Achievement Test really valid?," or my preservice teachers will often comment, "My students did poorly on the history test I gave them, but I'tm not sure it's an accurate representation of what they really know." Recently, I have also heard teachers discuss whether open-ended assessment strategies really measure their students' ability, and with the movement in the United States to the Common Core State Standards (CCSS) and the associated assessments (e.g., Smarter Balanced), there will no doubt be continued debate about whether the assessments accurately reflect what children know and are able to use as it relates to college readiness. The reauthorization of the Elementary and Secondary Education Act (ESEA) and its move from No Child Left Behind (NCLB) to the Every Student Succeeds Act (ESSA) in the United States signals yet another shift in how states will grapple with issues of teacher quality and student achievement. Specifically, ESSA allows for nonacademic measures as part of school scores of "school climate" and "social-emotional learning." All these trends will raise questions about **validity**, or how we know that the data we collect (e.g., test scores) accurately gauge what we are trying to measure. To put it technically, "validity refers to the degree to which scientific observations actually measure or record what they purport to measure" (Pelto & Pelto, 1978, p. 33).

Historically, validity was linked to numerically based research conducted in the positivistic tradition. For example, Cronbach and Meehl (1955) developed criteria for four different types of validity. These types of validity served to convince the researcher and the researchee that the "results" of the research were "right" and "accurate" and could withstand scrutiny from other researchers. In quantitative research, **internal validity** refers to the degree to which results are true for the participants in the study (Hendricks, 2017). For example, Alyson Marland's vignette at the start of this chapter attempted to determine whether the planned intervention of using students' conceptual understanding of the multiplication process along with efficient basic facts strategies affected students' scores on state math tests. The degree to which Marland's research results are attributable to the students' conceptual understanding of the multiplication process along with efficient basic facts strategies and not to another explanation is the degree to which the study is internally valid. In her study, Marland discovered that in fact 35 percent of her students were not meeting state standards in math in spite of her planned intervention. However, this discovery led her to a deeper understanding of the impact of her teaching strategies on student achievement on the statewide assessment test.

In quantitative research, we must also consider the external validity of the research. **External validity** is the degree to which study results are generalizable, or applicable, to groups and environments outside of the research setting. In other words, an examination of external validity focuses on threats or rival explanations that disallow the results of a study to be generalized to other settings or groups. Marland made no claims to external validity in her study of 35 fourth-grade students in her class. To make claims to findings that would have external validity, Marland would need to satisfy the tenets of quantitative research, including the random assignment of her students to a control group and an experimental group. This was clearly not the goal of her research, which focused on promoting student understanding and motivation while learning basic number facts.

As many types of qualitative research became more popular in classroom settings in the late 1970s and early 1980s, it became common for qualitative researchers to begin to justify and defend the validity of their studies according to the criteria that had previously been applied to quantitative studies. For example, as a graduate student completing a research-based master's thesis on the effects of high geographic mobility on the children of low-income families, I was required by my advisors to dedicate considerable time and effort to justifying and defending the accuracy of my account. They confronted me with the question, "How will your readers know that your case studies accurately portray the lives of these children?" (Mills, 1985).

In the early days of my career, this seemed like an overwhelming task because there was a paucity of literature that specifically dealt with the issue. Since then, individuals have been experimenting with a new vocabulary that captures the essence of the term *validity* in a way that applies specifically to the methods of qualitative research. Kincheloe (1991) asks, "Is *trustworthiness* a more appropriate word to use?" (p. 135), whereas Wolcott (1994) suggests that "*understanding* seems to encapsulate the idea as well as any other everyday term" (p. 367). Greenwood and Levin (2000) argue that because action researchers do not make claims to context-free knowledge (i.e., action research by its very nature is based in the context of our own classrooms and schools), issues of credibility, validity, and reliability in action research are measured by the willingness of teacher researchers (and the stakeholders in our studies) "to act on the results of the action research, thereby risking their welfare on the 'validity' of their ideas and the degree to which the outcomes meet their expectations" (p. 98). In short, the validity of our action research depends on whether the solution to a problem (our planned intervention) actually solves our problem!

Let's look at criteria for measuring the quality of qualitative research based on these two terms—*trustworthiness* and *understanding*—and then look at strategies for increasing the validity of your action research.

Guba's Criteria for Validity of Qualitative Research

Guba's article "Criteria for Assessing the Trustworthiness of Naturalistic Inquiries" (Guba, 1981) speaks directly to qualitative researchers. Guba argued that the

trustworthiness of qualitative inquiry could be established by addressing the following characteristics of a study: *credibility, transferability, dependability,* and *confirmability.*

Credibility

The **credibility** of the study refers to the researcher's ability to take into account the complexities that present themselves in a study and to deal with patterns that are not easily explained. To do this, Guba (1981) suggested that the following methods be used:

- *Do prolonged participation at the study site* to overcome distortions produced by the presence of researchers and to provide researchers with the opportunity to test biases and perceptions. By virtue of studying your own school, classroom, and students, you will be immersed in the setting and spend a prolonged amount of time at the site—probably close to 180 days per year!
- *Do persistent observation* to identify pervasive qualities as well as atypical characteristics.
- *Do peer debriefing* to provide researchers with the opportunity to test their growing insights through interactions with other professionals. For example, most of us will be able to identify a "critical friend," a colleague, or a "significant other"—somebody who is willing and able to help us reflect on our own situations by listening, prompting, and recording our insights throughout the process.
- *Practice triangulation* (discussed in Chapter 5) to compare a variety of data sources and different methods with one another in order to cross-check data.
- *Collect documents, films, video recordings, audio recordings, artifacts, and other "raw" or "slice-of-life" data items.*
- *Do member checks* to test the overall report with the study's participants before sharing it in final form.
- *Establish structural corroboration or coherence* to ensure that there are no internal conflicts or contradictions.
- *Establish referential adequacy*; that is, test analyses and interpretations against documents, recordings, films, and the like that were collected as part of the study.

Transferability

Guba's (1981) second criteria of **transferability** refers to qualitative researchers' beliefs that everything they study is context bound and that the goal of their work is not to develop "truth" statements that can be generalized to larger groups of people. To facilitate the development of descriptive, context-relevant statements, Guba proposed that the researcher should do the following:

- *Collect detailed descriptive data* that will permit comparison of a given context (classroom/school) to other possible contexts to which transfer might be contemplated.
- *Develop detailed descriptions of the context* to make judgments about fittingness with other contexts possible.

The transferability of an action research account depends largely on whether the consumer of the research can identify with the setting. Include as much detail as possible to allow the recipients of your work to "see" the setting for themselves.

Dependability

According to Guba (1981), **dependability** refers to the stability of the data. To address issues related to the dependability of the data we collect, Guba recommended the following steps:

- *Overlap methods* (similar to a triangulation process). Use two or more methods in such a way that the weakness of one is compensated by the strength of another. For example, interviews with students may be used to contribute to your understanding of what you observed happening during a lesson.
- *Establish an audit trail.* This process makes it possible for an external "auditor" (maybe a critical friend, principal, or graduate student) to examine the processes of data collection, analysis, and interpretation. This audit trail may take the form of a written description of each process and perhaps even access to original field notes, artifacts, video recordings, pictures, archival data, and so on.

Confirmability

The final characteristic that Guba (1981) addresses is the **confirmability** of the data, or the neutrality or objectivity of the data that have been collected. Guba argues that the following two steps can be taken to address this issue:

- *Practice triangulation* (discussed in Chapter 4), whereby a variety of data sources and different methods are compared with one another to cross-check data.
- *Practice reflexivity*; that is, to intentionally reveal underlying assumptions or biases that cause the researcher to formulate a set of questions in a particular way and to present findings in a particular way. One technique for doing this is to keep a journal in which reflections/musings are recorded on a regular basis. Key Concepts Box 6–1 lists Guba's criteria for validity of qualitative research.

KEY CONCEPTS BOX 6–1

Guba's Criteria for Validity of Qualitative Research

Criteria	Definition	Strategies
Credibility	The researcher's ability to take into account the complexities that present themselves in a study and to deal with patterns that are not easily explained.	Do prolonged participation at study site. Do persistent observation. Do peer debriefing. Practice triangulation. Collect "slice-of-life" data items. Do member checks. Establish structural corroboration or coherence. Establish referential adequacy.
Transferability	The researcher's belief that everything is context bound.	Collect detailed descriptive data. Develop detailed descriptions of the context.
Dependability	The stability of the data.	Overlap methods. Establish an audit trail.
Confirmability	The neutrality or objectivity of the data collected.	Practice triangulation. Practice reflexivity.

Wolcott's Strategies for Ensuring the Validity of Qualitative Research

Taken in concert with the previous discussion about validity criteria, the following strategies provide teacher researchers with practical options for making sure their research is the best it can be (adapted from Wolcott, 1994).

Talk Little; Listen a Lot

This strategy suggests that teacher researchers who are conducting interviews, asking questions, or engaging children, parents, and colleagues in discussions about the problem being studied ought to carefully monitor the ratio of listening to talking. For example, interviewing children can be difficult work—our best-thought-out questions elicit painfully brief replies, and we are left wondering what to do next. As teachers, we are in the business of talking for a living, so it comes quite naturally to us to jump in with our own answer for the child. The trustworthiness of our inquiries will be enhanced if we can bite our tongue, think of some other probing questions, and wait patiently (one thousand . . . two thousand . . . three thousand . . .). As a teacher, I have never been very comfortable with silence in my classroom, particularly when I thought that I had asked an engaging question. My advice is to be patient and allow the respondents time to respond. Avoid being your own best informant.

Record Observations Accurately

When conducting classroom research, recording observations while you are teaching is nearly impossible. However, you should record observations as soon as possible following a teaching episode to accurately capture the essence of what transpired. Although audio and video recordings can assist with our efforts to record accurately, there will still be many occasions when, as participant observers, we have to rely on our field notes, our journals, or our memories; and for me, relying on my memory is becoming an increasingly scary thing!

Begin Writing Early

In a workday already crunched by the pressures of time, finding time to write in journals is often difficult. However, if we rely solely on our memories of what has been happening in our classrooms over an extended period of time, we are likely to fall victim to writing romanticized versions of classroom and school life. Make time to write down your reflections. The act of writing down your recollections of a teaching episode or observation will make evident to you what blanks need to be filled in—for example, what questions need to be asked the next day or what should be the focus of your observations.

Let Readers "See" for Themselves

Include primary data in any account to let the readers of your action research accounts (colleagues, principals, university professors) see the data for themselves. As Wolcott (1994) suggests, "In striking the delicate balance between providing too much detail and too little, I would rather err on the side of too much; conversely, between overanalyzing and underanalyzing data, I would rather say too little" (p. 350). This is particularly true in a schoolwide action research effort in which you are seeking support for possible change based on data that you must present to colleagues who may not have had a central role in the conduct of the study. When sharing your research reports with colleagues, let them see the data. This may mean using charts, graphs, photographs, film—whatever you have collected. In doing so, you will bring the recipient of your work along in the process and perhaps earn his or her buy-in to the next action research cycle. Showing can be more persuasive than telling.

Report Fully

In our quest to find neat answers and solutions to our problems, it is often easy to avoid keeping track of discrepant events and data. Just when we think we know the answer, some data come along to shatter the illusion of having neatly resolved the problem! We do not need to be fearful of discrepant data. After all, it is all grist for the research mill, and although we do not need to report everything, it is helpful to keep track of the discrepant data and to seek further explanation to understand what is happening in our classrooms/schools.

Be Candid

Teacher researchers should be candid about their work, and if writing a narrative that they hope to publish or share with a broader audience, they should make explicit any biases that they may have about the inquiry they have undertaken. Teacher researchers should also make explicit the things about which they have made judgments because it is easy to slip into a narrative that seeks to validate one's position. Being candid may also provide an opportunity to be explicit about events that occurred during the study and that may have affected the outcomes. For example, high student turnover rates may provide an explanation for fluctuating test scores.

Seek Feedback

It is always a good idea to seek feedback from colleagues (and perhaps even students, parents, volunteers, and administrators) on your written study. Other readers will help raise questions about what you as the writer will have taken for granted. They will raise questions about the accuracy of the account and help you to go back to your classroom in your quest to get the story right (or, at least, not all wrong).

Write Accurately

Once you have written a description of your action research, it is a good idea to read the account aloud or to ask a close colleague to read the account carefully to look for contradictions in the text. Often we are too close to the investigation to really see the contradictions that may be blatantly obvious to an outsider. Nevertheless, the accuracy of the account (whether written or "performed") is critical to the validity of the study. (For further discussion of these points and a discussion of "When It Really Matters, Does Validity Really Matter?" see Wolcott, 1994, pp. 348–370.) See Research in Action Checklist 6–1 for Wolcott's strategies for ensuring the validity of qualitative research.

Reliability

In everyday English, *reliability* means "dependability" or "trustworthiness." The term means essentially the same thing with respect to measurement. Basically, **reliability** is the degree to which a test consistently measures whatever it measures. The more reliable a test is, the more confidence we can have that the scores obtained from the administration of the test are essentially the same scores that would be obtained if the test were readministered. An unreliable test is essentially useless; if a test is unreliable, then scores for a given sample would be expected to

RESEARCH IN ACTION CHECKLIST 6-1

Wolcott's Strategies for Ensuring the Validity of Qualitative Research

_____ Talk little; listen a lot.

_____ Record accurately.

_____ Begin writing early.

_____ Let readers "see" for themselves.

_____ Report fully.

_____ Be candid.

_____ Seek feedback.

_____ Write accurately.

be different every time the test was administered. If an intelligence test was unreliable, for example, then a student scoring an IQ of 120 today might score an IQ of 140 tomorrow and a 95 the day after tomorrow. If the test was reliable and if the student's IQ was 110, then we would not expect his or her score to fluctuate too greatly from testing to testing; a score of 105 would not be unusual, but a score of 145 would be very unlikely. If you have ever administered standardized tests to students, you will be familiar with the reliability coefficients that are presented in the administration manuals. The numbers are meant to convey to the test user the peace of mind that, if the test were administered on a future occasion, individual students would score roughly the same.

Reliability is expressed numerically, usually as a coefficient; a high coefficient indicates high reliability. If a test were perfectly reliable, the coefficient would be 1.00; this would mean that a student's score perfectly reflected his or her true status with respect to the variable being measured. However, no test is perfectly reliable. Scores are invariably affected by errors of measurement resulting from a variety of causes. High reliability indicates minimum error variance; if a test has high reliability, then the effect of errors of measurement has been reduced. Errors of measurement affect scores in a random fashion; some scores may be increased, while others are decreased. Errors of measurement can be caused by characteristics of the test itself (e.g., ambiguous test items that some students just happen to interpret correctly), by conditions of administration (e.g., directions not properly followed), by the current status of the persons taking the test (some may be tired, others unmotivated), or by a combination of any of the above. High reliability indicates that these sources of error have been eliminated as much as possible.

Errors of measurement that affect reliability are random errors; systematic or constant errors affect validity. If an achievement test was too difficult for a given group of students, all scores would be systematically lowered; the test would have low validity for that group (remember, "valid for whom?"). The test might, however, yield consistent scores (i.e., might be reliable); in other words, the scores might be systematically lowered in the same way every time. A given student whose "true" achievement score was 80 and who scored 60 on the test (invalidity) might score 60 every time he or she took the test (reliability). This illustrates an interesting relationship between validity and reliability: A valid test is always reliable, but a reliable test is not necessarily valid. In other words, if a test is measuring what it is supposed to be measuring, it will be reliable and do so every time, but a reliable test can consistently measure the wrong thing and be invalid!

For qualitatively oriented action researchers, the message is simple: As you think about the results of your inquiry, consider whether you think that your data would be consistently collected if the same techniques were utilized over time, or, if you are working as a member of a team that is collecting data, work out how to resolve any differences among observers so you can agree on the descriptive accuracy of an account.

Voices from the Field
Reliability

The teacher researcher in this vignette provides a compelling example of the challenges facing action researchers attempting to measure constructs such as "tenderness" as it relates to gender bias in basal readers. Jeanette explains that she relied on her own worldview based on her undergraduate education (and life) to "observe" specific traits and behaviors. Without connecting to the literature related to these traits and behaviors and without any attempt to establish inter-rater reliability, it raises questions about the dependability and trustworthiness of Jeanette's observations.

ENHANCEDetext
video example 6–1
In this video, Jeannette, a teacher researcher, notes that the data collection instruments and procedures she used in her action research project required subjective judgment and admits that she did not assess the reliability of her data collection and analysis. Her comments make it clear that, in the future, she plans to pay more attention to this important aspect of action research.

The Difference Between Reliability and Validity

To review, reliability "is the degree to which a test consistently measures whatever it is measuring" (Mills & Gay, 2016, p. 168), and validity is "the degree to which a test measures what it is supposed to measure" (Mills & Gay, 2016, p. 117). Reliability, however, is not the same thing as validity. Remember, a valid test that measures what it purports to measure will do so consistently over time. A reliable test may consistently measure the wrong thing.

Generalizability

Historically, research in education concerned itself with **generalizability**, a term that refers to the applicability of findings to settings and contexts different from the one in which they were obtained; that is, based on the behavior of a small group of individuals, researchers try to explain the behavior of a wider group of people. This view of generalizability, however, is not directly applicable to teacher action research—even though there is still a mind-set among some teachers, administrators, and policymakers that the findings of action research studies should be transferable. Many of these people believe that we should be able to generalize from the outcomes of a study in one classroom, one school, and one district to all similar classrooms in the state or country. This is not the nature of the research in which we are engaged.

The goal of action research is to understand what is happening in your school or classroom and to determine what might improve things in that context (Sagor, 1992). Therefore, action researchers don't need to worry about the generalizability of data because they are not seeking to define ultimate truths. However, one reviewer had the following reaction to this dismissal of generalizability:

> I fear, however, that this approach lends credence to many of my colleagues' beliefs that action research is unscientific, biased, and not generalizable. Some go so far as to call it "garbage research." The question that they often pose is what good is research that is not generalizable? (Anonymous reviewer)

Indeed, action research has faced a self-esteem problem among many "academics" who question the worthiness of the activity as "scientific" inquiry. Confronted with a similar argument, Stringer (1996) offered the following response:

> Whether or not action research is accepted as "scientific" depends on the way in which science is defined. Certainly it is, in one sense, rigorously empirical, insofar as it requires people to define clearly and observe the phenomenon under investigation. What is also evident, however, is that action research does not follow the carefully prescribed procedures that have become inscribed as scientific method. (p. 145)

Stringer goes on to argue that in spite of the success of the scientific method in advancing our knowledge in the "hard sciences," the applicability of this

Voices from the Field
Generalizability

The teacher researcher in this vignette makes a compelling case for the difference between external validity/generalizability and the goal of action research to understand what is happening in your school or classroom and to determine what might improve things in that context. Jureen is passionate in her belief that what she learned in her study can lead to changes in her teaching in order to better meet her students' needs.

ENHANCEDetext
video example 6–2
Jureen, the teacher researcher shown in this video, explains why, in her view, action research does not necessarily need to lead to generalizable results.

method to inquiries of human behavior has met with little success in increasing the predictability of human behavior. Other texts on educational research agree that action research is a different type of inquiry entirely and as such should not be focused on generalizability. For example, Vockell and Asher (1996) state,

> Action research refers to the practical application of the scientific method or other forms of disciplined inquiry to the process of dealing with everyday problems. It is particularly focused on teachers and other educators doing action research in order to make their particular educational activities more productive. It is more concerned with specific classes and programs and less concerned with generalized conclusions about other classes and programs. (p. 10)

Action research is not "garbage research" at the classroom/school level. As teacher researchers, we are challenging the experimental researcher's view that the only credible research is that which can be generalized to a larger population. Many examples of teacher research are generalizable to other classroom settings, but the power of action research is not in its generalizability. It is in the relevance of the findings to the researcher or the audience of the research.

Personal Bias in the Conduct of Action Research

Related to the issue of generalizability of research is the issue of personal bias. If we conduct our research in a systematic, disciplined manner, we will go a long way toward minimizing personal bias in our findings. However, in an intimate activity such as action research, it is a challenge to remain "objective" and open, to look into the mirror of our findings and reflect on what we see. It is relatively easy in any research, should we so choose, to collect data that simply validate our existing practices, to maintain the status quo, to pat ourselves on our collective backs, and to ignore discrepant data or discredit research results. The same can be said for reviewing related literature—we may choose to review only the literature that supports a particular thesis that we wish to promote. None of these are acceptable approaches for reconciling the biased collection of data.

Propositions

One way for teacher researchers to get in touch with their biases about the subject they are investigating is to develop a list of propositions about what they think they will find during the course of their investigations. These propositions provide a window into the belief system and personal biases that can—and often do— creep into the investigation. These statements also provide a good starting point for examining teacher researchers' theories about teaching and learning and for understanding where those theories came from.

For example, a teacher who wishes to investigate the effects of manipulatives on student achievement in mathematics may generate propositions such as the following:

1. The use of manipulatives when teaching mathematics will increase students' conceptual knowledge of mathematics.

Voices from the Field
Personal Bias in the Conduct of Action Research (Video 1)

The teacher researcher in this vignette makes a compelling case of action researchers to "embrace" their personal biases as a strategy for making explicit what they expect to find in their quests to understand causal relationships in teaching and learning. In so doing, teacher researchers can better understand the theories of teaching and learning that have impacted how they view their practices and to design systematic data collection strategies that will in all likelihood support and challenge their preconceived notions about what works in classrooms.

ENHANCEDetext
video example 6–3
Watch this video as Doug presents his views on some of the personal biases that affect action research.

Voices from the Field
Personal Bias in the Conduct of Action Research (Video 2)

The teacher researcher in this vignette provides a compelling example of the importance of action researchers to be aware of their preconceived notions and beliefs (perhaps through completing a "Propositions" activity) and how these beliefs potentially impact the research process, from the review of literature to data collection and data analysis and interpretation. Jureen recommends using the review of literature as a kind of instructional "check for understanding" to help teacher researchers link their findings to the existing body of knowledge of the phenomenon under investigation (in her case, the relationships between technology implementation and student achievement). Throughout the action research process, teacher researchers must remain vigilant to potential biases that emerge through the very nature of being engaged in an intimate and open-ended process.

ENHANCEDetext

video example 6–4
Watch this video as Jureen presents her views on some of the personal biases that affect action research.

2. The use of manipulatives will help overcome math anxiety because the children will have more fun doing math.
3. The use of manipulatives will improve students' basic number facts skills.

Teacher researchers will find it useful to examine their propositions closely so that they can explore what they believe they will find before they start their investigations and what they might do to ensure that they remain vigilant in the fidelity with which they collect their data (thus addressing the concerns of researcher bias). Similarly, this activity helps to clarify teacher researchers' conceptual frameworks for their investigations by making explicit the theories that affect what they do before, during, and after the research.

SUMMARY

1. Attention to the three important concepts of validity, reliability, and generalizability will help teacher researchers ensure the quality of their work. These concepts are also important for teacher researchers who are reviewing published and unpublished research.

2. Qualitative researchers, action researchers, and quantitative researchers disagree about the value of applying these concepts of validity, reliability, and generalizability to qualitatively oriented action research.

3. Teacher researchers must understand the meanings of validity, reliability, and generalizability to be knowledgeable consumers of research as well as producers of research that we hope will be trustworthy and persuasive in their own eyes and in the eyes of their audience.

Validity

4. Validity is "the degree to which scientific observations actually measure or record what they purport to measure" (Pelto & Pelto, 1978, p. 33).

5. Validity in quantitative research can be thought of in terms of internal validity and external validity.

6. Internal validity is the degree to which observed differences on the dependent variable are a direct result of manipulation of the independent variable, not some other variable.

7. External validity is the degree to which study results are generalizable, or applicable, to groups and environments outside of the research setting.

8. Action researchers do not make claims to context-free knowledge (i.e., action research by its very nature is based in the context of our own classrooms and schools); issues of credibility, validity, and reliability in action research are measured by the willingness of teacher researchers (and the stakeholders in our studies) "to act on the results of the action research" (Greenwood & Levin, 2000, p. 98).

9. The validity of our action research depends on whether the solution to a problem (our planned intervention) actually solves our problem.

10. Guba (1981) argued that the trustworthiness of qualitative inquiry could be established by addressing the following characteristics of a study: credibility, transferability, dependability, and confirmability.

11. The credibility of a study refers to the researcher's ability to take into account the complexities that present themselves in a study and to deal with patterns that are not easily explained.

12. Transferability refers to qualitative researchers' beliefs that everything they study is context bound and that the goal of their work is not to develop "truth" statements that can be generalized to larger groups of people.

13. Dependability refers to the stability of the data.

14. Confirmability of the data refers to the neutrality or objectivity of the data that have been collected.

15. Wolcott's (1994) strategies for ensuring validity of qualitative research are talk little, listen a lot; record observations accurately; begin writing early; let readers "see" for themselves; report fully; be candid; seek feedback; and write accurately.

16. Talk Little; Listen a Lot. This strategy suggests that teacher researchers who are conducting interviews ought to carefully monitor the ratio of listening to talking. The trustworthiness of our inquiries will be enhanced if we can bite our tongue, think of some other probing questions, and wait patiently. Avoid being your own best informant.

17. Record Observations Accurately. When conducting research in your own classroom, recording observations while you are teaching is nearly impossible. However, you should record observations as soon as possible following a teaching episode to accurately capture the essence of what transpired.

18. Begin Writing Early. The act of writing down your recollections of a teaching episode or observation will make evident to you what blanks need to be filled in—for example, what questions need to be asked the next day or what should be the focus of your observations.

19. Let Readers "See" for Themselves. Include primary data in any account to let the readers of your action research accounts "see" the data for themselves. This may mean using charts, graphs, and photographs—whatever you have collected—to provide the reader with a window into your research. Showing can be more persuasive than telling.

20. Report Fully. In our quest to find neat answers and solutions to our problems, it is often easy to avoid keeping track of discrepant events and data. We do not need to be fearful of discrepant data that may help us to seek further explanation to understand what is happening in our classrooms and schools.

21. Be Candid. Teacher researchers should be candid about their work, and if writing a narrative that they hope to publish or share with a broader audience, they should make explicit any biases that they may have about the inquiry they have undertaken.

22. Seek Feedback. It is always a good idea to seek feedback from colleagues on your written study. Other readers will raise questions about what you as the writer will have taken for granted and about the accuracy of the account.

23. Write Accurately. Once you have written a description of your action research, it is a good idea to read the account aloud or to ask a close colleague to read the account carefully to look for contradictions in the text.

Reliability

24. Reliability is the degree to which a test consistently measures whatever it measures. The more reliable a test is, the more confidence we can have that the scores obtained from the administration of the test are essentially the same scores that would be obtained if the test were readministered.

25. Remember, a valid test is always reliable, but a reliable test is not necessarily valid. In other words, if a test is measuring what it is supposed to be measuring, it will be reliable and do so every time, but a reliable test can consistently measure the wrong thing and be invalid!

26. For qualitatively oriented action researchers, the message is simple: As you think about the results of your inquiry, consider whether you think that your data would be consistently collected if the same techniques were utilized over time.

Generalizability

27. Historically, research in education concerned itself with generalizability, a term that refers to the applicability of findings to settings and contexts different from the one in which they were obtained; that is, based on the behavior of a small group of individuals, researchers try to explain the behavior of a wider group of people. This view of generalizability, however, is not directly applicable to teacher action research.

28. The goal of action research is to understand what is happening in your school or classroom and to determine what might improve things in that context (Sagor, 1992). Therefore, action researchers don't need to worry about the generalizability of findings because they are not seeking to define ultimate truths.

Personal Bias in the Conduct of Action Research

29. Related to the issue of generalizability of research is the issue of personal bias. If we conduct our research in a systematic, disciplined manner, we will go a long way toward minimizing personal bias in our findings.

30. Propositions. One way for teacher researchers to get in touch with their biases about the subject they are investigating is to develop a list of propositions about what they think they will find during the course of their investigations. These propositions provide a window into the belief system and personal biases that can—and often do—creep into the investigation. These statements also provide a good starting point for examining teacher researchers' theories about teaching and learning and for understanding where those theories came from.

TASKS

1. Describe how you have addressed the issues of validity, reliability, and generalizability in your action research inquiry. Specifically, how will you know that your planned intervention actually solves your problem?

2. Develop a list of propositions about the subject you are investigating (see the section "Personal Bias in the Conduct of Action Research"). What do each of these propositions tell you about your belief system and biases?

Data Analysis and Interpretation

After reading this chapter you should be able to:

7.1   Define data analysis and data interpretation.

7.2   Identify appropriate qualitative data analysis techniques for your action research project.

7.3   Identify appropriate quantitative data analysis and interpretation techniques for your action research project.

7.4   Identify appropriate qualitative data interpretation techniques for your action research project.

After collecting your data, the next steps in the action research process are to review what you have learned and to draw conclusions about what you think your data mean. This chapter provides guidelines and techniques for data analysis (the attempt to fully and accurately summarize and represent the data that have been collected) and data interpretation (the attempt to find meaning in those data, to answer the question "So what?").

Emphasizing Learning by Deemphasizing Grades

Lauren Fagel, Paul Swanson, John Gorleski, and Joe Senese
Highland Park High School

Lauren Fagel, Paul Swanson, John Gorleski, and Joe Senese are all members of the Action Research Laboratory (ARL) at Highland Park High School (HPHS) near Chicago, Illinois. This project provides a good example of a team approach to collaborative action research and the kinds of analysis and interpretations that can flow from various data sources.

*T*he scene is a common one for teachers: Papers are returned to students, who immediately search for the grade, sigh, take out calculators, tabulate quarter grades, and then compare grades with their neighbors! The rich comments and *constructive feedback on the papers usually go unheeded—the all-important grade is the prime focus of the students' gazes!*

This study was conducted at Highland Park High School, one of two large public high schools in Township District 113. Our student population consists of 1,509 students with an ethnic makeup of 3 percent Asian American, 2 percent African American, 13 percent Hispanic American, and 82 percent white. Ninety-two percent of the student body is college bound, and the parent community strongly encourages high student achievement. Many students enroll in Advanced Placement (AP) classes, strive to become members of the Highland Park Honor Society, and compete to become senior class valedictorian or salutatorian. This ARL group, which included an English teacher, a health teacher, and a history teacher, was concerned about the immense amount of pressure placed on students to receive good grades. We questioned the number system teachers use to assign grades, and we wondered whether grades actually represent what students have learned. We discussed the role of the teacher as assessor, questioning whether we act as true evaluators of student work or simply as "sorters" of students. We lamented the all-encompassing role grades play in the HPHS academic environment. We decided to conduct research in this area, investigating how a deemphasis of grades could, in turn, emphasize learning in the classroom. The research questions were as follows:

1. *How does an elimination of number and letter grades throughout the year (with the exception of quarter and semester grades) affect student attitudes toward learning?*
2. *How does an elimination of number and letter grades throughout the year (with the exception of quarter and semester grades) affect our teaching styles, use of assessments, and choice of curriculum materials?*
3. *How does an extensive use of student self-assessment affect student growth, improvement, and achievement over the course of a school year?*
4. *How does deemphasizing grades allow us to enrich our teaching?*

We began the year by informing students of our involvement in the ARL and presenting a rationale for deemphasizing grades and emphasizing learning. Teachers were still required to assign a grade at the end of each quarter, and students were curious about how their final grade would be determined. We explained how the system would work and followed up by asking students to write down what they thought they would like about the system, what they thought they would not like, and what they did not understand. A letter was also sent home to parents explaining the system and encouraging them to contact us with any questions, concerns, or comments.

Approximately once a month, we met as a team for an entire day of reflection, discussion, brainstorming, and future planning. We quickly found out that certain aspects of our system were working, while others needed refining, and still others needed to be eliminated or replaced.

With the exception of one major project during third quarter, we returned all student work without a number or letter grade. Instead, we used several different types of markings to indicate to students how well they performed on a particular assessment. On homework assignments, including journal entries, we wrote comments and then assigned a u, u1, or u2. On long-term projects, we either assessed different aspects of the final product on a scale of 1 to 5 and wrote one or two sentences to the student, or we did not use any scale and instead wrote extensive comments. On tests and quizzes we marked objective items wrong when appropriate, assigned a u, u1, or u2 to short-answer and other types of subjective questions, and wrote general comments throughout the test or quiz. Most students were able to tell how well they performed on a particular assessment, and only a very few students persisted by asking us how our comments would translate into a letter grade. In these cases, we found that students were less argumentative than our students had been in the previous year (prior to deemphasizing grades). This year we found ourselves more open to criticism about the way test questions were written and exams were formatted because students seemed to be more genuine in their questioning. They were not arguing for points because there were no points! This created a more community-like setting in the classroom, with all of us aiming for the same goal—learning.

Self-Assessment Worksheet

After some modification during the first semester, we adopted a self-assessment worksheet that encouraged students to reflect on their progress periodically throughout the year. The worksheet included the following headings: Content Mastery, Skill Mastery, Completion of Work, and In-Class Activity. This worksheet evolved into an end of quarter self-evaluation that asked students to select a grade they felt they deserved and then to provide evidence by referring to specific assignments, tests, quizzes, and projects. Finally, by the end of the school year, we were using an end-of-quarter evaluation sheet that listed the student's mid-quarter grade range, the marks they received on specific homework assignments completed since the previous student-teacher-parent conference, and a general comment for each major test, quiz, and project they had completed since mid-quarter. Students' grades were then assigned without holding an end-of-quarter conference.

Another important part of this project was that students accepted responsibility for their grades and participated in developing criteria that would be used to assess the quality of their work. The following criteria are an example of what evolved from involving students in the decision-making process:

"A" Criteria

> *Participates actively in class*
> *Shows a great deal of effort*
> *Does all homework*
> *Does well on tests*
> *Is on time for class*

Shows respect and works well with others
Is always prepared

"B" Criteria

Shows good participation
Misses no more than one to two assignments
Has one to two tardies
Shows good knowledge of material
Has no unauthorized absences
Shows some effort
Demonstrates respect for others

"C" Criteria

Demonstrates some knowledge of material and passes all tests
Work is frequently late or not turned in
Rarely participates in class
Shows little effort
Has several tardies
Has unauthorized absences
Is frequently not prepared

"D" Criteria

Doesn't show knowledge of material and performs poorly on tests
Has large number of assignments not turned in
Shows no effort or participation
Shows little respect for others
Has several unauthorized absences
Is disruptive in class
Is often tardy

By using this rubric, students had guidelines they could use as a reference to accurately assess their performance. The onus on defending a grade now became the students' responsibility and not the teachers't. If students could justify their self-evaluation grade, based on the criteria we had agreed to, that was the grade they received. As a result of this ownership, students had few complaints regarding their grades.

Student-Teacher Conferences

Students appeared to have a difficult time assigning and defending their grades during student-teacher conferences. For many years, students had been conditioned to accept the grades given to them by a teacher without question. They had rarely been asked to participate actively in assigning their own grade. The most valuable part of these conferences was the opportunity to speak with all students and to get a sense of how they were feeling about the class in general. Often the discussion of grade came at the end of the conference and was the shortest part of the conversation. Students were asked to suggest a grade (before the teacher), but there was a sense that a guessing game was in progress as we tried to balance the teacher's expectations with those of individual students.

The data collected from surveys, observations, and interviews with children suggest that the majority of students were either happy with the grading system or neutral about it. A majority of students indicated that the alternative grading system did affect their academic preparation and performance in class (in a positive way) and that they had a more positive attitude toward the class.

Grades

As we reflected on grade distributions, comparing this year to the previous year, there appeared to be a significant increase in the number of students whose grades fell in the A/A minus range (55 percent this year compared with 27 percent last year). There is no way of knowing exactly what accounted for the increase of As and A minuses; however, we believe that students' involvement in deciding their own grade, as well as the less objective nature of the way grades were assigned (i.e., not entirely based on the percentages scored on tests), had something to do with the outcomes. We believe that the increased focus on personal learning, growth, and improvement that evolved from deemphasizing grades made it less likely for students to fail and more likely for students to accept responsibility for their learning and to provide the evidence that they had learned.

The end-of-year survey revealed that 71 percent of students agreed with the following statement: "I feel that the grading practices used in this course helped me to focus more on my learning than on my grade." Seventy-four percent agreed that "they would recommend that this teacher continue using these grading practices because they help students learn better." We believe that these kinds of statements indicate student support for our deemphasized grading practices and that learning can occur in an environment where the pressure to earn grades is reduced. Students made supporting comments such as these:

> *"I felt I could concentrate on education."*
> *"It helped me concentrate on improving myself."*
> *"It helps you focus more on information and less on what the teacher wants."*
> *"It relieved a lot of stress and I was able to work at my ability without the competition of grades."*
> *"In comparison to the traditional grading system, this system is the most effective way of assessing my level of performance."*
> *"This method helps me perform best because it's personal to my needs."*

It was very reassuring to us to see the pride that students showed and the importance they placed on giving accurate self-evaluation grades. The following two comments illustrate the integrity with which the majority of students approached this responsibility:

"I knew I had to be honest with myself."

"Integrity defines you, and if you die tomorrow, people won't remember your grades or your statistics; they remember how true and real you were with yourself."

We learned a tremendous amount through this research, but as with any research, we were left with more questions than we answered. For example:

- *Is the total elimination of letter and number grades (with the exception of quarter and semester grades) the best way to deemphasize grades?*
- *Is there a way to deemphasize grades that requires less paperwork on the teacher's part? (After all, one of the things we learned through the implementation of this intervention is that grades are expedient and convenient for a harried teacher!)*
- *What is an appropriate role for students to play in determining their own grades?*
- *How can we deemphasize grades and still maintain very specific criteria/outcomes for students?*

By far the most rewarding part of working on an action research team was the opportunity to learn and grow with a small group of teacher colleagues. This experience of mutual commitment provided a wonderful staff development experience; by working with these colleagues consistently throughout the year, we were able to explore new ideas and take risks in the classroom with a type of "safety net" in place. For that reason alone, as well as our desire to explore the new questions and challenges raised by our research, we will continue to conduct action research into the effectiveness of our teaching and grading practices.

Giving up grading practices and beliefs that we have held for years can be a very scary proposition. It is not always easy to turn over some of our control to others. Perhaps our first action research steps need to be "baby steps." This action research project freed us from the grading merry-go-round and provided a new way to address assessment issues. By taking these steps, we were able to devote less time to pencil pushing and calculator crunching and to spend more time with our most important job: helping our students reach their full potential as we strive to reach our full potential as teachers.

Perhaps the most difficult part of action research is the process of trying to make sense of the mountains of data collected over the course of the study. This task is often daunting for action researchers who, while engaged in the regular, ongoing collection of data, must change their focus and adopt a more analytical and interpretive lens. They must move beyond the description of the phenomenon they have studied and make sense of what they have learned.

The Highland Park High School example richly illustrates how a team of teachers worked together to increase their understanding of how deemphasizing grades could help reemphasize student learning. In so doing, the teachers were able to encapsulate the "findings" of their research into "sound bites" that could be shared with other teachers and participants.

Considering how to best proceed with data analysis and data interpretation is critical before, during, and after the action research process and will be impacted by the type of research you have conducted: qualitative, quantitative, or mixed methods. It is important to think "How am I going to make sense of this data?" before conducting the study to avoid collecting data that are not important or that come in a form that cannot be understood. Similarly, during the study, teacher researchers should reflect on what they are finding and how it can inform their ongoing data collection efforts. Finally, as the systematic collection of data concludes, teacher researchers should determine what they want to "celebrate" and share in their findings.

Ongoing Analysis and Reflection

Action research studies provide teacher researchers with data that can be used formatively and summatively; that is, much of the data collected during the study can be used to positively affect teaching throughout the study. For example, teachers have always reflected on their teaching before, during, and after a particular teaching episode—it's part of our professional disposition. Action research is no different. We can and should take time to analyze our data during the study to decide whether what we are learning is what we had hoped to learn. For example, the Highland Park High School team discovered early in their research that some aspects of their deemphasized grading system were working, whereas others needed to be refined or eliminated. Pausing to analyze and reflect during the action research process is essential.

Anderson, Herr, and Nihlen (1994) maintained that "it is very important to recognize that at various intervals you must stop gathering data and reflect on what you have thus far" (p. 155). For example, these authors suggested that teacher researchers answer two questions to guide their work and reflections:

1. Is your research question still answerable and worth answering?
2. Are your data collection techniques catching the kind of data you wanted and filtering out the data that you don't? (p. 155)

Similarly, Hendricks (2017) discusses the importance of *interim analysis*, a step in the action research process that allows the researcher to make changes to data collection strategies during the research based on the kinds of questions and issues that arise during the ongoing data analysis process. Consciously "pausing" during the investigation will allow you to reflect on what you are attending to and what you are leaving out. Such a reflective stance will continue to guide your efforts (in process) as well as allow for early "hunches" about what you are seeing so far. As Anderson and colleagues (1994) suggested,

> Stopping periodically in the data collection process also allows you to see if you have any gaps in the data, holes where you need data to answer the questions. Seeing this early on in the research allows you to develop the correct techniques for a complete study. (p. 156)

Another way to think of this is in terms of Lewin's (1952) original action research model and the attention given to rethinking, reflecting, discussing, replanning, understanding, and learning during the action research process.

Avoid Premature Action

Although ongoing analysis and reflection is a natural part of the action research process, you should avoid premature actions based on early analysis and interpretation of data. Action researchers—especially those who are inexperienced—often make rash or impulsive decisions based on limited or no data. Neophyte teacher researchers engaged in the first systematic study of their own teaching tend to zealously collect, analyze, and interpret data in a rapid-fire fashion. Their efforts go awry as they become their own best informants and jump to hasty conclusions and impulsive actions.

The action research process takes time. Teacher researchers must be wary of the lure of quick-fix strategies and patient enough to avoid the pitfalls of basing actions on premature analysis. Rarely will a few days of observation provide enough insight to enact a quick-fix strategy! Although it is much easier to start a study with a preconceived notion about what you will find, it's a far greater test of patience, endurance, and integrity to let the action research inquiry slowly unfold over the course of a semester or two.

The Role of Analysis and Interpretation

You will reach a point in the research process where you will want to summarize what you have learned and what you think it means for your students. You will want to share your findings without having to share all of your data and use these

Voices from the Field
Avoid Premature Action

In this vignette, our teacher researcher, Rachelle, provides a good example of a neophyte teacher researcher grappling with the competing agendas of trying to find a "quick fix" while staying true to the research process. Rachelle references the temptation to change her data interpretation and to steer it toward outcomes that she had anticipated prior to the study. It is critical to the success of any action research effort that the teacher researcher avoid premature action based on preliminary and/or incomplete data collection, data analysis, and data interpretation. Similarly, teacher researchers must remain vigilant about the possible impact of their preconceived notions on the rigorous conduct of the action research process.

ENHANCEDetext
video example 7–1
Rachelle, the teacher researcher in this video, points out the link between early interpretation and researcher bias.

findings to identify what will happen next in the action research process. This critical component of the action research process is called data analysis and interpretation, and it needs to be carefully thought out.

Data analysis is an attempt by the teacher researcher to summarize collected data in a dependable and accurate manner. The type of data you collect will determine the data analysis techniques you will use. For example, if you collect narrative, descriptive, and nonnumerical data, such as field notes from observations or interviews, questionnaires, or pictures, qualitative data analysis will be best suited for your needs. It is not possible to "number crunch" and reduce this type of data to a manageable form, as is the case in quantitative data analysis. Sometimes, however, quantitative data analysis will be the most appropriate way to summarize your findings, such as when you need to summarize test scores. In this chapter, we will discuss how to analyze both qualitative and quantitative data sources.

After analyzing your data, you will be faced with the task of trying to understand it. **Data interpretation** is an attempt by the researcher to find meaning in the data, to answer the "So what?" question in terms of the implications of the study's findings. Put simply, analysis involves summarizing what's in the data, whereas interpretation involves making sense of—finding meaning in—that data.

Data analysis and interpretation are critical stages in the action research process that require the teacher researcher to both know and understand the data. When analyzing and interpreting data, challenge yourself to explore every possible angle and try to find patterns and seek out new understandings among the data. Remember Deborah South from the Chapter 1 vignette on "how to motivate unmotivated students"? At first, she was convinced that the only feasible interpretation of her data was that her class and her teaching were the causes of the dramatic drop in students' scores. After all, it was the only experience these 18 students had in common during the term! However, as Deborah revisited her data and as her fellow action researchers pushed her to examine other possibilities, it became clear that the homogeneous grouping of "low-achieving" and "unmotivated" students contributed to a "critical mass of negativity" in the classroom. As a result of her commitment to quality data analysis and interpretation, Deborah was able to use her action research findings to make a persuasive argument for the school principal to investigate other "interventions" that might more effectively address the problems of the "unmotivated" student.

Qualitative Data Organization

If data are to be thoroughly analyzed, they must be organized. Ideally, the teacher researcher will have carefully managed notes, records, and artifacts as they were collected; however, as a former classroom teacher, I know sometimes that chaos reigns! So, it is with this sensitivity to the realities of classroom life that I offer some additional organizational tips to "tidy up" your data, ensure their completeness, and make them easier to study. After the data are organized, the analysis can begin in earnest (see Figure 7–1).

figure 7–1 ▪ Data Organization Activities

- Write dates (month, day, year) on all notes.

- Sequence all notes with labels (e.g., 6th set of notes).

- Label notes according to type (such as observer's notes, memo to self, transcript from interview).

- Make two photocopies of all notes (field notes, transcripts etc.) and retain original copies.

- Organize computer files into folders according to data type and stages of analysis.

- Make backup copies of all files.

- Read through data and make sure all information is complete and legible before proceeding to analysis and interpretation.

- Begin to note themes and patterns that emerge.

One way to proceed with analysis is to follow three iterative, or repeating, steps: reading/memoing, describing what is going on in the setting, and classifying research data. The process focuses on (1) becoming familiar with the data and identifying potential themes (i.e., reading/memoing); (2) examining the data in depth to provide detailed descriptions of the setting, participants, and activity (i.e., describing); and (3) categorizing and coding pieces of data and grouping them into themes (i.e., classifying).

The interrelations among these steps are not necessarily linear. At the start of data analysis, the logical sequence of activities is from reading/memoing to description to classifying and finally to interpretation. However, as a researcher begins to internalize and reflect on the data, the initial ordered sequence may lose its structure and become more flexible. If you'tve ever driven home pondering some issue or problem and then out of the blue had a sudden flash of understanding that provides a solution, you have a sense of how qualitative data analysis takes place. Once you are *into* the data, it is not the three steps that lead to understanding; it is your ability to think, imagine, create, intuit, and analyze that guides the data analysis. Knowing the steps is not enough; the thinker, imaginer, and hypothesizer—that is, the teacher researcher—is the data analyzer, and the quality of the research analysis depends heavily on the intellectual qualities of the teacher researcher. Let me be very clear about this process: It is a process of digesting the contents of your qualitative data and finding related threads in it. You will not meaningfully accomplish these tasks with one or two or more readings of your data. To make the kinds of connections needed to analyze and interpret qualitative data, you must know your data—really know it, in your head, not just on paper. The process can be tedious, time consuming, and repetitious; however, the steps can help you understand, describe, and classify qualitative data.

Reading/Memoing

The first step in analysis is to read and write memos about all field notes, transcripts, and observer comments to get an initial sense of the data. To begin, find a quiet place and plan to spend a few hours at a time reading through the data. Krathwohl (1998) wisely pointed out that "the first time you sit down to read your data is the only time you come to that particular set fresh" (p. 309). It is important that you write notes in the margins or underline sections or issues that seem important to you so that you will have a record of your initial thoughts and sense of the data. Later, when you are deeper into the analysis, you may find that many of these early impressions are not useful; however, you may also find that some initial impressions hold up throughout. At this stage of analysis, you should also begin the search for recurring themes or common threads.

Describing

The next step, describing, involves developing thorough and comprehensive descriptions of the participants, the setting, and the phenomenon studied in order to convey the rich complexity of the research. The descriptions are based on your collected observations, interview data, field notes, and artifacts. The aim of this step is to provide a narrative picture of the setting and events that take place in it so you will have an understanding of the context in which the study is taking place. Attention to the research context is a common and important theme in qualitative research because the context influences participants' actions and understandings. Because meaning is influenced by context, analysis (and therefore interpretation) is hampered without a thorough description of the context, actions, and interactions of participants.

An important concern of teacher researchers is portraying the views of the research participants accurately. The descriptions of the research context, meanings, and social relations can be presented in a number of forms. For example, you can describe events in chronological order, create a composite of a typical day in the life of a participant in the setting, focus on key contextual episodes, or illuminate different perspectives of the participants. Regardless of the form, it is crucial that you describe thoroughly how participants define situations and explain their actions. Also, your descriptions should make note of how interactions and social relations among the participants may have changed during the course of the study.

Classifying

Qualitative data analysis is a process of breaking down data into smaller units, determining their import, and putting the pertinent units together in a more general, analytical form. Qualitative data are typically broken down through the process of classifying or *coding*; the pieces of data are then categorized. A *category* is a classification of ideas or concepts; categorization, then, is grouping the data into themes. When concepts in the data are examined and compared to one another and connections are made, categories are formed.

As an example, consider a teacher researcher who is conducting a qualitative study on characteristics of fifth-grade students' study methods. Suppose the researcher had collected 20 sets of field notes (i.e., based on observations) or 20 transcripts of interviews. The researcher's task is to read through all the notes or transcripts and categorize the meanings or understandings that emerge from the data. The categories provide the basis for structuring the analysis and interpretation—without data that are classified and grouped, a researcher has no reasonable way to analyze qualitative studies. However, the categories identified by one researcher would not necessarily be the same as those identified by another researcher, even if they analyzed the same data. There is no single "correct" way to organize and analyze the data. Different researchers produce different categories from the same data for many reasons, including researcher biases, personal interests, style, and interpretive focus.

Qualitative Data Analysis Techniques

Picture this: After weeks (months, years) of data collection using a variety of qualitative data collection techniques (observations, interviews, surveys, audio recordings, and the like), you sit in your living room (classroom, faculty lounge) with colleagues (or by yourself, perhaps being observed by a curious significant other!) surrounded by files (boxes) of stuff (data in all shapes and forms). This less-than-romantic image of the teacher researcher is a common one. Having immersed themselves in the systematic study of a significant problem, teachers (individually and collectively) are confronted with the somewhat daunting task of data analysis, engaging in analysis that will represent the mountains of descriptive data in a "correct," "accurate," "reliable," and "right" way. There is no easy way to do this work: It is difficult, time consuming, and challenging. Nevertheless, it is potentially the most important step in the action research process as we try to understand what we have learned through our investigations.

The strategies outlined in the following sections will serve as guideposts and prompts to move you through your analysis as efficiently as possible. There is no substitute for taking time to fully immerse yourself in your data. Literally bury yourself in what you have. Read and reread, listen and relisten, watch and rewatch. Get to know intimately what you have collected. Struggle with the nuances and caveats, the subtleties, the persuasive, the incomplete. Avoid premature judgment and action and try to remain aware of what will ultimately improve the lives of the children in your care. These are lofty goals, but they are at the heart of what we are trying to achieve with data analysis.

Identifying Themes

One place to start your analysis is to work inductively as you begin to analyze the data: consider the big picture and start to list "themes" that you have seen emerge in your literature review and in the data collection. Are there patterns that emerge, such as events that keep repeating themselves, key phrases that participants use to describe their feelings, or survey responses that seem to "match" one another? Consider the Highland Park High School action research team in the opening vignette of this chapter. As they gathered their data, they realized that they were dealing with many recurrent themes in their efforts to deemphasize grades—the stress on students created by grades, the satisfaction gained from the renewed focus on learning, the amount of time it took for teachers to assess student work not using traditional grades, and the issues of honesty and integrity, for example.

Coding Surveys, Interviews, and Questionnaires

One of the most frequent data analysis activities undertaken by action researchers is coding, the process of trying to find patterns and meaning in data collected through the use of surveys, interviews, and questionnaires. Working with these types of data is common because surveys, interviews, and questionnaires are generally accepted as part of the school culture, and they provide a great deal of information in a relatively short amount of time.

As you analyze your data, you may need to reduce that data to a manageable form. One way to proceed when working with field notes, transcripts of taped interviews, pictures, maps, charts, and so on is to try to record data on 3″ × 5″ index cards so your data will be manageable and allow for sorting. Visual data, such as pictures, maps, charts, and video recordings, may be reduced to a summary statement that captures the themes identified in the data. As you read and reread your data (possibly now reduced to fit on your cards), organize them into categories or themes. Although there is nothing magical about this process, it does take time and a willingness to check that the mountains of descriptive data have been analyzed in a "correct," "accurate," "reliable," and "right" way.

If you can imagine playing a game of cards and not knowing what the symbols on the cards mean, the following analogy might work: You have a deck of cards, each of which contains data. The order of the cards is random. As you initially scan the cards, you have an intuitive sense that the data on some of the cards looks similar to that on other cards. You finish carefully looking at all of the cards and reshuffle the deck. Again you look through the deck, but this time you group together the cards (data) that look alike. You end up with 13 collections of four cards that have some kind of trait in common (the number or face value of the card). Again, you reshuffle the cards. This time as you start to sort through the cards, you notice a different theme (the suit of the card) and end up with four piles of 13 cards. This is puzzling. Not to be thwarted in your efforts, you again reshuffle the deck and attempt to settle on an organizing theme. You group together cards (data) that have sufficient common characteristics, and you feel confident that your analysis of the data is undeniably accurate. But there is just one problem: What do you do with the Joker that found its way into the pack? And what about that wild card? Where did they come from, and where do they fit? Just when you thought you had it all worked out, in crept something that challenges the themes you have used to organize and represent the data you have collected. The process of shuffling and sorting continues.

A few commonsense guidelines may make this somewhat overwhelming activity of coding mountains of data more manageable:

1. Read through all the data and attach working labels to blocks of text. These labels ought to have meaning for you—a kind of shorthand that will serve as a reference point when you return to the text later in the process.
2. Literally cut and paste the blocks of text onto 3″ × 5″ cards (similar to the card-playing analogy earlier) so that your data are in a manageable form. Use some kind of numbering system so that you can track the block of text back to the original context in which it appeared. For example, noting date and time (1/26/02, 10:15) will help you to locate the reference in your journal or field notes. Remember: Context is important, and you will want to check that you have correctly labeled the text you are trying to funnel into a category with similar text. Trying to shuffle reams of paper can be a difficult task, so cards are beneficial.
3. Start to group together cards that contain the same or similar labels.
4. Revisit each pile of cards and see whether, in fact, the label still fits or whether similar labels actually warrant their own category. This process is somewhat similar to brainstorming and seeking categories that will encapsulate similar thoughts and ideas.

For example, in my study of school district change (Mills, 1988), I found myself with a large pile of 3″ × 5″ cards that included some of the following notations:

Card 1. Assistant superintendent urges principals not to reinvent the wheel but to share ideas with each other as they attempt to deal with an identified problem. (In this case, the problem was low test scores on the California Achievement Test [CAT].) The assistant superintendent states to the principals, "I don't want any of you to think that you are alone out there."

Card 2. One of the principals at the meeting comments, "Clearly, the CAT does not test what we teach in our schools. The test was designed for California, not Oregon."

Card 3. The next meeting of principals following the release of the CAT scores, and the directive from the superintendent that "all schools will develop action plans to address areas of weakness identified by the test scores" does not include any discussion of action plan development.

Card 4. A principal sums up his feelings about standardized testing as follows: "The district makes us go through a whole lot of garbage for little outcome or benefit to the teachers and the students."

Card 5. Principals' meeting 3 months following the release of test scores and action plan mandate. Action plans were due to the curriculum director 7 weeks ago. Principals are instructed that they can have another 2 weeks to complete the plans.

Card 6. The assistant superintendent announces that he will be meeting with principals on an individual basis to discuss how action plans for school improvement will be implemented. It is 4 weeks before the end of the school year and 16 weeks since the initial directive to develop school improvement action plans.

Card 7. One principal commented on the development of the action plan/school improvement plan, "Do I write plans of improvement just to let the central office know that it has been done so that they are satisfied and can get on with doing whatever it is that they do with all the paperwork? I admit that I have written plans and never followed up on them because I'tm too busy getting on with the real business of school."

By following the four commonsense guidelines presented earlier, the first step of "attaching working labels" to blocks of text that are then "cut and pasted" onto cards resulted in the following grouping of cards: Cards 1, 3, and 5 were labeled "Statement of school district approach to school change"; cards 2 and 4 were labeled "Principals' challenges to school district approach"; and cards 6 and 7 were labeled "Inaction of school district approach."

These cards are indicative of the comments that were captured during interviews with individual principals and observations of principals' meetings; collectively, the comments provided the context and understanding for the analysis that resulted in a statement of a theme titled "inaction." In writing about school change as it related to the McKenzie School District, I included in my data analysis a "Taxonomy of Managing and Coping Strategies for Educational Change," which incorporated such themes as "inaction" to describe the change process; that is, one of the ways that the McKenzie School District personnel managed and coped with educational change was to do nothing! Although the story of the change process was fascinating, I have included this example to demonstrate how a theme emerges from the data you collect. I chose the term "inaction" as a theme because it was descriptive (to me) of what was occurring in the district. The same will be true for your own analysis—as you code your data and reduce them to a manageable form, a label will emerge that describes a pattern of behavior. You will be well on your way to making sense of your data!

Analyzing an Interview

Another common form of qualitative data that action researchers analyze is interview data, most commonly in the form of a transcript from the audio recording of the interview. What follows is an annotated interview between a researcher and a bilingual education teacher as an example of the researcher's analysis of the themes that emerged from the interview.

As this example illustrates, the process of analyzing an interview transcript involves a careful reading of the transcript to identify broad themes emerging from the data that will help answer your research questions. This in-depth, intimate knowledge and examination of the data allows teacher researchers to categorize themes and ideas that will contribute to their understanding of the phenomenon under investigation. In this bilingual education teacher example, fear of change is a pervasive, recurring theme that contributes to the researcher's understanding of the phenomenon and possibly provides an answer to a research question.

Asking Key Questions

Another approach to data analysis involves the use of key questions. According to Stringer (1996), working through a series of questions can enable action researchers to "extend their understanding of the problems and contexts" (p. 87) they have investigated. These key questions may be the very ones with which you began your action research inquiry, the questions mentioned in Chapter 3 that involve the who, what, where, when, why, and how of the educational process. For example, Who is centrally involved? Who has resources? Which ones? What major activities, events, or issues are relevant to the problem? How do acts, activities, and events happen? When does this problem occur? and so on. Although not all these questions will be applicable to any single situation, they may provide a starting point for teacher researchers who are engaged individually or collectively in analysis.

To illustrate, the Highland Park High School team raised questions such as the following: What is an appropriate role for students to play in determining their own grades? How can grades be deemphasized while teachers maintain specific criteria/outcomes for students? Answers to these and other questions will help extend the team's understanding of the problems associated with deemphasizing grades while emphasizing the importance of learning.

Coding from a Sample Interview Transcript

Codes

Culture

Nativistic
   movements
Patriotic

Themes (and Other Ideas)

Fear
Fear of change

Job stability
Fear of new job

Q: Why do you think that English-only teachers fear bilingual education?

A: I think the fear factor is on a real gut-level and personal level. Teachers feel it's kind of a one-way system in that the teachers who are in the all-English program are fearful at a real basic visceral level that their jobs and their livelihood are at risk. Not to mention their culture, their society, and their known world is at risk by this other language coming into the schools and being acknowledged in the schools. And the teacher might say, "Oh well, because I don't have Spanish that means I am going to be out of a job. Am I going to be replaced by a bilingual teacher? If you have this program in my school that means you'tre going to need bilingual teachers. I am not bilingual so my job is at risk."

Q: Do you think that there is resistance towards expecting all children to learn English?

A: I think that's an interpretation that comes out of a model like a 90/10. When the child needs to come into the first year and has 90% in Spanish and 10% in English, it's easily perceived that we are withholding English from the child. That is a perception. A 50/50 model is a little more amenable to that because it's obvious that 50% of the time the child isn't getting English.

Q: There is the old adage that teachers who oppose bilingual education say, "My ancestors never received bilingual education services in public schools and they did just fine." How do you respond to that kind of attitude toward bilingual education?

A: I say that's old thinking. I think that what your parents or your grandparents had to do when they came here from Italy or Norway, or wherever they came from, to learn another language, the language demand was less than it is today. Employment was easier to obtain, let's say a hundred years ago on a manual labor kind of thing. So a person could come here and speak 80% Scottish and 20% English and still be able to get a job because he could manage to do the labor that was required with that little bit of English. It wasn't an academic level of English that he needed, or that my grandfather needed, coming here speaking Norwegian.

Q: What about the attitude, "Well they are in the United States, and we speak English here, so they can learn English. That's all there is to it." How would you respond to this attitude?

A: That's a big one. That's huge. I think that's a whole cultural, you know, it's based again in fear. Based again in the fact that the

Fear
Fear

United States is a very isolated island in that we are closed in by two oceans and we have never had the habit of stretching out beyond our borders much, or valuing much of what is beyond our borders. We are xenophobic in that sense. So we haven't traditionally learned other languages, or been interested in other languages. "Why bother, we'tre America, the biggest, the toughest, so why would we value anybody else's culture or language?" And I think that's an old thinking as well. It's an old habit.

Q: Do you think that this attitude is changing?

Nativistic
  movements
Patriotic

A: Well, I'tm not sure. With September 11th and Homeland Security and all that, I think we have had a big reversal. I think we were going to be able to look at a global perspective and we were on the track of maybe reaching out and saying, "Oh, yeah, this is interesting. Wow, this is great. Look at what we are getting from South America. Look at what we are learning from the Greeks. Look at what we are learning from folks traveling in Africa or traveling in Asia. We are gaining so much. We are taking in so much, it's been great." And then September 11th kind of closed that down and kind of put us back in our cave again and made us a little more fearful. I think the other phenomenon is, and I can speak from the point of view of my father, a good old Idaho boy, you know. Like, "If those folks are coming into our culture and they don't learn English. And they don't learn about Thanksgiving and the 4th of July and how we celebrate Valentine's Day and do it the same way we do, then they are going to change our culture. My culture. And if they change my culture then I won't know how to act. And it's my culture in the first place so if they want to be here they need to accept that."

Fear
Fear

Q: I hear in my class all the time, "If I go to Mexico they aren't going to speak English. They are going to expect me to speak Spanish and adhere to their culture." Why are we different? Why should we be more open?

A: Why should we be? Well, there is a big difference between a tourist going to Mexico and somebody coming here for two weeks, or somebody coming here to spend a lifetime and raise their children. That's a really big different set of elements that we are dealing with. So, one of the things about the United States is that we have always said we are a pluralistic culture. You can come here, settle, raise your family, bring your poor, humble, weak, and we will be collectively a nation. So it starts with the

Fear

idea, the salad bowl idea, that we can all be individuals but we are going to make a collective nation. And the contradiction of that is that we want to all be on the same page because we need to be united. I think the fear that we are not united is seen in the commonly held belief that the word "multicultural" is a nasty word. It's an eight-letter word or whatever it is, because it means that we are separating out into our little ghettos, into our little cultures, and we'tve got Latinos over here and Russians over here, and we'tve got the Afghanis over here and we'tve got the Vietnamese here in San Francisco, and they are going to be separated and not be pulling together in one United States. So that goes for elections and social security and achieving resources and services that are federally provided. Schools for example. The thinking would be "Why would we want all those really diverse thinkers? Like maybe we'tve got a whole bunch of people who are adhering to Islam and they want to come into the public schools and we should educate them? But Islam is apparently against the Anglo-Protestant way of the United States? Why would we let them access our services?" So that is from my father's point of view. Not from mine. But that is from that conservative, older generation in this country.

Doing an Organizational Review

Another approach that Stringer (1996) suggested is undertaking an organizational review that focuses on the following features of the organization (in this case, a school): vision and mission, goals and objectives, structure of the organization, operation, and problems, issues, and concerns (p. 90). Stringer noted, "As participants work through these issues, they will extend their understanding of the organization and aspects of its operation that are relevant to their problems, issues, and concerns" (pp. 90–91). A review of the school, with these features in mind, may provide insight into the data you have collected.

For example, in the Highland Park High School example that opened this chapter, an organizational review of the school's grading policies and communication policies with students and parents would include seeking answers to questions such as the following:

What is the school's mission and vision?
What is the school's policy on grading?
How is the school organized to provide effective communication with students and parents?
What issues arise when a change in grading policy is put into effect?

Answers to these questions would provide the teacher researchers at Highland Park High School with additional insights into the data they collected. However, the questions asked by teacher researchers as part of an organizational review will depend on the organization and the area of focus.

Developing a Concept Map

Stringer (1996) suggested that concept maps are another useful strategy that helps action research participants visualize the major influences that have affected the study. For example, what were the perspectives of the students? Parents? Teachers? Administrators? A concept map gives participants an opportunity to display their analysis of the problem and to determine consistencies and inconsistencies that may exist between the disparate groups. The steps for developing a concept map include the following:

1. List the major influences that have affected the study of your area of focus.
2. Develop a visual representation of the major influences (factors) connecting the influences with relationships you know exist (using solid lines) and influences you have a "hunch" about (using dotted lines).
3. Review the concept map to determine any consistencies or inconsistencies that exist among the influences. This forces you back to your data to see "what's missing."

For example, Jack Reston at Eastview Elementary School (see Chapter 8) concluded that the following factors were major influences on the success of the school's absenteeism policy: respectfulness, safety, conflict management, discipline, school rules, behavior, getting along, self-esteem, and academics. Further, Jack believed that some relationships (real and perceived) existed among these factors (see Figure 7–2).

Analyzing Antecedents and Consequences

Stringer (1996) also suggested a process of mapping antecedents (causes) and consequences (effects) to help action researchers identify the major elements of their analysis. Using this framework provides a visual representation of the causal relationships that you, the teacher researcher, now believe exist. It is also helpful to revisit the causal relationships uncovered in your review of the literature to determine challenges and support for your analysis and interpretations.

The steps for analyzing antecedents and consequences are as follows:

1. List the influences that emerged from the analysis for which there appear to be a causal relationship.
2. Revisit the review of literature to determine whether the analysis of the study supports or is challenged by the findings of previous studies.

figure 7–2 ▪ **Reston's Concept of the Factors Affecting Absenteeism at Eastview Elementary School**

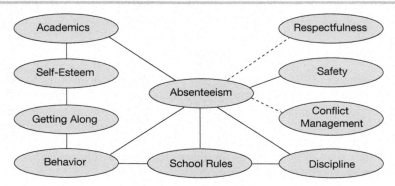

3. Revisit your data to determine whether anything is missing and suggest how your findings may influence the next action research cycle.

As an example, in the Eastview Elementary School study, the concept map (see Figure 7–2) could be expanded to include a mapping of antecedents (causes) and consequences (effects) as an outcome of the analysis. In this example, Jack Reston clearly identified (based on his analysis) that a causal relationship existed between absenteeism and academics (student performance) and absenteeism and discipline (student behavior). Based on these relationships, Reston revisited his review of literature to determine if his data analysis challenged or supported the findings of previous studies. Furthermore, Reston could use these reflections to help formulate the next action research cycle focused on another planned intervention to address absenteeism at Eastview Elementary School.

Displaying Findings

The information you have collected should be summarized in an appropriate and meaningful format that you can share with interested colleagues. To do this, teacher researchers should "think display" as they consider how to convey their findings to interested colleagues. You might use matrices, charts, concept maps, graphs, and figures—whatever works as a practical way to encapsulate the findings of your study. I have also witnessed teacher researchers who have made excellent use of other audiovisual media, such as video recordings and computer multimedia presentations (incorporating text, charts, matrices, audio, and video), to represent their findings. These visual displays of data serve an important function for teachers who wish to share findings and celebrate their insights in a public forum. Putting your data into a visual format might also help you "see" new aspects of your data. (See Appendix B for examples of visual displays of data.)

Stating What's Missing

Finally, as part of your full reporting, flag for the consumers of your research what pieces of the puzzle are still missing and identify any remaining questions for which you have not been able to provide answers. Often we find ourselves wanting and needing to provide answers, to move beyond our data with unwarranted assertions that may, in some cases, ultimately lead to embarrassing questions about what we actually did. In keeping with the theme of avoiding premature judgment (arriving at answers to problems without systematic inquiry), the data analysis technique of stating what's missing allows you to hint at what might or should be done next in your quest to better understand the findings of your study. (See Research in Action Checklist 7–1 for a list of data analysis techniques.)

Using Computer Software to Assist with Data Analysis

Increasingly, computer software is being developed to assist with the analysis of qualitative, narrative data. The important word in this sentence is "assist." This software will not do the analysis for you! Novice researchers need to remember that computers alone do not analyze or even code data. They are designed only to expedite these operations when researchers are working with large bodies of text and other kinds of data. The process of coding, retrieving, and subsequently mulling over and making sense of data remains a laborious process completely controlled by researchers. Even if a computer is used, researchers still must go through the process of punching each code into the data on the computer as they

RESEARCH IN ACTION CHECKLIST 7–1

Data Analysis Strategies

_____ Identify themes.

_____ Code surveys, interviews, and questionnaires.

_____ Analyze an interview.

_____ Ask key questions: who, what, where, when, why, and how?

_____ Do an organizational review of the school.

_____ Develop a concept map.

_____ Analyze antecedents and consequences.

_____ Display findings.

_____ State what is missing.

read through their interviews, field notes, and audio and video recordings. Computers are merely handy and extremely fast labeling and retrieval tools. Researchers also must remember that they alone can tell or program the computer to retrieve and count data in specific ways; the machines do not do these tasks automatically. Although computers can enhance and broaden qualitative research analysis, if you are not connected in some way with a research university, it is unlikely that you will have access to the software and the expertise of someone to teach you how to use the software.

To help you with your decision about whether to proceed with locating and learning a qualitative data analysis software package, let's review some of the factors that might affect the decision:

- Are you analyzing large amounts of data (e.g., more than 500 pages of field notes and transcripts)?
- Are you adequately trained in the use of the programs?
- Do you have the resources to purchase a program, or do you know someone who has the program?
- Do you need to be able to capture specific quotes from a large database? (Questions developed from Creswell, 2015, p. 240.)

Remember, computer software will not do the data analysis for you, but it will help retrieve categories from a large amount of narrative (text) data. Given the

Voices from the Field
Qualitative Data Analysis Techniques

The teacher researcher in this vignette provides some good examples of the kinds of data analysis techniques she used to analyze her field notes, observations, and surveys. Specifically, she identified themes from the field notes and observations by coding categories of student engagement (on task, off task, and enthusiastically on task) and applying a frequency count for each of the categories. She also coded student surveys and used descriptive statistical analysis to better understand how student perceptions changed over the course of her technology intervention.

ENHANCEDetext

video example 7–2
The teacher researcher in this video organized and coded her qualitative data for effective analysis. As she describes her procedures, try to identify some of the techniques she used.

time (and resources) it takes to learn new software programs and the relatively modest amounts of narrative data you are likely to encounter as a novice researcher, it is likely that you will resort to using the other "old-fashioned" techniques described in this chapter. The Digital Research Tools for the 21st Century feature on the next page discusses three common computer software packages available to assist teacher researchers with the analysis of qualitative data.

Qualitative Data Analysis: An Example

The example that follows is intended to provide a sense of qualitative analysis. A true qualitative study would entail more data analysis than shown here, but the basic ideas represent the process that a qualitative researcher would undertake when analyzing data throughout a study.

In this example, the topics under study are the concerns of parents regarding their first child's entrance into kindergarten and the kindergarten teacher's interactions with the students and families. The participants were four parents—three female and one male, representing four families—and the first child in each of the families. The children attend the same school; the kindergarten teacher was also a participant. Data collection procedures included observations and interviews with students, parents, and the kindergarten teacher.

Data analysis would proceed as follows:

1. From the field notes of your classroom observations, you begin to list some common items or topics that you noticed. You recorded in your notes that during classroom instruction, the teacher was using books, videos, and handouts. You also noted that at times, instruction was directed toward individual students, sometimes toward the whole class, and sometimes toward students who were working together in small groups.
2. From your interviews with the teacher, you realize that she gave you information about how she communicated with families about the children. You note that she talked about how she indirectly communicates through grading and report cards and how her lesson plans and tests are related to her overall assessment of the students' work. She also mentioned that she talks about report cards directly with families during conferences. Additionally, she communicates with families about their children through progress reports and phone calls.
3. From your initial analysis, you group the individual items or topics together into categories that show how the items or topics are related. For example, as shown in Figure 7–3, you could group books, videos, and handouts under a category called "Teaching Materials." You could group together the ways in which the instruction was carried out—individual, small group, and whole class—and label this category as "Classroom Interactions." Using information

DIGITAL RESEARCH TOOLS FOR THE 21ST CENTURY

Qualitative Data Analysis Computer Software

Computer software to assist with the analysis of qualitative, narrative data has been available to researchers for many years. The important word in this sentence is *assist*. This software will not do the analysis for you! It is important for novice qualitative researchers to remember that computers do not analyze or even code data. They are designed only to help expedite these operations when researchers are working with large bodies of text and other kinds of data. The process of coding, retrieving, and subsequently mulling over and making sense of data remains a laborious process completely controlled by researchers. Even if a computer is used, researchers still must go through the process of creating codes and labels and keying them into the computer as they read through their interviews, field notes, and audio- and videotapes. Computers are merely handy and extremely fast labeling and retrieval tools. Researchers also must remember that they must program the computer to retrieve and sort data in specific ways; the machines do not do these tasks automatically. Although computers can enhance and broaden qualitative research analysis, if you are not connected in some way with a research university, it is unlikely that you will have access to the software and the expertise of someone to teach you how to use it.

Three common and popular qualitative analysis software packages are NVivo 11, The Ethnograph v6, and HyperRESEARCH 3.7.3.

NVivo 11
NVivo 11 is designed for qualitative researchers who need to work with complex data, especially multimedia data. NVivo is designed to assist researchers with organizing, classifying, and analyzing data and allows the researcher to work with documents, PDFs, spreadsheets, audio, video, and pictures. More information on NVivo can be found on the QSR International website at http://www.qsrinternational.com.

The Ethnograph v6
The Ethnograph v6 is a program designed to help qualitative researchers work with text files (in any format) and search for and code segments of interest to the researcher. More information about The Ethnograph can be found on the Qualis Research website at http://www.qualisresearch.com.

HyperRESEARCH 3.7.3
HyperRESEARCH 3.7.3 is an advanced software program that allows the qualitative researcher to work with text, graphics, audio, and video sources and to code and retrieve data. More information about HyperRESEARCH can be found on the ResearchWare website at http://www.researchware.com.

Remember, computer software will not do the data analysis for you, but it will help you to retrieve categories from a large amount of narrative, audio, video, and photo data (Mills & Gay, 2016, p. 477).

figure 7–3 ▪ Diagram of Category Levels and Organization

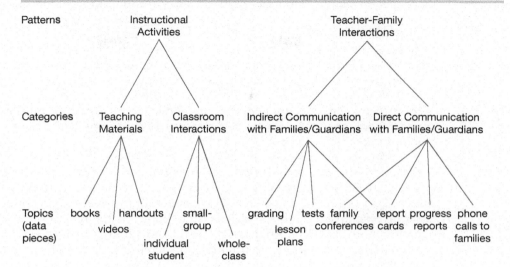

from the interviews, you could construct the category "Indirect Communication with Families/Guardians" to include grading, lesson plans, tests, and report cards. A category of "Direct Communication with Families/Guardians" could include family conferences, report cards, progress reports, and phone calls to families. Notice that report cards appear in both the indirect and the direct communication categories.

4. You organize your four categories into patterns, which are made up of two or more categories. For example, the categories of "Teaching Materials" and "Classroom Interactions" indicate a pattern of "Instructional Activities." The categories of "Indirect Communication" and "Direct Communication" fit together under a pattern of "Teacher-Family Interactions."

You then decide whether you need to collect additional data by interviewing students and parents about their experiences of interacting with the teacher to confirm your categories and patterns.

Analyzing and Interpreting Quantitative Data

Data analysis and interpretation can also involve the use of descriptive statistics to help make sense of your quantitative data. My advice here is simple: Count what counts! If it makes sense to tally and count events, categories, occurrences, test scores, and the like, use an appropriate descriptive statistic. However, do not feel compelled to include elaborate statistical measures simply to add a perceived sense of rigor or credibility to your inquiry. Action research is a very different kind of inquiry from experimental research and as such is less concerned with the statistically based claims that scientists make. However, if your research has used quantitative research approaches (e.g., survey research, correlational research, causal-comparative research, experimental research, single-subject experimental research, or mixed-methods research) that include quantitative measures, use the appropriate statistics to analyze and interpret your data. Treat statistics as one of an array of many tools that can help teacher researchers gain insight into their data and communicate them efficiently to others.

In this section, I will briefly discuss descriptive statistical measures of central tendency (mean, mode, and median) and variability (standard deviation). For a more detailed explanation of the appropriate use of these statistics, and of inferential statistics (e.g., *t* tests, analysis of variance, multiple regression, chi-square, and other investigative techniques, such as data mining, factor analysis, and structural equation modeling), I recommend Mills and Gay (2016). Inferential statistics are data analysis techniques for determining how likely it is that results obtained from a sample or samples are the same results that would have been obtained from the entire population. As stated previously, few (if any) action researchers concern themselves with making claims about the findings of their studies (based on the results obtained in their classrooms) that would generalize to a larger population (e.g., all fifth-grade students in the state).

Many readily available computer programs, such as SPSS for Windows and Microsoft Office Excel, may be accessible for computing statistics at your school or university. Remember, there are many excellent math specialists in your school or district, so don't hesitate to call on those resources with questions.

Preparing Quantitative Data for Analysis

Scoring Procedures

After data are collected, the first step toward analysis involves converting behavioral responses into some numeric system (i.e., scoring quantitative data) or categorical organization (i.e., coding qualitative data). When a standardized instrument is used for data collection, scoring is greatly facilitated. The test manual usually spells out the steps to follow in scoring each test, and a scoring key is usually provided. It is important that data are scored accurately and consistently; each participant's test results should be scored in the same way and with one criterion. If the manual is followed conscientiously and each test is scored carefully, errors are minimized. It is usually a good idea to recheck all or at least some of the tests (say, 25 percent, or every fourth test) for consistency of scoring. Scoring self-developed instruments is more complex, especially if open-ended items are involved, because the researcher must develop and refine a reliable scoring procedure. Steps for scoring each item and for arriving at a total score must be delineated and carefully followed, and the procedure should be described in detail in the final research report.

Tabulation and Coding Procedures

After instruments have been scored, the resulting data are tabulated and entered into a spreadsheet, usually on the computer. To demonstrate how a readily accessible software program can be applied, I have used Excel for the analysis of a hypothetical elementary school: Pinecrest Elementary School. Tabulation involves organizing the data systematically, such as by individual subject. If planned analyses involve subgroup comparisons, scores should be tabulated for each subgroup. Table 7–1 shows the data for the Pinecrest students, organized in an Excel spreadsheet. Each student's record is listed horizontally by student number, and then codes representing the values for each variable are placed in the vertical columns. For example, reading across the table for Student #1, we find Gender = 1 (male), Ethnicity = 1 (African American), Economic level = 1 (low), and so forth. The score or code for each categorical variable (a variable that has two or more named categories, such as sex (male, female) and ethnicity (African American, Native American, etc.)—should be included in a codebook (see Table 7–2), which serves as the key for the numerical values assigned to each variable. The ratio variables (variables with a true zero point, e.g., achievement scores), such as ReadF (reading score for fall), are defined by their range or maximum score (e.g., student scores can range from 0 to 100 for all the tests at Pinecrest).

Following tabulation, the next step in our analysis is to describe what is happening with our students or, in other words, to summarize the data using descriptive statistics. Choice of appropriate statistical techniques is determined to a great extent by your research design, hypothesis, and the kind of data you collect. Thus, different research approaches lead to different statistical analyses. Note, however, that the complexity of the analysis is not an indication of its "goodness" or appropriateness. Regardless of how well the study is conducted, inappropriate analyses can lead to inappropriate research conclusions. Data analysis is as important as any other component of research, and the statistical procedures and techniques of the study should be identified and described in detail in the research plan.

table 7–1 ▪ Excel Spreadsheet of Pacific Crest Elementary Data: Mrs. Alvarez's Third-Grade Class

ID	Gender	Ethnicity	Econ	ReadLevel	ReadF	ReadS	MathF	MathS
1	1	1	1	3	52.5	68.7	54.8	55.2
2	2	2	2	1	32.5	52.6	73.2	72.8
3	1	5	2	1	36.4	38.5	44.9	43
4	1	5	2	1	44.3	56.2	35.2	36.6
5	2	4	1	3	58.7	63.8	58.3	60.5
6	1	3	1	1	28.3	31.2	23.1	22
7	2	3	1	2	43.1	53.6	52.6	53.6
8	1	5	3	2	66.5	75.5	53.8	53.3
9	2	1	1	3	51.4	56.8	45.8	43.6
10	1	5	1	1	38.5	41.4	46.7	47.8
11	2	5	3	3	56	72.3	38.4	36
12	1	2	1	1	24.5	28.4	32.5	32.6
13	2	1	1	1	37.4	42.3	25.3	25.8
14	1	3	1	1	28.3	34.8	18.3	19.5
15	2	5	3	3	78.4	72.4	58.3	60.3
16	2	3	2	2	52.3	53.6	38.6	40.3
17	1	5	3	2	56.8	64.2	67.4	68.4
18	2	1	3	3	73.2	68.4	72.4	70
19	1	5	2	1	47.4	65.8	53.5	52
20	2	2	1	2	47.4	34.6	48.5	50.2
21	1	5	3	2	53.2	58.5	36.5	38.5
22	1	3	1	1	18.4	22	27.2	28
23	2	5	2	3	53.5	58.4	62.4	64
24	2	4	1	3	46.5	52.4	38.6	38
25	1	1	2	1	38.6	41.7	28.9	27

table 7–2 ▪ Pacific Crest Elementary Code Book

Variable	Name	Coding Values
Student ID	ID	1-25
Gender	Gender	1 = male, 2 = female
Ethnicity	Ethnicity	1 = African American, 2 = Asian, Pacific Islander, 3 = Hispanic, 4 = Native American, 5 = White
Economic Level	Econ	1 = low (free/reduced lunch), 2 = medium/working class, 3 = middle/upper class
Reading Level	ReadLevel	1 = low, 2 = middle, 3 = high
Fall Reading Score	ReadF	0-100 scale
Spring Reading Score	ReadS	0-100 scale
Fall Math Score	MathF	0-100 scale
Spring Math Score	MathS	0-100 scale

Why Use Descriptive Statistics?

Descriptive statistics provide a shorthand way of giving lots of information about a range of numbers using only one or two numbers, such as by using attitude scales (Likert scales and semantic differentials) to measure students' attitudes and other sources of quantitative data available to action researchers (e.g., teacher-made tests, standardized tests, and school-generated report cards). One way to provide a great deal of information about our students' attitudes (as measured by these instruments) is to use descriptive statistics to describe the students' attitudes. For example, we might describe students' attitudes to a new mathematics curriculum (see Chapter 5) by reporting the average response to the following item on a questionnaire:

1. I believe that the problem-solving skills I learn in class help me make good problem-solving decisions outside of school.

    SA A U D SD

    By assigning point values—SA = 5, A = 4, U = 3, D = 2, SD = 1—and calculating the average response, we would be able to describe, on average, what children believed about the transfer of problem-solving skills to decisions made outside of school. In other words, the use of a number, in this case an average, conveys a great deal of information about students' attitudes and helps us make sense of our questionnaire data. Without the use of numbers, we would be limited to talking about an individual student's response to each question and not in more general terms about the attitudes of all of our students.

Measures of Central Tendency

Simply put, a measure of central tendency is a single number that gives us information about the entire group of numbers we are examining. Three common measures of central tendency are the *mean* (the average), the *mode* (the most frequently occurring score/s), and the *median* (the middle score). In education, perhaps the most common descriptive statistic used by teachers is the mean. It allows us to talk in generalities and to compare how the students in our class have performed "on average" in comparison to other students or over a given time period. As a teacher, you have no doubt calculated many averages, but remember: The **mean** (M) is calculated by adding together all of the scores (observations) and dividing by the number of scores.

Mean = The sum of all the scores divided by the number of scores.

For example, you administer a mathematics test with 100 questions to the 30 students in your class. After grading the tests, you award the following scores: 95, 95, 92, 92, 90, 90, 90, 88, 88, 85, 85, 85, 82, 82, 82, 82, 79, 79, 75, 75, 75, 75, 75, 72, 72, 72, 69, 69, 69, 65.

$$\text{Mean}\ (\bar{x}) = \frac{\sum x\,(\text{the sum of scores})}{n\,(\text{the number of scores})}$$

$$= \frac{2,424}{30}$$

$$= 80.8$$

The mean is greatly affected by extreme scores because it is "pulled" in the direction of the atypical values. For that reason, the median is sometimes a better descriptor of the full range of scores. For the most part, though, the mean (or the average) is the easiest, most familiar measure to use.

The **median** (Mdn) is the middle score in a distribution when the scores are ordered from the highest to the lowest. If there is an odd number of scores (say, 31), then the middle score (the 16th one) is the median. But in the distribution of the math scores above, there is an even number of scores. To find the midpoint in the distribution when there is an even number of scores, we must add the two middle scores in the rank-ordered distribution and divide by two. In this case, we would add together the two scores that are at positions 15 and 16, and divide by two. In this case, it would be scores 82 and 82. Therefore, 82 is the median score.

The **mode** is the most frequently occurring score in a distribution. In the case of these math scores, the mode would be 75 because that score was received by five students in the class. A distribution of scores can have more than one mode (making it bimodal or multimodal) or have no mode at all. The mode is the least useful measure of central tendency in most educational research: It tells us only about the score received most often and doesn't give us any information about the other scores.

Measure of Variability: Standard Deviation

As a teacher, you may have been exposed to standard deviation (SD) but perhaps did not fully understand its meaning. For example, you may have received test scores for your students following administration of a standardized test with individual scores, a class average, and a standard deviation. For our purposes, it is not important to see and memorize the formula for the standard deviation or even to know its origins. It is more important to understand the concepts of variability and standard deviation, to know what they mean, and to recognize when they would be appropriate to use.

A measure of variability tells us "how spread out a group of scores are." The standard deviation is the most important measure of variability for our action research purposes. Whereas the mean is a measure of a position in a distribution of scores (in this case, 80.8 on a scale of 1 to 100), the **standard deviation** indicates the spread of a set of scores around the mean (Mills & Gay, 2016, p. 247). In essence, the standard deviation helps us to understand approximately how much a particular score deviates from the average score.

As a teacher researcher, I might also be puzzled about whether a relatively large or small standard deviation is "good" or "bad." Perhaps a better way to think of a standard deviation as it relates to our mathematics test scores is in terms of equity. For example, the mean is 80.8, and the standard deviation is 8.59. (I calculated the standard deviation using SPSS 18.0 for Windows. If you have a larger data set, this is not the kind of calculation you want to do by hand, but for a small data set, you can calculate the standard deviation by hand.) If the data set is too large to calculate by hand and you don't have access to SPSS, you can use computer programs, such as Excel or a calculator with a statistics function, to calculate the standard deviation.

In our example, where the mean is 80.8 and the SD is 8.59, the majority (68 percent to be precise) of the children scored (roughly) between 72 and 89 (±1 SD from the mean). In short, most of them probably succeeded on the test if, in fact, scoring within this range of scores suggests some kind of mastery of the content. Now, let's compare the standard deviation of 8.59 to a standard deviation of, say, 16. If this were the case, we might conclude that the majority of children scored between 64 and 97. Again the question is one of mastery and whether a score of 64 suggests mastery of the content. The larger standard deviation suggests that the children's scores on the math test are more spread out and, hence, leaves us to question the degree to which the children have achieved mastery on the test. For the classroom teacher seeking to confirm mastery of subject matter on a criterion-referenced test (teacher-made test), a higher mean and smaller standard deviation would be a desirable outcome.

All of this leads us to the question, "So how does this help me understand my students' mathematics test scores?" Armed with the knowledge that the average score for the 30 students in your class is 80.8 and the standard deviation of this distribution of scores is 8.59, you can make the following statements:

- On average, the children in the class scored 80 on the test.
- Approximately two-thirds of the children in the class scored between 72 and 89 on the test.
- The relatively small standard deviation and mean of 80 suggest that approximately two-thirds of the children achieved mastery of the content that the test covered.

Used in conjunction, the mean and standard deviation can provide you and your colleagues with a great deal of information about the data you have collected if you have determined that it is data that can be counted. See Key Concepts Box 7–1 for some of the uses of descriptive statistics.

KEY CONCEPTS BOX 7–1

Descriptive Statistics

Definition of Measure	Type Used in Action Research
A **measure of central tendency** is a single number that gives us information about an entire group of numbers.	• Mean (the average) • Mode (the most frequently occurring score/s) • Median (the middle score)
A **measure of variability** tells us how spread out a group of scores is.	• Standard deviation (a measure of distance from the mean that helps us understand approximately how much a *particular* score deviates from the *average* score)

An Illustration

In my study of change in the McKenzie School District (Mills, 1988), I administered a survey to classroom teachers. One of the items on the survey focused on the teachers' perceptions of how the district's at-risk program had changed classroom practices. Specifically, teachers were asked to respond to the following statement: To what degree has the at-risk program changed your classroom practice? The survey included an item that required teachers to circle a number between 1 and 5 (1 = no change, 5 = large change). A total of 52 teachers responded to the survey item with the following frequency:

Impact of At-Risk Program on Classroom Practices				
No Change				Large Change
1	2	3	4	5
Number of Respondents 7(13%)	18(37%)	17(35%)	10(15%)	0(0%)

I used the following descriptive statistics to describe the distribution of teachers' responses:

4,4,4,4,4,4,4,4,4,4,3,3,3,3,3,3,3,3,3,3,3,3,3,3,3,3,3,3,2,2,2,2,2,2,2,2,2,2,2,2,2,2,2,2,2,2,2,2,1,1,1,1,1, 1,1

$$\text{Mean } (\bar{x}) = \frac{\sum x}{n}$$
$$= \frac{134}{52}$$
$$= 2.58$$

Mode = 2.0 (most frequently occurring score—it occurred 18 times)
Median = 3.0 (the middle score in this distribution of 52 responses)
Standard Deviation = 1.02

However, numbers alone do not tell a complete story. They inform the reader about how a sample responded to a particular item. For example, the analysis of the earlier illustration related to classroom teachers' perceptions of how the district's at-risk program had changed classroom practices is incomplete using only descriptive statistics. To complete my reporting on this item, I included the following representative responses to the question, "To what extent do you think that the at-risk program changed your classroom practices?" The responses were grouped under the categories of "Positive Impact" and "No Impact."

Positive Impact

Reminded me and reinforced the concepts of learning styles and how to provide for them in my classroom.

Having insight to these kids has allowed me to be more sensitive and caring toward them and to act more compassionately.

I am more aware of needs of the "total child" as well as the student.

No Impact

No time to plan and implement all of those ideas!

I feel that the services needed for at-risk students are not available.

I was already using many of the skills.

I have been dealing with at-risk students since becoming a resource teacher, so I was already aware of the problem.

I believe that I have always been aware of the problem. It's only new at the district level.

The statistical analysis combined with the quotes from the teachers who responded provided me with a good understanding of the teachers' perceptions of the impact the at-risk program had on their classroom practices.

Be Careful About Your Claims

A final caveat: Be careful about how you "interpret" the descriptive statistics that you use to analyze your data and be careful about the claims you make based on a descriptive statistical analysis. Be clear about the limited significance that can be attached to averages and standard deviations. Remember that these statistics are used for description, not for identifying statistically significant relationships that can be generalized to the larger population.

Clearly, this discussion about descriptive statistics is quite brief. My experiences with teacher researchers is that, like me, they are somewhat math phobic and reluctant to incorporate statistics into their studies. But as Pelto and Pelto (1978) remind us,

> In fact, not only humans but also other animals are constantly counting things in the process of adapting to their environments. Basic processes of learning, as described by experimental psychologists, most often imply some kind of counting or measurement that permits an animal (human or other) to distinguish between one condition and another as a relevant stimulus for appropriate action. (p. 123)

If counting things positively contributes to understanding your research or suggests a relationship that warrants further investigation, then use whatever statistic is most appropriate to analyze and interpret your data. Moreover, if you are math phobic but still want to examine whether statistics can give you insight into your data, do not hesitate to call on the skills of your critical friends, colleagues, and university professors.

Voices from the Field
Analyzing and Interpreting Quantitative Data

In this vignette, the teacher researcher shares her analysis and interpretation of her quantitative data collection focused on better understanding how formative assessments (quizzes) changed student attitudes toward the class, learning language, and taking tests. Rachelle ultimately claims that there were some "very, very positive" results from her action research. These results rested with her interpretation of percentages and frequency counts. For example, after the use of formative assessments, the percentage of students who reported "no test anxiety" had gone from 13 to 26 percent. Rachelle's interpretation of this result was "very, very positive." This example is a good reminder for action researchers to be modest in their claims and interpretations of numerical data. Further, the example includes times of moving between percentages and numbers of students: quite different measures. Rachelle's analysis would have benefited from the use of other descriptive statistical analyses, including mean, mode, median, and standard deviation, in order to provide a more detailed analysis on which to base interpretations of the survey data.

ENHANCEDetext

video example 7–3
In this video, Rachelle summarizes some of her findings in her action research project, which focused on whether weekly quizzes changed students' attitudes toward the class, learning language, and taking tests. How does her presentation of the quantitative data help you to understand and draw conclusions about her students' test anxiety? Are there other descriptive statistics that you'td like to hear about?

Data Analysis in Mixed-Methods Designs

As I have discussed throughout this chapter, one of the most difficult aspects of any research endeavor is the analysis of data. This problem is showcased when we attempt to analyze quantitative and qualitative data sources concurrently or in sequence and then attempt to find points of intersection as well as discrepancies, as is the case in mixed-methods designs. To refresh your memory, mixed-methods research designs combine quantitative and qualitative approaches by including both quantitative and qualitative data in a single study. Many teacher researchers find themselves including both data sources in their studies, especially when capturing student achievement data. Table 7–3 summarizes the type of mixed-methods research designs and examples of data analysis and data interpretation techniques that teacher researchers can use (Creswell, 2015). Many of the suggestions in this table build on the information in the quantitative and qualitative analysis and interpretation sections in this chapter and therefore should be familiar to you. (For a comprehensive discussion of mixed-methods research designs, see Mills & Gay, 2016, Chapter 15.)

table 7-3 ▪ **Types of Mixed-Methods Designs and Data Analysis/Interpretation Procedures**

Types of Mixed-Methods Designs	Examples of Data Analysis and Data Interpretation Techniques
Convergent parallel (quantitative and qualitative data are collected simultaneously)	Quantify qualitative data coding by assigning a number to a code and counting the number of times it occurs. Quantitative data are descriptively analyzed for frequency of occurrence. The two data sets are compared.
Explanatory sequential (quantitative data are collected first, followed by qualitative data)	Follow up on outliers (extreme cases). Quantitative data are collected and outliers identified. Qualitative data are then collected on the outliers to increase understanding of these cases.
Exploratory sequential (qualitative data are collected first, followed by quantitative data)	Qualitative data are collected and analyzed and themes identified. The themes are used as the basis for identifying, or developing, an instrument that can be administered to collect quantitative data to measure the identified themes.

Source: Adapted from J. W. Creswell (2012, 2015). *Educational Research: Planning, Conducting, and Evaluating Quantitative and Qualitative Research.*

Qualitative Data Interpretation Techniques

You may wonder, why bother with interpretation, especially since interpretation involves taking risks and making educated guesses that might be off base? According to Wolcott (1994), qualitative (action) researchers must accept "the risks and challenges of the interpretive mode" because in doing so we can "demonstrate to others (and reassure ourselves) that, in spite of their undistinguished origins, our works and the implications to be drawn from them are socially significant" (p. 258). In other words, Wolcott argues for the importance of interpretation because as teacher researchers, our interpretations matter to the lives of our students. In addition, the process of interpretation is important because it can challenge teacher researchers' taken-for-granted assumptions and beliefs about the educational processes they have investigated.

The list of techniques for data interpretation that follow are adapted from Wolcott (1994, pp. 39–46) and Stringer (1996, pp. 87–96) but have been reframed to apply specifically to teacher researchers.

Voices from the Field
Data Analysis in Mixed-Methods Designs

In this vignette, the teacher researcher describes the mixed-methods design he used to study high school student interest and engagement. Doug's study can be classified as a convergent parallel mixed-methods design where he collected simultaneously qualitative and quantitative data and compared the data sets to better understand the impact of his intervention on student interest and engagement. Specifically, Doug used pre- and postsurveys that were analyzed using descriptive statistics (quantitative data) and student essays that were analyzed by coding and identifying themes (qualitative data). Doug characterizes his two data sets as "hard data" (data that can be reduced to numbers) and "affective data" (data that can be reduced to themes). However, Doug's assertion that "numbers reflect the significance of your intervention" should be viewed cautiously. The use of a mixed-methods design is specifically intended to provide the teacher researcher with multiple data sets to compare regardless of whether the data are numerical or narrative, and "significance" is a term best reserved for "statistical significance" and inferential statistical analyses.

ENHANCEDetext

video example 7–4
Doug, the action researcher in this video, describes the measures in his mixed-methods study. Which type of mixed-methods design did he use, and what recommendations might you give to him as he begins analysis of his data?

Extend the Analysis

One technique that is low on the data interpretation risk scale is to simply extend the analysis of your data by raising questions about the study, noting implications that might be drawn without actually drawing them. As Wolcott (1994) suggested, "This is a strategy for *pointing* the way rather than *leading* the way" (p. 40, emphasis added). For example, "While it appears as though the teen theater improvisation model positively impacts audience participation, a number of questions are raised by this strategy." In this example from Cathy Mitchell's Teen Theater group's use of improvisation (see Chapter 3), the analysis of data can be extended by raising questions about the intervention that were not asked as part of the original investigation but that may signal the beginning of the next action research cycle.

Similarly, in the Highland Park High School vignette, the research raised questions such as the following: Is the total elimination of letter and number grades the best way to deemphasize grades? Is there a way to deemphasize grades that requires less paperwork on the teacher's part? What is an appropriate role for students to play in determining their own grades? How can grades be deemphasized while teachers maintain specific criteria/outcomes for students?

Connect Findings with Personal Experience

Action research is personal business, so it makes sense to personalize our interpretations. For example, you may present your findings with the following prelude: "Based on my experiences in conducting this study, this is what I make of it all." Remember, you know your study better than anyone else; after all, it's been conducted in your classroom or school and focused on your students. You have been there for every twist and turn along the way, trying to make sense of discrepant events just when you thought you "had it right." Share your interpretations based on your intimate knowledge and understanding of schools and classrooms and teaching and learning. For example, recall that Deborah South (Chapter 1) had experienced the frustration of working with unmotivated children and the apparent futility of a study skills intervention. When faced with the "So what?" question, she based her interpretation not only on the analysis of data (test scores, surveys, interviews, and observations) but also on the memories and emotions of adolescent off-task behavior—a powerful interpretive lens.

Seek the Advice of "Critical" Friends

If you have difficulty focusing an interpretive lens on your work, rely on your trusted colleagues to offer insights that you may have missed because of your closeness to the work. Offer your accounts to colleagues with the request that they share with you their possible interpretations. For example, the group of teachers at Highland Park High School found that their interpretations were enriched by the multiple viewpoints that came as a result of their collaboration. Remember, these colleagues may be people you have never met face-to-face but with whom you

Voices from the Field
Seek the Advice of Critical Friends

The teacher researcher in this vignette provides a simple illustration of the role of critical friends in action research. A "car pool" of other MAT students provided a perfect venue for Rachelle to share her struggles and outcomes and to seek confidential feedback about how to move forward with her action research efforts specifically and her student teaching in general.

ENHANCEDetext

video example 7–5
Rachelle briefly describes her experience with a group of "critical" friends in this video.

have talked in action research chat rooms on the Internet. Similarly, you may ask your informants (students, parents, teachers, and administrators) for their insights.

But beware! The more opinions you seek, the more you will receive, and often these suggestions come with the expectation that you will accept the advice! Over time, you will develop reciprocity with a cadre of trusted, like-minded colleagues who will selflessly fulfill the role of critical friends. Take the time to build these relationships and reap the rewards they offer. For example, when Deborah South concluded from her data analysis and interpretation that her study skills class was the "cause" of her students' lack of motivation, her critical friends in her action research class protested that interpretation and provided her with ideas for alternate explanations. What Deborah gained from the feedback of her critical friends was a commitment to change the "intervention" that was being touted as "the solution" to the "unmotivated students" problem in the school.

Contextualize Findings in the Literature

Uncovering external sources as part of the review of related literature is a powerful way for teacher researchers to provide support for the study's findings. Wolcott (1994) suggested that qualitative (action) researchers "draw connections with external authority. Most often this is accomplished through informed references to some recognized body of theory in one's special field, or to the recognized classics, in the tradition of the literature review" (p. 34). Making these connections also provides teacher researchers with a way to share with colleagues the existing knowledge base in a specific area of focus and to acknowledge the unique contribution the teacher researcher has made to our understanding of the topic studied.

Turn to Theory

Let me first offer a modest definition of theory as "an analytical and interpretive framework that helps the researcher make sense of 'what is going on' in the social setting being studied" (Mills, 1993, p. 103). Theory serves a number of important roles for action researchers. First, theory provides a way for teacher researchers to link their work to broader issues of the day. As Wolcott (1994) suggested, "One interpretive tack is to examine a case in terms of competing theories and then proclaim a winner or, more often, attempt some eclectic resolution" (p. 43). Second, "theory allows the researcher to search for increasing levels of abstraction, to move beyond a purely descriptive account" (Mills, 1993, p. 115). That level of abstraction "allow(s) us to communicate the essence of descriptive work to our colleagues at research meetings" (Mills, 1993, p. 115). Finally, theory can provide a rationale or sense of meaning to the work we do. As educators, we have all been influenced by learning theories that provide a safe haven for our own work. Share the theories that appear to help make sense of your data. For example, Mills's story of the use of technology to enhance mathematics learning for the students at Billabong Elementary School (Chapter 2) is influenced by theories about how

RESEARCH IN ACTION CHECKLIST 7–2

Data Interpretation Techniques

_____ Extend the analysis by raising questions.

_____ Connect the findings with personal experience.

_____ Seek the advice of critical friends.

_____ Contextualize findings in the literature.

_____ Turn to theory.

students best learn math. Some of these theories are evident in the references to how students were using technology for "drill-and-kill" activities and how access to calculators was limited because calculator functions had been removed from the computers. The vignette suggests that other theories explain how students best learn math by challenging the "rote learning" theory that appeared well established at Billabong Elementary.

Know When to Say "When"!

Finally, if you don't feel comfortable with offering an interpretation, don't do it. Be satisfied with suggesting what needs to be done next and use that as a starting point for the next action research cycle. Restate the problem as you now see it and explain how you think you will fine-tune your efforts as you strive to increase your understanding of the phenomenon you have investigated. Wolcott (1994) cautioned, "Don't detract from what you have accomplished by tacking on a wimpy interpretation" (p. 41). (See Research in Action Checklist 7–2 for a list of data interpretation techniques.)

Sharing Your Interpretations Wisely

As educators, we have all, at some time, been exposed to what are variously called "fads," "the pendulum swing," the "bandwagon," and so on. Thus, many of us may hesitate to embrace anything new or different that comes our way in schools, calming ourselves with the mantra "This, too, shall pass!" If we, as professional educators, attempt to use our action research findings only to confirm our beliefs and values, then we risk being alienated by our colleagues. Avoid being evangelical about your interpretations, connect them closely to your data and analysis, and share your newfound understandings with colleagues in an appropriate manner.

SUMMARY

Ongoing Analysis and Reflection

1. Action research studies provide teacher researchers with data that can be used formatively and summatively; that is, much of the data collected during the study can be used to positively affect teaching throughout the study.
2. Use the following two questions to guide reflection:
   a. Is your research question still answerable and worth answering?
   b. Are your data collection techniques catching the kind of data you want and filtering out the data that you don't? (Anderson et al., 1994, p. 155)
3. Although ongoing analysis and reflection is a natural part of the action research process, you should avoid premature actions based on early analysis and interpretation of the data. Action researchers—especially those who are inexperienced—often make rash or impulsive decisions based on limited or no data.
4. The action research process takes time. Teacher researchers must be wary of the lure of quick-fix strategies and patient enough to avoid the pitfalls of basing actions on premature analysis.

The Role of Analysis and Interpretation

5. Data analysis is an attempt by the teacher researcher to summarize collected data in a dependable and accurate manner.
6. Data interpretation is an attempt by the researcher to find meaning in the data, to answer the "So what?" question in terms of the implications of the study's findings.
7. Put simply, analysis involves summarizing what's in the data, whereas interpretation involves making sense of—finding meaning in—those data.
8. Data analysis and interpretation are critical stages in the action research process that require the teacher researcher to both know and understand the data.
9. One way to proceed with analysis is to follow three iterative, or repeating, steps: reading/memoing, describing what is going on in the setting, and classifying research data.
10. Reading/Memoing. The first step in analysis is to read and write memos about all field notes, transcripts, and observer comments to get an initial sense of the data. To begin, find a quiet place and plan to spend a few hours at a time reading through the data.
11. Describing. The second step, describing, involves developing thorough and comprehensive descriptions of the participants, the setting, and the phenomenon studied in order to convey the rich complexity of the research. The descriptions are based on your collected observations, interview data, field notes, and artifacts.
12. Classifying. Qualitative data are typically broken down through the process of classifying or *coding*; the pieces of data are then categorized. A *category* is a classification of ideas or concepts; categorization, then, is grouping the

data into themes. When concepts in the data are examined and compared to one another and connections are made, categories are formed.

Qualitative Data Analysis Techniques

13. Identifying Themes. One place to start your analysis is to work inductively as you begin to analyze the data: Consider the big picture and start to list "themes" that you have seen emerge in your literature review and in the data collection. Are there patterns that emerge, such as events that keep repeating themselves, key phrases that participants use to describe their feelings, or survey responses that seem to "match" one another?

14. Coding Surveys, Interviews, and Questionnaires. One of the most frequent data analysis activities undertaken by action researchers is coding, the process of trying to find patterns and meaning in data collected through the use of surveys, interviews, and questionnaires.

15. Analyzing an Interview. Another common form of qualitative data that action researchers analyze is interview data, most commonly in the form of a transcript from the audio recording of the interview.

16. Asking Key Questions. Another approach to data analysis involves the use of key questions, such as those with which the teacher researcher started the study; they may take form of who, what, where, when, why, and how questions about the educational process.

17. Doing an Organizational Review. This approach to data analysis involves focusing on the following features of the organization (e.g., school): vision and mission, goals and objectives, structure of the organization, operation, and problems, issues, and concerns (Stringer, 1996, p. 90).

18. Developing a Concept Map. Concept maps are a useful strategy that helps action researcher participants to visualize the major influences that have affected the study (Stringer, 1996). The steps for developing a concept map include the following:
    a. List the major influences that have affected the study of your area of focus.
    b. Develop a visual representation of the major influences (factors) connecting the influences with relationships you know exist (using solid lines) and influences you have a "hunch" about (using dotted lines).
    c. Review the concept map to determine any consistencies or inconsistencies that exist among the influences. This forces you back to your data to see "what's missing."

19. Analyzing Antecedents and Consequences. A process of mapping antecedents (causes) and consequences (effects) helps action researchers identify the major elements of their analysis (Stringer, 1996). The steps for analyzing antecedents and consequences are as follows:
    a. List the influences that emerged from the analysis for which there appear to be a causal relationship.
    b. Revisit the review of literature to determine whether the analysis of the study supports or is challenged by the findings of previous studies.

    c. Revisit your data to determine whether anything is missing and suggest how your findings may influence the next action research cycle.

20. Displaying Findings. The information you have collected should be summarized in an appropriate and meaningful format that you can share with interested colleagues. "Think display" as one way to convey your findings.

21. State What's Missing. Flag for the consumers of your research what pieces of the puzzle are still missing and identify any remaining questions for which you have not been able to provide answers.

22. Use Computer Software to Assist with Data Analysis. Computer software is available to assist with the analysis of qualitative data. This software will not do the analysis for you. It is designed to help researchers who are working with large bodies of text and other kinds of data.

23. Three common and popular qualitative analysis software packages are NVivo 11, The Ethnograph v6, and HyperRESEARCH 3.7.3.

Analyzing and Interpreting Quantitative Data

24. Data analysis and interpretation can also involve the use of descriptive statistics to help make sense of your findings. My advice here is simple: Count what counts! If it makes sense to tally and count events, categories, occurrences, test scores, and the like, use an appropriate descriptive statistic.

25. Descriptive statistics give us a shorthand way of giving lots of information about a range of numbers using only one or two numbers.

26. A measure of central tendency is a single number that gives us information about the entire group of numbers we are examining. Three common measures of central tendency are the *mean* (the average), the *mode* (the most frequently occurring score/s), and the *median* (the middle score).

27. The mean (average) is calculated by adding together all of the scores (observations) and dividing by the number of scores. The mean is greatly affected by extreme scores because it is "pulled" in the direction of the atypical values.

28. The median is the middle score in a distribution when the scores are ordered from the highest to the lowest.

29. The mode is the most frequently occurring score in a distribution. The mode is the least useful measure of central tendency in most educational research.

30. Standard deviation is a measure of variability that tells us how spread out a group of scores are (Mills & Gay, 2016, p. 326). The standard deviation is the most important measure of variability for our action research purposes. The standard deviation helps us to understand approximately how much a particular score deviates from the average score.

31. Be careful about how you "interpret" the descriptive statistics that you use to analyze your data and be careful about the claims you make based on a descriptive statistical analysis. Be clear about the limited significance that can be attached to averages and standard deviations.

32. The challenges of data analysis are showcased when we attempt to analyze quantitative and qualitative data sources concurrently or in sequence and

then attempt to find points of intersection as well as discrepancies, as is the case in mixed-methods designs.

33. Mixed-methods research designs combine quantitative and qualitative approaches by including both quantitative and qualitative data in a single study.

Qualitative Data Interpretation Techniques

34. Extend the Analysis. One technique low on the data interpretation risk scale is to simply extend the analysis of your data by raising questions about the study, noting implications that might be drawn without actually drawing them.

35. Connect Findings with Personal Experience. Action research is personal business, so it makes sense to personalize our interpretations. Share your interpretations based on your intimate knowledge and understanding of schools and classrooms and teaching and learning.

36. Seek the Advice of "Critical" Friends. If you have difficulty focusing an interpretive lens on your work, rely on your trusted colleagues to offer insights that you may have missed because of your closeness to the work. But beware! The more opinions you seek, the more you will receive, and often these suggestions come with the expectation that you will accept the advice.

37. Contextualize Findings in the Literature. Uncovering external sources as part of the review of related literature is a powerful way for teacher researchers to provide support for the study's findings.

38. Turn to Theory. Share theories about teaching and learning that appear to help make sense of your data.

39. Know When to Say "When"! If you do not feel comfortable with offering an interpretation, don't do it. Be satisfied with suggesting what needs to be done next and use that as a starting point for the next action research cycle.

Sharing Your Interpretations Wisely

40. Avoid being evangelical about your interpretations, connect them closely to your data and analysis, and share your newfound understandings with colleagues in an appropriate manner.

TASKS

1. How will you analyze each data source that you have indicated in your data collection plan? Remember: Don't collect data when you don't know what you are going to do with it. For each data source identified in your data collection matrix, identify appropriate data analysis and data interpretation approaches.

Action Planning for Educational Change

After reading this chapter you should be able to:

8.1   Complete an action plan by working through a Steps to Action Chart.

8.2   Become aware of challenges that confront the action researcher in the action planning process.

8.3   Become aware of conditions that facilitate educational change in school environments.

8.4   Become aware of what teacher researchers gain by engaging in action research.

This chapter discusses different steps in action planning that help ensure that teacher researchers are able to implement positive educational change based on the insights they gain through action research. **Action planning** basically attempts to answer the question, "Based on what I have learned from my research, what should I do now?"

A Steps to Action Chart is presented to guide teacher researchers through the action planning process. The chart identifies the findings of the study, the recommended action that targets a given finding, who is responsible for specific actions, who needs to be consulted or informed about the findings of the study and the concomitant actions, how to monitor the effects of your actions through the collection of data, a time line for when the actions and monitoring will occur, and any resources that will be needed to carry out the action. A blank Steps to Action Chart is also included for your personal use.

Finally, this chapter will discuss action planning within the context of challenges that face the teacher researcher and the conditions under which action research and the educational change that follows it can occur.

Reflecting on an Absenteeism Policy

Jack Reston

This vignette is the story of an elementary school principal who modeled the process of action research for his teachers, many of whom were involved in their own action research projects at the same time. Jack's story is particularly powerful because it illustrates the willingness of a school principal to investigate the effect of a policy he had developed. Further, Jack tackled difficult problems facing many teachers and principals: how to keep children in school and the importance of being in school. The result of the study was an action plan that required the change of a district-wide absenteeism policy.

I was selected to serve on a committee of administrators to review current policies concerning students' absenteeism. The task of the committee was to write a new student absenteeism policy, which led to the adoption of a new absenteeism policy and procedure. I recognized throughout this process a need to look into student absenteeism with more depth and understanding, and for this reason I selected the topic of student absenteeism for my action research project.

I initiated my research project with a review of our school's attendance rate profile for the last 5 years. The profile showed little or no change in the attendance rate. This was a concern because I cross-referenced the attendance rate with the funds allocated for various attendance incentives designed to motivate students and could easily see that the dollars spent on incentives were not affecting the attendance rate. I sat at my desk and thought about all my current and past efforts. It was clear that I was not truly passionate about student absenteeism. I had never taken time to clearly understand its causes or researched the best solutions to prevent it. I was passionate about my belief that a child's success in life depends on a solid educational foundation. I was passionate about my belief that students cannot afford to miss class at any time. I was passionate about my belief that absenteeism is a symptom or gauge of a student experiencing failure in school.

I began by asking three questions:

1. *What student characteristics are associated with student absenteeism?*
2. *What are some longitudinal effects of student absenteeism?*
3. *What are some effective strategies to prevent student absenteeism?*

I reviewed current studies, literature, local and national profiles, written surveys, and interviews. I found that absenteeism was highly associated with dropping out of school, academic failure, and delinquency. I learned what students and parents in our school believed about the relationship between school and absenteeism. I concluded that I really did not understand the belief systems of families at risk for poor attendance in school. I conducted a massive survey of students and parents within a four-day period of time. Surveys gathered data concerning such things as respectfulness of students, safety in school, conflict management, discipline, school rules, self-esteem, and academics. In addition, the survey gathered data on mobility rates, volunteerism, and levels of education in parents. The identity of the families surveyed was kept unknown. Instead, the surveys were coded as "at risk" or "not at risk" data.

I collected data from the surveys in three stages. First, each family in the school was mailed a survey. The surveys arrived at the homes of students on a Saturday. Completed surveys were returned to the school prior to 9:00 a.m. on the following

Monday. Second, each student in the entire school was surveyed in their classroom at 9:00 a.m. on Monday. Third, selected students and parents were interviewed between Monday and Tuesday to collect data similarly gathered on the surveys.

Student teachers from a nearby university and local educators with experience in action research interviewed selected students and parents. The interviews were conducted over the telephone or face-to-face. I compiled all of the data and began searching for a better understanding of at-risk students and parents at my school. I found that these people believed the following:

- Other students did not respect them.
- They did not use conflict management skills.
- Adults in the school did not handle discipline effectively.
- School rules are not fair.
- There are behavior problems associated with this group.
- At-risk students perform poorly in academic areas.
- At-risk students in this school are not motivated by rewards such as drawings for prizes and certificates.

This information led to major changes in our approach to improving attendance in school. First, we stopped spending large sums of money for rewards and drawings. Although these are nice things for students, they are ineffective in dealing with the problem of poor attendance. Second, we recognized that punitive measures were having little effect on attendance. This led us to the belief that students succeeding in school were more likely to attend school regularly.

We began a concentrated effort to improve the success of students at school both academically and emotionally. This included the use of student/parent/teacher/principal contracts, daily planners for students, individual conferences between the student and the principal every 14 days to review grades and behaviors, better assessments to locate students having academic problems, improved instructional techniques and alignment of curriculum, and more concentrated efforts to improve the self-esteem of students.

In conclusion, I found the following to be true in our effort to improve student absenteeism:

1. Students need to be successful in school.
2. Students need to be connected to the school.
3. Students need friendships with students and adults at school.
4. Students need to develop the skills to deal with life's daily anxieties.
5. The school needs to develop meaningful relationships with the family.

Based on these findings, I worked with teachers and parents to develop quick responses that unite the student, parent, educator, and community in a preventive effort to minimize absenteeism.

To support Kurt Lewin's prophetic statement, "No action without research; no research without action" (cited in Adelman, 1993, p. 8), this chapter discusses how teacher researchers can ensure that action is a natural outcome of their action research efforts. Without action, we have done nothing more than replicate what we set out to avoid—doing research on someone for our own benefit, whatever that may be. But the reward for us all in this process is taking action to improve the educational experiences of our children—action is at the very heart of the action research endeavor.

In Jack Reston's vignette, we see a principal and members of the school community (children, parents, teachers, and student teachers) who persevered in trying to solve an important problem that faces many schools—how to keep children in school. Reston's action plan identified a number of actions targeted to the findings of the study: developing students' skills to deal with the anxieties of life and school, developing strategies to ensure student success in school, developing meaningful relationships with families, improving instructional techniques and curriculum alignment, using strategies to develop meaningful relationships/partnerships with families, and so on. In the action planning process, Reston had reflected on the findings of the study and what he now understood about the problem of absenteeism. As a result of this reflection, he was better able to plan the next steps in the action research process.

Action planning is a natural next step in the action research process. Using the guidelines in this chapter, you will be able to ensure that the necessary steps are taken to bring your efforts to fruition.

Developing Action Plans

At this phase of the action research process, the teacher researcher is basically trying to answer the following question: "Based on what I have learned from this investigation, what should I do now?" At this point, teacher researchers should reflect on the taken-for-granted assumptions that guided them to the investigation in the first instance and determine what course of action to take next. This reflection allows time for both teachers and administrators to determine what they have learned from their investigations and the related professional literature and to decide on the necessary steps to action.

To facilitate this process, consider using a Steps to Action Chart similar to those shown in Table 8–1 and Table 8–2. (Table 8–1 shows a generic Steps to Action Chart; Table 8–2 shows the Steps to Action Chart created by Jack Reston for his study of student absenteeism.) By working through the steps included on the chart, teacher researchers will have a list of the following:

- What they learned (findings)
- The recommended actions that target a given finding
- Who is responsible for specific actions (responsibility)

table 8–1 ■ **Steps to Action Chart**

Summary of Findings and Research Questions	Recommended Action Targeted to Findings	Who Is Responsible for the Action?	Who Needs to Be Consulted or Informed?	Who will Monitor/ Collect Data?	Time Line	Resources
1.0 Research question #1					When will action/ monitoring occur?	What will you need in order to carry out your action?
1.1 Finding #1		■ Teacher	■ Teacher			
1.2 Finding #2		■ Team	■ Team			
2.0 Research question #2		■ Department head	■ Department head			
2.1 Finding #1		■ Principal	■ Principal			
2.2 Finding #2		■ Parents	■ Parents			
2.3 etc.		■ Students	■ Students			

- Who needs to be consulted or informed about the findings of the study and the associated actions
- Who will monitor or collect the effects of actions
- Dates when the actions and monitoring will occur
- Any resources that will be needed to carry out the action

Elements of this chart will look familiar to you. Monitoring and data collection efforts will once again involve you in the action research process. In each case, you will focus on a new problem—such as "What are the effects of this action on student performance?"—and develop specific data collection/monitoring techniques to answer the question. Although not included on the chart, the monitoring/data collection techniques (see Chapter 5) would lead to data analysis and interpretation (see Chapter 7) with findings and further steps to action. Hence, the cycle repeats itself again and again. It may be that you are entirely satisfied with an intervention and that the proposed action is to continue with its implementation.

table 8–2 ▪ Jack Reston's Steps to Action Chart

Summary of Findings and Research Questions	Recommended Action Targeted to Findings	Who Is Responsible for the Action? T – Teacher S – Student P – Principal PA – Parent(s)	Who Needs to Be Consulted or Informed?	Who Will Monitor/ Collect Data?	Time Line	Resources
1.0 What student character-istics are attributed to student absenteeism?				T, P: 1. Observations 2. Intentions 3. Surveys 4. Test data	Ongoing throughout school year.	None
1.1 Lack of respect	1.1 Model respect for others.	1.1 T, S, P				
1.2 Poor conflict management skills	1.2–1.4 Develop skills to deal with life's daily anxieties.	1.2–1.4 T, S, P, PA	1.2–1.4 PA			
1.3 Lack of self-discipline						
1.4 Behavior problems						
1.5 Poor academic performance	1.5 Improve strategies to develop success in school.	1.5 T, P				
2.0 What are some longitu-dinal effects of student absenteeism?				T, P: 1. Observations 2. Intentions 3. Surveys 4. Test data	Ongoing throughout school year.	None
2.1 Dropouts	2.1–2.3 Students need to be connected to school.	2.1–2.3 T, P, S				

(Continued)

table 8–2 ▪ *(Continued)*

Summary of Findings and Research Questions	Recommended Action Targeted to Findings	Who Is Responsible for the Action? T – Teacher S – Student P – Principal PA – Parent(s)	Who Needs to Be Consulted or Informed?	Who Will Monitor/ Collect Data?	Time Line	Resources
2.2 Academic failure						
2.3 Delinquency	Develop strategies to build a sense of "belonging" at school.					
3.0 What are some effective strategies to prevent student absenteeism?						
3.1 Student/ Parent/ Teacher/ Principal contracts	3.1 Implement contracts.	3.1 S, PA, T, P	3.1 S, PA	T, P: 1. Observations 2. Intentions 3. Surveys 4. Test data	Ongoing throughout school year.	
3.2 Daily planners	3.2 Purchase and use planners.	3.2 P				3.2 $$ for planners
3.3 Diagnostic tools	3.3 Work with district office to administer diagnostic tests.	3.3 P	3.3 District office			
3.4 Self-esteem strategies	3.4 Implement self-esteem curriculum.	3.4 T				
3.5 Improved teaching and curriculum	3.5 Encourage ongoing professional development.	3.5 T, P				3.5 $$ for P.D.

RESEARCH IN ACTION CHECKLIST 8–1

Steps to Action

_____ Findings of the research

_____ Recommended action

_____ Responsibilities

_____ Sharing findings with colleagues

_____ Ongoing monitoring (data collection)

_____ Time line for action

_____ Resources

This routinization of instruction still suggests that as a reflective teacher, you will continue to collect data—to monitor the effects of your instruction on your students' performance and attitude. At that point, as a self-renewing school faculty or as an individual teacher with a reflective professional disposition, you will continue your systematic inquiry into some other aspect of your practice. (See Research in Action Checklist 8–1 for a list of steps to action.)

Levels of Action Planning

Action planning can occur at a number of different levels within the school—*individual*, *team*, and *schoolwide*—depending on the scope of the action research effort. Action planning also may take place at a number of these different levels during a single investigation. For example, the problem under investigation may have had a schoolwide focus, such as to determine the effects of an innovative reading curriculum (with an emphasis on constructing meaning) on student performance (as measured by statewide assessment scores and monthly criterion-referenced tests). Participation in the schoolwide effort might also have necessitated that teachers meet in grade-level teams to plan appropriate reading interventions and to analyze regularly collected data. Finally, individual teachers would need to adapt the intervention as appropriate for their own students' needs. In this case, action planning should be undertaken at all levels within the school.

Individual

Typically, *individual action planning* will be characterized by teacher researchers who have worked through an action research cycle as part of a course, licensure, or grant requirement or by teacher researchers who are undertaking action research as a regular component of their practice. Individual teachers can still work through the Steps to Action Chart (see Table 8–1) and in so doing remind themselves of the steps that need to be taken to implement action and monitor the effects of the action.

In all likelihood, individual teacher researchers will have focused their action research projects and interventions on an issue related to curriculum, instruction, assessment, classroom management, or community involvement. In these areas, the resulting action plan will focus on activities such as the following:

- *Curriculum development.* Findings of a study related to curriculum development (and implementation) would provide the teacher researcher with specific actions for the next cycle of curriculum development (e.g., the inclusion of new and/or revised lessons), additional learning artifacts (resources and materials), and so on. Following the Steps to Action Chart, the individual teacher researcher would be responsible not only for all actions but also for consulting with grade-level colleagues, department heads, district-level curriculum specialists, parents, and the school principal.

- *Instructional strategies.* Findings of a study related to the implementation of new instructional strategies (e.g., cooperative learning, high-level questioning strategies, increase in "wait time," teaching reading across the curriculum, and so on) would provide the teacher researcher with specific actions for the next cycle of developing and implementing any new instructional strategies. Following the Steps to Action Chart, the individual teacher researcher would be responsible for all actions, including consulting with grade-level colleagues, department heads, district-level teaching specialists (e.g., a teacher on special assignment [TOSA]), parents, and the school principal. The teacher may identify specific additional professional development activities that need to be undertaken (and budgeted for) before the next action research cycle.

- *Assessment strategies.* Findings of a study related to the use of innovative assessment strategies (e.g., the Highland Park High School "Emphasizing Learning by Deemphasizing Grades" example in Chapter 7) would provide the teacher researcher with specific actions for the next cycle of implementing an innovative assessment strategy. Following the Steps to Action Chart, the individual teacher researcher would be responsible for all actions, including consulting with grade-level colleagues, department heads, district-level curriculum and instruction specialists, parents, and the school principal.

- *Classroom management strategies/plans.* A common area of focus for beginning teachers (preservice and in-service) is classroom management. Findings of a study related to implementation of a new classroom management plan would provide the teacher researcher with specific actions for the next cycle of teaching. Following the Steps to Action Chart, the individual teacher researcher would be responsible not only for all actions but also for consulting with grade-level colleagues, department heads, district-level curriculum and instruction specialists, parents, and the school principal.

- *Community involvement.* Findings of a study related to community involvement (e.g., Jack Reston's vignette at the start of this chapter) would provide the teacher researcher with specific actions for the next cycle of how to improve community involvement in solving local school problems. Following the Steps to Action Chart, the individual teacher researcher would be responsible for all actions, including consulting with grade-level colleagues, department heads, district-level curriculum specialists, parents, the school principal, and probably the district superintendent.

Blank Steps to Action Chart

Summary of Findings and Research Questions	Recommended Action Targeted to Findings	Who Is Responsible for the Action?	Who Needs to Be Consulted or Informed?	Who Will Monitor/ Collect Data?	Time Line	Resources

Although the primary audience for the findings from any of these studies is the individual teacher, it is important for teacher researchers to tap into the kind of support networks one will find at universities. As Elliott (1991) suggested,

> A small band of isolated teacher researchers can tap into a reflective counter culture in the form of an action-research network which transcends school boundaries and is linked to a teacher education institution. Membership of such a network can provide the kind of cultural resources which strengthen the capacity of aspiring teacher researchers to resist the time pressures operating on them from inside schools. (pp. 66–67)

This networking transcends not only school boundaries but also global boundaries via participation in online action research listservs and chat rooms. This kind of cyberspace network can strengthen the resolve of teachers who must work in isolation to continue with the process through the action planning stage and into the next revolution of the cycle.

Team

In an era when schools have increasing authority to make decisions about curriculum and instruction, it is common to see teams of teachers, administrators, and sometimes parents working collaboratively on action research projects. Often these groups grow out of networks developed in an action research course among teachers with similar areas of interest and expertise. At other times, they grow out of grant requirements for grade-level or discipline-based teams to work collaboratively on a school improvement focus. Regardless of the catalyst for the network, these **teams** all share a common focus at this stage in the action research process—to mobilize their collective energies to move forward with action. This process can be facilitated by working through the Steps to Action Chart and collaboratively determining who has responsibility for what, when, and where. Resolution of any issues that emerge at this stage is critical to the continued success and longevity of the action research team. At this stage, the primary audience for the action plan consists of the team members. However, action research teams must seek appropriate ways to transcend the traditional boundaries that have historically seen small teams of teachers burn out without feedback and support from the environments in which they work.

Schoolwide

Schoolwide action research, as the name implies, is about all of the members of the school community working together with a single goal in mind. For example, a schoolwide emphasis on improving reading, writing, or math is a common area of focus in elementary schools. Similarly, and sadly, it is not uncommon to see a high school focus on the effects of a drug and alcohol curriculum on student attitude, understanding, and levels of use. However, the distinguishing feature in these examples is that they have been agreed on by the whole school faculty as the focus for a schoolwide improvement effort that will be driven by the findings of an action research effort. Cooperation, collaboration, and communication are no less important in the action planning phase than they were during the other steps of the process.

The challenge at the schoolwide level is how to actively engage all the participants in goal setting that is integral to the action planning process. There will always be finger-pointing and denial, and it will take a skilled facilitator to move a faculty through the Steps to Action Chart if progress is to be made. Do not underestimate the necessity of meaningfully engaging all of the school community in this action planning process, or you will risk perpetual isolation in the world of playground supervision—been there, done that, bought the umbrella!

Action Should Be Ongoing

This discussion about action planning is not meant to suggest that action occurs only at the end of the action research process. The very dynamic nature of teaching necessitates that teachers make many changes to instruction during the course of a day based on the formative feedback (data) collected as an integral part of the teaching process. For example, preservice teachers are often requested to include on lesson plans "Evaluation" statements to the effect of "How will you know if your students have achieved your instructional objectives?" In other words, what data will you collect that informs your postplanning at the end of

Voices from the Field
Action Should Be Ongoing

In this vignette, the teacher researcher speaks passionately about how the findings of her study will lead to changes in her future instructional practices. Specifically, Rachelle plans to continue using formative assessments with her students as her study indicated that students performed better on their summative assessments, students better retain information, students do a better job of "keeping on track," and it resulted in an improved classroom climate. These are powerful insights for a beginning teacher who will continue to make changes in her classroom practices as a result of her action research.

ENHANCEDetext

video example 8–1
Rachelle, the action researcher in this video, found that giving weekly quizzes in her classes had a number of positive effects for the students. Would you agree with her statement that she has "completed" her action research project?

the day? Often these data are collected intuitively and informally in noninvasive ways. It is such a normative aspect of teaching that we take it for granted. As teachers, we have been programmed to collect, analyze, and interpret data quickly and efficiently so that we can suggest "findings" and take necessary "actions" (remediation, reteaching, related material, extension activities) that enable learning to proceed in a connected fashion.

The Importance of Reflection

Action planning is also a time for reflection—reflection on where you have been, what you have learned, and where you are going. Action planning and reflection give you an opportunity to identify your individual or collective continuing professional development needs. This reflection is facilitated by the review of the related literature you collected early in the action research process in concert with your own findings. The following questions may also be helpful prompts for reflection:

- What were the intended and unintended effects of your actions?
- What educational issues arise from what you'tve learned about your practice?

Clearly, these are not questions that elicit quick and easy responses. They urge you to look back at your practice from the enlightened viewpoint of someone who has

Voices from the Field
The Importance of Reflection

In this vignette, Jureen speaks eloquently about the importance of reflection for teachers. As she states, "With all research, answers lead to more questions!" For Jureen, this translates to new questions about emerging technologies and how they can effectively be used with and by students in an increasingly digital world. Given her previous action research experience, Jureen will be able to continue to reflect on her use of technology and to replicate her research in another context with a focus on emerging technologies and how they can effectively be integrated into classroom instruction.

ENHANCEDetext
video example 8–2
Jureen, the action researcher in this video, is very reflective about her project and about the important educational issue it addressed. It is clear that her action research project was very meaningful to her and that it changed the way she thinks about her own teaching.

systematically inquired into the effects of teaching on student outcomes. In undertaking such reflection, you will position yourself to act responsively to the findings of your study. The remaining sections of this chapter will help you to further identify challenges that you may face when attempting to implement change and will guide you in meeting those challenges and effecting positive educational change in your school.

Some Challenges Facing Teacher Researchers

As you reflect on the critical steps to action, consider the challenges that all teacher researchers face both when doing action research and when attempting to effect educational change based on the results of their inquiry. If indeed we are going to avoid living out Sarason's (1990) prophecy of "the more things change, the more they will remain the same" (p. 5), then we must be prepared to address these obstacles. These hurdles include a lack of resources, resistance to change, reluctance to interfere with others' professional practices, reluctance to admit difficult truths, the challenge of finding a forum to share what you have learned, and the difficulty of making time for action research endeavors.

Lack of Resources

The scarcity of resources is perhaps the greatest obstacle to action planning you will face. Many excellent action research and change efforts have been blocked by the lack of classroom resources and materials. But by being innovative and remaining energized by what you have learned about your practice, you will find ways to make change happen. This may mean using creativity to solve materials management issues. Don't wait for an administrator, central office person, or philanthropist to offer what you need to be successful. Go after the grants, however small, to fund the resources you identify as critical to the success of your intervention. (See Chapter 9 for further discussion of grant sources available for teacher researchers.) Use the data you have collected, analyzed, and interpreted as a way to build a case for resources that may be presented to Parent-Teacher Associations, district-wide committees, school boards, granting agencies, and so on to make a case for what you need.

Action researchers also need professional as well as material resources. If action research is to become a part of your professional disposition and be continued over time, it must benefit both your own continued professional development and student outcomes. Identification of promising practices will suggest the kinds of professional development you need to seek, either individually or collectively. If your local university or school district can't provide the professional development you seek, use the Internet to find out who does. Again, use your findings to make a compelling, persuasive case for the kind of professional development you need—not what someone else thinks you need.

Resistance to Change

Any type of change, however small, may be viewed as threatening by some. After all, the status quo is familiar and comfortable. But the era of schools that refuse to innovate is past. The ever-changing social and political environment in which we live necessitates that teachers become sophisticated instructional leaders and decision makers who have the skills to empower students and other individuals in their learning communities. Participation in and support of the action research process is critical if there is to be a shift in the culture of schools to the reflective practitioner culture of the self-renewing school. Living the commitment to a dynamic school culture as opposed to living the traditional "advocate of constraint" persona will go a long way toward revitalizing an individual school's culture and bringing about positive change.

For example, Jack Reston's investigation of the effect of the school/district policy on absenteeism showed that attendance rates had remained the same despite costly student incentives that were an integral part of the policy. Once he realized that the current intervention was having no impact, Jack knew he had to take responsibility for trying to change the system to make Eastview Elementary School an environment where all children (especially those at risk for absenteeism) would want to come to school. That meant changing even fundamental things, such as the way administrators interacted with students and the amount of time he spent with them individually. In doing so, he overcame several factors, including the institutional resistance to change.

Reluctance to Interfere with Others' Professional Practices

Unfortunately, there seems to be a prevailing cultural value in schools of "Don't mess around in someone else's professional practice"—especially if you are not invited. The dilemma here for the teacher researcher arises from a conflict between the desire to persuade colleagues to experiment with or embrace new practices that have been shown via action research to have positive effects and a "respect for the professional expertise of colleagues and their right to exercise authority within the confines of their own classroom" (Elliott, 1991, p. 59).

Often teacher researchers faced with this dilemma back away from their investigations and change efforts to "keep the peace" with colleagues. However, if we are to learn from our own and others' professional practice, we must be willing to set aside the traditional protection of each other's classrooms and to embrace as a community of learners the proposed action plan that emerges from our research.

How you approach this professional collaboration with other teachers in your school is as important as trying it at all. It is critical to the success of your action research and change efforts, particularly at the schoolwide level, not to have alienated yourself from others by appearing to be a member of some "enlightened elite" who now knows all of the answers to the problems that affect students' inability to do well on statewide assessments! You will have gone a long way to revitalizing the professional disposition of teaching if you have been able to nurture your own and your colleagues' understanding of the problems you have investigated and built a teamwide commitment to implementing action based on your findings. Collaboration can help break down these stubborn professional barriers.

Reluctance to Admit Difficult Truths

If we view action research and action planning as one way to empower teachers, we should also be aware of the increased accountability that these efforts place on teacher researchers. We can't have it both ways: If we want the authority to make the changes we have recommended based on our action research findings, then we must be prepared to look into the mirror and face what we see. After all, if each of us has the power to make the most important decisions in our schools—that is, the ones that have the greatest impact on students—then we must also not abdicate responsibility when things don't go our way. If what we learn is that, despite our best efforts and intentions, our interventions have not succeeded, then we must be prepared to look objectively at the data and make new recommendations for change in our quest to provide the best education possible for our students.

Voices from the Field
Reluctance to Interfere with Others' Professional Practices

In this vignette, our teacher researcher explains the challenges she faced conducting action research as a student teacher in her cooperating teacher's class. This is a common challenge for preservice teachers, as they try to collaborate with another teacher in all areas related to curriculum, instruction, assessment, and classroom management. This can be particularly problematic for a beginning teacher who is willing to systematically investigate the impact of his or her presence in a classroom on student outcomes and to share those outcomes. Further, the teacher researcher may need to decide what to share and what not to share with a colleague in order to sustain a collegial working relationship where action research and sharing of findings may not be the norm.

ENHANCEDetext

video example 8–3
As a "student" teacher, Rachelle had constraints on both the measures she could use in her action research and the kinds of action she could take. However, many teachers have similar experiences, especially when they are concerned about interfering with another teacher's professional practice.

For example, Deborah South (Chapter 1) had hoped to find in her action research project that the group of "unmotivated" students in her study skills class would respond positively to her instruction and guidance. Instead, she noticed an alarming and demoralizing trend: Students' grades were dropping. Deborah had to wrestle with this "difficult truth" and carefully consider her own responsibility for the students' performance before coming to a conclusion about the best way to effect change to benefit these "unmotivated" students.

Finding a Forum to Share What You Have Learned

The potential for an action plan to serve as the catalyst for reflective conversation between professionals is limitless. Elliott (1991) argued that such data sharing "promotes a reflective conversation and is at the heart of any transformation of the professional culture" (p. 60). However, an open conversation about what the data from the study suggest (analysis and interpretation) and how these findings have been transformed into a proposed action plan will not always be an easy one.

Voices from the Field
Finding a Forum to Share What You Have Learned

The teacher researchers in this vignette discuss how they plan to use a professional learning community (PLC) to collaboratively share the findings of their research. They also plan to use this forum as a way to develop future collaborative action research projects with a possible K–12 focus. Clearly, there are many face-to-face and virtual opportunities for teacher researchers to share their work. What is perhaps missing in schools is a culture of research and leaders who value classroom-based research. The research on professional learning communities is persuasive, and action research provides a process whereby individual, team-level, and school-level groups can and should work collaboratively to tackle important educational issues.

ENHANCEDetext

video example 8–4
The three action researchers in this video plan to share their findings with their colleagues in their teaching program. How might they find an even broader audience?

What is needed is a forum (local, national, or global!) for teachers to share their accounts and a recognition by the profession that change-oriented action research is an important part of the professional competencies of being a teacher. For example, some preservice teacher preparation programs are incorporating action research into their requirements. Individual schools are providing teachers with opportunities to showcase their action research skills as part of an annual teacher evaluation cycle, state and federal grants incorporate action research as part of the instructional improvement cycle, school-based decision-making teams are embracing an action research model to guide their school improvement efforts, and state teacher-licensing agencies are incorporating action research into continuing license renewal requirements.

Although teacher researchers typically have not published their findings, the sharing of teacher researchers' stories has also been facilitated by Web-based action research sites. Teachers can now use a global forum to share their stories, the actions they have taken based on their research, and what they have learned in subsequent action research cycles. (These online journals include *Educational Action Research*, *Networks*, *Action Research International*, and *Action Research Electronic Reader*.) The sharing of action plans and what teacher researchers learn in the process is critical to the emerging teacher-as-researcher culture. (See Chapter 9 for practical guidelines for "getting the word out.")

Voices from the Field
Make Time for Action Research Endeavors

The teacher researcher in this vignette makes a strong case for making action research a part of who you are as a professional educator and includes it as a set of proficiencies along with curriculum, instruction, assessment, and classroom management. She also makes the point that there is a time demand at the start of the process when you need to clarify your area of focus, research questions, and data collection strategies but that the process itself (data collection, data analysis, data interpretation, and action planning) can occur as a normative part of your teaching practice.

ENHANCEDetext
video example 8–5
In this video, Rachelle talks about some ways to make action research part of your daily life as a teacher. What other suggestions can you offer?

Making Time for Action Research Endeavors

We have already discussed the challenge of making time for action research in your busy daily schedule. Just when you thought the action research cycle was over and you are ready to return to "just teaching," you are thrust back into the process with further reflection about the actions suggested by the findings of your study and the who, what, and when of the next cycle.

"You mean I need to take more action and monitor its effects? But I don't have the time to do one more thing!" This exasperated call for putting the brakes on the process is not uncommon or unreasonable. By the time you have arrived at action planning, you may be all but spent and happy to claim that the status quo is working just fine. If you fall into this category of teacher, I would suggest that you follow your instincts. Allow yourself time to reflect and plan at a bearable pace. You are no good to the students in your care if you are burned out. (As the parent of a child in eleventh grade, the last thing I want is my child's teacher all worn out from a year of doing action research!) The goal is to evolve to the point where action and research become a part of your professional life but not at the expense of the energy that you need to be vital, creative, and exciting in your daily teaching. After all, if the action research process cannot be normative and undertaken without adversely affecting your primary focus of teaching children, then it *should not be done*.

On the other hand, if you have arrived at the action planning phase with renewed energy and enthusiasm for your work, if you are committed to implementing a locally contextualized innovation that you believe will contribute to the well-being of the students in your care, and if you have maintained a clear sense of direction, mission, and purpose, then move forward in the process and share your stories by whatever medium you can! It will be your stories of success and being a lifelong learner that will change the culture of teaching. These are intimate changes that cannot be forced on any of us from outside—they must come from the passion within.

Regardless of international, national, state, and local trends and initiatives, the individual teacher researcher's ability to resolve the issue of time constraints will ultimately determine whether action research is routinized into the classroom. However, if we as professionals cannot find time to do the work associated with it, then action research will be discarded on the dustheap of other promising educational initiatives.

Facilitating Educational Change

The goal of action research is to enhance the lives of students and teachers through positive educational change. We have just discussed several common challenges that teachers face when attempting to effect educational change based on action research findings. In addition to being prepared to address those challenges, you can help create an environment that is conducive to change. The following are eight conditions that facilitate educational change (adapted from Fullan, 1993; Miller & Lieberman, 1988; Sarason, 1990).

Teachers and Administrators Need to Restructure Power and Authority Relationships

The first condition for fostering action research and encouraging educational change is that teachers and administrators need to restructure power and authority relationships. Power relationships in schools have the potential to empower or underpower action planning efforts. **Power** is not being used in a pejorative sense here—teacher researchers have the potential to harness the collective power of their colleagues, including administrators, to bring about meaningful change through a democratic, liberating, and life-enhancing process. For this to happen, participants in the action research process must be prepared to ask the hard questions related to implementing action based on the findings of the study: What is the recommended action? Who is responsible for doing what? Who needs to be consulted or informed? How will the effects of the implementation be monitored? When will tasks be completed? What resources are needed?

Asking these questions invariably leads to discussions about who has the final decision-making power in the school. In an era of school-based decision making, it is likely that a team of teachers, parents, students, and administrators will have the authority to answer action planning questions and to make decisions. However, whether your school has a professional or a bureaucratic model of school-based decision making in place will determine the amount of influence you will have individually or as a team. According to Conley (1991), the bureaucratic model emphasizes the formal authority of administrators to delegate responsibilities to subordinates, to formulate rules to govern subordinate behavior, and to implement centralized control, planning, and decision making. In contrast, the professional model emphasizes the professional discretion and expertise of teachers in diagnosing and addressing student needs, with an aim to provide teachers the rights they expect as professionals.

Power should be seen as an investment, not as a means of controlling people. According to Miller and Lieberman (1988), "If we look at power this way, teachers and principals can hold leadership roles, and, working together, they can help the schools build a professional culture" (p. 653). This view emphasizes a reflective practitioner culture that empowers rather than underpowers teachers.

Deborah South was empowered, for example, to make changes to the study skills program for unmotivated students based on what she learned from her action research study. Jack Reston was empowered to change the absenteeism policy for his school and to recommend changes to the district's absenteeism policy based on his new understandings of what worked and didn't work for keeping children in school. Viewed in this way, power was an investment in the quality of the educational experiences of many children.

Both Top-Down and Bottom-Up Strategies of Change Can Work

In effecting educational change, both top-down and bottom-up strategies of change can work (Hord, Rutherford, Huling-Austin, & Hall, 1987). **Top-down strategies** can be thought of as changes that are mandated by school/district/state administrators without giving teachers an equal voice in the decision-making process (bureaucratic model). Alternatively, **bottom-up strategies** can be thought of as change that is driven by teachers when given the authority to make decisions (professional model). The debate over whether top-down or bottom-up efforts at change produce the greatest effects has flourished for many years. Fullan (1993) concluded, "What is required is a different two-way relationship of pressure, support and continuous negotiation" (p. 38), such as a continuous discourse between administrators and teachers involved in a collaborative action research project.

For example, the teachers at Highland Park High School worked collaboratively with the school's assistant principal and involved him in the team's action research activities. In this respect, there was obvious support from the school's administration for the action research effort. Alternatively, the teachers at Billabong Elementary School (Chapter 2) were quite resentful that the principal had mandated a math text for the school without consulting teachers in the process.

Teachers Must Be Provided with Support

Additionally, teachers involved in change efforts brought about by action research must be provided with support. Support for teachers in their endeavors ideally would come from all quarters: students, other teachers, the school administration, students' families, government officials, and so on. For example, Jack Reston's investigation into absenteeism could not have occurred had it not been for the support of the parents, teachers, and student teachers (who helped with interviews). Deborah South relied heavily on the emotional support of her critical friends in the action research class when she shared the analysis and interpretation of her study of unmotivated students.

Every Person Is a Change Agent

Both individual and collective efforts are critical to successful change, and every person has the potential to be a change agent. The action research vignettes in this book illustrate the potential for change to happen at the individual, team, and schoolwide levels. But perhaps the key point of all these examples is that it took the desire of an individual teacher or principal to initiate the action research process and to effect positive educational change based on the findings. As Fullan (1993) reminds us, "Each and every teacher has the responsibility to help create an organization capable of individual and collective inquiry and continuous renewal, or [change] will not happen" (p. 39).

Change Tends Not to Be Neat, Linear, or Rational

Equally important, those involved in action research must recognize that change tends not to be neat, linear, or rational. Consider as an example the work of Cathy Mitchell and the Duct Tape Theater (Chapter 3). Although Cathy was able to confirm

Voices from the Field
Every Person Is a Change Agent

In this vignette, the teacher researcher provides a good example of how change in her classroom is possible (locus of control) in spite of not being able to directly impact district-wide policy about a basal reading textbook adoption. Based on the outcomes of her study focused on gender bias in basal reading texts, Jeanette clearly explains how she plans to implement critical thinking questions and supplementary reading materials with her students. Change starts with individual teachers, and Jeanette's work may lead to future collaborative action research efforts targeting a common perceived problem.

ENHANCEDetext
video example 8–6
Jeannette, the action researcher in this video, studied the basal readers her district requires. In what ways can she be an agent of change? What constraints and challenges might she face?

that her objective of making teen theater a more meaningful experience was sound, she also recognized that the approach of interactive improvisation did not have the desired effects. The audience did not respond to the "Violence Improv" scene as she expected, and as a result, her action research project did not provide her with the tidy solutions she hoped for. Although recommitted to her goal, Cathy is still faced with figuring out new ways to make teen theater a more meaningful experience. For Cathy, the processes of action research and change will be recursive and cyclical.

Teacher Researchers Must Pay Attention to the Culture of the School

A sixth condition is that teacher researchers must pay attention to the culture of the school. Change efforts should always be viewed in the context of the culture of the school and classroom in which the action research effort is being conducted. For example, until Jack Reston investigated the effectiveness of his school's absenteeism policies, it was assumed that the current reward system of drawings and certificates was effective. Instead, he found that the reward system made no difference for at-risk students. As a result, he tried to isolate what intervention would make a difference to these children. He used surveys and interviews to attempt to thoroughly understand the culture, values, and belief systems of the families of children at risk for absenteeism. Based on his findings, he was able to recommend meaningful changes to the school's policy on absenteeism that specifically responded to the needs of this group, especially their need to feel connected to the school.

The Outcome of Any Change Effort Must Benefit Students

A somewhat obvious condition for doing action research and effecting educational change is that the outcome of any change effort must benefit students if it is to be continued. Action research can provide a method for recording, measuring, and analyzing the results of an educational practice or intervention. For example, as discussed in Chapter 5, the data collected by James Rockford in his study of the effectiveness of keyboarding software on the class word processing rate provided conclusive evidence that the keyboarding software being tested was very effective and that time spent on computers at schools was critical. These persuasive data gave James confidence in the benefits of this educational intervention and supported his recommendation that teachers take students to the computer lab every day, monitor keyboarding habits, and see that each student received a minimum of 10 minutes of practice per day.

Being Hopeful Is a Critical Resource

Finally, being hopeful is a critical resource if teachers are to perform action research and stay the course of change. Recall the words of Cathy Mitchell, whose teen theater action research project was described in Chapter 3:

The most important part of this project is that I felt renewed energy for my work. Last year at this time I was busily seeking a replacement for myself and announcing to everyone that I wasn't going to direct teens anymore. I didn't even consider that there was a problem that could be addressed and remedied. It feels really good to expect something to happen in my working life as a result of the research and reflection that I myself have done.

As a result of her action research inquiry, Cathy has created a powerful resource for herself—the hope that she will discover new ways to make her work meaningful for teens. Even though she once felt like quitting, she writes that this new hope is powerful enough to sustain her through future change efforts.

For educational change to be successful, all those involved must be optimistic about the results of the transformation. (Of course, they also need to be realistic: Being hopeful is not the same as being naïve.) Reform efforts can sometimes generate negative emotions and a sense of hopelessness because the individuals involved may be on the defensive from external attack or part of small groups of reformers suffering burnout (Fullan, 1997). But if we are going to make progress with reform efforts, we have to weather the negative emotions to succeed.

At the action planning stage of the action research process, you may again have to confront negative emotions from other stakeholders in the process. This is a critical turning point in the action research process: You can easily adopt the position that this is a lost cause, or you can rely on the most critical resource any of us have—*hope*. Individually, we all must take a stand on whether our investigations have yielded findings that warrant taking action. If we have done a good job, we should have collected findings that are trustworthy and true. Reflect on the hope you felt when you first began your project, then use that hope to sustain you through the action planning process. "Being hopeful and taking action in the face of important lost causes may be less emotionally draining than being in a permanent state of despair" (Fullan, 1997, pp. 231–232).

Recognize that we can do little to really change how a colleague thinks, acts, and feels—we must all answer to ourselves and the search for self-efficacy that comes with being a professional educator. If any of us reach a point in our professional lives when we feel that we can no longer make a difference or no longer struggle in the face of adversity (e.g., limited time or resources), then it is probably time to try another professional calling. In education, whether it's a lack of chalk, paper, or RAM for the computer, none of us have ever had a blank check to finance the time and resources we think we need to be the best we can be. But what sets us apart from other professionals is the belief that we can make a difference in children's lives, with or without the resources.

Schools are complex social settings, and those of us who have taught at a number of different schools know how they can differ from community to community. You are in the best position to know what lessons you can apply from this broad discussion of educational change to your own situation, but we can all learn from each other's experience by sharing our stories. Whenever possible, share your action research stories with others. In doing so, you will help revitalize the professional disposition of teachers.

What Do Teachers Gain Through All of This Work?

If you are now living this process, perhaps in a quiet, unassuming way, what follows will validate your work as a professional—contribute to your sense of self-efficacy—for it is within that we all find the rewards that teaching has to offer. Returning to our earlier discussion about critical/postmodern perspectives of action research, you will recall that what we believe as a professional community and what we as individual teacher researchers have gained through all of this work has systematically guided us to action.

Having invested a great deal of time and energy into investigating the taken-for-granted relationships and practices in your professional life, you have now arrived at the point where the "rubber meets the road." Will you really initiate action and continue the process? If you answer in the affirmative, you have gone a long way toward embracing some of the tenets of a socially responsive approach to research: You have engaged in a democratic process that has encouraged the participation of your colleagues. The process has been equitable, with the participants all having one voice. The experience has been liberating and has freed you from accepting with blind faith something that may have been forced on you. Finally, the experience has been life enhancing for you as a professional and for the students who will benefit from your teaching.

Voices from the Field
What Do Teachers Gain Through All of This Work?

As the teacher researcher in this vignette asserts, no matter where she teaches, she will be better prepared to tackle problems because of the skills she has learned through the action research process. This is an important takeaway for action researchers: No matter what challenges they confront in their teaching careers, action research provides a systematic, disciplined, step-by-step process for moving forward and contributing to our collective understandings about what works in schools.

ENHANCEDetext
video example 8–7
In this video, Jeannette reflects on what she gained from her research project.

For me, the ultimate payoff for teacher researchers who have stuck with the process, have learned and internalized the action research skills, and are now committed to action and self-renewal is the belief and knowledge that the real beneficiaries of your work are the students in your care. There can be no argument against this powerful and altruistic goal.

SUMMARY

Developing Action Plans

1. Action planning is an effort to answer the question, "Based on what I have learned from my research, what should I do now?" Without action, we have done nothing more than replicate what we set out to avoid—doing research on someone for our own benefit, whatever that may be. But the reward for all of us in this process is taking action to improve the educational experiences of our children—action is at the very heart of the action research endeavor.

2. To facilitate the action planning process, consider using a Steps to Action Chart that addresses issues related to what you as a teacher researcher have learned (findings), what recommended action targets a given finding, who is responsible for specific actions (responsibility), who needs to be consulted or informed about the findings of the study and the concomitant actions, how you will monitor the effect of your actions by collecting data, on what dates the actions and monitoring will occur, and what resources will be needed to carry out the action (see Tables 8–1 and 8–2).

3. Action planning can occur at a number of different levels within the school: individual, team, and schoolwide.

4. Individual action planning is done by teacher researchers who have worked through an action research cycle and can still work through a Steps to Action Chart and, in so doing, remind themselves of the steps that need to be taken to implement action and monitor the effects of the action.

5. Team action planning is most commonly done by teams of teachers, administrators, and sometimes parents working collaboratively on action research projects. An action research team shares a common focus at this stage in the action research process—to mobilize their collective energies to move forward with action.

6. Schoolwide action research is about all of the members of the school community working together with a single goal in mind. The challenge at the schoolwide level is how to actively engage all the participants in goal setting that is integral to the action planning process.

7. Action planning, at all levels, is also a time for reflection—reflection on where you have been, what you have learned, and where you are going. Action planning and reflection give you an opportunity to identify your individual or collective professional development needs.

Some Challenges Facing Teacher Researchers

8. Some of the challenges faced by action researchers who seek to implement positive educational change include lack of resources, resistance to change, reluctance to interfere with others' professional practices, reluctance to admit difficult truths, difficulty of finding a forum to share what you have learned, and lack of time for action research endeavors.

Facilitating Educational Change

9. Eight factors for facilitating educational change in a school environment are that (1) teachers and administrators need to restructure power relationships; (2) both top-down and bottom-up strategies for change can work; (3) teachers involved in change efforts brought about by action research must be provided with support; (4) every person is a change agent; (5) those involved must recognize that change tends not to be neat, linear, and rational; (6) teacher researchers must pay attention to the culture of the school; (7) the outcome of any change effort must benefit students to be continued; and (8) being hopeful is a powerful resource.

What Do Teacher Researchers Gain Through All of This Work?

10. The ultimate payoff for teacher researchers who have stuck with the action research process, have learned and internalized the action research skills, and are now committed to action and self-renewal is the belief and knowledge that the real beneficiaries of your work are the students in your care. There can be no argument against this powerful and altruistic goal.

TASKS

1. Develop an action plan based on your action research findings and present it using the Steps to Action Chart format.
2. How would you apply what you have learned about the challenges of implementing educational change to overcome potential obstacles that you may encounter in taking action?

Writing Up
Action Research

After reading this chapter you should be able to:

9.1 Describe the value of writing about action research.

9.2 Utilize strategies for writing about action research.

9.3 Describe guidelines for submitting your action research write-up for publication.

There is little point to writing up qualitative research if we cannot get anyone to read what we have to report, and no point to research without reporting.

(Wolcott, 2001, p. 7)

*P*erhaps one of the most difficult tasks confronting teacher researchers is finding the time and inclination to commit to paper what they have learned about their area of focus. For university researchers who live in a "publish or perish" world, the motivation to write up and publish their research is far more extrinsic. However, teacher researchers are more concerned about the pressures and complexities of daily classroom life—after all, their number one priority is the planning, implementation, and evaluation of engaging learning experiences for the children in their classrooms.

Still, teacher researchers can help fellow teachers as well as themselves by writing about action research in a prescribed way—in an organized report. Think of this last step as helping to close the gap that has historically existed between research and practice. It is important to be familiar with a form that is most commonly accepted for publication in journals and certainly for satisfying traditional university course requirements.

There are two primary motivations for writing up your action research:

1. *The act of writing helps each of us better understand the story we are trying to tell.*
2. *A written account provides us with a permanent, accessible record for our professional and personal use.*

Many of my students find themselves writing not by choice but by mandate (you may well be in the same situation!). In fact, some of you may see the very act of writing up your studies as unpleasant—just one more term paper to complete, another hoop to jump through. On the other hand, you may not mind writing but still may be frustrated by some of the nuts-and-bolts issues associated with writing and finding an audience for your work. Read on! I can't guarantee that the outcome of your writing journey will be publication in a prestigious journal or text. I can guarantee, however, that if you invest the time and energy into writing your research story, you will at least benefit your students as well as give yourself the opportunity to have it read by like-minded folks. And what could be more altruistic than helping other teachers help their students? What's that saying about if a tree falls in the forest and nobody hears it, did it make a sound? The same is true for writing up our research efforts. If you don't share your stories, how will anyone know you ever did anything that contributed to the teachers' body of knowledge?

Before our discussion about formally writing about your action research, we need to discuss the value of writing up your action research experience and findings.

Why Should I Formally Write About My Action Research?

Perhaps one of the most difficult concepts I have to "sell" to teacher researchers is the importance of "writing up" their research efforts; they struggle to see the value of it. These teachers are focused on understanding the impact of what they do in classrooms and on how and what their students learn. In short, these professional teachers are committed to improving their own practice but do not necessarily see the purpose of sharing what they have learned with a wider audience. Often teacher researchers have declared to me,

> I developed my action plan based on what I learned. . . . I am making a difference in my own classroom for my own kids. What does it matter if somebody else reads about what I did and learned?
>
> Writing up what I have done and trying to publish the story is not rewarded or recognized as important by my school and district. Why bother if nobody cares?

Again, this is a difficult argument to win when one argues on the basis of giving back to the profession and contributing to the knowledge base, and blah, blah, blah! Yet as members of a profession, we have to get beyond the point that writing up research is something that is done by academics in ivory towers.

The value in writing up your research is that the process of writing requires the writer to clarify meaning—to choose words carefully, thoughtfully describe that which is experienced or seen, reflect on experiences, and refine phrasing when putting words on a page. You may learn something important about your students and their learning—something you may have missed had you not considered your words on the page—as you formally write about your research. Furthermore, the act of putting information on paper for your peers necessitates honesty, accuracy, clarity, and thought, thereby encouraging you to create a better product than if you had simply made a mental note of your action research as you left school at the end of the day. So keep this reason in mind as you engage in this writing phase of your research:

- *Clarification.* Writing your research requires clarity and accuracy of expression. Writing about your research activities encourages thought and reflection and perhaps creates new questions that are resolved, a process that shapes and completes your research.

Other reasons to write up your research include the following:

- *Validation.* Publishing your research and the feedback you will receive from your reviewers and readers will validate who you are as a professional educator and what you do.
- *Empowerment.* Reflecting on your practices through writing will empower you to continue to challenge the status quo and be an advocate for your children.
- *It is generative.* Writing is a generative activity that culminates in a product, something tangible that you can share with colleagues, supervisors, and parents.
- *Accomplishment.* Writing up your research will provide you with a sense of accomplishment. It is both humbling and exciting when colleagues read your work and compliment you on your accomplishments!

Format and Style

Format refers to the general pattern of organization and arrangement of the research report. The number and types of headings and subheadings to be included in the report are determined by the format used. Style refers to the rules of grammar, spelling, capitalization, punctuation, and word processing followed in preparing the report. Formats may vary in terms of specific headings included, and research reports generally follow a format that parallels the steps involved in conducting a study. For example, although one format may call for a discussion section and another format may require a summary or conclusions and a recommendations section (or both), all formats require a section in which the results of the study a discussed and interpreted. All research reports also include a condensed description of the study, whether it be a summary of a dissertation or an abstract of a journal article.

Most colleges, universities, and professional journals either have developed their own required style manual or have selected one that must be followed. Check with your instructor about the style used in your institution. Do this before beginning writing, because rearranging a format after the fact is tedious and time consuming. One such manual, which is increasingly being required as a guide for theses and dissertations, is the *Publication Manual of the American Psychological Association* (American Psychological Association, 2009), also called the *APA Style Manual* (currently in its sixth edition). If you are not bound by any particular format and style system, the APA manual is recommended, as it is the most widely accepted academic format and style system used by colleges, universities, and journals. In addition to acquiring and studying a copy of the selected manual, it is also very helpful to study several reports that have been written following the same manual. For example, look at existing action research write-ups to get an idea of format and what is expected. To the degree possible (e.g., with respect to tables, figures, references, and student examples of tasks), this text you are reading reflects APA guidelines, as does the following discussion. Are you sold on the idea of writing? If so, let's forge ahead with examining an example of an action research article.

Sample Annotated Action Research Article

The following research article is reprinted here so that you may examine the general structure and components of written action research. I hope that you will refer to this example frequently as you write your first action research report. Just as you'tve been trained to observe your students, be observant as you read the following article and consciously note the various components of this written report: the headings, some of the phrases that are characteristic of particular sections of the write-up, and the meaning of each section. As you will soon see (or perhaps you came to this realization earlier), the organization of an action research write-up is not rocket science. In fact, the sections that follow predictably mirror the core chapters of this text and the Steps in the Action Plan: the Area of Focus Statement, Research Questions, Review of Literature, Data Collection, Data Analysis, and the Action Plan. (Look at the Contents of this text—look familiar?)

Now that you'tve seen a sample of something you might produce, let's discuss some nuts-and-bolts ideas on writing up action research.

"Come to My Web (Site)," Said the Spider to the Fly: Reflections on the Life of a Virtual Professor

Geoff Mills

This paper was presented at the Third Conference of the Self-Study in Teacher Education Practices group at Herstmonceux Castle, East Sussex, England, July 2000, and is included in the proceedings for the conference.

Abstract

Intervention or Innovation ➔

The purpose of this paper is to share the results of a 2-year study that focused on the effects of teaching action research via a web-based class. In a market-driven economy in which many universities now find themselves, web-based delivery of education classes has become increasingly popular. This paper will share the findings of a study that looked at the experiences of teaching and learning action research in a web-based environment.

Introduction

In recent years, Oregon universities have moved to decrease the amount of "satellite" time associated with distance learning classes and to increase the amount of support made available to students "on-line." As a result of the Learning Anywhere, Anytime Project (LAAP) grant by the Oregon University System, the Education Department at Southern Oregon University is pioneering the development and implementation of completely web-based graduate classes in education. This paper is based on my experiences of teaching a web-based version of action research for two terms in 2 consecutive years.

Context ➔

The Action Research course is a 10-week introductory, graduate level class focused on the development, implementation, and evaluation of action research. One of the goals of the web-based class is to maximize the interaction between the instructor and the students, and among the students. In order to encourage this interaction, students "post" their responses to weekly tasks as well as respond to other students in the class. Additionally, the class utilizes a listserv and a discussion board (chat room). In order to complete the course, students are required to write a review of related literature, respond to weekly postings and tasks, and complete an action research project. Students register for the class and request a copy of the required text by calling a toll-free number or registering on-line. The course is based around the text *Action Research: A Guide for the Teacher Researcher* (Mills, 2000) and is supplemented with PowerPoint presentations that can be downloaded from the course web site. A complete overview of the class can be accessed at the following URL using the password "research" to enter the class: http://www.collegecourse.com/sou/ed/ed519/.

Action research involves teacher researchers in a four-step process that includes the following: identifying an area of focus, data collection, data analysis and interpretation, and action planning. In doing action research, teacher researchers have developed solutions to their own problems and as such are the authoritative voices as to what works in their particular settings. They exhibit a professional disposition that is encapsulated in their willingness to challenge the taken-for-granted assumptions that influence their daily instructional practices. By modeling the action research process for my graduate education students, I believe that I am able to nurture the development of a teacher researcher professional disposition and, in some ways, to demystify the process. My students are able to witness the development of an emerging action research project that involves them in the data collection process. They are also able to see a teacher who is committed to improving his own teaching through the use of an action research model. For many of my students, this is a revelation in itself—that someone who teaches at a university would actually want to improve his practice! Therefore, this paper is structured using the action research conceptual framework I use to teach action research: The Dialectic Action Research Spiral.

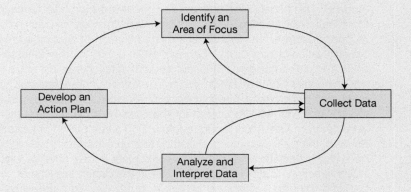

Area of Focus Statement

Area of Focus Statement →

The purpose of this study was to describe the effects of web-based instruction in a distance learning action research class on student outcomes and attitudes. This area of focus statement satisfies my central tenets of action research in that it involves teaching and learning, is something that is within my locus of control, is something I feel passionate about, and is something I would like to change or improve (Mills, 2000, p. 27).

Research
Questions →

Research Questions

1. What is the effect of web-based instruction on students' communication with each other? With the instructor?
2. How do students' learning styles affect their success in a web-based class?
3. How do on-line resources meet students' needs to access course materials?

Review of Related Literature

Literature
Review →

As an expatriate Australian, I am positively predisposed to distance learning. As a young teacher in a small rural "outback" town in Australia, my only option for continuing my education was via correspondence education. In the United States, correspondence education is not widely accepted as an acceptable form of education by those of us working in universities. But why is this the case when other developed countries (like Australia!) have wide acceptance of distance learning via correspondence? I believe that this issue gets to the heart of the propositions many of us hold about effective pedagogy, whether it is in a live or web-based learning environment, and provides the framework for the related literature to be considered here.

There is a dearth of literature that addresses what is for me one of the most critical aspects of classroom learning environments—the nature and quality of the interaction between teachers and students, and between students and other students. This pedagogical concern can be viewed in broader terms to include "the identification of learning goals, philosophical changes in teaching and learning, reconceptualization of the teacher's role, evaluation of student and instructor, and the stimulation of interactivity" (Schrum, 1998, p. 56). In order to foster interaction in a virtual classroom, Berge (1999) points out that teachers must utilize interactions of a synchronous (communication occurs in real time) or asynchronous (technologically mediated in time) nature. I taught my action research class based on an asynchronous model—students who registered for the class could take it anywhere, anytime— although they were encouraged to follow a 10-week outline of tasks and activities. Similarly, the class was characterized by asynchronous communication—there was never the expectation that the class would meet in "real time" or with any face-to-face interaction. But as I will discuss later in this paper, this kind of communication provided me with a significant challenge in the way I developed rapport with my students. Levin (1997) characterizes this challenge in the following way:

> I can neither see the puzzlement in an online learner's eyes or the "aha" twinkle when a student gets the point. One of the attractions of asynchronous computer mediated communication also poses another challenge: anytime, anywhere, but alone. If you believe as I do that learning should be viewed as the social construction of meaning and knowledge, then this isolation poses a stiff challenge to learning. Online learning is conducted largely within text. (p. 6)

As you will see, I find this inability to see the twinkle of my students' eyes a drawback in my ability to develop a rapport and understanding of the complex worldviews they bring to the learning environment. However, there is little evidence in the literature to suggest that students of web-based instruction (WBI) classes perform differently compared with traditional classes.

Teachers and students who participate in WBI classes appear to hold somewhat contrasting views of the distance learning experience that are challenging to reconcile. For example, faculty are consistently concerned about the quality of the teaching/learning experience and the degree of interactivity that occurs. Alternatively, students are generally positive about the experience and report that the convenience of this medium meets the needs of the nontraditional (distance learning) student who balances work, family, and study (Daugherty & Funke, 1998). The same study reports that faculty perceptions of WBI can be categorized as follows: lack of technical support, lack of software/adequate equipment, lack of faculty/administrative support, the amount of preparation time required to create and grade assignments, and student lack of knowledge and resistance to the technology. Alternatively, students tend to acknowledge the utility of the Internet and the "discovery" learning that occurred through the use of Internet resources and, according to Daugherty and Funke (1998), "appeared genuinely impressed by the variety and quality of the learning materials offered via the Web" (p. 30). In an earlier study, Harasim (1987) reported an even greater list of perceived advantages of on-line learning, from an increased interaction in quantity and intensity to motivational aspects related to text-based communication (p. 124). Students value being able to communicate in a text-based environment to a far greater degree than they would in a traditional live class—a finding that is supported in my own study and to which I will speak later in this paper.

Data Collection

Qualitative data collection techniques were used as the primary research methods for this study. However, the traditional ethnographic technique of "participant observer" was limited to written communication and postings at the course listserv and discussion board (chat room). The only time I met with students "face-to-face" was in the rare instance when a student drove to the university to talk to me, or when I interviewed the students at the end of the course. There was never an opportunity to observe the students in their own learning environments at home (where all of the students "attended" the course).

Data
Collection

Data Sources

- *Surveys*—Students filled out surveys throughout the class in order to provide insights into their experiences during the term in which the class was taught and follow-up surveys during which time they reflected on their experience in the class and its application to their regular teaching environment.

- *Interviews*—Following the surveys, students were invited to meet with me to further discuss their experiences throughout the class. As Agar (1980) suggests, information from interviews can serve as the "methodological core" against which observational data can be used to "feed" ongoing informal interviews. The interviews can best be categorized as informal ethnographic interviews that allowed me to inquire into the experiences of the students in the on-line class and to follow-up on comments individual students had made in response to survey items.
- *Matrix*—All of the listserv postings were printed and analyzed in terms of the number of postings and the types of communication that were occurring. This constant "lurking" on the Web was a valuable data source.
- *Artifacts*—Students submitted final action research projects in "display" form, which varied from multi-media presentations posted to the course's web page to audio and video presentations with accompanying poster boards.

Data Analysis and Interpretation

The following themes emerged from the analysis of the surveys, interviews, observations, and students' projects.

Theme ➞ *The Frequency and Type of Communication*

The frequency and types of communication varied considerably throughout the length of the course. Frequently, students reported being "overwhelmed" with the volume of e-mail that was an integral part of the weekly class participation. Although not every e-mail required a response from the instructor, like the students in the class, I found the daily task of responding to e-mail quite daunting.

Theme ➞ *The Benefits and Drawbacks of Listserv Communication*

Students considered the benefits of listserv communication as follows:

- Comfort level of being able to give feedback in an on-line setting. Many students expressed high levels of satisfaction with being able to give and receive feedback without feeling pressured to "talk" in class.
- Frequency of responses individual students received appeared related to their area of focus and the frequency of responses they made to other students in the class, that is, if the content area was something a number of students had in common, they tended to gravitate toward each other. The matrix of frequency and kinds of responses indicated that quiet students received less feedback on their projects.

Students considered the drawbacks of listserv communication as follows:

- The overwhelming volume of e-mail messages. It did not appear to matter whether there were 10 or 20 students registered in the class—both groups described the volume of e-mail as "overwhelming."

- Delay in receiving feedback. Some students expressed frustration with not receiving "immediate" feedback from the instructor and/or colleagues in the class.
- Lack of nonverbal cues. A number of students requested that we "post" digital photographs so that we could "put a face with a name." There appeared to be interest in getting to know each other but a virtual classroom environment was not the ideal setting for establishing rapport.

Related to the use of the listserv and e-mail was the use of a discussion board (chat room) during the second offering of the class. My intent in implementing the discussion board was to cut down on the frequency and total number of e-mail postings. However, the use of the chat room appeared to cause more problems than it solved due to technical problems of access to the discussion board. Students were given the option of using one communication network or the other. Ultimately, this did not work and caused a division in the class that challenged the continuity of the communication among all students.

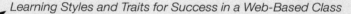

Learning Styles and Traits for Success in a Web-Based Class

The completion rate for students in the first offering of the class was 50% and increased to 63% in the second offering. I believe that this completion rate raises questions about matching students' learning styles with the medium of instruction. For example, my traditional "live" offerings of this action research class average about an 85% completion rate. The majority of students (70%) indicated that if traveling distance to the university was not a factor, they would have preferred a "live" class.

Themes

On-Line Resources

Students indicated a high level of satisfaction with the availability and quality of on-line resources available on the Internet. However, there were some students who expressed concern about the "black hole" of time that accompanied searching for materials on the Web. Similarly, students who were new users ("newbies") expressed concern about the amount of time it took for them to acquire the skills to search the Internet in an effective and efficient manner.

Action Plan ➤ *Action Plan*

Based on the themes that have emerged from this study, I plan to make the following changes in the future offerings of my web-based, distance learning action research:

- Restructure the class tasks so that the interaction between students, and between the students and the instructor, are manageable. Any future use and implementation of the chat room strategy would have to come with an assurance that *all* students would be able to access the discussion board. This is critical for effective communication—perhaps the one aspect of a web-based learning environment that is critical to success.

- Learning styles—Although there appears to be a dearth of literature that discusses the importance of students' learning styles as they relate to web-based learning, I believe that it is critical that students are somehow screened in order to determine the likelihood that they will succeed in a virtual classroom environment. For example, in future offerings of the class I will interview all students prior to giving permission to register for the class to determine their comfort level with (a) the use of computers and the Internet, and (b) their comfort level with being an independent, "self-starter" learner who can work on tasks in a relatively self-directed fashion. I will try to identify an instrument that can assist with this task and for which there is predictive validity.
- On-line resources—I will continue to explore the use of on-line resources to facilitate independent teacher research, such as supporting students' efforts to retrieve copies of journal articles, which is an otherwise expensive activity.
- Rapport building—In order to build rapport with my students, and between students, I will include an interactive, face-to-face communication facilitated by distance learning technologies. Rapport may also be facilitated by the use of cameras mounted on the top of computers. Finally, I will incorporate the use of a dial-up teleconference during which time students can present their term projects. For example, students could "post" their projects to the listserv, which could then be downloaded prior to a designated class session. Using a toll-free university phone tree, students could participate in a teleconference and be able to scroll through each other's projects during a presentation. All of these strategies will function to facilitate the development of rapport and decrease feelings of isolation.

Final Thoughts

As I mentioned earlier, I am positively predisposed to distance learning modalities. I believe that it addresses issues of equity and access to education for all. This is particularly true at my university, which provides services to many teachers working in rural communities.

However, with spiraling tuition costs, many of these teachers also question whether or not they are getting "value for money" when they choose to learn in isolation. Do equity and access equal good pedagogy? How is it that on-line courses maintain the integrity of a graduate education? What characteristics distinguish an on-line course from a correspondence course? This study has raised more questions for me than it has answered. I am challenged by the opportunities that current distance learning modalities offer and strive to balance issues of equity and access against quality. Ultimately, perhaps, the responsibility for choosing to learn via an on-line environment rests with the learner. Similarly, the responsibility for overcoming some of the inherent problems associated with teaching in an on-line environment must rest with the teacher. Through the implementation of an action research approach, I have reflected on the limitations of teaching in a web-based environment and am committed to address them in future class offerings.

References

References

Agar, M. (1980). *The professional stranger: An informal introduction to ethnography.* Orlando, FL: Academic.

Berge, Z. (1999). Interaction in post-secondary web-based learning. *Educational Technology, 39*(1), 5–11.

Daugherty, M., & Funke, B. L. (1998). University faculty and student perceptions of web-based instruction. *Journal of Distance Education, 13*(1), 21–39.

Harasim, L. (1987). Teaching and learning on-line: Issues in computer-mediated graduate courses. *CJCE, 16*(2), 117–135.

Levin, D. (1997). *Institutional concerns: Supporting the use of Internet discussion groups.* ED 416481.

Mills, G. E. (2000). *Action research: A guide for the teacher researcher*. Upper Saddle River, NJ: Merrill.

Schrum, L. (1998). On-line education: A study of emerging pedagogy. *New Directions for Adult and Continuing Education, 78*, 53–61.

Rituals and Writing

One of my favorite books on writing is Howard Becker's (1986) *Writing for Social Scientists: How to Start and Finish Your Thesis, Book, or Article.* As Becker points out, many writers hold certain irrational rituals as necessary precursors to the act of writing:

> From one point of view, my fellow participants (in the writing workshop) were describing neurotic symptoms. Viewed sociologically, however, those symptoms were magical rituals. According to Malinowski (1948, pp. 25–36), people perform such rituals to influence the result of some process over which they think they have no rational means of control. (p. 3)

A survey of friends and colleagues suggested that the following magical rituals were powerful predictors of successful writing sessions. How do they compare with your own?

- Writing can only occur between the hours of 7:00 a.m. and 12:00 p.m.
- At least six sharpened pencils and a yellow legal pad must be in place next to the computer.
- Writing can only be done longhand using a blue pen and white legal pad.
- The house must be clean before writing starts.
- Everything must be in order (materials, lighting, soft music, etc.) before writing can commence.

Establishing a Writing Routine

There is no easy way around the pragmatic issue of time—writing takes time, and we never have enough time to do all that we have to do, professionally and personally. The only advice I can offer here is to somehow make writing part of your professional life and responsibility. Capture the minutes and hours where they fall—before school, after school, preparation periods, canceled faculty meetings, failed parent conferences, and professional development days. Argue for the time as part of your faculty meetings and professional development days—and be prepared to ante up when asked to share the outcome of your efforts.

I know of no other way besides attacking personal family time to get my writing done. In the short term, our loved ones will put up with "I need to stay home and get this writing (or grading, lesson planning, or test development tasks that teachers take home) done. You go ahead and enjoy the movie (dinner, picnic, hike, river rafting, skiing)." We could all fill in the blanks based on our professional life as a teacher.

However you make it happen, I am assuming that there will come a time when you sit down in front of a keyboard or with a blank pad of paper and start the task of writing up your action research. I can picture you now—pencil in hand, keyboard at the ready—poised to pen the story of your action research! Go to that place for a while. Get ready to write!

In the spirit of sharing tips for successful writing, see Figure 9–1 for some tips on what *not to do*. You might identify with some of these.

figure 9–1 ▪ Geoff's Tips for Being Able to Avoid Writing

- Think about all the things at school that I need to do before tomorrow.
- Scan my desk to see if someone has left me a note about a meeting, sports practice, birthday party that I need to go to NOW.
- Check my voicemail.
- Check my e-mail.
- Check my checkbook to see if it is balanced.
- Call my wife/child/colleague/friend/enemy to see what they are doing.
- Walk down the hallway to see if I can find someone to talk to.
- Dream about winning the lottery.
- Make an appointment to see my dentist.

On a more practical note, here are some guidelines for writing and editing:

- Write at the same time every day, a time when you know you won't be disturbed.
- Write up your story as though you're sending an e-mail to a friend. Pretend that your friend needs it explained in simple terms.
- Tell a story as you write. Most teachers are good storytellers. Whether it is telling third graders about Columbus's voyages, how chicks hatch in an incubator, or an embarrassing incident that occurred "way back when" when you were in school, teachers are compelling storytellers who can capture the imagination of their students. This is true regardless of the content matter. These skills can be transferred to the way in which we share our action research stories. And I do not use the term *storyteller* in a pejorative sense here—storytellers can still employ rigor in their work.
- If you're having trouble getting started, "write it the way you talk." The editing can come later. Tell your story with an audience of colleague teacher researchers in mind, and the words will flow naturally. If you get hung up on writing for a larger "academic" audience, the words will not come easily, and sentences may be stilted and formal. There is also no reason to use big words.
- Organize your thoughts around an outline and tell your story in a way that stays true to the facts of your study. Make it coherent and make sure your story flows.
- In the early stages, don't worry too much about how well the text reads or whether it is full of grammatical errors. Write without consideration for grammar, syntax, or punctuation—just write. Concentrate on getting the story out. Look for progress, not perfection.
- Write whatever comes to mind. Then go back and hunt for what you are really trying to say—it's there.
- Have you ever thought to yourself, "I wish I had done that differently"? Writing is like that, and then you get to do it differently—editing your own work is a delight. Write boldly and then say it again—better.
- Writing, then editing, then rewriting, and then reediting clarifies thoughts into a coherent package. Even a gem needs to be mined roughly, cut ruthlessly, then buffed.
- Nobody knows my work better than I do. Writing is an exercise in learning about your own work. I'm always surprised how much better I know it when I've discussed it with my computer a few times.
- Edit after you have all your thoughts on paper. I may be a poor writer, but I am a fast writer! I churn out words faster than you can imagine. The problem is they take a lot of editing, wordsmithing, revising, rethinking, and replacing along the way. What you see here is not my first draft—or my last. It also has benefited from the collective wisdom and skills of a development editor, copy editors, people with Ph.D. degrees in English and literature, and friends who are pretty good writers. In short, as readers of research, we should not hold ourselves to unrealistic expectations of grandeur. Any of us can write well given the

time, effort, and assistance needed to produce "good" writing. Set realistic expectations for yourself somewhere between "The first draft is the last draft!" and "This will never be perfect—I'll just stick with it for another few years!"

- If you accept that your first draft is not your last draft, living with mediocre text becomes easier to accept. Put another way,

> The only way I can get anything written at all is to write really, really sh— first drafts. . . . All good writers write them. This is how they end up with good second drafts and terrific third drafts. (Lamott, cited in Wolcott, 2001, p. 55)

I am sure that you can add to these lists with your own rituals and tips. My advice to you is consistent with the advice I once gave to my third-grade students when teaching them to play the recorder: "Make as much noise as you want to for the next 2 minutes. Get it out of your system. When the time is up, we will focus on playing the music on the page. Go ahead and blow!" A suggestion: Write down your avoidance list and stick it next to wherever it is that you write. Check it occasionally but get the behaviors out of your system. Consider it therapeutic and try and catch yourself being "good," that is, staying on task with your writing. Think of a little reward system (if you are somewhat extrinsically motivated like me, that is). Here are a few things I "treat" myself to when I have dedicated myself to some writing time (not in order of preference): a run, time to play with my son and wife,

Voices from the Field
Establishing a Writing Routine

The teacher researcher in this vignette provides support for the other suggestions in this chapter and the importance of establishing a writing routine. For example, she dedicated some time every day to keep up with field notes and data analysis rather than waiting until later in the process to reflect on her data. Similarly, she "wrote as she went" and in so doing found the writing to be manageable. Finally, at the end of the process, she dedicated a block of time to read, reflect, and edit her work without other interruptions. There is no substitute for scheduling time to write!

ENHANCEDetext
video example 9–1
Jureen, the action researcher in this video, describes her writing routine. Reflect on your own rituals and routines. How might you make your own writing more efficient?

something sweet (you know, some sugar to help with the fatigu
age, food, sleep, or all of the above.

Now that you have identified your avoidance techniques
down to the business of writing: structure, how to submit the
nal, using a consistent style, and assessing content. Later v
length, choosing a title, getting feedback, and final editing.

An Outline for an Action Research Report

Review the following list. Does it look familiar?

- Area-of-focus statement ("The purpose of this study was to . . .")
- Related literature
- Defining the variables
- Research questions
- Description of intervention or innovation
- Data collection
- Data considerations (issues of validity, reliability, and ethics)
- Data analysis and interpretation
- Action plan (e.g., "Steps to Action Chart")

This is the basic outline I have used with teacher researchers for many years, and it has proved to be a valuable approach. You may need to adapt the structure of your article to fit your audience. This outline is not set in stone—a statement that will no doubt be supported by your own professor (if you are taking a class), school (if you are writing up your action research as part of an evaluation model), or journal editor (if you are submitting your story to an action research journal). Nevertheless, this outline is a useful way to start organizing your thoughts about your story. Later in this chapter, you will see a rubric of essential elements to include in your report and points to consider for each of the items in this list.

Other Structures in Action Research Reports

As an alternative to using this outline, you can look at the "Notes for Contributors" or "Author Guidelines" in action research and teacher research journals that you might want to target for publishing your story. These sections provide guidelines for authors to consider before submitting work to the journal's editor or editorial board. For example, *Networks*, an online action research journal, offers the following guidelines for submissions:

When submitting a contribution, please indicate the section for which your submission is intended.

- Full-length articles (normally 2,000–3,500 words). These will typically report a completed investigation or offer a critical review of a number of investigations that share a common theme or topic.
- Shorter articles and notes (about 300–750 words). These might describe work in progress, raise issues arising from such work, or discuss general issues related to methodologies, ethics, collaboration, and so on.
- Book reviews (about 750–1,000 words). These will typically provide a sense of the main arguments and presentation style of the author. In addition, reviews will take the perspective of a critical friend in terms of the author's assumptions, arguments, and evidence—drawing, where possible, on other work on the same topic or issue.
- Resources for teacher research. These notices will keep teacher researchers informed of upcoming events, opportunities, and resources.

Submission Preparation Checklist

As part of the submission process, authors are required to check off their submission's compliance with all of the following items, and submissions may be returned to authors that do not adhere to these guidelines:

1. The submission has not been previously published, nor is it before another journal for consideration (or an explanation has been provided in Comments to the Editor).
2. The submission file is in Microsoft Word, RTF, or WordPerfect document file format.
3. All URL addresses in the text (e.g., http://pkp.sfu.ca) are activated and ready to click.
4. The text is single spaced, uses a 12-point font, and employs italics rather than underlining (except with URL addresses), and all illustrations, figures, and tables are placed within the text at the appropriate points rather than at the end.
5. The text adheres to the stylistic and bibliographic requirements outlined in the Author Guidelines, which is found in About the Journal.
6. The text, if submitted to a peer-reviewed section (e.g., Articles), has had the authors' names removed. If an author is cited, "Author" and year are used in the bibliography and footnotes instead of author's name, paper title, and so on. The author's name has also been removed from the document's Properties, which in Microsoft Word is found in the File menu. (Visit the journal at http://journals.library.wisc.edu/index.php/networks.)

Similarly, *Educational Action Research* (http://www.tandf.co.uk/journals/authors/reacauth.asp) calls for contributions from practitioner researchers (in fields varying from education to nursing, medicine, and other "social settings") with the following guidelines:

Two kinds of papers are particularly welcome: (1) accounts of action research and development studies; and (2) contributions to the debate on the theory and practice of action research and associated methodologies. Readability and honest engagement with problematic issues will be among the criteria against which contributions will be judged. The journal can be construed as carrying out, through its contributors and reviewers, action research on the characteristics on effective reporting, and the Editors will, therefore, welcome exploratory forms of presentation. (Notes for Contributors)

As a teacher researcher reading these guidelines, you are probably struck by one overriding feeling—anxiety! What is meant by "honest engagement with problematic issues" anyway, and how will it be judged? What are the criteria? To take this anxiety one step further, let's look at who the people are who publish in journals. My hunch is that 99 percent of articles published (and probably submitted) to **refereed journals** (a fancy way of saying that more than one "qualified" person reads the submission) are by teachers teaching and researching in higher education. However, this does not mean that it must continue to be that way, and I have been delighted with the teacher researcher articles published in *Networks*, a journal that seems to live up to its billing as a journal by teachers and for teachers. (For a comparison of action research journals that you may want to target for publication, see Figure 9–2.)

So, what do these "Notes to Contributors" and my outline have in common? Is there a rubric that will help me decide whether I am meeting the publication's benchmark? Unfortunately, there is no easy answer to this conundrum. I have a drawer full of rejection letters for what I thought were "reader-friendly" journal articles that addressed an "issue of significance"! I also know "published" academics who, despite their reputation and experience, still manage to get rejected on occasion. Of course, this is the magic of the **blind review** process, a practice by which articles submitted for publication are presented to reviewers without name and institutional affiliation to avoid bias. The editorial board wants to ensure that the article is accepted on its merit, not the author's reputation. Therefore, let me offer the following modest advice for attending to contributors' notes.

General Guidelines for Submissions to Journals

- *Attend to the context of your study.* Craft a narrative that guides your audience to the site at which your study occurred. For example, let's compare a good and a bad context narrative from the sample paper "'Come to My Web (Site),' Said the Spider to the Fly."

Good example: "As a result of the LAAP grant by the Oregon University System, the Education Department is pioneering the development and implementation of completely web-based graduate classes in education. This paper is based on my experiences of teaching a web-based version of action research for two terms in consecutive years."

figure 9–2 ■ Action Research Journals

Name of Publication	Link to Publication	Description
Networks: An Online Journal for Teacher Research	http://journals.library.wisc.edu/index.php/networks	An online journal that provides a forum for teachers working in classrooms to share their experiences and learn from each other. Also publishes book reviews and discussions on current issues in teacher research.
Educational Action Research	http://www.tandfonline.com/toc/reac20/current	A refereed journal that publishes accounts of action research in education and across the professions. Also provides a forum for dialogue about current action research issues.
Action Research	http://arj.sagepub.com	A refereed journal that provides a forum for the development of theory and practice of action research.
ie: Inquiry in Education	http://digitalcommons.nl.edu/ie/	A refereed journal that provides a forum for scholarly work pertaining to practitioner research.

Poor example: "This study is based on my experiences of teaching a web-based class on action research."

The good example provides the reader with information about the setting (a university), the audience (graduate education students), the length of the study (two terms in consecutive years), and that the course development and implementation was funded by a grant (Learning Anywhere, Anytime Project grant). This brief statement provides the reader with helpful information about the study that is otherwise overlooked (in the poor example).

■ *Use a clear, reader-friendly writing style.* Don't try to model your writing after the kinds of articles you have read in prestigious research journals. Be realistic in your goal and write using the same voice that you use to tell the story of your research to your colleagues. (See the guidelines for writing listed earlier in this chapter.)

- *Peruse the journals you are considering* for your submissions and notice the structure and writing style of the researchers whose work has been accepted and published.
- *Include a brief description of what you did.* Attend to issues related to data collection, analysis, interpretation, and data collection considerations (e.g., validity, reliability, and ethics).
- *Write in an honest, open manner.* Don't try to hide behind jargon and don't make statements that you can't substantiate. Let your data speak for themselves. In other words, what is the gist of what your data show? Say it. Remember what Kennedy (1997) said (see Chapter 1) about teachers not reading research because it is not accessible. Now is your chance to explain it as if you were discussing it over coffee with a colleague or with your Uncle Fred, who may not know about your research. Make it understandable.
- *Keep readers' attention.* If you are like me, you read something that is "published" and make a judgment like "Not bad," "Engaging," "Pretty bad," or "I'tll give it another few pages before I put it in the round file." For whatever reason, we intuitively know what will keep our attention. For example, I read fiction books, not texts, for pleasure. Indeed, these are different genres, and we should not be surprised by the fact that we are engaged in reading best-selling novels and not academic writings. (I joke with my nonteacher friends that I know a good cure for insomnia—and its title starts with Action Research!) But does enjoyable, engaging reading (and, hence, writing) have to be mutually exclusive from academic writing? Consider writing up your teacher researcher studies in a way that makes them engaging for you and your audience.
- *Follow a style* (e.g., APA style) used in action research journals.

Perhaps the underlying lesson here is that if we have a story to tell and a compelling way in which to tell it, then there is a good chance that an editorial board will agree with you!

Choosing a "Journal" Style

Teacher researchers often ask me what "convention" they should follow when writing a term paper or preparing an action research study for publication. There is no simple answer to this. I usually suggest one of the following approaches:

- Choose an article from the journal you are targeting for your write-up and follow the conventions used by the author. Rationale: If the journal published the article using the conventions contained therein, then the editor will probably accept your mirroring of it!
- Follow the conventions outlined in the *APA Style Manual.* For those of us trying to publish in education journals, it is the most widely accepted style to follow.

At the risk of trying to oversimplify a complete style manual, the list given in the following section suggests conventions that you should attend to in your writing; and remember, if in doubt, go to the manual itself or visit the APA style website at http://www.apastyle.org. The APA also provides a free tutorial for new APA users focused on how to structure and format their work, recommended ways to avoid bias in language, and how to avoid plagiarism charges and shows how to cite references (http://www.apastyle.org/learn/tutorials/basics-tutorial.aspx).

I now offer the following as a simple reminder of the conventions that most often plague my teacher researcher colleagues.

APA Publication Manual Conventions

Punctuation

- *Period*. Use a period to end a complete sentence.
- *Comma*. Use a comma between elements in a series of three or more items.
- *Semicolon*. Use a semicolon to separate two independent clauses that are not joined by a conjunction.
- *Colon*. Use a colon between a complete introductory clause and a final explanatory phrase or clause.
- *Dash*. Use an em dash (—) to indicate only a sudden interruption in the continuity of a sentence.
- *Quotation marks*. Use double quotation marks to introduce a word or phrase used in an ironic comment, to set off the title of an article or chapter, or for a direct quotation of fewer than 25 words.
- *Parentheses*. Use parentheses to set off structurally independent elements, for citations, and to introduce abbreviations.

Preferred Spelling

- *Merriam-Webster's Collegiate Dictionary* is the standard spelling reference for APA journals and texts. (Consult http://www.apastyle.org for current information.) For example, appendix, appendices; criterion, criteria; phenomenon, phenomena; curriculum, curricula *or* curriculums.
- *Check part of speech*. write up (verb), write-up (noun).
- *Hyphenation*. Refer to the dictionary to determine whether you should use a hyphen. For example, is "follow-up" or "followup" the correct form to use?

Abbreviations

- APA prefers that authors use abbreviations sparingly.

Reference Style

- *Periodical*. Mills, G. E. (1999). Teacher research and the professional disposition of teaching. *New England Mathematics Journal, 31*(2), 5–17.
- *Book*. Mills, G. E. (2000). *Action research: A guide for the teacher researcher.* Upper Saddle River, NJ: Merrill Prentice Hall.

- *Online reference*. Hansen, L. (2000). The inherent desire to learn: Intrinsically motivating first grade students. *Networks*, 4(2). Retrieved January 15, 2002, from www.oise.utoronto.ca/nctd/networks.
- Six or more authors in a reference, use "et al."

This listing of APA editorial style cannot really summarize a chapter on editorial style! Once you identify the journal you are going to target for publishing your work, find out the preferred editorial style for your manuscript. Consult the complete *APA Style Manual* for specific details. Most of the teacher researchers with whom I work, however, struggle with simple issues related to punctuation, spelling, and references. To this end, I offer the guide just presented—for everything else, go to the source.

Like other aspects of an action research project, there are technology tools to help you manage your citations that will save you an enormous amount of time when it comes to preparing your research report. A few of these tools are outlined in the Digital Research Tools for the 21st Century: Managing Citations feature.

DIGITAL RESEARCH TOOLS FOR THE 21ST CENTURY

Managing Citations

The Internet offers a variety of reference management software choices, depending on the needs, operating system, and budget available to you. Here I will discuss three of the most commonly used and accessible citation management software packages available to you.

RefWorks
Many universities have adopted RefWorks as an online citation management tool that they make available to their students at no cost (otherwise, you will need to purchase a subscription). RefWorks is a commercial citation manager that provides users with the ability to manage and store references online at a personal database that can be accessed and updated from any computer. It also allows users to link to electronic editions of journals to which universities subscribe (perhaps as part of a consortium agreement) and to easily capture and format bibliographic information.

Zotero
Zotero is a free plug-in for Firefox that allows users to instantly pull bibliographic information from websites into Zotero. For example, if you are browsing Amazon.com and find a book you want to add to your reference list, you simply click a button in your Firefox browser window, and whatever bibliographic information is available from the site is instantly downloaded to your personal Zotero account. You can later return to your account and quickly generate citations and references in whatever format you choose. Similarly, if your source is an online journal article, Zotero can store a copy of the source for you. Did I mention that this is free?!

(Continued)

DIGITAL RESEARCH TOOLS FOR THE 21ST CENTURY

Managing Citations (*Continued*)

EndNote

EndNote is a commercial (read as pay-to-use) reference management software package that allows users to manage bibliographies and references while writing a research report. Also, EndNote X4 now meets the complete *APA Style Manual* requirements as well as offering quick links to create footnotes, all while creating lists of references in Word documents (Mills & Gay, 2016, p. 537).

Self-Assessing Your Write-Up

The following rubric (Figure 9–3) may be one way of self-assessing whether your write-up is ready to be sent to a journal for consideration. If you rank yourself with 3s on all of these categories, you are probably ready to submit your article for publication. What follows is an example of how the rubric was applied to the article "'Come to My Web (Site),' Said the Spider to the Fly."

Assessing an Article Using Rubric Criteria

In the following outline, I have self-assessed my article reprinted in this chapter using the criteria in the rubric.

a. *Organization and Use of Conventions—3*. The article complies with an acceptable format and uses correct grammar, spelling, and punctuation.

b. *Area of Focus—3*. The article includes a clear area-of-focus statement: "The purpose of this study was to describe the effects of web-based instruction in a distance learning action research class on student outcomes and attitudes."

c. *Data Collection—3*. The article includes a clear statement outlining the data sources used for the study: surveys, interviews, matrix, and artifacts. This section might have been improved by including a data collection matrix (see Chapter 4).

d. *Review of Literature—3*. The article includes a succinct literature review that is directly related to the area of focus. Specifically, the review focused on the challenges of synchronous and asynchronous components of online courses. This section might have been strengthened by the use of subheadings to guide the reader or by the inclusion of a literature matrix (see Chapter 3).

e. *Context—3*. The article provides the reader with a context for the study and how it is related to the Learning Anywhere, Anytime Project grant.

f. *Writing Style—3*. I wrote it so it must be good, right?! The narrative is reader friendly.

g. *Action Plan—3*. The article includes an action plan that clearly outlines the next steps in the search for excellence in online teaching and learning. There is a clear connection between the data and the suggested future changes.

figure 9–3 ▪ Action Research Write-Up Rubric

Category	1	2	3
A. Organization of Conventions	• Write-up does not follow any format • Many errors in grammar, spelling, and punctuation	• Write-up partially follows a format • Grammar, spelling, and punctuation are generally accurate	• Write-up follows a format • Grammar, spelling, and punctuation are free of errors
B. Area of Focus	• There is no clear area of focus for the study • Research questions are vague (e.g., "Is on-line learning good?")	• The area of focus is too broad or too narrow • Research questions are poorly written (e.g., "What is the effect of on-line learning?")	• There is a clear area of focus statement ("The purpose of this study was to…") • Research questions are clear and appropriate (e.g., "What are the effects of web-based instruction on student outcomes?")
C. Data Collection	• Few data sources are evident • Data sources do not match the research questions	• Multiple data sources are evident • Data sources roughly match the research questions	• Multiple data sources are evident and there is an attempt to triangulate the data • A variety of data sources is used • Data sources match the research questions
D. Review of the Literature (Refer to Chapter 2 "Writing a Review of the Literature" for suggestions about writing this section)	• There is no attempt to connect the study to existing research	• Five recent sources (within the past 3 years) are cited • One or more sources that do not relate to the study are cited • One or more sources are incorrectly cited	• Five or more recent sources are cited • Irrelevant sources are not cited • Citations are made correctly, per APA style or another style required for the audience
E. Context	• No context for the study is provided	• Context is provided but is vague	• Context is well-written and provides the audience with a clear understanding of where the study was conducted
F. Writing Style	• Narrative is hard to read	• Narrative uses headings that guide the reader • Writer uses jargon	• Narrative is clear, coherent, and reader friendly • Evidence is provided to support statements (e.g., see reprinted research paper in this chapter)
G. Action Plan	• There is no action plan	• Components of the action plan are missing or incorrectly stated • There is not a clear connection between data analysis and the action plan	• There is a clear connection between the findings of the study and proposed changes in practice (e.g., an action plan may start with the following: "Based on the themes that have emerged from this study, I plan to make the following changes….")

After you'tve completed the second draft of your write-up, consider each of these points to assess whether you are ready to share your work with others.

Integrating Teaching, Research, and Writing

Classroom teachers face a stressful challenge every day—they must inspire children in their classes for eight hours each school day, and, of course, the day doesn't end there—there is always planning, grading, perpetual cleaning of the classroom, organizing, creating, professional development, and parent-student-teacher conferences. No wonder that teacher researchers express concern about finding time to write.

So, if writing is not a way of life for teacher researchers, what advice can I offer that may help encourage and nurture writing? Let's assume for one moment that you have a story that you *want* to tell; then the issues become finding the time to tell the story to an interested audience and finding enjoyment in committing the story to words. So, as a teacher researcher, how can I find the time to write a story that I want to share with like-minded teacher researchers?

I believe that the secret lies in the ability to integrate teaching, research, and writing. For the teacher researchers with whom I have worked, the secret to writing has been a commitment to integrate the writing as part of their daily routine. It usually does not mean committing a large block of time to writing, but every little bit helps, especially when it is done on a daily basis. What follows is a list of creative strategies that teacher researchers have used to make time for writing.

- *Journal Writing Time.* Many teachers provide their students with dedicated class time to journal each day. Teacher researchers will often use this time to write their research. Furthermore, teacher researchers who practice this often tell me that if they model writing for their children during "journal time," children are more likely to spend the time writing! Keep your journal or legal pad within easy reach in or on top of your desk. Your observations should be fresh, so ideally you should jot down conversations or classroom observations while you'tre in school.
- *"Down Time" in School.* In rare cases, teacher researchers are able to carve out writing time by committing a planning period, a supervisory study hall, a period that might be freed up by student teachers or art and physical education specialists, or library time to writing. And although I would not recommend that teachers always leave their students during these times, it can be an effective way to find some writing time during the contract day.
- *Professional Development Days.* Many school districts have collective bargaining agreements that allow for a day per term for teacher professional development. Teacher researchers can negotiate with their building administrators to use some of this time for writing. This argument can be enhanced when teacher researchers incorporate action research as a component of their annual evaluation process.

- *Vacation.* A commitment of one day during each vacation period on the school calendar can make huge inroads into the writing task. I know many teachers who take a day out of each vacation period to simply clean their classroom. Writing could become the new "cleaning" or "catching up" priority.
- *Time Dedicated to Grant Writing.* Grants from professional organizations, such as the International Literacy Association and the National Council of Teachers of Mathematics, may be used to fund release time for the purpose of writing and publishing teacher research. The Teacher as Research Grants of the International Literacy Association provides up to $4,000 annually for a completed action research study. Details of the award can be found at http://www.literacyworldwide.org/blog/literacy-daily/2012/09/13/teacher-as-researcher-grant-proposals-due-november-1. Similarly, the National Council of Teachers of Mathematics (NCTM) also offers the Classroom Research Grants or Teachers of Grades Pre-K–6 and Grades 7–12 (http://www.nctm.org/News-and-Calendar/News/NCTM-in-the-News/NCTM-Accepting-Applications-for-Classroom-Research-Grants-for-Teachers-of-Grades-7-12/). The purpose of this grant is to provide up to $6,000 for classroom-based research conducted as a collaborative by university faculty, preservice teacher(s), and classroom teacher(s) seeking to improve their understanding of mathematics in pre-K–12 classroom(s).

How Long Should the Write-Up Be?

This is always a burning question for teacher researchers who are required to write up their action research projects in order to earn academic credit. My answer, "It depends," is usually not very helpful. It depends on the scope of the study, the kind of research that was conducted, the audience, the time allowed for writing, what the professor has stated in the syllabus, or what the "Notes to Contributors" for the targeted journal suggests.

For Submission to a Journal

Let's assume that you are targeting a journal for your write-up. The average length for a journal article typically is 2,500 to 3,500 words. I suspect that this is about twice the length of an average "term paper" (approximately 6 to 10 double-spaced, $8\frac{1}{2}'' \times 11''$ pages). Again, don't worry about length. I know how overwhelmed I felt when I received the contract for the first edition of this text that stated it would be approximately 90,000 words! I couldn't conceive of the idea that I had 90,000 words to say on the topic, but like any teacher, I found that talking (and writing) about the focus of my writing, in this case action research, was easier than I had thought. If you break the task down into pieces of manageable length (as per an outline or table of contents), the task becomes less overwhelming.

For Distribution to Local Colleagues

The length of your write-up will also depend on your audience. For example, for colleagues in your school, you may want to keep it to an "executive summary" of a page or two. Similarly, if you are sharing your study with a school board, principal, or PTA, then a brief summary probably is appropriate. However, if you are developing a paper that will be presented at a professional development seminar or conference, you might think about something along the lines of 1,000 to 2,000 words in length. Ultimately, you are the best person to decide whether you have included enough context and detail in the write-up so that you can affirmatively answer the question, "What happened in this study?" If in doubt, err on the side of detail rather than be criticized for providing readers with an incomplete picture.

Seeking Feedback

I would recommend that you seek feedback from trusted friends and colleagues, with one caveat: Be careful what you ask for because you will get it! Interpretation: If you ask someone for feedback, they will probably give it to you; however, you may not like what they have to say and not know what to do with it! The feedback I receive from my family and friends is, "Why do you want to spend your leisure time writing and not playing with us?" I have a few trusted colleagues who work with me and who also teach action research. I know that when I ask them for feedback, they will be brutally honest with me. Similarly, I often ask my students for feedback on my writing (in an anonymous, nonthreatening way)—after all, they are the audience with whom the success or failure of the text rests.

The point here is simple: Different audiences will give you different kinds of feedback that, if taken seriously, will ultimately result in a better outcome. This process is no more evident than in the development of a commercial text such as this one. The publishers use folks who are experts in grammar and content experts who check the content validity of the material in an effort to get it right. But for teacher researchers, seeking feedback should be a far more pragmatic activity. You will know your study better than anybody else; therefore, you provide your own content validity to your write-up. The feedback you will seek is more along the lines of the following:

- Does the write-up provide a complete picture of the research?
- Is the write-up reader friendly?
- Is the write-up engaging?
- Will someone (besides loved ones!) want to read it?

I offer one last suggestion here: Do not expect your friends and colleagues (and professors, for that matter) to do your editing for you. Before you send them a draft, make sure that you have attended to the basic editorial needs of grammar and punctuation. Otherwise, you run the risk of focusing their attention on the structure of the narrative rather than the story itself.

What's in a Title?

When it comes to giving your write-up a title, I would suggest that you be somewhat creative. I think that we all probably underestimate the power of the title for attracting our readers. After all, if we can't get folks past the title, there is probably little chance that they will get into the story that follows. The following examples are illustrative of the importance of titles and the roles they play:

It's Memorable!

I have a friend who reads applications for competitive grants. His advice to me about successful grant writing has been this: Make sure you have a catchy title or acronym—something that the reader will remember. Now, I don't want to suggest that grant readers are so shallow as to be solely attracted to a title; however, folks are attracted to engaging titles and are more likely to pick up a text or journal article if their curiosity is piqued by the title. Of course, you are probably thinking, "Oh sure, what does this guy know? He came up with a really engaging title for his text"! I remember discussing the title with my friend and mentor Harry Wolcott. He suggested that I write down all of the descriptors that would convey the content of the text and try to organize them in a way that is engaging. With a text (or journal article, for that matter), you need a title that will also be found by a keyword search, such as on ERIC. I remember asking friends for advice and receiving suggestions like "Lights, Camera: Action Research!" I also think that I have written some pretty good conference papers that utilized catchy titles, such as the article reprinted in this chapter, "'Come to My Web (Site),' Said the Spider to the Fly: Reflections on the Life of a Virtual Professor," "Talking Heads and Techno-Pages: Reflections on the Development of a Graduate Distance Learning Program," and "Herding Cats and Nailing Jello: Reflections on Being a Dean of Education." You may also notice that I have a habit of using a colon in my titles. I tend to use a catchy opening and follow the colon with a subtitle that clarifies what the paper is about. I like to have fun with titles and hope that my readers will find them fun as well—enough fun so that they will at least pick up the report in the first place.

It Provides a Focus

The other more practical purpose that a title can serve is to provide a focus for your writing. For example, the title for my article was both memorable and a focus for my writing. Specifically, the subtitle "Reflections on the Life of a Virtual Professor" kept me on track during the writing. That is, I was constantly reminded that I was writing about what it was like to be a "virtual professor. " However, it may also be that the title changes during the write-up—a fact that reflects the writer's better understanding of the meaning of the study.

Polishing the Text

Let's assume that you have made it to the point where you are ready to submit your write-up for publication or presentation and you want to take one last shot at making the text as tight as possible. Wolcott (2001) provides a useful analogy to help with this process:

> Some of the best advice I'tve ever found for writers happened to be included with the directions for assembling a new wheelbarrow: Make sure all parts are properly in place before tightening. (p. 109)

I'tve never assembled a wheelbarrow, but if my experience with assembling a barbecue grill is anything to go by, I can relate to the analogy. The directions for the barbecue were quite explicit: "Ensure assembly is complete before igniting."

To apply the assembly metaphor to our polishing task, be sure to take the time to carefully read the narrative (instructions!) and attend to all details. Working with the narrative and getting it ready for publication is not the time to be in a hurry. You have endured many days, weeks, and months of doing action research. You are close to meeting your personal and professional goal and want to get the text off your desk (or hard drive). Now is not the time to be foolhardy and to try and light the barbecue before all the pieces are correctly positioned and tightened! Take time to do a word-by-word edit and delete unnecessary words and "excessive anythings" (Wolcott, 2001, p. 116).

In this chapter, I have provided some simple suggestions for getting the word out. There is no substitute for perseverance and perspiration when it comes to writing. Your commitment to getting your word out and the positive impact it will have on your students and colleagues is the ultimate reward.

SUMMARY

1. There are two primary motivations for writing up your action research:
   a. The act of writing helps each of us better understand the story we are trying to tell.
   b. A written account provides us with a permanent, accessible record for our professional and personal use.

Why Should I Formally Write About My Action Research?

2. Other reasons to write up your action research include clarification, validation, empowerment, that it is a generative activity, and accomplishment.

Format and Style

3. Format refers to the general pattern of organization of the research report. Formats may vary in terms of specific headings included, and research reports generally follow a format that parallels the steps involved in conducting a study.
4. Style refers to the rules of grammar, spelling, capitalization, punctuation, and word processing followed in preparing the report.

5. Most colleges, universities, and professional journals either have developed their own required style manual or have selected one that must be followed.
6. One of the more popular style manuals is the *APA Style Manual*. Additional information about the APA manual can be found at http://www.apastyle.com.

Rituals and Writing

7. There is no easy way to get around the pragmatic issue of time when it comes to writing. One suggestion to overcome this issue is to somehow make writing a part of your personal and professional life.
8. Practical tips for writing include the following:
   a. Write at the same time every day, a time when you know you won't be disturbed.
   b. Write up your story as though you'tre sending an e-mail to a friend. Pretend that your friend needs it explained in simple terms.
   c. Tell a story as you write.
   d. If you'tre having trouble getting started, "write it the way you talk."
   e. Organize your thoughts around an outline and tell your story in a way that stays true to the facts of your study. Make it coherent and make sure your story flows.
   f. In the early stages, don't worry too much about how well the text reads or whether it is full of grammatical errors. Write without consideration for grammar, syntax, or punctuation—just write. Concentrate on getting the story out. Look for progress, not perfection.
   g. Write whatever comes to mind. Then go back and hunt for what you are really trying to say—it's there.
   h. Write boldly and then say it again—better.
   i. Writing, then editing, then rewriting, and then reediting clarifies thoughts into a coherent package. Even a gem needs to be mined roughly, cut ruthlessly, then buffed.
   j. Nobody knows my work better than I do. Writing is an exercise in learning about your own work.
   k. Edit after you have all of your thoughts on paper.
   l. If you accept that your first draft is not your last draft, living with mediocre text becomes easier to accept.

An Outline for an Action Research Report

9. An outline for an action research report may include the following headings:

- Area-of-focus statement
- Related literature
- Defining the variables
- Research questions
- Description of intervention or innovation
- Data collection

- Data considerations
- Data analysis and interpretation
- Action plan

Other Structures in Action Research Reports

10. As an alternative to using the outline suggested in this text, you can also look at the "Notes for Contributors" or "Author Guidelines" in action research and teacher research journals that you might want to target for publishing your story.
11. A refereed journal is a journal in which articles are reviewed by a panel of experts in the field and are thus seen as more scholarly and trustworthy than articles from nonrefereed or popular journals.
12. The blind review process is a practice by which articles submitted for publication are presented to reviewers without name and institutional affiliation to avoid bias.

General Guidelines for Submissions to Journals

13. Attend to the context of your study.
14. Use a clear, reader-friendly writing style.
15. Peruse the journals you are considering for your submissions and notice the structure and writing style of the researchers whose work has been accepted and published.
16. Include a brief description of what you did.
17. Write in an honest, open manner.
18. Keep readers' attention.
19. Follow a style used in action research journals, such as the *APA Style Manual*.
20. The following rubric may be one way of self-assessing whether your write-up is ready to be sent to a journal:
    a. Organization and use of conventions
    b. Area of focus
    c. Data collection
    d. Review of literature
    e. Context
    f. Writing style
    g. Action plan
21. The secret to writing lies in the ability to integrate teaching, research, and writing. Creative strategies that teacher researchers have used to make time for writing include the following:
    a. Journal writing time
    b. Downtime" in school
    c. Professional development days
    d. Vacation
    e. Grant writing to secure funding to support writing time

22. The length of the write-up depends on the intended audience. Journals are typically 2,500 to 3,500 words, while summaries of projects to be shared with colleagues might be in the 1,000- to 2,000-word range.
23. Different audiences will give you different kinds of feedback that, if taken seriously, will ultimately result in a better outcome.
24. A title should be memorable for the reader and provide a focus for the writer.
25. Be sure to take the time to carefully read the narrative and attend to all details. Working with the narrative and getting it ready for publication is not the time to be in a hurry. Take time to do a word-by-word edit and delete unnecessary words.

TASKS

1. Develop a list of your personal writing rituals and how they help (or hinder!) your writing.
2. Develop an outline for your action research write-up that includes the headings provided in this chapter with an accompanying brief descriptive statement that captures what you will include in each section.
3. Review the "Notes for Contributors" for the following journals and decide which journal you will submit your action research report to *Networks: An Online Journal for Teacher Research*, *Educational Action Research*, *Action Research*, or *ie: Inquiry in Education*.
4. Develop a writing schedule for the development of your write-up and stick to it!

Evaluating Action Research

After reading this chapter you should be able to:

10.1 Identify criteria for evaluating the quality of action research.

10.2 Apply the criteria for evaluating action research to a published article and/or your own action research project.

Whereas Chapter 8 showed teacher researchers how to ensure that action is planned with consideration of the findings of the study and the potential obstacles to implementing change and Chapter 9 described the writing process and suggestions for how to "get the word out," this chapter addresses the criteria for evaluating action research reports in terms of area of focus, research questions, locus of control, data collection, ethics, reflective stance, action, the relationship between action and data, and format. A published journal article is included at the start of the chapter for evaluation.

"Let's Talk": Discussions in a Biology Classroom: An Action Research Project

Penny Juenemann

Introduction

Action research has provided me with the opportunity to engage in professional development, enabling me to reflect on my teaching and determine whether I am living up to my values. In this action research project, I have been studying how my teaching has changed in order to facilitate meaningful discussions in the classroom, and I have been assessing how these changes impact my students. The motivation for this study came from my desire to have students make connections between what they already know and new knowledge they encounter in biology. By reflecting upon my teaching I discovered that I was doing most of the biology-related talking. As an undergraduate we discussed the importance of a student-centered classroom and when I graduated I was confident that I would always be a student-centered teacher. It has been almost ten years since I received my undergraduate degree and I haven't always lived up to that value. By increasing my ability to facilitate meaningful discussions I hope to swing the pendulum back to the students. I teach biology to all tenth-grade students and believe that it is important that students are able to make connections between biology content we cover in the classroom and the world around them. By engaging in more discussions I believe students' learning will become more meaningful.

Context

During the 2003–2004 school year at Two Harbors High School I taught five sections of tenth-grade biology, one section of twelfth-grade Advance Placement biology and one section of eleventh- and twelfth-grade physics daily. Each class had approximately 22 students except AP biology, which had 8 students. My action research focused on my tenth-grade biology students.

Research Questions

How will incorporating more meaningful discussions into my biology classroom affect my teaching and the ability of students to learn?

Sub-questions

1. *How do I need to change my teaching to facilitate more meaningful discussions in my biology classroom?*
2. *Will having more meaningful discussions allow students to learn content at a higher level?*
3. *Will having more meaningful discussions help students make connections between biology content and the world around them?*
4. *Will having more meaningful discussions increase students' ability to make informed decisions regarding socially and/or ecologically significant issues?*

Theoretical Framework

This paper is about my journey as a teacher through action research. Action research is a process by which teachers attempt to study their problems scientifically in order to guide, correct, and evaluate their decisions and actions concerning their teaching and learning. Action research requires the researcher to be reflective of his or her practice. Through action research the researcher is striving to live his or her values in the classroom.

I feel it is important for students to make connections between what they already know and what we learn in class. To acquire a deep understanding of complex ideas (meaningful learning), students need to make connections between what they know and new knowledge that they encounter. Such an epistemology is referred to as constructivism. One of the first philosophers to explain constructivism was Piaget. The idea can be traced back even further to Giambattista Vico in 1710 who proclaimed, "To know means to know how to make." He substantiates this notion by arguing that one knows a thing only when one can explain it (Yager, 2000, p. 44).

Through better discussions, students can develop a better understanding of the content being covered in class. As Lord (1994) suggests, "By attempting to explain what one knows about a topic to someone else, explainers test the fit of their understanding. Similarly, while trying to understand what a colleague is saying, listeners question and challenge their own understanding and try to fit the material into their already established cognitive foundations" (Lord, 1994, pp. 346–347).

Students must talk about what they are doing, relate it to past experience, and then apply it to their daily lives. By discussing topics that are relevant to students' lives but also contain the biological concepts students are required to know, students will construct their knowledge in a meaningful way. By monitoring these discussions, teachers can obtain immediate feedback. If one student is incorrectly explaining material aloud to another, the teacher can do immediate re-teaching. More optimistically, teachers can also give immediate praise.

Early on in my project I realized that it would be important to ask good questions and monitor student responses and cognition. There are three domains of learning: cognitive, affective and psychomotor. In 1956, Benjamin Bloom defined the cognitive (the mental process or faculty of knowing) domain for educators (Henson, 1993, p. 124). He developed a taxonomy for categorizing questions, objectives, or responses. His six categories can be divided into two groups, low order and high order. The low-order categories are the simplest and the least demanding, whereas high-order categories require greater understanding and are thus more demanding. Low-order categories are knowledge and comprehension. High-order categories involve application, analysis, synthesis, and evaluation. Asking higher-order questions challenges students to think while promoting learning, as higher-order questions require students to process information in ways associated with greater comprehension and understanding. In order for me to stimulate meaningful discussions, I need to ask questions of a higher order on Bloom's taxonomy. Simple knowledge-based questions elicit little discussion. Another important concept regarding questioning is wait time. It is recommended to wait three to five seconds after asking a question, and again after the response, in order to give students a chance to think and formulate a high-order response. A third important consideration in questioning is the use of Socratic dialogue. In Socratic dialogue, teachers respond to students' questions with questions. It is also very important that students ask questions. "If we want to engage students in thinking through content we must stimulate their thinking with questions that lead them to further questions" (Elder, 1998, p. 298).

After monitoring discussions for about a month, I discovered that the make-up of the group conducting the discussion is important, as people learn in different ways. The main learning styles are visual, auditory, and kinesthetic. Visual learners learn best by seeing, auditory learners learn best by hearing and talking, and kinesthetic *learners learn best by doing. People can possess any combination of these learning styles, but often one is dominant. Through discussions with a critical friend, I decided to try grouping students heterogeneously by their learning styles. Later on, after reading more literature, I discovered that many teachers have had success grouping their students heterogeneously by ability. I then tried arranging my students heterogeneously by learning style and ability in an attempt to improve discussions.*

Another path my action research has taken me on is cooperative learning. Cooperative learning models also recommended that groups be arranged heterogeneously. In a study conducted on cooperative learning at the college level the researcher said, "We experienced first hand that homogenous teams are a prescription for disaster in a cooperative learning driven course. . . . It is important for students from different backgrounds to work together and learn from each other's perspectives and strengths" (Trempy, 2002, p. 32). To facilitate meaningful discussions, students need to work together cooperatively. This practice was reinforced by the results of a questionnaire I gave my students in which they stated that participation was important for quality discussions to take place. To address this concern, I began using some cooperative learning techniques. Cooperative learning is an approach that encourages students to collaborate with each other to achieve common learning goals. According to Johnson and Johnson (1985) one of the main elements of cooperative learning is "individual accountability," where every student is responsible for contributing to the group. This can be done by assigning and checking individual contributions to the group, assigning roles or jobs to every member, randomly quizzing every member over the material, and/or giving individual tests. Another essential element is "positive interdependence" when students feel they need each other in order to complete the task successfully. According to Holubec (1992), cooperative learning is also a style that leads toward higher-level thinking. When students are working together and discussing the material, they will work beyond the lower-order questions. Within discussion groups, students need to accept and learn from each other's opinions, strengths and contributions. Lotan's research found that students can be empowered by this type of group work. "Group-worthy tasks require students to share their experiences and justify their beliefs and opinions. By assigning such tasks, teachers delegate intellectual authority to their students and make their students' life experiences, opinions and points of view legitimate components of the content to be learned" (Lotan, 2003, p. 72).

The affective domain, which addresses students' attitudes and values, is also important in the classroom. Part of my research examined socially and/or ecologically significant issues, with the hope of encouraging moral growth in my students, helping them become more aware of their values and to allow them to make connections between biology and the world around them (between new and preexisting knowledge). In addition to making necessary connections, hopefully students will improve their critical thinking skills. Woodruff explains how discussing these issues can increase students, critical thinking skills, "Ethical thinking is neither a matter of pure intellect nor of gut feelings and prejudices. What is important here is one's reasoning and critical thinking skills. Thus, by strengthening and expanding these skills, the student will be able to view our ever-changing biological world from a new perspective, and not be limited by the past or previous belief-systems" (Woodruff, 1992, p. 2).

In summary, through my action research and my desire to be more of a constructivist teacher, I have found it necessary to research good questioning skills, higher-order learning, learning styles, and cooperative learning.

Changes in My Teaching Practices

The main focus of my research is on small group discussions, as that is where more students can participate in a more comfortable environment. Though I didn't have a defined method of research as I began, I collected and analyzed data and made what I thought were appropriate changes in my teaching as I progressed through my action research. The following is a list of changes that I made.

1. *I increased the number of discussion opportunities in my classroom.*
2. *I administered a learning style inventory, then arranged students into groups heterogeneously based on their learning style, and later on arranged students heterogeneously by learning style and ability.*
3. *I increased the number of high-order questions. Throughout my research I tried to ask higher-order questions according to Bloom's taxonomy in hopes that students would increase their higher-order responses. When preparing discussion questions I referred to Bloom's taxonomy. Also, I tried to keep myself from directly answering a student's question, instead guiding them to their own understanding through an increase in Socratic dialogue.*
4. *I used more cooperative learning techniques. From the first questionnaire that I gave students I discovered that students wanted everyone to participate more, including themselves. I used roles or jobs within a group, the numbered heads technique, the round robin technique, and the jigsaw technique. In the numbered heads technique, the students were numbered off within a group and told that I would randomly pick a person from their table to answer a question. They must work together to make sure everyone understands the topic. The round robin technique is when each group has one paper and it is passed around the table for everyone to contribute to. I used this technique to review the plant kingdom. Students were instructed to make a dichotomous key as a group going around the table until the key was finished. The jigsaw method uses two groups, a "home" group (their original group) and the "jigsaw" group. First, students start in their home group to discuss the issue; then they break into their jigsaw group (students are numbered within their home group, then all like numbers get together to make the jigsaw group). Last, students return to their home group to share information they collected. While using cooperative learning groups, I had a student mention that discussions should be "worth more," referring to points, and it was suggested by a colleague to have students evaluate each other on their participation.*

In response to this I developed a rubric for students to evaluate each other on their participation.

5. *As a way to involve students in discussions, I designed and facilitated discussions on socially and ecologically significant issues. Ten of the twenty discussions focused on socially and/or ecologically significant issues. Some discussions involved scientific articles. First, students read the articles and answered questions independently. Then they discussed their answers to the articles using a cooperative learning technique. Another type of activity I used was dilemma cards, for example, "Deer Dilemma" modified from an activity in Project Wild where students had to respond to the ecological impacts that the growing deer population has in our environment and design a solution as a group. I used the jigsaw method for this activity.*

6. *Another way to involve students in discussions was by having them design and carry out labs as a group. I provided them with the question and with some guidelines—guided inquiry. Four of the twenty planned discussions were designing labs.*

Data Collection and Analysis

Data collection for this study came from several sources. To analyze this data I read through my journal on a regular basis, analyzed student questionnaires, and discussed results with my validation team while searching for themes within the data.

Teacher Journal

While reflecting on my journal entries I was able to verify the need for this action research project. In an early entry I was concerned about "down time"—students not engaged—and a couple months later was very excited about initiating a good discussion. Reading journal entries helped guide my teaching.

Student Questionnaires

Students responded to two questionnaires. The greatest benefit from the first questionnaire was that students let me know that participation was critical for group work success. One open-ended question on the questionnaire was: What can I (the teacher) do to improve discussions in the classroom? Eight percent of the students responded that I should make sure everyone participated. The second open-ended question was: What can you (the student) do to improve discussions in the classroom? Forty-six percent of the students responded that they should participate more. From this first questionnaire I also noticed that students want to make connections between what we are doing in biology and the world around them. Two students made the comment, "Have things we may run into later in life." One student seemed to be aware of the benefit of discussions to constructivism: "Have a weekly class discussion that involves not only what we learned but what we know."

chart 1 ▪ Triangulation of Data

Research Questions	Data Collection Techniques			
	1	2	3	4
How do I need to change my teaching to facilitate more meaningful discussions in my biology classroom?	Teacher Journal	Student Questionnaire	Student Interviews	Lesson Plan Book
Will having more meaningful discussion allow students to learn content at a higher level?	Audiotape of discussions	Student Questionnaire	Unit Tests	
Will having more meaningful discussion help students make connections between biology content and the word around them?	Audiotape of discussions	Student Questionnaire	Student Interviews	
Will having more meaningful discussions increase students' ability to make informed decisions regarding socially and/or ecologically significant issues?	Student Questionnaire	Mock situations where students use their biology knowledge and skills to address a social or ecological problem.	Student Interviews	

chart 2 ▪ Analysis of Biology Test

Date	Test name	Point total for higher-order question/ total point	% of points from higher-order questions	Number of tests analyzed	Students' average score on higher-order questions	% of points earned for higher-order questions
9/12/03	Microscope and Scientific Method	10/47	21%	111	6.7	67%
10/10/03	Eukarya Test	13/60	22%	95	8.1	62%
10/29/03	Animal Kingdom	7/22	32%	107	5.4	78%
11/11/03	Bacteria and Viruses	4/22	18%	99	2.6	65%

In the second questionnaire I noticed that students were still concerned about participation, but they noted several instances when discussions were better because everyone participated. For example, with the round robin virus articles a student said, "Everyone participated because they had different information." And with the deer dilemma some student comments were: "It got everyone involved and participating." "We had to decide something as a group." "We had good conversations." From the second questionnaire I also noticed that students enjoyed discussing socially and ecologically significant articles. A student said, "We shared our point of views and opinions on the article. So I learned others' thoughts on the article."

In summary, the questionnaires helped guide me in my research by showing how important it was to the students that everyone participates. I also discovered that students feel it is necessary to make connections between the biology content and the world around them and that they felt that engaging in these discussions helped them to do that.

Unit Tests

When analyzing my tests I used Bloom's taxonomy to determine whether questions were low- or high-order questions. Then I studied the students' responses to determine the percent of points earned on the higher-order questions. The purpose was to see if increases in discussions would lead to more points earned on higher-order questions throughout my research.

From this data I can conclude that I still need to work on writing higher-order questions. I believe the content type influences the amount and type of questions that are asked.

Audiotapes of Discussions

On seven different occasions I audiotaped discussions. Using Bloom's taxonomy I categorized the discussion questions that I designed prior to the discussions and questions that developed during the discussion. When I audiotaped more than one group, I averaged the number of high- or low-order questions.

From this graph I can see that I have increased the number of questions that I am asking as well as the amount of high-order questions that I am asking. However, because this graph combines different types of activities, I graphed the difference between high-order and low-order questions in graph 2.

As indicated by this graph, I am making progress towards asking more high-order questions compared to low-order questions over time.

Student responses from the audiotapes were also categorized using Bloom's taxonomy.

GRAPH 1   An evaluation of teacher questions

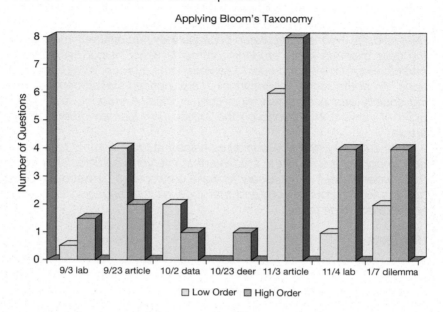

Applying Bloom's Taxonomy

GRAPH 2   Change in higher order questions

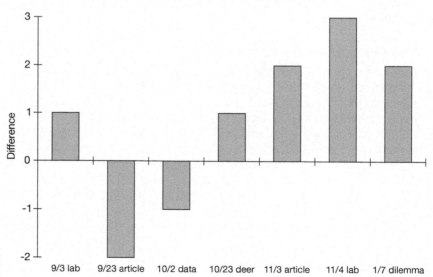

High Order minus Low Order Questions

Again it is important to note that the six discussions in these graphs are from different types of activities. On 9/3 and 11/4 students designed and conducted their own labs within their discussion group. On 9/3 students had chosen their discussion groups, and on 11/4 they were arranged heterogeneously by ability and learning style. On 9/23 and 11/3 students read articles and answered questions independently and then discussed their answers. On 11/3 they answered their questions using the numbered together cooperative learning technique. On 10/2 students were analyzing data from a lichen field study. On 10/23 students solved the deer dilemma. On 1/7 students responded to an ethical dilemma based on articles they read about stem cell research.

I graphed the difference between high-order and low-order questions from graph 3 in graph 4.

I was excited when I unexpectedly noticed that students had more high-order responses than low-order responses when they were involved in student-centered activities. The three positive bars are from designing their own experiments and from the deer dilemma. Even though I increased the number of higher-order questions with the antibiotic article on 11/3/03, students responded with a higher number of low-order statements. However, I can also see that as discussions have increased, more is being said during the discussions.

Student Interviews

From the student interviews, I found that students believe and appreciate that I am trying to get everyone involved, but two of the four students were still concerned that everyone doesn't always participate. In response to the question "What do you like about my teaching?" one student seemed to recognize that discussions help her make connections, "You teach from the book but then we do other things and we discuss them. It sticks really well. When I first read the chapter I think I'tm never going to remember but after a while it all clicks together and by the end it's stuck in my brain." Three of the four students felt that having roles during discussions helped improve the participation, and one felt that it worked really well in the deer dilemma. All four students felt that grading students on their participation would improve discussions. Three of the four students felt that discussing socially or environmentally significant issues was meaningful to them. I asked the following question: We discussed a couple of socially or environmentally controversial issues—the deer population and the antibiotics. How do you feel about discussing these types of issues? Is it meaningful to you? One student responded, "I like to discuss them because it gives you more understanding of the world around you. Cause like I never knew there were so many antibiotic resistant bacteria. I learned a lot from that. And then with the deer it gave me different perspectives because I'tm not the deer hunting type so it gave me a different perspective of where people are coming from. And it is something you could relate to in your life." A second student responded, "Oh yeah I take what I think of it and then with the deer you gave us the things that we had to be, the thing that you gave me was not what I was originally thinking so it made me think in their point of view which was a lot better than just staying focused on my point of view."

Results

As a result of this study many themes emerged. In the following chart I will triangulate the themes that emerged with the data that was collected.

How do I need to change my teaching to facilitate more meaningful discussions in my biology classroom?

With the goal of facilitating meaningful discussions in my classroom I have been more systematic when designing discussion groups and using more cooperative learning techniques. I have been more thoughtful when designing questions and have required students to be more responsible for their role within their discussion group. I have been focusing more on topics of concern to our society. The numbers of discussions that students participated in are greater this year than in the past. Students are doing more guided inquiry activities than in the past. With the greatest challenge, I have increased the number of higher-order questions that I ask.

GRAPH 3 An evaluation of student responses

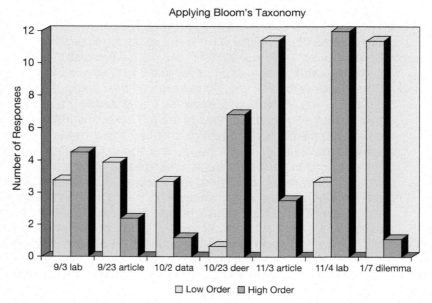

GRAPH 4   Change in higher order responses

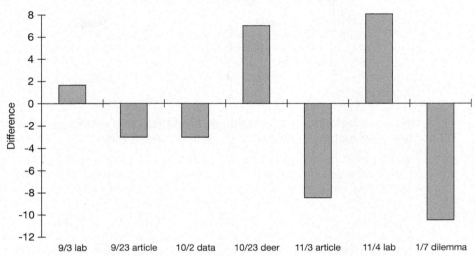

High Order minus Low Order Responses

Theme	Data Source	Data Source	Data Source
Increase in discussion opportunities.	Lesson Plans	Teacher Journal	Student Questionnaire
Increase in cooperative learning techniques.	Lesson Plans	Teacher Journal	Student Interviews
Increase in higher-order questions being asked of students.	Audiotapes of discussions	Unit Test	Teacher Journal
Increase in authentic learning through discussion of socially and ecologically significant issues.	Lesson Plans	Audiotapes of discussions	Teacher Journal
A more student-centered classroom.	Audiotapes of discussions	Student Interviews	Teacher Journal

Will having more meaningful discussions allow students to learn content at a higher level?

From analyzing the audiotape transcriptions, the length of student discussions appears to have increased over time; however, this could be due to the type of discussion. Depending on the type of activity, students increased the number of higher-order responses made during discussions. Student-centered or student-directed activities seemed to elicit higher-order responses. From student responses to a questionnaire, 77% of my students believe that discussions help them learn biology content. I was unable to see any changes in my students' test scores by analyzing points they earned on higher-order questions. Throughout the course of this project, lower-ability students have increased their participation. This could be the result of a variety of factors such as the heterogeneous grouping, maturity, the increase in discussions, and/or other factors.

Will having more meaningful discussions help students make connections between biology content and the world around them?

Yes. Having meaningful discussions does help students make connections between biology content and the world around them. One piece of data that supports this result is from an audiotape transcription of a discussion on an article about using hydrogen produced from algae as a fuel source. The question was: Why would you want to fuel your car with pond scum? One student responded, "So we reduce carbon dioxide." Another student in the same group responded, "And we don't need to borrow it (oil) from foreign countries." The article does not discuss, nor had we discussed in class where our fuel supply currently comes from. The deer dilemma clearly helped students connect biology to the world around them because many of my students hunt and there were a lot of varying strong opinions. But as students said on the questionnaires and in interviews, they found it valuable to role-play a perspective other than their own. It was rewarding to learn from parents that students were discussing these issues at home.

Will having more meaningful discussion ncrease students' ability to make informed decisions regarding socially and/or ecologically significant issues?

From the second questionnaire 74% of my students felt that discussing socially and ecologically significant issues will help them make informed decisions. From the interviews I discovered that it is through these types of issues that students are really able to make the connections between biology and their life. These issues provide the hook that gets students interested in the topic of study. From interviews students agreed that it is a good idea to discuss these issues, and they are glad that they are informed.

Conclusions

To achieve meaningful learning, I have also considered the four commonplaces: teacher, learner, curriculum, and governance.

Teacher

Through action research I have become a more reflective teacher. I have studied my teaching and used the data I collected to guide my actions while continuing to collect data for self-evaluation. Throughout my pilot study conducted last year and my current project, action research has connected me to my students. It is their feedback combined with my journal that I have used to make changes in how I teach!

Because of this project I am living closer to my values. One of the main motivations for this study was to help students make connections. I have gained a lot of satisfaction from hearing students say that discussions have helped them connect biology to their world.

My classroom is a more student-centered environment—I am more learner-sensitive, and constructivism is taking place as I am facilitating more meaningful discussions. By monitoring students' discussions, I listen more, detecting misconceptions and giving students immediate feedback. I learn from my students.

Action research has given me a systematic way to make changes in my classroom and determine if those changes are worthwhile. I will continue to facilitate meaningful discussions and use action research as a tool to evaluate the impact that these discussions are having on my students and myself.

Learner

Students are talking about science more in the biology classroom! These discussions give students the opportunity to share their knowledge and beliefs, which deepens their understanding through actively discussing and listening. In the course of these discussions students have acquired meaningful learning. Through cooperative learning techniques, students began helping each other in a productive way. Students can learn more in a group than individually. We are more together than alone.

Curriculum

This project has not required much change in the biology curriculum. We studied the same topics while I used articles and/or activities to complement these topics. Any extra time these discussions take is worth it, because when students can discuss what they know it reinforces their learning and makes them active learners.

Governance

Currently, the state of Minnesota is in the process of developing a new set of standards, which at this time means that biology will have to cover an even broader range of topics. As teachers are asked to cover more material in the same amount of time, it becomes more difficult to set up a learning environment conducive to meaningful learning. I am confident that student discussions will be integral to the meaningful learning of these new standards.

Discussion

Action research has given me the opportunity to study my profession in a systematic way. The part of action research that has always been most appealing to me is the *opportunity to live closer to my professional values. As McNiff (1996) says, "Another difference of action research is that it has an explicit value basis. Your intention as an action researcher would be to bring about a situation that was congruent with your value position." I have long believed that students need to visualize that what they are studying fits into the broader scheme of life. Through constructivist methodologies students can connect what they know and what they have experienced to new pieces of information. Through this action research project I have been able to live closer to my values as I facilitated discussions that helped students make the biology knowledge fit their prior experiences. Through these discussions students are able to learn content at a higher level because they are discussing the issues, formulating the information in their own words. I believe that students need to think critically about the world around them. By studying and discussing social and ecological issues, students are better able to relate these important issues to the biology content they are being exposed to.*

The journey we make is not alone—the teacher and the student must both be active participants. Through this project I have learned a lot from my students and myself. This has been the most important lesson of action research—that I can effectively make changes in my teaching profession if I reflect on my own thoughts and the thoughts of my students.

Bibliography

Council for Environmental Education. (2000). *Project Wild K12 Curriculum & Activity Guide*.

Elder, L., & Paul, R. (1998). The Role of Socratic Questioning in Thinking, Teaching, and Learning. *Clearing House, 71*(5), 297–301.

Henson, Kenneth T. (1993). *Methods and Strategies for Teaching in Secondary and Middle Schools*, 2nd ed. New York: Longman.

Holubec, E. J. (1992). How Do You Get There From Here? Getting Started With Cooperative Learning. *Contemporary Education, 63*(3), 181–184.

Johnson, D. W., Johnson, R. T., Holubec, E. J., & Roy, P. (1985). Circles of Learning: Cooperation in the Classroom. *Association for Supervision and Curriculum Development*.

Lord, Thomas R. (1994). Using Constructivism to Enhance Student Learning in College Biology: *Journal of College Science Teaching, 23*(6), 346–348.

Lotan, Rachel A. (2003). Group Worthy Tasks. *Educational Leadership*. March. 72–75.

McNiff, Jean, Lomax, P., & Whitehead, J. 1996. *You and Your Action Research Project*. London: RoutledgeFalmer.

Novak, J. D. & Gowin, D. B. (1984). *Learning How To Learn*. Cambridge: Cambridge University Press.

SchoolNet Grass Roots Program. (2003). *GrassRoots Taxonomy of Thinking Skills*. Retrieved October, 2003, from http://www.schoolnet.ca/grassroots/e/project.centre/shared/Taxonomvy.asp.

St. Edward's University Center for Teaching Excellence. (2001). *Bloom's Wheel*. Retrieved October 2003, from http://www.easykayaker.com/school/reading/bloom.xhtml.

Trempy, J. E., Siebold, W. A., & Skinner, M. M. (2002). Learning Microbiology Through Cooperation: Designing Cooperative Learning Activities that Promote Interdependence, Interaction, and Accountability. *Microbiology Education*, 3(1), 26–36.

Woodruff, Brian. (1992). Woodrow Wilson Biology Institute.

Yager, Robert E. (2000). The Constructivist Learning Model. *The Science Teacher* 67(1), 44–45.

Note: From "'Let's Talk': Discussion in a Biology Classroom: An Action Research Project" by P. Juenemann, 2004, *AR Expeditions*. Reprinted with permission.

It is unlikely that by the time you have arrived at this point in the text, you will have actually been through the full action research cycle and will be ready to immerse yourself in the next cycle. It is likely, however, that you are currently engaged in the process, perhaps collecting data, undertaking early analysis, monitoring the appropriateness of your data collection, and so on. As the title suggests, this chapter is about evaluating action research. And although it may be premature, given the stage you are at in the process, to discuss its critical evaluation and "public debut," it is appropriate to consider some of those issues now and how they impact your view of your own research and the published research of others.

Knowing how to conduct research and how to produce a research report are valuable skills, but as a professional, you should also know how to consume and evaluate research. Anyone who reads a newspaper, listens to the radio, or watches television is a consumer of research. Many people uncritically accept and act on medical and health findings, for example, because the findings are presented by someone in a white lab coat or because they are labeled "research." Very few people question the procedures utilized or the generalizability of the findings. You have a responsibility to be informed about the latest findings in your professional area and to be able to differentiate good from poor research when investigating a topic. A researcher critically evaluates each reference and does not consider poorly executed research.

To evaluate a research study competently, you must have knowledge of each component of the research process. Your work in previous chapters has given you that knowledge. In this chapter, then, we discuss the criteria on which to evaluate an action research report.

General Evaluation Criteria for Educational Research

Many research studies have flaws. Just because a study is published does not necessarily mean that it is a good study or that it is reported adequately. The most common flaw is that the author has failed to collect or report information about data-gathering procedures, such as tests, observations, questionnaires, and interviews. Other common flaws in a study itself include weaknesses in the research design and inappropriate or biased selection of participants; flaws in the report include failure to state limitations in the research and a general lack of description about the study. Watching for these problems is part of being a competent consumer of research reports; the problems also highlight common pitfalls to avoid in your own research.

At your current level of expertise, you may not be able to evaluate every component of every study. However, you should be able to detect a number of basic errors or weaknesses in research studies. You should, for example, be able to detect obvious indications of researcher bias that may have affected qualitative or quantitative research results. For example, a statement in a research report that "the purpose of this study was to **prove** . . ." should alert you to a probable bias. Remember, we start a study not to *prove* anything but rather to better understand our area of focus.

As you read a research report, either as a consumer of research keeping up with the latest findings in your professional area or as a producer of research reviewing literature related to a defined problem, you should ask and answer a number of questions about the adequacy of a study. The answers to some of these questions are more critical than the answers to others. An inadequate title is not a critical flaw; an inadequate research plan is. Some questions are difficult to answer if the study is not directly in your area of expertise. If you specialize in reading, for example, you are probably not in a position to judge the adequacy of a review of literature related to anxiety effects on learning, and, admittedly, the answers to some questions are more subjective than objective. Whether a study was well designed is pretty clear and objective; most quantitative researchers would agree that the randomized posttest-only control group design is a good design. On the other hand, the answer to whether an author used the most appropriate design, given the problem under study, often involves a degree of subjective judgment. For example, the need for a pretest may be a debatable point; it depends on the study and its design.

Despite the lack of complete agreement in some areas, most professionals recognize that evaluation of a research report is a worthwhile and important activity. Major problems and shortcomings are usually readily identifiable, and you can formulate an overall impression of the quality of the study. Moreover, you should be able to transfer the skills you need to evaluate published research to the evaluation of your own research. In the sections that follow, I list for your consideration evaluative questions that can be applied to action research. This list is by no means exhaustive, and as you read it, you may very well think of additional questions. You may also note that not every criterion applies equally to both quantitative and qualitative research studies.

Criteria for Evaluating Action Research

As discussed in Chapter 1, action research conducted in school settings is research done *by* and *for* teachers and students, not research done on them. As such, the methods for doing action research and the methods for sharing action research are uniquely suited to its special purposes. Given these distinctions, what are the criteria for evaluating action research? Each of us who accepts the responsibility of being a self-governing professional must apply some or all of the criteria for evaluating the quality of the action research accounts that we encounter.

Based on a number of evaluative schema, I have devised a list of criteria and questions, shown in Research in Action Checklist 10–1, to help you evaluate your own action research efforts and the efforts of others. These questions are intended to capture the essence of the multitude of evaluation criteria described earlier in the chapter and to bring together the criteria for the action research process described throughout the text.

✓ RESEARCH IN ACTION CHECKLIST 10–1

Criteria for Evaluating Action Research

_____ **Area of focus**—Does the area of focus involve teaching and learning?

_____ **Research questions**—Does the researcher state questions that were answerable given the researcher's expertise, time, and resources?

_____ **Locus of control**—Was the area of focus within the researcher's locus of control?

_____ **Data collection**—Did the researcher use appropriate data collection techniques (qualitative and/or quantitative) to answer the study's research questions?

_____ **Ethics**—Did the research face any ethical challenges? If so, how were they resolved?

_____ **Reflective stance**—In what ways has the action research effort contributed to the researcher's reflective stance on the ways teaching and learning are viewed?

_____ **Action**—Did the outcomes of the study lead to action?

_____ **Action-data connection**—How is the proposed action connected to the study's data analysis and interpretation?

Applying Action Research Evaluation Criteria

In this section, I will apply the action research evaluation criteria listed in Research in Action Checklist 10–1 to this chapter's opening vignette, "'Let's Talk': Discussions in a Biology Classroom: An Action Research Project," by Penny Juenemann.

Area of Focus

Ideally, an action research study conducted by a teacher should have an area of focus that involves teaching and learning, is within the teacher's locus of control, and is something the teacher feels passionate about and would like to change or improve. Some of these characteristics are difficult to evaluate based on reading an action research account. For example, how do we know that the researcher is passionate about the area of focus and that it is something that she would like to change or improve on? However, when reviewing the article presented at the beginning of the chapter, you can see that Juenemann's focus is on her own biology classroom ("How will incorporating more meaningful discussions into my biology classroom affect my teaching and the ability of students to learn?"). Juenemann makes a strong connection between her area of focus and the context that led her to the desire to have students make connections between what they already know and the new knowledge they encounter in her biology classroom. Juenemann also connects her area of focus to a strong theoretical framework based in constructivism and cooperative learning principles.

A poor-quality research article lacks clarity of focus, or it has an area of focus that narrows the focus a bit but does not address a specific teaching and learning intervention, for example, "How do biology students learn?" A research question such as this does not provide the researcher with the required level of specificity related to a specific teaching and learning intervention. The word *focus* suggests clarity, and an area of focus that lacks clarity does not provide the action researcher with the guidance necessary to implement a study.

Research Questions

Research questions breathe life into the area-of-focus statement and help provide a focus for the action researcher's data collection plan. These questions should provide the researcher with a workable way to proceed with the research. When reviewing the Juenemann article, you can see that she lists the following research questions:

1. "How do I need to change my teaching to facilitate more meaningful discussions in my biology classroom?"
2. "Will having more meaningful discussions allow students to learn content at a higher level?"

3. "Will having more meaningful discussions help students make connections between biology content and the world around them?"
4. "Will having more meaningful discussions increase students' ability to make informed decisions regarding socially and/or ecologically significant issues?"

These questions clearly link to the area of focus and strongly suggest sources of data needed to determine the effectiveness of an instructional intervention.

In contrast, a poor-quality research article would include questions that did not relate to the area of focus and specifically to teaching and learning. For example, a poor-quality study might ask, "How do higher-level analysis and application questions enable students to be better citizens?" While an interesting question, it would be impossible for an action researcher to "measure" what it means to be a good citizen.

Locus of Control

By definition, an action research area of focus and research questions must be answerable and in the teacher researcher's locus of control. For example, Juenemann states, "My action research focused on my tenth-grade biology students." A poor-quality action research article would include an area of focus and research questions that are outside the teacher researcher's locus of control, for example, "My action research focused on my teaching partner's eleventh-grade physics students." Clearly, Juenemann's teaching partner's eleventh-grade physics students would be outside her locus of control! It is a common pitfall for a teacher researcher to overly broaden the scope of the research to include data sources outside the teacher's locus of control, in this case, to compare tenth-grade biology student performance against student performance in other areas of study.

Data Collection

When reviewing an action research report, you should carefully consider the appropriateness of the sources of data the teacher researcher has identified. Will these data sources provide the teacher researcher with the information necessary to answer the research questions? For example, if the teacher researcher was studying the impact of a specific teaching intervention on student achievement on statewide assessment tests, did the teacher researcher collect test scores and analyze the results using appropriate descriptive statistical analysis? Similarly, if the teacher researcher was studying the impact of a classroom management intervention on student attitudes towards school, did the teacher researcher use a semantic differential to measure student attitude changes along with individual and/or focus group interviews? The Juenemann article lists the following data collection sources: teacher journal, student questionnaires, unit tests, audiotapes of discussions, student interviews, and the teacher's lesson plan book (see Chart 1: Triangulation of Data). These data sources can be matched to the four research questions in the study and also allowed Juenemann to triangulate her findings. For example:

Research question 1. How do I need to change my teaching to facilitate more meaningful discussions in my biology classroom? Data sources: teacher journal (based on observations of student discussions in class), student questionnaire, student interviews, and lesson plan book.

Research question 2. Will having more meaningful discussions allow students to learn content at a higher level? Data sources: transcriptions of audiotapes of discussions, student questionnaire, and unit test results.

Research question 3. Will having more meaningful discussions help students make connections between biology content and the world around them? Data sources: transcriptions of audiotapes of discussions, student questionnaire, and student interviews.

Research question 4. Will having more meaningful discussions increase students' ability to make informed decisions regarding socially and/or ecologically significant issues? Data sources: student questionnaire, social problem simulation, and student interviews.

Juenemann's research report would have been of inferior quality if she had included any data sources that did not contribute to her understanding of her research questions. For example, collecting data about another teacher's tenth-grade biology class would not have been relevant to Juenemann's study. This kind of data would be outside Juenemann's locus of control and would not provide any insights into the effectiveness of her own teaching of biology.

Ethics

When reviewing an action research article, the reader should be sensitive to any possible ethical challenges faced by the researcher. For example, were students' individual test scores made public in a manner that would have resulted in student embarrassment and ridicule? While Juenemann does not address any specific ethical challenges that she faced conducting the study, it appears as though student scores were shared only as group data, thus protecting individual students from being identified. There is no indication that Juenemann experienced any problems related to the confidentiality and anonymity of her students. Juenemann's research report would have been unacceptable had she violated any of the ethical tenets of conducting action research, for example, had she specifically singled out students by name and test score.

Reflective Stance

Ideally, an action research study results in the researcher adopting a reflective stance on the ways teaching and learning are viewed. Juenemann was very clear about the impact of the action research process on the way she views teaching and learning when she states the following:

> Through action research I have become a more reflective teacher. I have studied my teaching and used the data I collected to guide my actions while continuing to collect data for self-evaluation. Action research has connected me to my students. It is their feedback combined with my journal that I have used to make changes in how I teach!

Juenemann's article would have been of an inferior quality if she had failed to discuss how the action research process had impacted her classroom practices.

Action

As Kurt Lewin reminds us, "No action without research; no research without action" (cited in Adelman, 1993, p. 8). Ideally, an action research study should lead to action by the teacher researcher. In Juenemann's article, several statements make it clear that the outcomes of the research led her to take action: "My classroom is a more student-centered environment." "I am more learner-sensitive and constructivism is taking place as I am facilitating more meaningful discussions." "By monitoring students' discussions, I listen more, detecting misconceptions and giving students immediate feedback." Juenemann's research report would be of inferior quality had it failed to discuss how she is taking action based on what she learned about her teaching and her students' learning.

Action-Data Connection

Juenemann clearly links data analysis to her actions in the section of her research titled "Data Collection and Analysis." For example, she states, "The questionnaires helped guide me in my research by showing how important it was to the students that everyone participates." "When analyzing my tests I used Bloom's taxonomy to determine if questions were low- or high-order questions. . . . From this data I can conclude that I still need to work on writing higher-order questions." Juenemann also does an excellent job of visually displaying her data (see graphs 1–4) to provide the reader with a clear connection between her data and the actions embedded in the research project. Juenemann's research report would have been of inferior quality had she failed to connect proposed actions to the analysis of data.

This Is Just the Beginning!

It should come as no surprise that I suggest toward the end of this text that now is really the beginning of your work. At this point, you have invested considerable time and energy reading about action research, learning how to do action research,

Voices from the Field
Applying Action Research Evaluation Criteria

Table 10-1 provides an evaluation summary evaluation for each student's written action research project included in the text. All of these projects were completed as part of an action research preservice teacher education program requirement. They were completed under the constraints common to student teachers and conducted in a "cooperating teacher's" classroom during a 10-week student teaching placement. They provide us with rich narratives of neophyte teachers and teacher researchers. They are included in this book not as exemplars but rather as authentic examples of teachers implementing action research in their classrooms for the first time. One of the challenges for neophyte researchers, especially student teachers, is to make explicit the action that the findings of their studies will lead to in terms of their teaching practices. Perhaps in part this is due to the fact that these four teachers were student teachers and didn't connect their findings to life in their own classrooms. Nevertheless, we can infer from the findings of their projects the kinds of actions they would take when faced with the same teaching and learning problem.

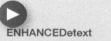

ENHANCEDetext
video example 10–1
The action researchers shown in the videos featured in this text very graciously offered the write-ups of the research projects they describe throughout the text for you to review and evaluate. In your view, what are the strengths of each project, and what recommendations might you offer to these first-time action researchers—**Doug**, **Jureen**, **Jeannette**, and **Rachelle**?

locating action research within the broader framework of socially responsive research, developing your own action research efforts, clarifying an area of focus, establishing data collection techniques, undertaking data analysis and interpretation, and formulating an action plan through the use of a Steps to Action Chart. In short, you have done much work in a relatively short amount of time.

But now comes the real test of any educational innovation. Can it become a critical component of your regular, ongoing teaching practice? If you have found ways to overcome the potential obstacles to incorporating action research into the reflective practice stance you now have, you are well on your way to living the life of a reflective teacher researcher. Living this professional life, in the ways described here, can enable us to change the culture of schools so that we can once again evoke the faith and confidence of our communities in our schools and in our profession of teaching.

We can all think of reasons why we shouldn't be incorporating action research into our craft culture—most notably because we are challenged by the

table 10-1 ▪ **Applying Action Research Evaluation Criteria to Student Projects**

	Doug	Jureen	Jeanette	Rachelle
Area of focus	The purpose of this study was to examine how a teacher could improve student motivation through including expressed student interest in instruction.	The purpose of this study was to determine the effect of integrating technology into a classroom that was not addressing the National Education Technology Standards (NETS).	The purpose of this study was to determine if the basal reading program in the school district showed evidence of gender bias.	The purpose of this study was to determine the effect of formative assessments on students' summative assessments scores, morale, and attitude toward the class.
Research questions	1. What do unmotivated students look like? What are their characteristics? 2. What are the current options for freshman year? 3. What are students' physical, academic, and career goals? 4. What are the current tools for freshmen for interest and goals? What do they need?	1. What impact does the use of technology have on the students' attitudes toward subject content? 2. What impact does the use of technology have on promoting interest in learning further technology skills? 3. Does the introduction of technology lead to the increased use of technology? 4. Does the inclusion of technology complicate or simplify lesson plans and time resources?	What messages are these basal reading programs sending to students in regards to gender and social roles?	1. Do formative assessments motivate students to study harder? 2. Do formative assessments reduce test anxiety for students? 3. Do formative assessments improve summative assessment scores? 4. Do formative assessments improve class morale?
Locus of control	Yes	Yes	No Jeanette has no control over the district's choice of basal reader. However, the findings of her study could lead to changes in her own instructional strategies, critical thinking, and questioning skills.	Yes

(Continued)

table 10-1 ■ (Continued)

	Doug	Jureen	Jeanette	Rachelle
Data collection	Grade book Classroom observations Pre and post student surveys	Student surveys Student performance tasks Student self-evaluations Classroom observations	Analysis of basal reader series *Reading Street* for first, third, and fifth grades using the Bem Sex Role Inventory (BSRI).	
Ethics	Informed consent	Informed consent	Did not follow ethical guidelines and faced an ethical dilemma when confronted by the principal.	Informed consent
Reflective stance	Yes	Yes	Yes	Yes
Action	The results of the study suggest that when teachers include expressed interests and goals in instruction, there is a positive impact on student motivation.	The results suggest that increased access and exposure to technology can promote student confidence, leading to the desire for further computer usage and increased student engagement and motivation.	The analysis of the basal readers suggests that there were more male main characters than female characters and that masculine traits were more frequently represented than feminine traits. The intended action at this point is to make a more concentrated effort to discuss gender bias and stereotypes in literature with my students, to expose my students to more authentic characters that depict a truer complexity of human emotions and experiences.	The results of the study suggested that formative assessments are valuable for several reasons: (1) formative assessments have a positive impact on summative test scores, (2) formative assessments motivate students to study on a more regular basis, (3) formative assessments help to reduce students' test anxiety, and (4) formative assessments positively affect class morale.
Action-data connection	Yes	Yes	Yes	Yes

impediments of time and resources. However, if you believe in what you are doing, you will find a way to make it happen. Call me an idealist if you will, but I am constantly impressed by the positive nature of teachers who, faced with adversity and challenges, are able to find ways to make a positive difference in children's lives. Make no mistake, that is what this action research journey has been about.

Armed with your knowledge, skills, values, and attitudes about action research, the work now begins as you routinize the practice and continue to monitor the effects of your innovations on students' learning, openly accepting the credo for professional practice and living the life of a lifelong learner. What you are learning about your practice will ultimately enhance the lives of the children in your care. If you are now motivated to continue with the action research process, the next logical step is to "Get the word out!"

SUMMARY

Criteria for Evaluating Action Research
1. *Area of focus*—Does the area of focus involve teaching and learning?
2. *Research questions*—Does the researcher state questions that were answerable given the researcher's expertise, time, and resources?
3. *Locus of control*—Was the area of focus within the researcher's locus of control?
4. *Data collection*—Did the researcher use appropriate data collection techniques (qualitative and/or quantitative) to answer the study's research questions?
5. *Ethics*—Did the research face any ethical challenges? If so, how were they resolved?
6. *Reflective stance*—In what ways has the action research effort contributed to the researcher's reflective stance on the ways teaching and learning are viewed?
7. *Action*—Did the outcomes of the study lead to action?
8. *Action-data connection*—How is the proposed action connected to the study's data analysis and interpretation?

TASK

1. Apply the criteria for evaluating action research to your own action research report.

Action Research in Action

A Case Study of Curtis Elementary School and an Article Critique

After reading this appendix you should be able to:

A.1 Describe what good action research looks like in practice.

A.2 Apply the criteria for evaluating action research to the case study of Jonathan Stewart at Curtis Elementary School.

A.3 Discuss how you will represent your own action research projects.

This appendix includes a case study of Jonathan Stewart, a fifth-grade teacher at Curtis Elementary School. This account of Jonathan's study of the effects of an "altered curriculum" on student achievement in reading follows the framework for action research outlined in this text and includes a critique using criteria for judging action research from Chapter 9. The case is offered not as an ideal for action research but rather as yet another example (this time, a more detailed one) of what action research looks like in practice. This case also illustrates how action research can be embedded into the culture of a Professional Development School (PDS) through cooperative work between public school and university faculty.

The Setting: Curtis Elementary—A Professional Development School

Curtis Elementary School is a small K–5 urban elementary school with 256 children and 12 teachers. Located in the Pacific Northwest town of Cedarwood (population 18,000), Curtis Elementary was built in 1949. The limitations of the structure became evident when the school, like others in Cedarwood, received a grant to purchase computers for each classroom. The result—the school needed to be rewired to cope with the extra strain on the electrical system! The building is also considered to be "at risk" in the event of an earthquake and regularly undergoes structural inspections. A new wing was recently added to the school to house music and drama classes. The school also has an extensive playground that abounds with activity during the school day and a soccer/softball field that is used by community groups (such as the YMCA) for after-school sports.

For the most part, the teachers and principal have been working at the school for an average of 10 years, and all report high levels of satisfaction with the teaching/learning environment. Curtis Elementary boasts a high level of parental involvement in school activities and a supportive Parent-Teacher Association as well as a supportive community. This support manifests itself in regular school-sponsored field trips, materials to enhance the curriculum (in particular, computer software), and teacher appreciation luncheons.

The demographics of the school are as follows: 256 students, 12 classroom teachers, and 10 certified support personnel. The ethnic backgrounds of the students are Native American (2 percent), Hispanic American (4 percent), African American (5 percent), Asian American (5 percent), and White (84 percent). All of the teachers are White, and most of them live in Cedarwood. Some of the teachers have children who attend the school. The general socioeconomic status of the community is revealed by the fact that 27 percent of the students are eligible for "free or reduced lunch," making the school eligible for federal Chapter 1 funding.

The principal has been at the school for 15 years and is highly respected by the teachers, children, and parents for his leadership, particularly through a period of embedding technology in the school to improve teacher productivity and enhance curriculum. The principal is described by his teachers as being "caring, thoughtful, and an educational leader," and he facilitates many of the decisions affecting curriculum and instruction through a consensus, school-based decision-making process. The principal has also worked closely with faculty from the local university in areas of program development and student teacher selection and placement in public schools in the region.

Curtis Elementary is a **Professional Development School (PDS)**, or "partner" school, with the local university. PDSs (analogous to teaching hospitals in the medical profession) are based on the following principles:

- **Reciprocity**—Mutual exchange and benefit between research and practice
- **Experimentation**—Willingness to try new forms of practice and structure
- **Systematic inquiry**—The requirement that new ideas be subject to careful study and validation
- **Student diversity**—Commitment to the development of teaching strategies for a broad range of children with different backgrounds, abilities, and learning styles

PDSs such as Curtis Elementary are "settings for teaching professionals to test different instructional arrangements, for novice teachers and researchers to work under the guidance of gifted practitioners, for the exchange of professional knowledge between university faculty and practitioners, and for the development of new structures designed around the demand of a new profession" (Holmes Group, 1986, p. 67). In PDSs, experienced teachers help teach and induct new members into the profession. In doing so, these experienced teachers also continue their quest to become better teachers themselves.

Curtis has used its PDS relationship with the university to drive school improvement efforts through action research. The partnership has created a synergistic relationship of public school teachers, preservice teachers, and university professors who can complement each other's skills. These are not research projects developed by professors to study teachers and children. They are collaborative, systematic, long-term efforts focused on improving teaching and learning. They are activities that can ultimately enhance the lives of children in classrooms. What follows is a description of the action research process as experienced by one teacher during a year at Curtis Elementary.

The Area of Focus: Constructing Meaning in Reading

The educators at Curtis Elementary have collectively agreed to make reading instruction a priority. As a team, they have decided that the general focus for action research efforts at Curtis Elementary will be on how children construct meaning in reading and how teachers can enhance student learning. After many collaborative discussions and reconnaissance activities, the members of the action research teams determined the school's area of focus would be: What is the effect of an "altered curriculum" on student performance? They defined an altered curriculum as an individual teacher's changes in what reading was taught and how it was taught based on professional development activities focused on constructing meaning in reading.

These decisions (and others like them) were based on reflective conversations like this one held at the weekly early morning faculty meetings at the beginning of the year:

Principal: As you know, I've been working for the past few weeks trial-running interview questions and strategies with students in grades 3, 4, and 5. From these interviews, it's clear that children use a variety of techniques for constructing meaning in their reading.

Teacher 1: One of the things I've been sitting here thinking about is the difference for our students between reading fiction and nonfiction.

Principal: I think that you're right. I wonder what this means for the way that we teach children to construct meaning in their reading.

Teacher 2:   I read some research recently that indicated that children construct meaning by connecting what they are reading to other concepts they have learned.

Teacher 3:   That's real similar to what happens in mathematics when children construct meaning. They link their new knowledge to existing knowledge.

Principal: Let me share with you one more story from a third grader. It appears as though she felt unable to trust her guesses about what was happening in the story, but she also gave me a vivid example of how she used visualization to construct meaning. I think that some of these examples point to how children use prior knowledge and context to construct meaning.

Teacher 4:   It makes me think about how we create opportunities for students to create meaning in all of the different strategies I use in my classroom. But to be honest with you, while the information you have collected from the interviews with the students is so rich, I think that it's unrealistic to expect us to interview all of our students.

Principal: I think that you're right about that, which is why I think we should involve our preservice teachers in data collection. It will also satisfy a university course requirement for them. But I do think that these data are very rich and can help us understand how our students create meaning and what the effects of our reading strategies are on increasing their ability to construct meaning.

Reviewing the Literature

A subcommittee of the teachers conducted a review of literature. They consulted sources already present in the school: professional journals, teachers with advanced preparation in reading, and faculty from the university. They also accessed literature via the Internet through the AskERIC Service for educators and the AskERIC Q&A service (askeric@askeric.org). A list of sources provided by ERIC for teachers at Curtis Elementary is shown in Figure A–1.

Creating an Action Plan

To guide them through their yearlong action research projects, the teachers created action plans in conjunction with the principal. These action plans were used to guide and document the teachers' action research projects. Fifth-grade teacher Jonathan Stewart's action plan looked like this:

figure A–1 ■ Sources Provided by ERIC for Teachers at Curtis Elementary

Web Sites
- ERIC Clearinghouse on Reading, English, and Communication
  http://www.indiana.edu/~eric_rec
- Reading for Meaning
  http://www.sasked.gov.sk.ca/docs/ela_mean.html
- Vocabulary Instruction and Reading Comprehension
  http://www.indiana.edu/~eric_rec/ieo/digests/d126.html
- Reading Comprehension Instructional Strategies—Elementary Level
  http://www.indiana.edu/~eric_rec/ieo/bibs/rdcompel.html
- How to Improve Reading Comprehension
  http://www.marin.cc.ca.us/~don/Study/7read.html

Readings
- Barrentine, Shelby, et al. (1995). *Reading mini-lessons: An instructional practice for meaning centered reading programs.* Grand Forks, ND: Center for Teaching and Learning, University of North Dakota.
- Cote, Nathalie, et al. (1995). Children's use of prior knowledge and experience in making sense of informational text. Paper presented at the annual meeting of the American Educational Research Association, San Francisco, CA. April 18–22, 1995.
- Cothern, Nancy B., et al. (1990). Using readers' imagery of literacy characters to study text meaning construction. *Reading Research and Instruction, 30* (1), 15–29.
- Dugan, JoAnn-Rubino, & Bean, Rita M. (1997). Side-by-side reading: Scaffolding meaning-making through literature discussions. Paper presented at the annual meeting of the American Educational Research Association, Chicago, IL. March 24–28, 1997.
- Hass, Christina, & Flower, Linda. (1988). Rhetorical reading strategies and the construction of meaning. *College Composition and Communication, 39* (2), 167–183.
- Keene, Ellin Oliver, & Zimmermann, Susan. (1997). *Mosaic of thought: Teaching comprehension in a reader's workshop.* Portsmouth, NH: Heinemann.
- Kucer, Stephen L. (1985). The making of meaning: Reading and writing, as parallel processes. *Written Communication, 2* (3), 317–336.
- Langer, Judith A. (1986). Reading, writing, and understanding: An analysis of the construction of meaning. *Written Communication, 3* (2), 219–267.
- Mosenthal, Peter B. (1987). Research views: Understanding meaning in reading. *Reading Teacher, 41* (2), 206–209.
- Oded, Brenda, & Stavans, Anat. (1994). The effect of "false" schema activation on the construction of meaning. *System, 22* (4), 497–507.
- Rowell, Jack A., et al. (1990). The construction of meaning from text: Possible effects of different reading strategies. *Educational Psychology: An International Journal of Experimental Educational Psychology, 10* (1), 39–55.
- Tierney, Robert J. (1990). Redefining reading comprehension. *Educational Leadership, 47* (6), 37–42.
- Wangberg, Elaine G. (1983). Instructional strategies for implementing a reading for meaning approach. *Reading Horizons, 23* (4), 259–262.

Creating Meaning in Reading
Jonathan Stewart

I am concerned about the ability of students in my classroom to construct meaning as they read. I teach fifth grade and feel that in my teaching of reading I have resorted more to emphasizing volume (the number of books children read) than to creating meaning (whether or not children really understand what they are reading). I guess that by the time children come to my fifth-grade class, I have started to take for granted that they already know how to read and how to create meaning from what they read. As last year's statewide assessment scores indicated, I (and other teachers in this school) need to challenge the assumption that older children have already developed the skills to read and create meaning by the fifth grade. Therefore, the purpose of this study is to describe the effect of an "altered curriculum" on student achievement in reading.

Defining the Variables

As a whole faculty, we defined an altered curriculum as an individual teacher's changes in how reading was taught based on professional development activities focused on constructing meaning in reading. Student performance was defined as the scores children earned on statewide assessment tests and teacher-made tests administered regularly during the year.

Research Question

What is the effect of an altered curriculum on student performance?

Intervention

The reading intervention that I implement in my class will be developed on the basis of the professional development activities we engage in as a faculty. I anticipate that these activities will include a renewed emphasis on comprehension skills and diagnostic techniques and a greater understanding of exactly how children create meaning from what they read. I am also hoping that the literature will reveal some promising practices that I might consider for use in my classroom.

Membership of the Action Research Group

All of the teachers in the school have adopted the same action research goal for the year. However, we are working individually with the specific interventions that we feel are most appropriate for the students in our individual classrooms.

Negotiations to Be Undertaken

The principal fully supports the action research process and will use individual teacher's documentation of the process and classroom observations of teaching as major components of the annual teacher evaluation cycle. I will need to negotiate my individual action research project with the principal, especially if I need to purchase any resources.

Time Line

- *Summer—Search ERIC for literature. Do professional reading. Attend professional development activities offered by the university. Take graduate class in reading.*
- *Fall—Work with other teachers to determine appropriate professional development opportunities. Develop the specifics of my "creating meaning" reading intervention. Develop data collection strategies and collect some baseline data.*
- *Winter–Spring—Implement intervention and collect data. Meet regularly with colleagues to discuss the effects of the intervention.*
- *Spring—Analyze and interpret data and present findings to the faculty during an action research celebration. Plan the next cycle in the action research process.*

Resources

- *Paid noncontract time during summer to work on reviewing the literature*
- *Support to attend summer institute on reading*
- *Tuition reimbursement for cost of graduate credit*

Data Collection Ideas

- *Interviews with students in my class*
- *Observations during reading activities*
- *Statewide assessment scores*
- *Regular collection of student work*

Following the summer activities, Jonathan developed a formal data collection plan that included multiple-choice activities, cloze activities, and oral storytelling activities, as outlined below.

Data Collection

During the school year, I will use three different sources of data to help me "see" how my fifth graders are able to construct meaning when interacting with given passages of printed text. These data sources will include the following:

1. *Multiple-choice, comprehension/recall activities using reading passages from grade levels 3 through 6.*
2. *Cloze procedures involving the students in the oral reading of a passage, at grade level, on Paul Bunyan, in which they will orally supply missing words from the text that complete the meaning of the passage.*
3. *Reading and retelling of a passage, at grade level, about the Bermuda Triangle (to name one example), in which the students will be allowed to read the passage as many times as they wish and to write/draw a retelling of the passage in their own words.*

Data Analysis and Interpretation

Obviously, the only way I have of "knowing" that my students have reacted favorably to the curriculum and instruction changes used to implement my vocabulary focus on constructing meaning from the written work is to witness those students as they read, write, and interpret those same written words, both in context and individually. For the sake of brevity, I will simply share one situation that I have seen this year relating to each of the goals of increased vocabulary and meaning.

In the middle of a total group reading of Thunder Cave *by Roland Smith, I was stopped by the class to recognize just how important it was that Jake, the young hero of the story, had been said to have handed a "folded" letter to a foreign official as part of a visa request process. This carried great meaning to me in that they had to realize (construct meaning) that, since the letter was to have come from his father in Africa and that he had just forged the letter on his own computer only blocks away, the insight to fold the letter rather than just bring it in flat was absolutely neces-sary for the story to hold credibility to both the official and the reading audience. (Note: When my class brought this passage up to the author, who visited our school in person, he had to admit he had never thought about it in quite that much detail, but he was glad that he had done it correctly by their critical standards of reading!)*

During our annual Storytelling Unit this year, it was specifically brought to my mind by several of my 25 students, as they were "learning by heart" their tell-able tales, that some words used by the retellers of the chosen tales you just "had to memorize to use well" or the meaning of the story would change. As one student put it, "If they [the audience] can't understand that her venomous personality was snake-like, then I'll just have to add a line that lets them know that she really behaved like a snake and even looked like one at times." (Note: One student asked to be allowed to perform the same story she had done last year in fourth grade because she felt that this year she really understood what the story was about and could tell it in a more believable way.)

Student writings and rewritings show how they are constructing meaning ei-ther as a response to something they have already read or in thinking about how they want their readers to react to what they have put down on paper. For example, the following student dialogue evolved between a classmate and a peer proofreader and captures the essence of creating meaning:

"Charlie, how badly is this guy supposed to be hurt in this part of the story?"

"Not too bad. He's just got a cut on his forearm from the knife, and it's ban-daged up already."

"Then don't you think that gushed is a little strong for the way the blood was coming out of the bandage? Maybe it should be ooze or seep?"

When the children are having the discussions, asking the questions, and making the clarifying statements with each other, the teaching is invisible and at its highest level. Words weave wondrous webs!

Of the various factors of meaning construction I observed through the use of the data collection techniques, the most striking to me was the pivotal importance of each student "knowing or not knowing" the meaning of the vocabulary used in the story—not just the words "at grade level" that are the basic glue for the verbal presentation but also the "extended or specialized" terms that truly gave personality, character, and depth to the writing. Especially through the cloze procedure, I was able to witness, with my own ears, the mental processing that some readers could (and others could not) employ to generate a meaningful and appropriate word choice to continue, complete, and, in many cases, enrich a preinitiated idea.

I was most aware of my students' reactions to and use of heightened vocabulary to increase their construction of meaning through three different activities:

1. *Students recognize through a word replacement activity that it is very difficult to maintain the meaning of a well-written passage or sentence if you are trying to replace certain specifically selected words in that segment.*
2. *Students have "voiced" the feelings and mental pictures brought forth in their minds by different passages, both read and listened to, during various curricular reading assignments.*
3. *Student writing samples demonstrate how well they absorb and use different writing styles, voice, and word selection to create a more interesting, engaging, and detailed piece of writing.*

The Findings

Based on my data analysis and interpretation, I will present the following findings of my study of the effects of an altered curriculum on student achievement to the other teachers and the principal:

- *A high level of the skills and knowledge developed in professional development settings transferred to my classroom practice.*
- *Students understand the difficult nature of word replacement in activities where they try to replace words and maintain the meaning of a passage.*
- *As students have learned to create meaning during reading, they can discuss the feelings and mental pictures evoked by the passage.*
- *Students' ability to create meaning of what they read is also evident in their abilities to create interesting, engaging, and detailed writing of their own.*

Action Planning

Though I have long been a person who loves to play with words and understands their massive power, I have never really tried to pass on that idea of literal word power. I plan to continue to emphasize looking for, reading, discussing, understanding, and employing the added power that well-used vocabulary can create in both oral and written expression.

My focus on vocabulary reinforcement will be extended through the following areas of reading and written expression with my students: group novels, published poetry, current events magazines, storytelling collections, student-created stories, narratives, opinion papers, descriptions, research papers, and oral presentations.

I plan to use the following in-class techniques to monitor, modify, and evaluate the impact and effectiveness of my vocabulary intensification efforts: observations of student learning, reflections with students (oral, written, individual, and group), and continued assessment using the data-gathering techniques mentioned earlier (multiple-choice activities, cloze activities, and oral storytelling activities). Students will also make regular journal entries recording their own observations of how different wording has affected their construction of meaning.

I have already implemented several teaching and curriculum changes as a result of this action research project. One helpful technique was my asking students to look up certain vocabulary words from novel selections, to know the meaning of the word as it was used in the selection, and then to try to replace the word with another word or phrase that maintained the flow and intent of the chosen sentence. Students are already finding out why the author chose a particular word for the intent of the sentence.

I am sure that as I start the next cycle of action research I will be "constructing meaning" of my own about how children construct meaning. The constant inquisitive nature of my fifth-grade learners will ensure that we are continually thinking together about our reading and how to improve ourselves. (See Table A–1.)

Online Resources

Throughout the year, I visited the following online sites to research the literature, check for promising practices and current trends within the professional organizations in the area of reading, and discuss my action research work in progress with other teachers across the nation:

- *ERIC—I used the AskERIC Q&A service to conduct an electronic search of the literature related to my area of focus.*
- *Association for Supervision and Curriculum Development (http://www.ascd .org).*
- *International Reading Association (http://www.reading.org)—The IRA offers grants to support teacher research (up to $5,000) through their Teacher as Researcher Grants. I also discovered that the IRA home page had links to their Research and Policy Division and links to upcoming research conferences and meetings.*
- *PARnet—I visited the PARnet website (http://www.parnet.org) to see if any other teachers were working on similar action research projects.*
- *Arlist—I subscribed to the action research listserv and monitored conversations.*

table A—1 ▪ Jonathan Stewart's Steps to Action Chart

Summary of findings of research questions	Recommended action targeted to findings	Who is responsible for the action? T – Teacher S – Student P – Principal PA – Parent(s)	Who needs to be consulted or informed?	Who will monitor/ collect data?	Time line	Resources
1.0 What is the effect of an altered curriculum on student performance?					Ongoing through-out school year.	
1.1 High level of transfer of P.D. skills and knowledge to classroom practice.	1.1 Continue to monitor transfer of P.D. skills and to modify and evaluate vocabulary intensification efforts.	1.1 T	1.1 T, P	1.1–1.4 Multiple-choice activities. Cloze procedures.		1.1 $$ for P.D. and tuition reimburse-ment.
1.2 Students' understand-ing of word replacement strategies was high.	1.2–1.4 Continue to implement strategies that improve stu-dents' abilities to create meaning in their reading and writing.	1.2–1.4 T, S	1.2–1.4 T, P, S, PA	Retelling passage/ story activities.		1.2–1.4 $$ for curriculum materials.
1.3 Students were able to create meaning during reading and to discuss feelings and mental pictures.				Student journal writing.		
1.4 Students were able to cre-ate meaning through their own writing.						

Sharing the Findings

The faculty at Curtis Elementary met once a month for regular professional development activities related to the "creating meaning in reading" area of focus. Most of these activities were held after school and culminated with a dinner discussion at a restaurant or a faculty member's house. These forums for discourse are embedded in the culture of Curtis Elementary and are funded by the school's professional development fund.

Evaluating Action Research

Now, let's take a few moments to apply the criteria for evaluating action research (from Chapter 9) to Jonathan Stewart's action research project. Before proceeding with this activity, take a few minutes to write down your reactions to the study and whether you think that it is "good" action research.

1. *Area of focus* —Does the area of focus involve teaching and learning?

   Jonathan provided the reader with the context to his study, explained why it was that the teachers at Curtis Elementary School wanted to focus on how children construct meaning in reading, and described how in his own classroom an "altered (reading) curriculum" can enhance student learning.

2. *Research questions* —Does the researcher state questions that were answerable given the researcher's expertise, time, and resources?

   Jonathan's study involved one specific question that was answerable given his expertise, time, and resources: "What is the effect of an altered curriculum on student performance?" Jonathan operationally defined his "altered curriculum" intervention and how he was going to measure its impact on student performance.

3. *Locus of control* —Was the area of focus within the researcher's locus of control?

   Although part of a schoolwide focus on how children construct meaning in reading, Jonathan's focus was clearly on the performance of the children in his classroom and how his "altered curriculum" impacted the children in his care.

4. *Data collection* —Did the researcher use appropriate data collection techniques (qualitative and/or quantitative) to answer the study's research questions?

Jonathan used the following appropriate data collection techniques to answer his research question:

- Interviews with students in his class
- Observations during reading activities
- Statewide assessment scores
- Regular collection of student work

5. *Ethics* —Did the research face any ethical challenges? If so, how were they resolved?

There is no evidence to suggest that Jonathan was confronted by any ethical challenges during the conduct of his action research study.

6. *Reflective stance* —In what ways has the action research effort contributed to the researcher's reflective stance on the ways teaching and learning are viewed?

Jonathan's professional disposition now appears to embrace a reflective stance and shows a willingness to continue with the action research process to monitor the impact of his intervention during the next year.

7. *Action* —Did the outcomes of the study lead to action?

Jonathan implemented a reading curriculum that enhanced vocabulary development through reading and written expression activities involving group novels, published poetry, current events magazines, storytelling collections, student-created stories, narratives, opinion papers, descriptions, research papers, and oral presentations. Students also incorporated regular journal entries, recording their own observations of how different wording has affected their construction of meaning. Furthermore, Jonathan will continue with his reading intervention as it was originally developed, but he is open to incorporating any new promising practices that emerge from his continued professional development opportunities. Jonathan will also add to his data collection strategies the use of journal writings in which students reflect on how they create meaning in reading.

8. *Action-data connection* —How is the proposed action connected to the study's data analysis and interpretation?

Jonathan's narrative includes some references to data that informed his decision making, including observations of students as they read, write, and interpret written words in context; multiple-choice comprehension/recall activities; cloze procedures involving oral reading tasks; and writing, drawing, and retelling passages from stories. The data presented in Jonathan's case suggest a strong action-data connection. That is, Jonathan's proposed actions are connected to the data he collected, analyzed, and interpreted.

Final Thoughts

We have now been through the full cycle of the action research process. We have read about the historical antecedents and theories that underpin action research. We have read about (and, ideally, put into practice) each of the four steps in the process. We have read action research vignettes that breathe life into the process and demystify what action research might look like in practice. We are now ready to move on to the next action research cycle.

Action research is a process, but it is also a way of thinking and being. Becoming a teacher researcher means making a commitment to continually reflect on the way things are in our classrooms and schools and striving to learn what we can do to make them better. Your decision to do action research—your commitment to this way of thinking and being—contributes to the revitalization of the teaching profession. Your willingness to embark on this intimate, open-ended, creative journey called action research will be rewarded with the knowledge that our students are the benefactors of our search for excellence in education.

Summary

This appendix provided a case study of Jonathan Stewart, a fifth-grade teacher at Curtis Elementary School. This case study captured much of what Jonathan did during his study of the effects of an "altered curriculum" on student achievement in reading. The case study also included a critique of the study using criteria for evaluating action research from Chapter 9. This case also exemplified how action research can be embedded into the culture of a PDS through cooperative work between public school and university faculty.

Tasks

1. What did you learn from Jonathan Stewart's case study that can help with your own action research?
2. How would you apply the criteria for judging the quality of action research to Jonathan Stewart's case?
3. How can you develop a collaborative action research network that involves your school's principal and teachers with other educators (such as preservice teachers, university faculty, etc.)?

Appendix B

Standard Deviation and Action Research

In this appendix, I will briefly discuss standard deviation as a measure of variability, having already discussed measures of central tendency (mean, mode, and median). For a more detailed explanation of the appropriate use of these statistics, I recommend Mills and Gay (2016). Many readily available computer programs, such as SPSS and Excel, may be accessible for computing statistics at your school or university. Remember, there are many excellent math specialists in your school or district, so don't hesitate to call on those resources with questions.

Measure of Variability: Standard Deviation

As a teacher, you may have been exposed to standard deviation (SD) but perhaps did not fully understand its meaning. For example, following the administration of a standardized test, you may have received test scores for your class, including individual scores, a class average, and a standard deviation. For our purposes, it is not important to see and memorize the formula for the standard deviation or even to know its origins. It is more important to understand the concepts of variability and standard deviation, to know what they mean, and to recognize when they would be appropriate to use.

A measure of variability tells us "how spread out a group of scores are" (Mills & Gay, 2016). The standard deviation is the most important measure of variability for our action research purposes. Whereas the mean is a measure of a position in a distribution of scores, the standard deviation is a measure of distance from that mean (Witte, 1985, pp. 53–56). In essence, the standard deviation helps us to understand approximately how much a particular score deviates from the average score.

As a teacher researcher, I might also be puzzled about whether a relatively large or small standard deviation is "good" or "bad." Perhaps a better way to think of a standard deviation as it relates to our mathematics test scores is in terms of equity. Take the example from Chapter 6 for a mathematics test administered to 30 students with the following scores: 95, 95, 92, 92, 90, 90, 90, 88, 88, 85, 85, 85, 82, 82, 82, 82, 79, 79, 75, 75, 75, 75, 75, 72, 72, 72, 69, 69, 69, and 65. In this case, the mean is 80.8, and the standard deviation is 8.59. (I calculated the standard deviation using IBM SPSS Statistics for Windows. If you have a larger data set, however, this is not the kind of calculation you want to do by hand, although for a small data set, you can calculate the standard deviation by hand—something we will tackle later in this appendix!) If the data set is too large to calculate by hand and you don't have access to SPSS, you can use computer programs such as Excel or a calculator with a statistics function to calculate the standard deviation.

In this example, where the mean is 80.8 and the SD is 8.59, the majority (68 percent to be precise) of the children scored (roughly) between 72 and 89 (±1 SD from the mean). In short, most of them probably succeeded on the test, if in fact scoring within this range of scores suggests some kind of mastery of the content. Now, let's compare the standard deviation of 8.59 to a standard deviation of, say, 16. If this were the case, we might conclude that the majority of children scored between 64 and 97. Again, the question is one of mastery and whether a score of 64 suggests mastery of the content. The larger standard deviation suggests that the children's scores on the math test are more spread out and, hence, leaves us to question the degree to which the children have achieved mastery on the test. For the classroom teacher seeking mastery of subject matter on a criterion-referenced test (teacher-made test), a higher mean and smaller standard deviation would be a desirable outcome.

All of this leads us to the question, "So how does this help me understand my students' mathematics test scores?" Armed with the knowledge that the average score for the 30 students in your class is 80.8 and the standard deviation of this distribution of scores is 8.59, you can make the following statements:

- On average, the children in the class scored 80 on the test.
- Approximately two-thirds of the children in the class scored between 72 and 89 on the test.
- The relatively small standard deviation and mean of 80 suggest that approximately two-thirds of the children achieved mastery of the content that the test covered.

Used in conjunction, the mean and standard deviation can provide you and your colleagues with a great deal of information about the data you have collected if you have determined that such data can be counted. See Key Concepts Box B–1 for some of the uses of descriptive statistics.

KEY CONCEPTS BOX B–1
Descriptive Statistics

Definition of Measure	Type Used in Action Research
A measure of **central tendency** is a single number that gives us information about an entire group of numbers.	■ Mean (the average) ■ Mode (the most frequently occurring score[s]) ■ Median (the middle score)
A measure of **variability** tells us how spread out a group of scores are.	■ Standard deviation (a measure of distance from the mean that helps us understand approximately how much a *particular* score deviates from the *average* score)

An Illustration

In my study of change in the McKenzie School District (Mills, 1988), I administered a survey to classroom teachers. One of the items on the survey focused on the teachers' perceptions of how the district's at-risk program had changed classroom practices. Specifically, teachers were asked to respond to the following question: "To what degree has the at-risk program changed your classroom practice?" The survey included an item that required teachers to circle a number between 1 and 5 (1 = no change, 5 = large change). A total of 52 teachers responded to the survey item with the following frequency:

Impact of At-Risk Program on Classroom Practices

	No Change				Large Change
	1	2	3	4	5
Number of Respondents	7 (13%)	18 (37%)	17 (35%)	10 (15%)	0 (0%)

I used the following descriptive statistics to describe the distribution of teachers' responses:
4,4,4,4,4,4,4,4,4,4,3,3,3,3,3,3,3,3,3,3,3,3,3,3,3,3,3,3,2,2,2,2,2,2,2,2,2,2,2,2,2,2,2,2,2,2,1,1,1,1,1,1

$$\text{Mean } (\bar{x}) = \frac{\sum x}{n}$$
$$= \frac{134}{52}$$
$$= 2.58$$

Mode = 2.0 (most frequently occurring score—it occurred 18 times)
Median = 3.0 (the middle score in this distribution of 52 responses)
Standard Deviation = 1.02

For fun, let's calculate a standard deviation by hand so that we have a good understanding of what was involved in arriving at a standard deviation of 1.02! Since we are doing this example "for fun," let's use the following data set of student test scores. Although sample sizes of 5 are hardly ever considered acceptable, I will use this number of participants for illustration purposes.

To summarize, symbols commonly used in statistical formulas are as follows:

	X	*X²*
Iggie	1	1
Hermie	2	4
Fifi	3	9
Teenie	4	16
Tiny	5	25

$$\Sigma X = 15 \qquad \Sigma X^2 = 55$$
$$(\Sigma X)^2 = 225$$

X = any score
Σ = the sum of; add them up
ΣX = the sum of all the scores
$\overline{X}$ = the mean, or arithmetic average, of the scores
N = total number of subjects
n = number of subjects in a particular group
ΣX^2 = the sum of the squares; square each score and add up all the squares
$(\Sigma X)^2$ = the square of the sum; add up the scores and square the sum, or total

If you approach each statistic in an orderly fashion, it makes your statistical life easier. A suggested procedure is as follows:

1. Make the columns required by the formula (e.g., X, X^2), as just shown, and find the sum of each column.
2. Label the sum of each column; in the previous example, the label for the sum of the X column is ΣX, and the label for the sum of the X^2 column is ΣX^2.
3. Write the formula.
4. Write the arithmetic equivalent of the formula [e.g., $(\Sigma X)^2 = (15)^2$].
5. Solve the arithmetic problem [e.g., $(15)2 = 225$].

The Standard Deviation

The standard deviation is the square root of the variance, which is based on the distance of each score from the mean. To calculate the standard deviation, however, we do not have to calculate variance scores; we can use a raw score formula that gives us the same answer with less grief. Now, before you look at the formula, remember that no matter how bad it looks, it is going to turn into an easy arithmetic problem. Ready?

$$SD = \sqrt{\frac{SS}{N-1}}, \text{ where } SS = \sum X^2 - \frac{(\sum X)^2}{N}$$

or

$$SD = \sqrt{\frac{\sum X^2 - \frac{(\sum X)^2}{N}}{N-1}}$$

In other words, the *SD* is equal to the square root of the sum of squares (*SS*) divided by $N - 1$.

If the standard deviation of a *population* is being calculated, the formula is exactly the same, except we divide the sum of squares by N instead of $N - 1$. The reason is that a sample standard deviation is considered to be a biased estimate of the population standard deviation. When we select a sample, especially a small sample, the probability is that participants will come from the middle of the distribution and that extreme scores will not be represented. Thus, the range of sample scores will be smaller than the population range, as will be the sample standard deviation. As the sample size increases, so do the chances of getting extreme scores; thus, the smaller the sample, the more important it is to correct for the downward bias. By dividing by $N - 1$ instead of N, we make the denominator (bottom part!) smaller, and thus $\frac{SS}{N-1}$ is larger, closer to the population *SD* than $\frac{SS}{N}$. For example, if $SS = 18$ and $N = 10$, then

$$\frac{SS}{N-1} = \frac{18}{9} = 2.00 \quad \text{and} \quad \frac{SS}{N} = \frac{18}{10} = 1.80$$

Now just relax and look at each piece of the formula; you already know what each piece means. Starting with the easy one, N refers to what? Right—the number of subjects. How about $(\sum X)$? Right—the sum of the scores. And $(\sum X)^2$? Right—the square of the sum of the scores. That leaves $\sum X^2$, which means the sum of what? Fantastic. The sum of the squares. Okay, let's use the same scores we used to calculate the mean. The first thing we need to do is to square each score and then add those squares up. While we are at it, we can also go ahead and add up all the scores.

	X	**X²**	
Iggie	1	1	
Hermie	2	4	$\sum X = 15$
Fifi	3	9	$\sum X^2 = 55$
Teenie	4	16	$N = 5$
Tiny	5	25	$N - 1 = 4$
	$\sum X = 15$	$\sum X^2 = 55$	

Do we have everything we need? Yes. Does the formula ask for anything else? No. We are in business. Substituting each symbol with its numerical equivalent, we get

$$SS = \sum X^2 - \frac{(\sum X)^2}{N} = 55 - \frac{(15)^2}{5}$$

Now what do we have? A statistic? No! An arithmetic problem? Yes! A hard arithmetic problem? No! It is harder than $\frac{15}{5}$, but it is not hard. If we just do what the formula tells us to do, we will have no problem at all. The first thing it tells us to do is to square 15:

$$SS = \sum X^2 - \frac{(\sum X)^2}{N} = 55 - \frac{(15)^2}{5} = 55 - \frac{225}{5}$$

So far so good. The next thing the formula tells us to do is divide 225 by 5, which equals 45. It is looking a lot better; now it is really an easy arithmetic problem. Next, we substract 45 from 55 and get a sum of squares (*SS*) equal to 10.00. Mere child's play.

Think you can figure out the next step? Terrific! Now that we have *SS*, we simply substitute it into the *SD* formula as follows:

$$SD = \sqrt{\frac{SS}{N - 1}} = \sqrt{\frac{10}{4}} = \sqrt{2.5}$$

To find the square root of 2.5, simply enter 2.5 into your calculator and hit the square root button ($\sqrt{\ }$); the square root of 2.5 is 1.58. Substituting in our square root, we have

$$SD = \sqrt{2.5} = 1.58$$

The standard deviation is 1.58. Now you know how to do two useful descriptive statistics.

However, numbers alone do not tell a complete story. They inform the reader about how a sample responded to a particular item. For example, the analysis of the earlier illustration related to classroom teachers' perceptions of how the district's at-risk program had changed classroom practices is incomplete using only descriptive statistics. To complete my reporting on this item, I included the following comments that were representative of the remarks that accompanied the question, "To what extent do you think that the at-risk program changed your classroom practices?" The responses were grouped under the categories of "Positive Impact" and "No Impact."

Positive Impact

"Reminded me and reinforced the concepts of learning styles and how to provide for them in my classroom."

"Having insight to these kids has allowed me to be more sensitive and caring toward them and to act more compassionately."

"I am more aware of needs of the "total child" as well as the student."

No Impact

"No time to plan and implement all of those ideas!"

"I feel that the services needed for at-risk students are not available."

"I was already using many of the skills."

"Have been dealing with at-risk students since becoming a resource teacher so was already aware of the problem."

"I believe that I have always been aware of the problem. It's only new at the district level."

The statistical analysis combined with the quotes from the teachers who responded provided me with a good understanding of the teachers' perceptions of the impact that the at-risk program had on their classroom practices.

Appendix

Displaying Data Visually

This appendix includes examples taken from action research projects where the teacher researcher has displayed data visually for ease of data analysis and data sharing with other teacher researchers who wish to "see for themselves." Visual displays of data help the researcher to summarize information that in any other format may be clumsy and difficult to reduce to a manageable format. For the most part, the data collected, using the data collection techniques outlined in Chapter 4, earlier, have been recorded as narrative in field notes. However, as we will see in this appendix, there are other ways to think about data reduction so that the teacher researcher can work with the data in a way that leads to a trustworthy analysis. As Miles and Huberman (1994) assert,

> Valid analysis requires, and is driven by, displays that are focused enough to permit a viewing of a full data set in the same location, and are arranged systematically to answer the research questions at hand. (pp. 91–92)

The examples provided in this appendix are intended to be illustrative of the ways in which teacher researchers can display their data visually in order to assist with analysis of the data as well as share the data with their audiences.

Example 1: Writers' Workshop and ESL Students' Written Work and Attitudes

The following visual displays have been taken from a teacher researcher's study of the impact of a writing intervention (Writers' Workshop) on the quality of seventh- and eighth-grade ESL students' written work and their attitudes toward writing. Students' writing was assessed using a scoring rubric that measured "voice" and "ownership" in their writing (adapted from the Oregon Department of Education Writing Scoring Guide).

The teacher researcher's use of bar graphs to summarize and represent the pre-, mid-, and postassessments for all ESL students is a helpful way of sharing the kinds of numerical data that would have been recorded in a grade book. These graphs also allow the teacher researcher to work with the data in a manageable way and to draw conclusions about individual student performance over the course of the writing intervention. Similarly, it provides the reader of the study with access to the same data—a powerful way of providing an "audit" for the outcomes of the study (see Figures C–1 and C–2).

figure C–1 ▪ Overall Student Performance Gains—VOICE

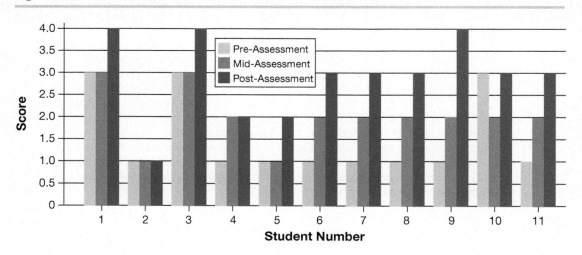

figure C–2 ▪ Overall Student Performance Gains—OWNERSHIP

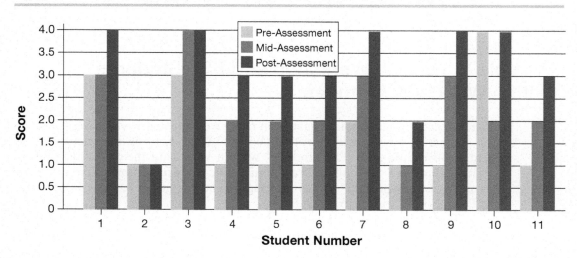

Also, this teacher researcher utilized a summary table of students' responses on a postassessment questionnaire to the questions, "Do you like to write? Why or why not?" This summary of data, once again, allows the teacher researcher to provide illustrative examples of how the ESL students felt about writing in support of the themes "Likes to write" and "Does not like to write" (see Table C–1).

In addition, this teacher researcher used a similar format to summarize student responses to the questions, "Do you think your writing has improved this term? How? What have you learned?" (see Table C–2). This visual display of data allows the teacher researcher to reduce the students' responses to a

table C–1 ■ Postassessment Questionnaire

Question 1: Do you like to write? Why or why not?		
STUDENT NUMBER	**LIKES TO WRITE**	**DOES NOT LIKE TO WRITE**
1	Yes, 'cause that's how I let out my expressions.	
2	Yes, because I just like it.	
3	I like to write a little bit, not much. The reason I like to write is because you can express your feelings.	
4		No, because I do not like to write a lot.
5	Yes, I do.	
6	Sometimes, I like writing when I'm bored.	
7	Yes, because it expresses.	
8		No, because we have to write a lot at school and I get tired to write all day and to think about all different topics to write about. After a while you run out of topics to write about.
9	Yes, because I can express myself.	
10	Yes, because it expresses my feelings.	
11	Yes, because I can tell about myself.	

table C–2 ▪ Postassessment Questionnaire

Question 3: Do you think your writing has improved this term? How? What have you learned?		
STUDENT NUMBER	**WRITING HAS IMPROVED**	**WRITING HAS NOT IMPROVED**
1	I've learned that it's better to make your own stories because you got more ideas.	
2	Yes, I learned to write better.	
3	I think my writing has improved a little bit, but not much.	
4	Yes, I have improved because every day I learn something new at school. I learned how to spell better.	
5	Yes, my writing is better because I wrote about what I wanted.	
6	Yes, by writing it longer.	
7	Yes, because I know how to spell more better.	
8	Yes, on spelling and commas, periods and more. I have learned where to put in my commas and periods.	
9	When I write about me or someone else I know, I learn a lot more things like writing everyday or express more myself.	

manageable level while at the same time capturing the essence of the students' comments. This activity also assists the teacher researcher's efforts to find themes that emerged from the students' comments. For example, all the students in this study believed that their writing had improved as a result of their participation in the Writers' Workshop intervention—even though the overall student performance gains graphs indicated that at least two of the students did not improve—as measured by the rubric.

Example 2: Teaching Mathematics Using Manipulatives

This example is taken from a second-grade teacher researcher's project that focused on the impact of math manipulatives on students' learning and "on-task" behavior. This project also involved five other teachers' perceptions (six in all) of the impact of math manipulative use on student on-task behavior. Figure C–3 summarizes the six teachers' perceptions of the impact of the use of math manipulatives on student learning and on-task behavior. It is interesting to note that the teacher of classroom 4 indicated that while there was no change in student learning, there was a decrease in on-task behavior. This anomaly is evident in the visual representation of the data.

The following figures also use bar graphs to display the data that compares on-task behavior (Figure C–4), strategy/process (Figure C–5), and completion/accuracy (Figure C–6) for six students in a second-grade math class over the course of a "Math Mystery" series of lessons that were taught with and without manipulatives. Again, the use of the visual display allows the teacher researcher to reduce all of the data for the six students to a manageable format for analysis.

figure C–3 ▪ **Results of Teacher Questionnaire: Effects of Math Manipulative Use on Student Learning and On-Task Behavior**

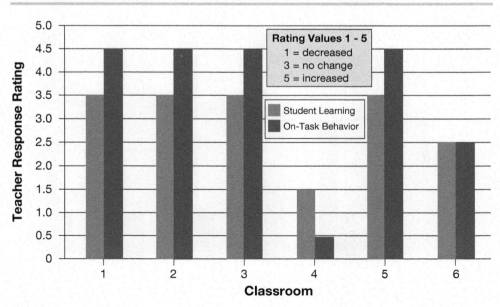

figure C–4 ▪ Math Mystery Format—On-Task Behavior

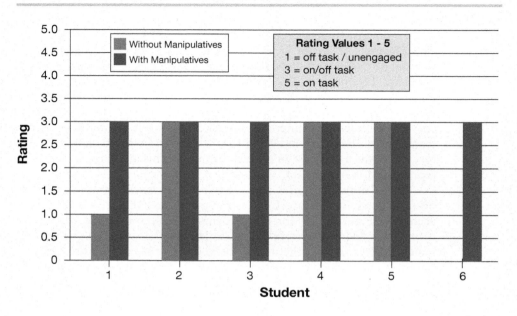

figure C–5 ▪ Math Mystery Format—Strategy/Process

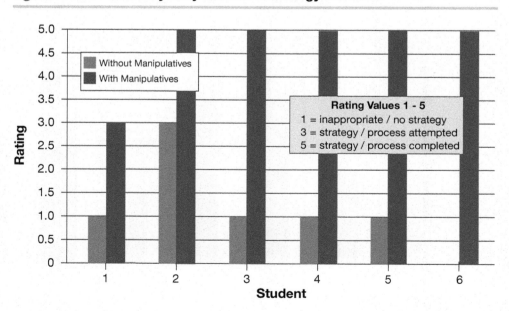

figure C–6 ▪ **Math Mystery Format—Completion/Accuracy**

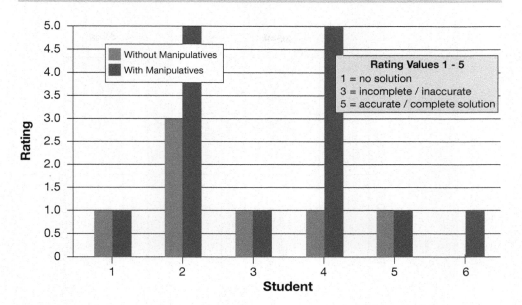

In this case, the teacher researcher concluded that while most students' abilities to develop problem-solving strategies and processes improved with the use of manipulatives, only two students' completion and accuracy improved with the use of manipulatives.

Example 3: The Impact of Book Sharing on Student Motivation to Read

This example is taken from a first-grade teacher's study of the impact of a "book sharing" intervention on students' motivation to read. This teacher researcher used a matrix to summarize the 15 students' responses to a series of questions that were given as a pre- and postassessment and allowed the teacher to classify the responses as either a "positive change" or "no change" in attitude (see Table C–3). The teacher researcher was able to use this data display (along with bar graphs showing positive changes in student attitude toward reading) to support concluding statements such as "More students enjoyed reading during play time than before the intervention."

table C–3 ■ Comparison of Student Responses from Pre- to Postassessment Survey

STUDENT NUMBER	Do you like to read?		Do you like to be read to?		Do you read every day?		Do you like going to the library?		Do you like to read during free time at school?		Do you like to read instead of play?	
	PRE	POST	PRE	POST	PRE	POST	PRE	POST	PRE	POST	PRE	POST
1	Yes	Sometimes	Yes	Yes	Sometimes	Sometimes	Yes	Yes	Sometimes	Sometimes	Sometimes	Yes
2	Yes	Sometimes	Yes	Yes	No	No	Yes	Yes	Sometimes	Sometimes	No	No
3	Sometimes	Sometimes	Yes	Yes	No	Sometimes	Yes	Yes	Sometimes	Sometimes	No	Sometimes
4	Sometimes	Yes	Sometimes	Yes	Yes	Yes	Sometimes	Sometimes	No	Sometimes	Sometimes	Sometimes
5	Sometimes	Sometimes	Yes	Yes	Sometimes	Sometimes	No	Sometimes	Sometimes	Sometimes	No	Sometimes
6	Yes	Sometimes	Yes	Yes	Sometimes	Sometimes	Yes	Sometimes	Yes	Yes	No	No
7	Sometimes	Sometimes	Sometimes	Sometimes	No	Sometimes	Sometimes	Sometimes	No	Sometimes	No	Sometimes
8	Sometimes	No	Yes	Yes	No	No	Yes	Yes	No	No	No	No
9	Yes	Sometimes	Sometimes	No	No	Yes	No	Yes	Sometimes	Yes	No	Yes
10	Yes	Yes	Sometimes	No	Yes	Yes	Yes	Yes	Yes	Yes	No	Yes
11	Sometimes	Yes	Yes	Yes	Yes	No	Sometimes	Sometimes	Sometimes	Yes	Yes	Yes
12	Yes	Yes	Yes	Yes	No	Yes	Yes	Yes	Yes	Sometimes	Sometimes	Sometimes
13	Sometimes	Sometimes	Yes	Yes	No	Yes	No	Sometimes	No	No	No	No
14	Yes	Sometimes	Yes	Sometimes	Sometimes	Yes	Yes	Yes	Yes	Yes	Sometimes	No
15	Yes	Yes	Yes	Yes	Sometimes	Yes	Sometimes	Yes	Sometimes	Sometimes	Yes	Sometimes

Dark—Positive Change in Attitude; White—No Change in Attitude; Light—Negative Change

Example 4: Mapping Teachers' "Locus of Control" and "Movement"

Sometimes, teachers may want to track their "locus of control," that is, whether a particular individual child or group of children in a classroom demand a majority of the teacher's time and effort. This kind of data collection is greatly enhanced by the use of a visual display that records the frequency of student-teacher interactions during a lesson. In this particular example, the teacher researcher would ask a colleague to record the frequency of interactions between the teacher and the students and to keep a tally (see Figure C–7). Similarly, the privileged observer can keep track of the teacher's movement around the classroom (lines connected to numbers). From this visual display of data, the teacher researcher may conclude, for this particular teaching episode, that most of the teacher's time and energy was focused on a few children seated in a group at the rear of the classroom. This kind of data would challenge the teacher to consider other questions such as "Why?" and "What was happening to cause this lopsided attention to a few children?" Again, this visual display provides the teacher researcher with a powerful way of capturing data that would not otherwise be easily recorded.

figure C–7 ■ Locus of Control/Teacher Movement

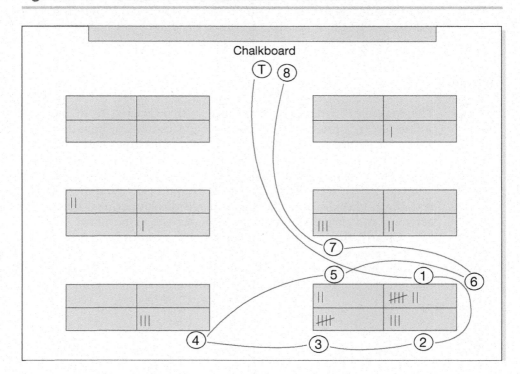

figure C–8 ▪ Eastview's Concept Map of the Factors Affecting Absenteeism

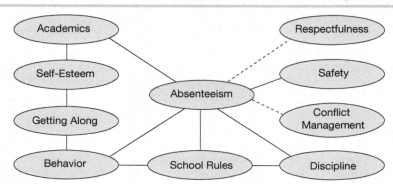

Example 5: Concept Map

Another visual representation that is a useful tool to aid data analysis and interpretation is the concept map. In this example, I have used a map to outline the factors that affected absenteeism in Eastview's study (discussed earlier). Again, this display provides the teacher researcher and reader with a conceptual view of all the factors that might affect absenteeism at the school (see Figure C–8).

Summary

The examples in this appendix have been extracted from preservice teachers' action research projects and are simple illustrations of how displaying data visually can enhance teacher researchers' data collection, data analysis, and sharing efforts. However, for the ultimate statement on the kinds of data displays that can be used to enhance data analysis, I would urge the reader to consult Miles and Huberman (1994), who provide concrete examples of visual displays, such as a context chart, checklist matrix, time-ordered display, critical incident chart, causal network, and partially ordered meta-matrix—to name a few!

Clearly, there are perhaps as many ways to display data visually as there are teacher researchers. The challenge for each of us is to "think display" so as to enhance our ability to work effectively and efficiently with the mountains of data that emerge from our qualitatively oriented research efforts.

References

Adelman, C. (1993). Kurt Lewin and the origins of action research. *Educational Action Researcher, 1*(1), 7–25.

Agar, M. H. (1980). *The professional stranger: An informal introduction to ethnography.* Orlando, FL: Academic.

American Educational Research Association. (2011). *Educational Researcher, 40*(3), 145–156.

American Psychological Association. (2009). *Publication manual of the American Psychological Association* (6th ed.). Washington, DC: Author.

Anderson, G. L., Herr, K., & Nihlen, A. S. (1994). *Studying your own school: An educator's guide to qualitative practitioner research.* Thousand Oaks, CA: Corwin.

Becker, H. S. (1986). *Writing for the social scientists: How to start and finish your thesis, book, or article.* Chicago: University of Chicago Press.

Bogdan, R. C., & Biklen, S. K. (1998). *Qualitative research for education: An introduction to theories and methods* (5th ed.). Needham Heights, MA: Allyn and Bacon.

Calhoun, E. F. (1994). *How to use action research in the self-renewing school.* Alexandria, VA: Association for Supervision and Curriculum Development.

Christians, C. G. (2000). Ethics and politics in qualitative research. In N. K. Denzin & Y. S. Lincoln (Eds.), *Handbook of qualitative research* (2nd ed., pp. 133–155). Thousand Oaks, CA: Sage.

Cochran-Smith, M., & Lytle, S. L. (1993). *Inside outside: Teacher research and knowledge.* New York: Teachers College Press.

Conley, S. (1991). Review of research on teacher participation in school decision making. *Review of Research in Education, 17,* 225–266.

Creswell, J. W. (2012). *Educational research: Planning, conducting, and evaluating quantitative and qualitative research* (4th ed.). Upper Saddle River, NJ: Merrill/Prentice Hall.

Creswell, J. W. (2013). *Qualitative inquiry and research design: Choosing among five approaches* (3rd ed.). Thousand Oaks, CA: Sage.

Creswell, J. W. (2014). *Research design: Qualitative, quantitative, and mixed methods approaches* (4th ed.). Thousand Oaks, CA: Sage.

Creswell, J. W. (2015). *Educational research: Planning, conducting, and evaluating quantitative and qualitative research* (5th ed.). Upper Saddle River, NJ: Merrill/Prentice Hall.

Cronbach, L. J., & Meehl, P. E. (1955). Construct validity in psychological tests. *Psychological Bulletin, 52*(4), 281–302.

Daugherty, M., & Funke, M. (1998). *University faculty and student perceptions of web-based instruction.* Edmonton, Canada: Athabasca University Press.

Eisner, E. W. (1991). *The enlightened eye: Qualitative inquiry and the enhancement of educational practice.* New York: Macmillan.

Elliott, J. (1991). *Action research for educational change.* Bristol, PA: Open University Press.

Flinders, D. J. (1992). In search of ethical guidance: Constructing a basis for dialogue. *Qualitative Studies in Education, 5*(2), 101–115.

Fueyo, V., & Koorland, M. A. (1997). Teacher as researcher: A synonym for professionalism. *Journal of Teacher Education, 48*(5), 336–344.

Fullan, M. (1993). *Change forces: Probing the depths of educational reform.* New York: Falmer.

Fullan, M. (1997). Emotion and hope: Constructive concepts for complex times. In A. Hargreaves (Ed.), *Rethinking educational change with heart and mind* (pp. 216–233). Alexandria, VA: Association for Supervision and Curriculum Development.

Gay, L. R., Mills, G. E., & Airasian, P. W. (2012). *Educational research: Competencies for analysis and application* (10th ed.). Boston, MA: Pearson Education.

Gay, L. R., Mills, G. E., & Airasian, P. W. (2016). *Educational research: Competencies for analysis and application* (11th ed.). Boston, MA: Pearson Education.

Greenwood, D. J., & Levin, M. (2000). Reconstructing the relationships between universities and society through action research. In N. K. Denzin & Y. S. Lincoln (Eds.), *Handbook of qualitative research* (2nd ed., pp. 85–106). Thousand Oaks, CA: Sage.

Guba, E. G. (1981). Criteria for assessing the trustworthiness of naturalistic inquiries. *Educational Communication and Technology, 29*(2), 75–91.

Gunz, J. (1996). Jacob L. Moreno and the origins of action research. *Educational Action Research, 4*(1), 145–148.

Hammersley, M. (1993). On the teacher as researcher. *Educational Action Research, 1*(3), 425–441.

Harasim, L. (1987). *Teaching and learning on-line: Issues in computer-mediated graduate courses.* Washington, DC: Institute of Education Sciences.

Hendricks, C. (2017). *Improving schools through action research: A comprehensive guide for educators* (4th ed.). Boston: Allyn and Bacon.

Henson, K. T. (1993). *Methods and strategies for teaching in secondary and middle schools.* New York, NY: Pearson Education.

Holmes Group. (1986). *Tomorrow's schools of education.* East Lansing, MI: Author.

Hord, S., Rutherford, W. L., Huling-Austin, L., & Hall, G. E. (1987). *Taking charge of change.* Alexandria, VA: Association for Supervision and Curriculum Development.

Jackson, P. (1968). *Life in classrooms.* New York: Holt, Rinehart and Winston.

Jones, J. H. (1998). *The Tuskegee syphilis experiment.* New York: Free Press.

Joyce, B. R., Hersh, R. H., & McKibben, M. (1983). *The structure of school improvement.* New York: Longman.

Juenemann, P. (2004). "Let's talk": Discussion in a biology classroom: An action research project. *AR Expeditions.* http://arexpeditions.montana.edu

Kemmis, S. (1988). Action research in retrospect and prospect. In S. Kemmis & R. McTaggart (Eds.), *The action research reader.* Geelong, Victoria, Australia: Deakin University Press.

Kennedy, M. M. (1997). The connection between research and practice. *Educational Researcher, 26*(7), 4–12.

Kincheloe, J. (1991). *Teachers as researchers: Qualitative inquiry as a path to empowerment.* Philadelphia: Falmer.

Krathwohl, D. R. (1998). *Methods of educational and social science research: An integrated approach* (2nd ed.). Reading, MA: Addison-Wesley.

Lewin, K. (1952). Group decision and social change. In G. E. Swanson, T. M. Newcomb, & E. L. Hartley (Eds.), *Readings in social psychology.* New York: Holt.

Lord, T. R. (1994). *Using constructivism to enhance student learning in college biology.* Washington, DC: Institute of Education Sciences.

Lortie, D. C. (1975). *Schoolteacher.* Chicago: University of Chicago Press.

Lotan, R. A. (2003). *Educational leadership.* Alexandria, VA: Association for Supervision and Curriculum Development.

Lytle, S. (1997). *Action research keynote address.* Kansas City, MO: The Learning Exchange.

Marshall, C., & Rossman, G. B. (1995). *Designing qualitative research* (2nd ed.). Thousand Oaks, CA: Sage.

McMillan, J. H. (1996). *Educational research: Fundamentals for the consumer* (2nd ed.). New York: HarperCollins.

McNiff, J., Lomax, P., & Whitehead, J. (1996). *You and your action research project.* New York, NY: Routledge.

Miles, M. B., & Huberman, A. M. (1994). *Qualitative data analysis: An expanded sourcebook* (2nd ed.). Thousand Oaks, CA: Sage.

Milgram, S. (1964). Group pressure and action against a person. *Journal of Abnormal and Social Psychology, 69,* 137–143.

Miller, L., & Lieberman, A. (1988). School improvement in the United States: Nuance and numbers. *International Journal of Qualitative Studies in Education, 1*(1), 3–19.

Mills, G. E. (1985). *Transient children.* Unpublished M.Ed. thesis. Western Australian Institute of Technology, Perth.

Mills, G. E. (1988). *Managing and coping with multiple educational change: A case study and analysis.* Unpublished doctoral dissertation. University of Oregon, Eugene.

Mills, G. E. (1993). Levels of abstraction in a case study of educational change. In D. J. Flinders & G. E. Mills (Eds.), *Theory and concepts in qualitative research: Perspectives from the field* (pp. 103–116). New York: Teachers College Press.

Mills, G. E. (2000). *Action research: A guide for the teacher researcher.* New York, NY: Prentice Hall.

Mills, G. E., & Gay, L. R. (2016). *Educational research: Competencies for analysis and application* (11th ed.). Upper Saddle River, NJ: Pearson

National Council of Teachers of Mathematics. (1991). *Professional standards for teaching mathematics.* Reston, VA: Author.

Nguyen, Q. T. (2007). Understanding high school black male students' achievement and school experience. In C. Caro-Bruce, R. Flessner, M. Klehr, & K. Zeichner (Eds.), *Creating equitable classrooms through action research* (pp. 78–100). Thousand Oaks, CA: Corwin.

Noffke, S. (1994). Action research: Towards the next generation. *Educational Action Research, 2*(1), 9–18.

Nolen, A. L., & Vander Putten, J. (2007). Action research in education: Addressing gaps in ethical principles and practices. *Educational Researcher, 36*(7), 401–407.

Osterman, K. F., & Kottkamp, R. B. (1993). *Reflective practice for educators: Improving schooling through professional development.* Newbury Park, CA: Corwin.

Patton, M. Q. (1990). *Qualitative evaluation and research methods* (2nd ed.). Newbury Park, CA: Sage.

Paul, R., & Elder, L. (1998). *The role of Socratic questioning in thinking, teaching, and learning.* Tomales, CA: Foundation for Critical Thinking.

Pelto, P. J., & Pelto, G. H. (1978). *Anthropological research: The structure of inquiry.* Cambridge, MA: Cambridge University Press.

Sagor, R. (1992). *How to conduct collaborative action research.* Alexandria, VA: Association for Supervision and Curriculum Development.

Sagor, R. (2000). *Guiding school improvement with action research.* Alexandria, VA: Association for Supervision and Curriculum Development.

Sagor, R. (2005). *The action research guidebook: A four-step process for educators and school teams.* Thousand Oaks, CA: Corwin.

Sarason, S. B. (1990). *The predictable failure of educational reform: Can we change course before it's too late?* San Francisco: Jossey-Bass.

Schrum, L. (1998). *On-line education: A study of emerging pedagogy.* New York, NY: John Wiley & Sons.

Smith, L. M. (1990). Ethics in qualitative field research: An individual perspective. In E. W. Eisner & A. P. Peshkin (Eds.), *Qualitative inquiry in education: The continuing debate* (pp. 258–276). New York: Teachers College Press.

Soltis, J. (1990). The ethics of qualitative research. In E. W. Eisner & A. P. Peshkin (Eds.), *Qualitative inquiry in education: The continuing debate* (pp. 247–257). New York: Teachers College Press.

Spradley, J. (1980). *Participant observation.* New York: Holt, Rinehart and Winston.

Stenhouse, L. (1981). What counts as research? *British Journal of Educational Studies, 29*(2), 103–114.

Stringer, E. T. (1996). *Action research: A handbook for practitioners.* Thousand Oaks, CA: Sage.

Stringer, E. T. (2004). *Action research in education.* Upper Saddle River, NJ: Merrill/Prentice Hall.

Tickle, L. (1993). Testing for quality in educational action research: A terrifying taxonomy? *Educational Action Research, 3*(2), 233–236.

Trempy, J. E., & Skinner, M. M. (2002). *Learning microbiology through cooperation: Designing cooperative learning activities that promote interdependence, interaction, and accountability.* Siebold, WA: National Center for Biotechnology Information.

Van de Walle, J. A. (2003). *Elementary school mathematics: Teaching developmentally.* New York: Longman.

Vockell, E. L., & Asher, J. W. (1996). *Educational research.* Upper Saddle River, NJ: Merrill/Prentice Hall.

Wells, G. (Ed.). (1994). *Changing schools from within: Creating communities of inquiry.* Portsmouth, NH: Heinemann.

Witte, R. S. (1985). *Statistics.* New York: Holt, Rinehart and Winston.

Wolcott, H. F. (1982). Differing styles of on-site research, or "If it isn't ethnography, what is it?" *Review Journal of Philosophy and Social Science, 7*, 154–169.

Wolcott, H. F. (1988). Ethnographic research in education. In R. M. Jaeger (Ed.), *Complementary methods for research in education* (pp. 187–210). Washington, DC: American Educational Research Association.

Wolcott, H. F. (1989). *Kwakiutl village and school.* Prospect Heights, IL: Waveland Press.

Wolcott, H. F. (1990). On seeking—and rejecting—validity in qualitative research. In E. W. Eisner & A. Peshkin (Eds.), *Qualitative inquiry in education: The continuing debate* (pp. 121–152). New York: Teachers College Press.

Wolcott, H. F. (1992). Posturing in qualitative inquiry. In M. LeCompte, W. L. Millroy, & J. Preissle (Eds.), *Handbook of qualitative research in education* (pp. 3–52). San Diego, CA: Academic.

Wolcott, H. F. (1994). *Transforming qualitative data: Description, analysis, and interpretation.* Thousand Oaks, CA: Sage.

Wolcott, H. F. (1997). Ethnographic research in education. In R. M. Jaeger (Ed.), *Complementary methods for research in education* (2nd ed., pp. 325–398). Washington, DC: American Educational Research Association.

Wolcott, H. F. (2001). *Writing up qualitative research* (2nd ed.). Thousand Oaks, CA: Sage.

index